高校英语选修课系列教材

英汉互译
实践与技巧

A Practical Course of E-C & C-E Translation

第五版
Fifth Edition

许建平 编著

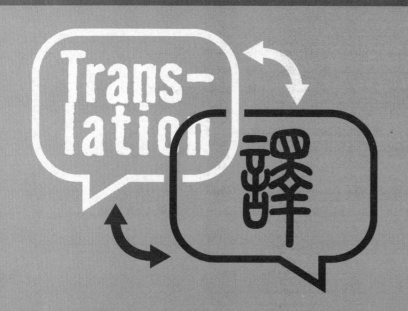

清华大学出版社
北京

内 容 简 介

本书是为非英语专业的大学生及研究生编写的英汉互译教程。其主要内容包括：翻译基本理论知识与原则；常用翻译方法、技能与技巧；实用英汉互译训练和指导；有针对性的各类文体英汉互译独立练习。本教材内容经过清华大学等众多高校课堂教学长期反复使用，效果良好。所有练习均附有参考译文，便于自学。

本书亦可供有志于提高翻译技能并具有中等以上水平的自学者使用。

版权所有，侵权必究。举报：010-62782989，beiqinquan@tup.tsinghua.edu.cn。

图书在版编目（CIP）数据

英汉互译实践与技巧. / 许建平编著. —5版. —北京：清华大学出版社，2018（2023.9重印）
（高校英语选修课系列教材）
ISBN 978-7-302-50114-5

Ⅰ.①英… Ⅱ.①许… Ⅲ.①英语–翻译–高等学校–教材 Ⅳ.①H315.9

中国版本图书馆CIP数据核字（2018）第106245号

责任编辑：刘细珍
封面设计：平　原
责任校对：王凤芝
责任印制：丛怀宇

出版发行：清华大学出版社
网　　址：http://www.tup.com.cn，http://www.wqbook.com
地　　址：北京清华大学学研大厦A座　　邮　编：100084
社 总 机：010-83470000　　邮　购：010-62786544
投稿与读者服务：010-62776969，c-service@tup.tsinghua.edu.cn
质量反馈：010-62772015，zhiliang@tup.tsinghua.edu.cn

印 装 者：三河市科茂嘉荣印务有限公司
经　　销：全国新华书店
开　　本：185mm×260mm　　印　张：22　　字　数：492千字
版　　次：2000年1月第1版　2018年5月第5版　印　次：2023年9月第13次印刷
定　　价：75.00元

产品编号：072235-04

第五版前言

《英汉互译实践与技巧》自 2000 年 1 月出版发行以来,深受广大读者的欢迎,分别于 2003 年、2007 年、2012 年出版发行了第二版、第三版、第四版。与之配套的《英汉互译实践与技巧教学参考书》《英汉互译入门教程》也陆续出版发行,总印刷量达 20 余万册。本教材 2008 年荣获清华大学优秀教材二等奖,2012 年、2016 年两度荣获一等奖。以该书为指定教材的英汉互译选修课于 2007 年、2010 年、2013 年三度被评为清华大学精品课。开课 20 余年来,该教材先后用于上百个教学班的数千名本科生、研究生教学,受到历届同学的普遍好评。除用于大学英语、研究生英语的后续课、提高课之外,此教材亦用于全国数十所高校英语专业本科生、研究生、翻译专业硕士等翻译课程的教学。

《英汉互译实践与技巧(第四版)》自 2012 年 8 月修订出版以来,转眼又 5 年多了。在这期间,国内英语教学改革力度加大,翻译越发受到重视,无论是中学还是大学本科或研究生阶段,都对翻译教学提出了更高的要求。为了与时俱进,跟上并适应外语教学的新形势,我们对《英汉互译实践与技巧(第四版)》做了适当的调整和修订,形成了目前的《英汉互译实践与技巧(第五版)》,主要从以下几个方面对第四版做了升级换代:

1. 与时俱进,淘汰更换了 7 个单元相关翻译技巧训练的英译汉、汉译英素材,新增添替换的内容均为近 5 年清华大学教学的一手资料或六级考试真题;

2. 审订修改了每个单元的文字叙述,增添、更换、精简了其中的一些例句和练习;

3. 对每个单元后面的配套练习做了相应的增删,同时对各单元的参考译文做了必要的调整和修改;

4. 更新、增补了 16 个单元之后的英汉互译独立作业练习及参考译文;

5. 修订了第四版教学参考书,新版教参与教材同步出版发行;

6. 将教材改为大开本,以方便学生使用,迎合教材装帧设计的潮流趋势。

编　者
2017 年 10 月
于清华大学荷清苑

第一版前言

　　翻译是一门实践性极强的学问,需要长期下苦功夫才能真正学到手。翻译能力的形成不能单靠学习理论知识、强化技巧训练,而是需要扎扎实实的双语功底及大量的翻译实践。因此,从某种意义上讲,一个人的翻译能力不是课堂上学出来,也不是翻译技巧所能造就的,而是要靠自己脚踏实地地干出来的。本书正是基于这方面的考虑,为培养和增进读者英汉互译的实际动手能力而编写成的,其主要对象为非英语专业研究生及已完成了大学英语基础阶段学习的同学,亦可供英语专业研究生、本科生选用。

　　本书的主要内容包括:

　　1. 翻译的基本知识及原则,包括翻译的性质、标准、直译与意译等问题;

　　2. 翻译中的常见基本方法技巧(选词用字、字词的增减、词类转换、词序调整、正反表达、语态转换、长句的处理等);

　　3. 不同体裁的文类(如科技英语、各类文献等)的一般翻译原则和方法;

　　4. 不同类别、不同风格的译文欣赏对比;

　　5. 各类文体的英汉互译练习。

　　与传统翻译教材相比,本教程的最大特点是用英语编写,旨在让读者通过阅读、对比,有效地培养和形成自己的双语语感,潜移默化地掌握翻译的一般技巧、方法。书中的主要内容来自作者近年来为清华大学研究生、本科高年级学生所开设的"高级翻译"课程,也可以说是作者十余年来的翻译研究理论、观点、方法的浓缩。本书的大体结构是:英译汉、汉译英同行并举,分头阐述;内容按章节逐次展开,循序渐进。每章正文之前用汉语拟写了章节概述,作为简要的归纳,章后配有适量练习,并附以答案,便于读者自学。各章既可单独使用,方便查阅,亦可与其他各章合为一体,互为参照。此外,为了进一步提高读者的实操能力,在通篇讲解论述之后,另设了两个附录,分别安排英—汉、汉—英翻译对照欣赏以及篇章、段落翻译作为翻译综合练习。各章所选译例及练习大都出自国内近年出版的教材、专著,以及外刊、原版书籍等;还有一些来自日常生活、工作的翻译实例,如出国申请、个人简历、自传及推荐信等;另有少部分选自翻译公司的翻译测试题及涉外业务往来实例。

感谢外语界老前辈李相崇先生逐字审阅、修改拙稿，耳提面命，受益匪浅；感谢清华大学出版社的热心扶持、鼎力资助。没有他们的关心和提挈，本书只不过是一堆凌乱的讲义稿。

用英语编写英汉互译教程是一种新尝试。文无定法，译无定论，仁者见仁，智者见智。本人才疏学浅，错误疏忽在所难免，不当之处，还望译界同人及读者朋友批评指正。

编　者

1999 年 11 月 15 日

于清华园

目 录

Unit 1 Introduction: Translation and Translation Techniques 绪论：翻译与翻译技巧 1

Practice of the Relevant Skill 相关翻译技巧训练 1
    I. Important Role of Translation 翻译的重要作用 4
    II. Nature and Scope of Translation 翻译的性质和范围 5
    III. Principles or Criteria of Translation 翻译的原则标准 6
    IV. Literal Translation and Free Translation 直译与意译 7
    V. Translation Techniques 翻译技巧种种 10
Reflections and Practice 思考与练习 11

Unit 2 Diction 遣词用字 15

Practice of the Relevant Skill 相关翻译技巧训练 15
    I. Equivalence Between English and Chinese at Word Level
       英汉字词层面的对等关系 20
        1. Word-for-Word Equivalence 字词对等 20
        2. One Word with Multiple Equivalents of the Same Meaning 多词同义 20
        3. One Word with Several Equivalents of Different Meanings 一词多义 21
        4. Equivalents Interwoven with One Another 词义交织 21
        5. Words Without Corresponding Equivalents 无对等词语 21
    II. Methods to Make out the Meaning of a Given Word 英语词义辨析法 22
        1. Judging by Word Formation 通过构词法确定词义 22
        2. Judging by References 通过指代关系确定词义 22
        3. Judging by Context and Collocation
           通过上下文及习惯搭配确定词义 23
        4. Judging by Branches of Learning and Specialties
           按不同学科或专业门类确定词义 24

III. Techniques of Translating a Given English Word 英语词语翻译技巧 24
1. Deduction 推演法 24
2. Transplant 移植法 25
3. Extension 引申法 25
4. Substitution 替代法 25
5. Explanation 释义法 25
6. Combination 合并法 26
7. Transliteration 音译法 26
8. Pictographic Translation 图形法 26

IV. Diction in C-E Translation 汉译英的选词用字 26
Reflections and Practice 思考与练习 28

Uuit 3 Conversion 转换 31
Practice of the Relevant Skill 相关翻译技巧训练 32
I. Conversion in E-C Translation 英译汉的词类转换 35
1. Converting into Verbs 转换成动词 35
2. Converting into Nouns 转换成名词 36
3. Converting into Adjectives 转换成形容词 37
4. Converting into Adverbs 转换成副词 38
5. The Conversion of Sentence Elements 句子成分转换 38

II. Conversions in C-E Translation 汉译英的词类转换 39
1. Converting Verbs into Other Parts of Speech 汉语动词转换成其他词类 39
2. Conversions Between Different Parts of Speech 各种词类相互转换 40

Reflections and Practice 思考与练习 41

Unit 4 Amplification 增添法 43
Practice of the Relevant Skill 相关翻译技巧训练 44
I. Amplification in E-C Translation 增词法在英汉翻译中的运用 48
1. Putting in Words Omitted in the Original 加入原文所省略的词语 48
2. Putting in Necessary Connectives 加入必要的连接词语 48

3. Putting in Words to Convey the Concept of Plurality 增词以表达复数概念 48

4. Putting in Words to Indicate Different Tenses or Sequences
增词以表现不同的时态或先后顺序 48

5. Amplification by Common Sense 常识性增词 49

6. Amplification for the Purpose of Rhetoric or Coherence 修辞性或连贯性增词 49

7. Amplification by Repetition 重复性增词 49

II. Amplification in C-E Translation 增词法在汉英翻译中的运用 49

1. Adding Necessary Pronouns 增添必要的代词 49

2. Adding Necessary Articles 增添必要的冠词 50

3. Adding Necessary Connectives 增添必要的连接词语 50

4. Adding Necessary Prepositions 增添必要的介词 50

5. Adding Necessary Background Words 增添必要的背景词语 50

Reflections and Practice 思考与练习 51

Unit 5 Omission 省略法 53

Practice of the Relevant Skill 相关翻译技巧训练 54

I. Omission in E-C Translation 省略法在英汉翻译中的运用 57

1. Omitting the Pronoun 省略代词 57

2. Omitting the Article 省略冠词 57

3. Omitting the Preposition 省略介词 57

4. Omitting the Conjunction 省略连词 58

5. Omitting the Verb 省略动词 58

6. Omitting the Impersonal Pronoun "It" 省略非人称代词"It" 58

II. Omission in C-E Translation 省略法在汉英翻译中的运用 59

1. Omitting Redundant Words 省略冗词赘语 59

2. Omitting Words of Conceptual Category 省略概念范畴类词语 59

3. Omitting Meticulous Descriptions 省略过详的细节描述 59

Reflections and Practice 思考与练习 60

Unit 6   Restructuring 结构调整 63

Practice of the Relevant Skill 相关翻译技巧训练 64
I. Different Word Orders in English and Chinese 英汉语言的词序差异 67
    1. Different Modes of Thinking 不同的思维模式 67
    2. Different Inversion Structures 不同的倒装结构 68
II. Restructuring in E-C Translation 英汉翻译的结构调整 69
    1. Keeping the Original Sequence 保持原文顺序 69
    2. Reversing the Original Sequence 颠倒原文顺序 70
    3. Restructuring by Time Sequence 按时间顺序调整 70
    4. Restructuring by Logical Sequence 按逻辑顺序调整 70
III. Restructuring in C-E Translation 汉英翻译的结构调整 71
    1. Different Sequences in Customary Word Combinations
       不同的词语习惯表达顺序 71
    2. Cases of Restructuring in C-E Translation 汉英翻译的结构调整情况 71
Reflections and Practice 思考与练习 72

Unit 7   Affirmative vs. Negative 肯定与否定 75

Practice of the Relevant Skill 相关翻译技巧训练 76
I. Negation in E-C Translation 英译汉的正反调换 79
    1. Affirmative in English, but Negative in Chinese 英语为肯定，汉语译作否定 80
    2. Negative in English, but Affirmative in Chinese 英语为否定，汉语译作肯定 80
    3. Same English Wording, Either Affirmative or Negative in Chinese
       译作肯定否定均可 81
    4. Double Negative for Emphasis 强调性双重否定 81
    5. Roundabout Affirmative 间接式肯定 81
    6. Some Traps in Negative Structures 否定的陷阱 82
II. Negation in C-E Translation 汉译英的正反调换 83
    1. Negation According to English Usage 按英语表达习惯译作肯定或否定 83
    2. Negation for Emphasis or Rhetorical Effect

从强调或修辞角度考虑译作肯定或否定 83

3. Negation to Convey Exactly the Original Meaning
用正反调换传达出原文的确切意思 83

Reflections and Practice 思考与练习 84

Unit 8 The Passive Voice 被动语态 87

Practice of the Relevant Skill 相关翻译技巧训练 87

I. The Passive Voice in E-C Translation 英汉翻译的被动语态 91

1. Converting the Passive Voice into the Active 将被动语态转为主动结构 91
2. Converting the Passive Voice into a Subjectless Sentence
   将被动语态转为无主句 92
3. Keeping the Passive Structure Unchanged 被动语态保持不变 92
4. Replacing the Passive Voice with Other Means 用其他手段代替被动语态 93

II. Passive Structures in C-E Translation 汉英翻译的被动结构 93

1. Chinese Sentences with Passive Labels 带有被动标签的汉语句子 94
2. Chinese Sentences Without Passive Labels 不带被动标签的汉语句子 94
3. Converting the Active Structure into the Passive Voice
   将主动结构转换为被动语态 94
4. The Translation of Some Idiomatic Chinese Expressions
   一些汉语习惯表达的翻译套路 95

Reflections and Practice 思考与练习 95

Unit 9 Nominal Clauses 名词性从句 99

Practice of the Relevant Skill 相关翻译技巧训练 99

I. The Translation of English Nominal Clauses 英语名词性从句的翻译 103

1. Subject Clauses 主语从句 103
2. Object Clauses 宾语从句 103
3. Predicative Clauses 表语从句 104
4. Appositive Clauses 同位语从句 104

ix

II. The Translation of Chinese Complex Sentences 汉语复句的翻译 105
    1. Sentence Combination 句子的合并 105
    2. Sentence Sequence 句序 106
Reflections and Practice 思考与练习 107

Unit 10 Attributive Clauses 定语从句 110
Practice of the Relevant Skill 相关翻译技巧训练 111
I. A Comparative Study of English and Chinese Attributive Structures 英汉定语结构的对比 113
II. Restrictive Attributive Clauses 限制性定语从句 114
    1. Combination 合并法 114
    2. Division 分译法 115
    3. Mixture 混合法 115
III. Non-Restrictive Attributive Clauses 非限制性定语从句 116
    1. Division 分译法 116
    2. Combination 合并法 117
IV. Attributive Clauses Functioning as Adverbials 兼有状语功能的定语从句 117
    1. Translating into Adverbial Clauses of Cause 译作原因句 118
    2. Translating into Adverbial Clauses of Result 译作结果句 118
    3. Translating into Adverbial Clauses of Concession 译作让步句 118
    4. Translating into Adverbial Clauses of Condition 译作条件句 118
    5. Translating into Adverbial Clauses of Purpose 译作目的句 119
Reflections and Practice 思考与练习 119

Unit 11 Adverbial Clauses 状语从句 122
Practice of the Relevant Skill 相关翻译技巧训练 122
I. The Translation of English Adverbial Clauses 英语状语从句的翻译 124
    1. Adverbial Clauses of Time 时间状语从句 125
    2. Adverbial Clauses of Place 地点状语从句 125

3. Adverbial Clauses of Cause 原因状语从句 126

4. Adverbial Clauses of Condition 条件状语从句 126

5. Adverbial Clauses of Concession 让步状语从句 126

6. Adverbial Clauses of Purpose 目的状语从句 127

II. Adverbial Clauses in Chinese Complex Sentences 汉语复句中的状语分句 127

1. Discerning Subordination 分清主次关系 127

2. Using Inanimate Subjects 使用无灵主语 127

Reflections and Practice 思考与练习 128

Unit 12 Long Sentences 长句 131

Practice of the Relevant Skill 相关翻译技巧训练 132

I. Long Sentences in E-C Translation 英汉翻译的长句处理 134

1. Two Stages and Five Steps 长句翻译的两个阶段和五个步骤 134

2. Sample Analysis 长句分析示例 134

II. Methods of Translating Long English Sentences 英译汉长句的翻译方法 136

1. Embedding 内嵌法 136

2. Dividing 切分法 137

3. Splitting 拆分法 138

4. Inserting 插入法 139

5. Recasting 重组法 139

III. Long Sentences in C-E Translation 汉译英的长句处理 140

Reflections and Practice 思考与练习 142

Unit 13 English for Science and Technology and Its Translation 科技英语及其翻译 146

Practice of the Relevant Skill 相关翻译技巧训练 146

I. Formation of English Technical Terms 英语科技词语的构成 149

1. Affixation 缀合法 149

2. Compounding 复合法 150

    3. Blending 缩合法 150
    4. Acronyms 首字母缩略 150
    5. Proper Nouns 专有名词 151

  II. Characteristic Syntax of EST 科技英语的句法特点 152
    1. Long and Complicated Sentences 使用结构复杂长句 152
    2. High Frequency of Noun Phrases 频繁使用名词短语 153
    3. Extensive Use of the Passive Voice 广泛使用被动语态 153
    4. More Non-Finite Forms of the Verb 多使用非限定动词 153
    5. Different Uses of the Tense 时态的使用差异 154
    6. The Post-Position of the Attributive 定语后置 154

  III. Methods of Translating EST 科技英语的翻译方法 155
    1. Expanding Noun Phrases into Separate Clauses
       将名词性短语扩展成汉语分句 155
    2. Converting Noun Phrases into Verb-Object Structures
       将名词性短语转换成动宾结构 155
    3. Converting Attributive Elements into Independent Sentences,
       Adverbial Clauses, etc. 将定语成分转换成独立句、状语分句等 155
    4. Converting the Passive into the Active 将被动转换成主动 155
    5. Supplementing Necessary Words to Indicate Given Time
       补充适当的词语表示特定的时间 156

  Reflections and Practice 思考与练习 156

Unit 14 The Translation of Documentation 文献的翻译 159
  Practice of the Relevant Skill 相关翻译技巧训练 160
  I. The Translation of Contracts and Agreements 合同与协议的翻译 162
  II. The Translation of Proposals, Reports and Reviews
      建议、报告与评论的翻译 164
  III. The Translation of Patents and Trademarks 专利与商标的翻译 166
  IV. The Translation of Copyright Documents 版权文献的翻译 168
  V. The Translation of Bid-Documents 招标文献的翻译 169
  VI. The Translation of Abstracts, Indexes and Bibliographies

摘要、索引与文献目录的翻译 171
Reflections and Practice 思考与练习 174

Unit 15   Application Documents for Studying Abroad
出国留学申请翻译 179

Practice of the Relevant Skill 相关翻译技巧训练 179
I. Orienting Your Target 留学目标定位 181
II. Résumé (Curriculum Vitae) 个人简历（履历） 182
III. School Transcript (Academic Record) 学习成绩单 185
IV. Letters of Recommendation 推荐信 188
V. Personal Statement (Statement of Purpose) 自我陈述 190
Reflections and Practice 思考与练习 194

Unit 16   Developing Comprehensive Abilities Through Comparative Studies and Practice
通过比较研究与实践培养翻译综合能力 197

Practice of the Relevant Skill 相关翻译技巧训练 198
I. A Comparative Study of English and Chinese Languages 英汉语言宏观对比 200
   1. Synthetic vs. Analytic 综合性与分析性 200
   2. Compact vs. Diffusive 紧凑与松散 201
   3. Hypotactic vs. Paratactic 形合与意合 201
   4. Complex vs. Simplex 繁复与简单 201
   5. Impersonal vs. Personal 物称与人称 202
   6. Passive vs. Active 被动与主动 202
   7. Static vs. Dynamic 静态与动态 203
   8. Abstract vs. Concrete 抽象与具体 203
   9. Roundabout vs. Straightforward 间接与直接 203
   10. Substitutive vs. Repetitive 替换与重复 203
II. Developing Practical Abilities Through Comparative Studies and Practice
通过比较研究和实践提高翻译动手能力 204
   1. Language Sensibility 语感能力 204

2. Contextual Analysis 语境分析能力 205
3. Logical Thinking 逻辑思维能力 207

Reflections and Practice 思考与练习 **209**

Appendix A **Translation Exercises for Independent Work
英汉互译独立作业练习** **212**

Appendix B **Keys to Practice of the Relevant Skill and Exercises
相关翻译技巧及练习答案** **248**

Appendix C **Keys to Translation Exercises for Independent Work
英汉互译独立作业练习参考译文** **301**

Bibliography **参考文献** **335**

Unit 1　Introduction: Translation and Translation Techniques

> ● 单元要点概述
>
> 相关翻译技巧训练英译汉：Proverbs in Latin American Talk
> 相关翻译技巧训练汉译英：谚语
> I. 翻译的重要作用
> II. 翻译的性质和范围
> III. 翻译的原则和标准
> IV. 直译与意译
> V. 翻译技巧种种

　　本单元为全书的绪论，简要回顾了我国的翻译史，阐述了翻译的重要性，举例说明了翻译不当所造成的问题，界定了翻译的性质和类别，对翻译的原则及标准、直译与意译等问题展开了讨论，并就翻译技巧与实践的关系进行了阐述。

　　严复的"信、达、雅"标准，仁者见仁，智者见智，我们一般采用"忠实、通顺"的标准即可。直译与意译是一个相对的概念，没有截然的划分，无论采用哪一种，均须以理解原文为前提。需要注意的是，直译要近情理，便于读者理解、接受，否则就会变成硬译、死译；意译应当注重事实依据，不能无中生有、随意杜撰，否则就会变成曲译、胡译。

　　翻译的种种技巧方法源于翻译实践，翻译能力的形成不能单靠学习理论知识、方法技巧，必须通过扎扎实实的训练完成大量的翻译实践方能凑效。

Practice of the Relevant Skill

1.　E-C Translation

Proverbs in Latin American Talk

　　Proverbs are the popular sayings that brighten so much Latin American talk, the boiled-down wisdom that you are as apt to hear from professors as from peasants, from beggars as from élégantes. Brief and colorful, they more often than not carry a sting.

When a neighbor's dismally unattractive daughter announced her engagement, Imelda remarked, "You know what they say, Senora: 'There's no pot so ugly it can't find a lid.'" And when her son-in-law blustered about how he was going to get even with the boss who had docked his pay, Imelda fixed him with a cold eye and said, "Little fish does not eat big fish."

One afternoon I heard Imelda and her daughter arguing in the kitchen. Her daughter had quarreled with her husband's parents, and Imelda was insisting that she apologize to them. Her daughter objected, "But, Mama, I just can't swallow them, not even with honey. They talk so big until we need something; then they're too poor. So today when they wouldn't even lend enough to pay for a new bed, all I did was saying something that I've heard you say a hundred times: 'If so grand, why so poor? If so poor, why so grand?'"

"Impertinent!" snorted Imelda. "Have I not also taught you, 'What the tongue says, the neck pays for'? I will not have it said that I could never teach my daughter proper respect for her elders. And before you go to beg their pardon, change those trousers for a dress. You know how your mother-in-law feels about pants on a woman. She always says, 'What was hatched a hen must not try to be a rooster!'"

Her daughter made one more try, "But Mama, you often say, 'If the saint is annoyed, don't pray to him until he gets over it.' Can't I leave it for tomorrow?"

"No, no and no! Remember: 'If the dose is nasty, swallow it fast.' You know, my child, you did wrong. But, 'A gift is the key to open the door closed against you.' I have a cake in the oven that I was making for the Senora's dinner. I will explain to the Senora. Now, dear, hurry home and make yourself pretty in your pink dress. By the time you get back, I will have the cake ready for you to take to your mother-in-law. She will be so pleased that she may make your father-in-law pay for the bed. Remember: 'One hand washes the other, but together they wash the face.'"

Notes and Explanations

1. the boiled-down wisdom 浓缩的智慧
2. élégante *n.* [法语]风雅的人，淑女
3. more often than not carry a sting 往往不无带刺；sting *n.* 刺，讽刺
4. dismally unattractive 直译：难看得令人忧虑；dismally *adv.* 沉闷地，忧郁地，根据上下文，此处可考虑译作"丑陋的""其貌不扬的"
5. There's no pot so ugly it can't find a lid. 直译：世上没有丑得找不到盖子的罐子。（暗示：丑女不愁嫁。）

UNIT 1 Introduction: Translation and Translation Techniques

6. senora *n.* [西班牙语]夫人，太太

7. get even with the boss who had docked his pay 找克扣了他工资的老板算账；get even with 扯平，进行报复，算账；dock *v.* 剪掉……，扣……工资

8. I just can't swallow them, not even with honey. 我就是受不了他们那一套，哪怕是拌了蜜也咽不下呀！swallow *v.* 咽，吞下，忍受

9. talk big 吹牛，说大话

10. If so grand, why so poor? If so poor, why so grand? 既然那么阔，干嘛要叫穷？既然那么穷，干嘛摆阔气？grand *adj.* 壮观的，显赫的，摆阔的

11. I will not have it said that... 我可不愿意让人家说……（注意have something done结构的译法）

12. What was hatched a hen must not try to be a rooster! 直译：孵出来是母鸡就别想冒充公鸡！

13. If the saint is annoyed, don't pray to him until he gets over it. 直译：要是圣徒恼了，在他消气之前不要向他祈祷。

2. C-E Translation

谚　　语

　　谚语是广泛用于民间的短小精悍的格言，通常经口头流传下来，大都反映了劳动人民的生活实践经验。谚语类似成语，但口语性强，通俗易懂，因而很有感染力。

　　谚语往往多少能反映一个民族的地理、历史、社会制度、社会观点和态度。比如，有些民族住在沿海一带，靠海为生，他们的谚语往往涉及海上航行、经受风雨、捕鱼捉蟹。像阿拉伯人这样的游牧民族的谚语则多涉及沙漠、草原、羊、马、骆驼和豺狼。尊敬老人的社会就会有颂扬老人足智多谋的谚语。妇女地位不高的社会就有许多轻视、贬低妇女的谚语。

　　人们的经历和对世界的认识在不少方面是相似的。因此，尽管中国人和讲英语的人文化背景不同，但在英语和汉语中有很多相同或相似的谚语。

Notes and Explanations

1. 经口头流传 pass down by word of mouth
2. 有感染力 appeal to
3. 游牧民族 nomads
4. 足智多谋 resourcefulness
5. 轻视、贬低 despise or disparage

I. Important Role of Translation

Translation means a conversion of one language to another, i.e. the faithful representation in one language of what is written or said in another language.

As a means of communication, translation plays an important role in human civilization. In the West, literary translation can be traced back to 300 BC, while in China, recorded translation activities are even earlier, dating from the Zhou Dynasty (1100 BC). However, not until recent centuries, especially by the end of the 19th century did systematic study of translation get underway. In the past decades translation theories and activities have developed fast both at home and abroad.

Translation plays an even more important role in modern times and serves as a powerful tool to promote mutual understanding between peoples of different cultural and social backgrounds. A proper and dexterous translation is meaningful and appealing, easy to gain acceptance on the part of the reader, such as humor（幽默）, club（俱乐部）, Coca Cola（可口可乐）, hacker（黑客）, etc. Whereas a misunderstanding or improper rendering of words or expressions may lead to confusion, and sometimes even cause disasters. For instance, the mistranslation of the Japanese telegram sent to Washington just before the bomb was dropped on Hiroshima, when mokusatsu（默殺）was allegedly translated as "ignored" instead of "considered", and the ambiguity in UN Resolution 242, where "the withdrawal from occupied territories" was translated as *le retrait des territoires occupés*, and therefore as a reference to all of the occupied territory to be evacuated by the Israelis. Another example is the rendering of "Renaissance". The original word refers to the period in Europe between the 14th and 17th centuries, when the art, literature, ideas of ancient Greece were discovered again and widely studied, causing a rebirth of activity in all these things. It is commonly known as "文艺复兴" in Chinese via translation—although we know today this movement extended far beyond literature and art circles; actually the connotation of "Renaissance" is much more profound than that of the Chinese term. Similar fallacies also occur in C-E translation. For example, a popular Chinese brand of lipstick "芳芳" is translated as "Fangfang", a hideous image in English—the English word "fang" happens to have two disagreeable definitions: a. a long, sharp tooth of a dog; b. a snake's poisonous tooth. Similar translation blunders are not rare in domestic affairs. For instances, rendering "五讲四美、三热爱" into "five stresses, four beauties and three loves"; "抓紧施肥" into "grasp manure"; "街道妇女" into "street women"... Had the translators mastered enough translation knowledge, such blunders should have been avoidable.

UNIT 1 Introduction: Translation and Translation Techniques

II. Nature and Scope of Translation

What is translation? Some people believe it is a science, others take it as an art; and yet many consider it a craft, or rather, a skill.

Of these varied opinions, which one holds true for our purpose? The answer depends on how we understand or interpret the word "translation", for the very word "translation" itself is ambiguous, and the Chinese equivalent "fanyi" sounds even fuzzier. "Fanyi" in Chinese, may either stand for a subject in the curriculum, a job or profession people are engaged in, a piece of literary work, or the translating or interpreting activities or profession. Sometimes, "fanyi" may even refer to the translator or interpreter himself/herself, as illustrated in the following diagram.

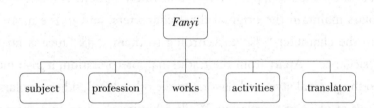

If the word "translation" refers to a subject, namely, the study of translation theory and skills, it is no doubt a science, just as any subject is, with its own rules and principles for translators to abide by; however, if it refers to some specific pieces of translation, then it is more like an art, with each piece manifesting its own charms and style by the creative work of the translator; whereas, if it refers to a process, in which something is translated, then we may regard it as a craft or a skill. For unlike any branch of natural science, the process of translation has its peculiarity, and none of its rules and principles is universally applicable. Besides, translation entails a lot of practice—particular craftsmanship and skills are displayed by the touches of different translators.

Translation covers a very broad range. In terms of languages, it can be divided into two categories: from native languages into foreign languages and vice versa. In terms of working mode, it can be divided into oral interpretation, written translation and machine translation. In terms of materials to be translated, there is translation of scientific materials, translation of literary works such as novels, stories, prose, poetry, drama, etc., translation of political essays such as treatises on social problems, reports, speeches, etc., and translation of practical writing such as official documents, contracts and agreements, notices, receipts, etc. In terms of translator's disposal, it can be either full-text translation（全文翻译）, abridged translation（摘译）or adapted translation（编译）.

III. Principles or Criteria of Translation

The so-named principles and criteria of translation are actually two aspects of the same thing. The former lays emphasis on the translator, who should follow these principles while translating; while the latter on the reader or critic, who may use the criteria to evaluate translation works. Whenever principles or criteria of translation are under discussion in China, Yan Fu's（严复）"three-character guide", which was first proposed in 1898, would be mentioned, namely, the principle of "信、达、雅" (faithfulness, expressiveness and elegance).

In the past decades, Mr. Yan's principle of translation has been generally regarded as a yardstick to measure the professional level of translation and a goal for translators to strive after. However, in the application of this principle, many scholars come to see its limitations and at the same time, put forward some new standards instead.

Some scholars maintain the original three characters, and in the meantime add some new concepts to the character "雅". According to them, "雅" means far more than the English word "elegance". Apart from the traditional interpretation, it also means classicism, the adherence to the original style and flavor. On the other hand, other scholars argue that the word "雅" is out of place in translation. While adopting the first two characters of Mr. Yan Fu's principle, they discard the character "雅" and replace it with some other criteria. Noticeably, there are such revisions as "信、达、切" (faithfulness, expressiveness and closeness), "信、达、贴" (faithfulness, expressiveness and fitness), etc. Besides, some scholars disagree with Yan Fu's principle on the whole. By casting away the three-word guide, they propose some new principles or translation criteria of their own. Of the various popular theories "spiritual conformity"（神似）and "sublimed adaptation"（化境）are most influential in the translation circles. The former, proposed by Fu Lei（傅雷）, emphasizes the reproduction of the spirit or the flavor of the original, while the latter, advocated by Qian Zhongshu（钱钟书）, focuses on the translator's smooth and idiomatic Chinese version for the sake of the Chinese reader.

Despite the variety of opinions, two criteria are almost unanimously accepted, i.e. the criterion of faithfulness/accuracy（忠实/准确）and that of smoothness（流畅）. These two criteria may serve as our principles of translation in general. By faithfulness/accuracy, we mean being faithful not only to the original contents, to the original meaning and views, but also to the original form and style. By smoothness, we mean not only easy and readable rendering, but also idiomatic expression in the target language, free from stiff formula and mechanical copying from dictionaries.

UNIT 1 Introduction: Translation and Translation Techniques

IV. Literal Translation and Free Translation

The process of translation consists of two phases: comprehension and expression. Generally speaking, comprehension is of foremost importance, and expression is the natural consequence of thorough comprehension. However, in the practice of translation we may find that now and then some words in their usual senses are very difficult to deal with because of the disparity between the English and the Chinese languages. In this case, we have to resort to some special means of translation. Literal translation and free translation are two alternative approaches to tackle this problem.

Literal translation does not mean word-for-word translation. Superficially speaking, it means "not to alter the original words and sentences"; strictly speaking, it strives "to keep the sentiments and style of the original". It takes sentences as its basic units and takes the whole text into consideration at the same time in the course of translation. Furthermore, it strives to reproduce both the ideological content and the style of the original works and retains as much as possible the figures of speech.

For example, the concept of "death" may be expressed as follows: breathe one's last（断气）, go to one's eternal rest（安息）, the long sleep（长眠）, pass away（去世）, see God（见上帝）, see Marx（见马克思）, see one's ancestors（见祖先）, go west（归西）, go to heaven（进天国）, kick the bucket（蹬腿儿了）, etc. Actually, quite a lot of successful literal translations have been adopted as idiomatic Chinese expressions. For example, crocodile tears（鳄鱼的眼泪）, be armed to the teeth（武装到牙齿）, chain reaction（连锁反应）, gentlemen's agreement（君子协定）, and so on. Similarly, some Chinese words and expressions may also find their English counterparts through literal translation. For example, "三教九流"(the three religions and the nine schools of thought), "四书五经"(the Four Books and the Five Classics), "纸老虎"(paper tiger), "一国两制"(one country, two systems), and so on.

Free translation is an alternative approach generally used to convey the meaning and spirit of the original without trying to copy its sentence patterns or figures of speech. This approach is most frequently adopted when it is really impossible for the translator to translate the original meaning literally. For example:
- Adam's apple 喉结
- rest room 公用厕所，洗手间
- stopwatch 秒表，跑表
- white wine 白葡萄酒
- It rains cats and dogs. 大雨滂沱。

- Do you see any green in my eye? 你以为我是幼稚可欺的吗?
- Don't cross the bridge till you get to it. 不必担心过早。（不必自寻烦恼。）

The above illustrations cannot be translated literally, otherwise, the Chinese rendition would either cause confusion or simply make no sense at all, let alone the original meaning.

More often than not, literal translation and free translation may be alternately used in the process of translation, as illustrated by the following examples from Practice of Relevant Skill of this unit:

- There's no pot so ugly it can't find a lid.
  Literal translation：再丑的罐儿也不愁配个盖儿。Or：罐儿再丑，配个盖儿不犯愁。
  Free translation：再丑的姑娘也不愁找不到婆家。Or：丑女不愁嫁。
- Little fish does not eat big fish.
  Literal translation：小鱼吃不了大鱼。
  Free translation：胳膊拧不过大腿。
- What the tongue says, the neck pays for.
  Literal translation：舌头说话，脖子还账。
  Free translation：舌头闯祸，脖子遭殃。
- What was hatched a hen must not try to be a rooster!
  Literal translation：孵出来是母鸡就别想冒充公鸡！
  Free translation：生就是个女人就别想冒充男人！
- A gift is the key to open the door closed against you.
  Literal translation：礼物是打开把你关在门外的房门的钥匙。
  Free translation：大门把你关在外，礼物送到门自开。

The above illustrations show clearly that literal translation and free translation are relative concepts. In other words, there is no absolute "literal", nor entirely "free" version in the practice of translation, and overemphasizing either of them would result in ridiculous consequences. Let's scrutinize the following two samples of translation excerpted from the reminiscences of Helen Snow.

Original English 1: I love *tiger cat*... British movies on public television, fluffy blouses, the *nuclear family*... (Helen Snow, *My China Years*)

Chinese Version A: 我爱虎猫……（爱）电视上放映的英国影片，有绒毛的短衫，核心家庭……

Chinese Version B: 我喜欢豹猫……喜欢公共电视台播放的英国电影，喜欢蓬松柔软的棉毛衫，喜欢一夫一妻制的家庭……

Comment: Apparently, both of these two Chinese versions leave much room for improvement.

UNIT 1 Introduction: Translation and Translation Techniques

In the first place, version A and B literally render "tiger cat" respectively as 虎猫 and 豹猫. Actually, this species of wild animal has nothing to do with the family life. Consulting an English-English dictionary may shed light on the answer: tiger cat, a striped or sometimes blotched tabby cat (虎纹家猫/豹斑家猫)。

Second, the phrase "nuclear family" is rendered as "核心家庭" by version A and "一夫一妻制家庭" by version B respectively. The former seems a bit too stiff, for most of the Chinese readers have hardly any idea of "核心家庭". The latter, in contrast, seems to have gone too far as to distort the author's original intention.

Therefore, neither of the above versions is desirable. A close examination of its definition in an E-E dictionary may reveal its true meaning: nuclear family, a family group that consists only of father, mother and children. Therefore, the proper rendering of the phrase should be worded to this effect: a cozy small family, namely, the Chinese equivalent "小家庭".

Revised Version: 我喜欢虎纹家猫……爱看公共电视台播放的英国影片，爱穿蓬松的罩衫，向往小家庭生活……

Original English 2: Mao Tse-tung was well bred, but inside he was made of steel, of hard resistance, of tough tissue—the kind of tissue the Boxers thought they had by magic, and bared their solar plexuses to foreign bullets. (ibid.)

Chinese Version A: 毛泽东有很好的教养，内部是钢，有坚强的抗力，是由坚韧的材料制成的：这是义和团设想的由于神力具有的、可以把腹部袒露给外国人的子弹的那种材料。

Chinese Version B: 毛泽东教养有素，精神支柱铁铸钢打，不怕高压，是由坚韧的组织构成的。这种组织，就是义和团认为他们通过魔法得到的那种组织——袒胸露体，刀枪不入。

Comment: The word "tissue" can hardly be rendered into Chinese either in literal translation or free translation, nor could the metaphor "inside he was made of steel" be properly rendered without grasping the essence of the whole sentence. As we may see from the above, the former is freely rendered as "材料" and "组织"; the latter is rendered as "内部是钢" and "精神支柱铁铸钢打"—both fail to reflect the connotation of the original. By adopting translation skills such as amplification, omission, conversion and restructuring, we may revise the above Chinese versions as follows:

Revised Version: 毛泽东外表温文尔雅，实际上却是钢筋铁骨，坚韧不拔——从他身上可以看到当年义和团自信所具有的那种神力，面对洋枪洋炮也敢袒胸露怀。

Based on the above analysis, we come to the conclusion that there is no obvious distinction between literal translation and free translation, nor is it necessary to distinguish one from the other. The key point for a translator to grasp is to comprehend the original thoroughly, and then put it into idiomatic Chinese. In the process of translation, specific approaches such as literal or free translation may be of some help, but we should avoid the two extremes. In the application of literal translation, we should endeavor to rid ourselves of stiff patterns and rigid adherence to translation rules, trying to be flexible; while in the practice of free translation, we should be cautious of subjectivity, avoiding groundless affirmation or arbitrary fabrication. Whatever the circumstances, we may alternate or combine these two approaches when it is necessary.

V. Translation Techniques

When it comes to translation techniques, we differ from those who tend to ignore them, or dismiss them lightly as something inconsequential. On the other hand, we should not exaggerate the function of "translation techniques", and in no circumstances should we take them as almighty remedies.

Different kinds of materials to be translated require different stresses in their rendition. Scientific materials stress their preciseness; novels and stories, their plots and characters; poetry, the emotion; document translation, the form and wording, etc.

Generally speaking, the basic translation techniques that merit our attention and are to be applied in E-C and C-E translations include: (1) Diction（选词用字）; (2) Amplification（增添法）; (3) Omission（省略法）; (4) Repetition（重复）; (5) Conversion（转换）; (6) Restructuring（结构调整）; (7) Negation（正反调换）; (8) division（长句拆译）. Of course, there are different opinions on the labels of translation techniques. For example, some consider subordination a technique, assuming it to be an inseparable link in the process of comprehension; others do not consider repetition itself as a technique, categorizing it as amplification; while quite a few scholars add the disposal of the passive voice, the rendering of technical terms, the rendering of long sentences, etc. to translation techniques, which, however, in the eyes of others, are not techniques at all but methods or approaches in tackling specific problems. Regardless of these controversies, this textbook aims at taking all these practical means of translation into consideration. Besides, it also offers a brief comparative study and analysis of E-C and C-E translation. And in the following units we are going to elaborate these translation techniques and methods one by one.

Last but not least, translation techniques alone cannot guarantee faithful and smooth

UNIT 1 Introduction: Translation and Translation Techniques

rendition—we may make use of them, but should not rely completely on them. Apart from translation techniques, a mastery of general knowledge and knowledge of the subject matter is of vital importance. In many cases, we can hardly do our translation well unless we have acquired adequate knowledge of the subject matter and the relevant background. As an experienced senior translator has pointed out: "The importance of the translator's store of general knowledge—and of his/her knowledge of the subject matter cannot be overemphasized, and it can almost be accepted as a rule that, given the required language proficiency, the greater the translator's knowledge of the subject matter, the less arduously understanding occurs, and the more accurate his/her representation in the target language."

In order to expand his/her scope of knowledge, a conscientious translator should always do two things on his/her own: (1) constantly exposing himself/herself to various reading materials on all subjects relevant to his/her work; (2) conscientiously consulting relevant background materials or reference materials on the subject dealt with so as to keep up with the latest developments of the branch of knowledge he/she works in.

Reflections and Practice

I. Discuss the following questions.
1. What is the definition of translation? What kind of role does it play in our society?
2. What is the nature of translation? Do you agree with the author's point of view? Why or why not?
3. How is translation generally categorized? Which of the categories are you familiar with?
4. How do you understand Yan Fu's three-character guide "信、达、雅"? What's your opinion on the principles or criteria of translation?
5. What is literal translation? What is free translation? What principles should a translator abide by when applying them to translation?
6. What do you know about translation techniques? Name a few of them and try to cite some examples.

II. Put the following sentences into Chinese, using either literal or free translation.
1. Every life has its roses and thorns.
2. I'll have Lisa where I want her.

3. He carried his age astonishingly well.
4. She'd never again believe anything in trousers.
5. He was a dead shot. However, he met his Waterloo this time.
6. Valuable left in full view can be open invitation to theft.
7. Yet China was a land of constant surprise and shifting impression.
8. After the failure of his last novel, his reputation stands on slippery ground.
9. In dealing with a challenge on such a scale, it is no exaggeration to say "unity we stand, divided we fall".
10. He walked at the head of the funeral procession, and every now and then wiped his crocodile tears with a big handkerchief.
11. It is the same old story of not being grateful for what we have until we lose it, of not being conscious of health until we are ill.
12. Mr. Lowenhaupt recalls an acquaintance from China teaching him a Chinese saying, "rice paddy to rice paddy in three generations".
13. It was the best of times, it was the worst of times; it was the age of wisdom, it was the age of foolishness; it was the epoch of belief, it was the epoch of incredulity; it was the season of the Light, it was the season of Darkness; it was the spring of Hope, it was the winter of Despair; we had everything before us, we had nothing before us; we were all going to Heaven, we were all going direct the other way.
14. A greeting card can warm a heart, hold a hand, lend an ear, pat a back, light up a face, tickle a funny bone, dry an eye, surprise a child, woo a sweetheart, toast a bride, welcome a stranger, wave a good-bye, shout a bravo, blow a kiss, mend a quarrel, ease a pain, boost a morale, stop a worry and start a tradition.

III. Compare the following different Chinese versions with the English text, paying attention to literal translation and free translation.

1. Motto
   All other things above
   Are liberty and love;
   Life would I gladly tender
   For love: yet joyfully
   Would love itself surrender
   For liberty. (Petőfi: *Liberty and Love*)

UNIT 1　Introduction: Translation and Translation Techniques

译文 A　座右铭

我一生最宝贵：
恋爱与自由。
为了恋爱的缘故，
生命可以舍去；
但为了自由的缘故，
我将欢欢喜喜地把恋爱舍去。

译文 B　格言

生命诚可贵，
爱情价更高；
若为自由故，
二者皆可抛！

2. *Evolution and Ethics*

　　It may be safely assumed that, two thousand years ago, before Caesar set foot in southern Britain, the whole countryside visible from the windows of the room in which I write, was in what is called "the state of Nature". Except, it may be, by raising a few sepulchral mounds, such as those which still here and there, break the flowing contours of the downs, man's hands had made no mark upon it; and the thin veil of vegetation which overspread the broad-backed heights and the shelving sides of the coombs was unaffected by his industry. (Huxley)

译文 A　《天演论》

　　赫胥黎独处一室之中，在英伦之南，背山而面野。槛外诸境，历历如在几下。乃悬想二千年前，当罗马大将恺撒未到时，此间有何景物。计惟有天造草昧，人功未施，其借征人境者，不过几处荒坟，散见坡陀起伏间。而灌木丛林，蒙茸山麓，未经删治如今日者，则无疑也。

译文 B　《进化与伦理》

　　可以有把握地想象，二千年前，当恺撒到达不列颠南部之前，从我正在写作的这间屋子的窗口可以看到，整个原野是一种所谓"自然状态"。也许除了若干突起的坟墓已在几处破坏了连绵的丘陵的轮廓以外，此地未经人工修葺整治。薄薄的植被笼罩着广阔的高地和峡谷的斜坡，还没有受到人类劳作的影响。

13

3. **Of Studies**

　　Studies serve for delight, for ornament and, for ability. Their chief use for delight is in privateness and retiring; for ornament, is in discourse; and for ability, is in the judgment and disposition of business. For expert men can execute, and perhaps judge of particulars, one by one; but the general counsels and the plots and marshaling of affairs, come best from those that are learned. (Bacon)

译文 A 《论读书》

　　读书可以怡情，足以傅彩，足以长才。其怡情也，最见于独处幽居之时；其傅彩也，最见于高谈阔论之中；其长才也，最见于处事判事之际。练达之士虽能分别处理细事或一一判别枝节，然纵观统筹、全局策划，则舍好学深思者莫属。

译文 B 《论读书》

　　读书可以作为消遣，可以作为装饰，也可以增长才干。孤独寂寞时，阅读可以消遣。高谈阔论时，知识可供装饰。处世行事时，正确运用知识意味着才干。懂得事务因果的人是幸运的，有实际经验的人虽能够处理个别性的事务，但若要综观整体、运筹全局，却唯有学识方能办到。

Unit 2 Diction

> ● 单元要点概述
>
> 相关翻译技巧训练英译汉：Euphemism in British Speech
> 相关翻译技巧训练汉译英：中文热词
> I. 英汉字词层面的对等关系
> II. 英语词义辨析法
> III. 英语词语翻译技巧
> IV. 汉译英的选词用字

本单元介绍了翻译中的遣词用字技巧。首先用对比的方式归纳了英汉字词层面的五种对应情况，即字词对等、多种同义、一词多义、词义交织、无对等词语。

接着从 4 个角度探讨了如何判断某一英语词语的准确含义，即：通过构词法、通过指代关系、根据上下文或词的搭配词义、根据不同学科或专业门类来确定词义。

在词义辨析的基础上归纳了英语词语翻译的 8 种常用技巧：推演法、移植法、引申法、替代法、释义法、合并法、音译法、图形法。

汉译英的遣词用字问题与英译汉的情况有所不同。英译汉只要读懂了就能翻译，因为我们输出的是自己所熟悉的语言文字，而汉译英则需要在大量不那么熟悉的词语中做出取舍，然后再去套用英语语法规则，因此往往会感到力不从心——这就是为什么汉译英比英译汉费力的原因所在。

Practice of the Relevant Skill

1. E-C Translation

Euphemism in British speech

The British are probably the world champions of euphemism. The best of these are widely understood, creating a pleasant sense of complicity between the euphemist and his audience. British newspaper obituaries are a rich seam: nobody likes to speak ill of the dead, yet many enjoy a hint of the truth about the person who has "passed away". A drunkard will be described as "convivial" or "cheery". Unbearably garrulous is "sociable" or the dread "ebullient"; "lively wit" means a penchant for telling cruel and unfunny stories. "Austere" and "reserved" mean joyless and depressed. Someone with a foul temper "did not suffer fools gladly". The priapic will have "enjoyed female company"; nymphomania is "notable vivacity". Uncontrollable appetites of all sorts may earn the ultimate accolade: "He lived life to the full."

Such euphemisms are a pleasant echo of an age when private lives enjoyed a degree of protective discretion that now seems unimaginable in Britain. That left room for "a confirmed bachelor" (a homosexual) or someone "burdened by occasional irregularities in his private life" (leaving the reader guessing whether the problem was indecent exposure, adultery or cross-dressing).

Writing about dead people is a question only of taste, because they can't sue. Describing the living (especially in libel-happy jurisdictions such as England) requires prudence. "Thirsty" applied to a British public figure usually means heavy drinking; "tired and emotional" (a term that has moved from the pages of *Private Eye*, a satirical magazine, into general parlance) means visibly drunk. "Hands-on mentoring" of a junior colleague can be code for an affair, hopefully not coupled with a "volatile" personality, which means terrifying eruptions of temper. References to "rumbustious" business practices or "controversial", "murky" and "questionable" conduct usually mean the journalist believes something illegal is going on, but couldn't stand it up in court if sued.

In the upper reaches of the British establishment, euphemism is a fine art, one that new arrivals need to master quickly. "Other Whitehall agencies" or "our friends over the river" means the intelligence services (American spooks often say they "work for the government"). A civil servant warning a minister that a decision would be "courageous" is saying that it will be career-cripplingly unpopular. "Adventurous" is even worse: it means mad and unworkable. A "frank discussion" is a row, while a "robust exchange of views" is a full-scale shouting match.

Euphemism is so ingrained in British speech that foreigners, even those who speak fluent English, may miss the signals contained in such bland remarks as "incidentally" (which means, "I am now telling you the purpose of this discussion"); and "with the greatest respect" ("You are mistaken and silly").

Notes and Explanations

1. euphemism *n.* 委婉语
2. complicity *n.* 共谋，串通
3. obituary *n.* 讣告
4. speak ill of 诋毁，说……的坏话
5. garrulous *adj.* 唠叨的，喋喋不休的
6. ebullient *adj.* 热情洋溢的，沸腾的
7. penchant *n.* 爱好，嗜好
8. suffer fools gladly 耐着性子与蠢人相处
9. priapic *adj.* 阴茎的，崇拜男性生殖器的
10. nymphomania *n.* 慕男狂，花痴
11. ultimate accolade 最高褒奖
12. homosexual *n.* 同性恋
13. indecent exposure *n.* 有伤风化的暴露，露阴（特指男性）
14. adultery *n.* 通奸
15. cross-dressing *n.* 穿异性服装
16. libel-happy jurisdictions 以审理诽谤案件为乐的司法区域
17. *Private Eye*《私家侦探》
18. the intelligence services 情报部门
19. career-cripplingly 削弱就业
20. ingrained *adj.* 根深蒂固的，积习成性的

2. C-E Translation

中文热词

中文热词通常反映社会变化和文化，有些在外国媒体上愈来愈流行。例如，"土豪"和"大妈"都是老词，但已获取了新的意义。

"土豪"以前指欺压佃户和仆人的乡村地主，现在用于指花钱如流水或喜欢炫耀财富的人，也就是说，土豪有钱，但是没有品位。"大妈"是对中年妇女的称呼，但是现在特指不久前金价大跌时大量购买黄金的中国妇女。

"土豪"和"大妈"可能会被收入新版《牛津英语词典》，至今约有120个中文词条加进了牛津英语词典，成为英语语言的一部分。

Notes and Explanations

1. 热词 hot words/buzzword
2. 反映社会变化和文化 reflect social changes and culture
3. 外国媒体 foreign media
4. 愈来愈流行 be increasingly popular
5. 老词 obsolete saying
6. 获取新的意义 get different new meanings
7. 欺压佃户和仆人 oppress the tenants and servants
8. 花钱如流水 spend money like water
9. 炫耀财富 show off one's wealth
10. 没有品位 have no taste
11. 特指 refer in particular to
12. 大跌 plunge/tumble
13. 新版《牛津英语词典》 the latest *Oxford English Dictionary*
14. 加进词典 add to the entries

By "diction" we mean the proper choice of words and phrases in the process of translation to fit their context.

In the practice of translation, it has always been an arduous task for the translator to find the right equivalent to the target language. Great care is called for in the translation of "familiar" English words into Chinese, as their meanings vary with the change in collocation or context. Take the following simple sentence for example:

- Tension is building up.

Simple as it is, the above sentence cannot be translated into Chinese without a given context. Actually, we may have different Chinese versions accordingly:

- 形势紧张起来。
- 张力在增大。
- 电压在增加。
- 压力在增强。
- ……

Another example:

- I'll *finish* the book next week.

We cannot fix the exact meaning of "finish" without context. If we have the contextual information such as "I've been reading/writing/editing the book", or "I'll go to library/the press", the translation would be quite easy:

下周我要看完/写完/审完这本书。

As a noted linguist has observed, "the meaning of a word is its use in the language", and "each word, when used in a new context, is a new word". Sometimes, even the same word or expression may evoke different meanings.

More examples:
- *As luck would have it*, no one was in the building when the explosion occurred. **真幸运**，发生爆炸时大楼里没有人。
- *As luck would have it*, there was rain on the day of the picnic. **真不巧**，野餐那天下雨了。

Even more examples may be found in the above Practice of the Relevant Skill, such as: not suffer fools gladly 没有耐心与蠢人周旋；enjoy female company 大受女性欢迎，男色情狂； nymphomania 慕男狂，花痴；notable vivacity 特别精力充沛，女性的好色；uncontrollable appetites of all sorts 欲望无度的人；the ultimate accolade 最高褒奖；live life to the full 人生完满无憾；leave room for 留下想象空间；be burdened by occasional irregularities in his private life 私生活因偶尔违规而受拖累；indecent exposure 有伤风化的露阴癖；cross-dressing 易装癖；tired and emotional 又累又情绪化；*Private Eye*《私家侦探》；hands-on mentoring 手把手指导；affair 风流韵事；visibly drunk 喝得烂醉如泥； frank discussion 坦率讨论；robust exchange of views 强有力的交换意见；with the greatest respect 以最大的尊重……；and so on.

In comparison with Chinese, English words are generally more flexible both in form and in meaning; therefore, it is often a hard task for a translator to find their Chinese equivalents that are suitable to the occasion. Take the word "story" for example:

(1) This war is becoming the most important *story* of this generation.

(2) It is quite another *story* now.

(3) Some reporters who were not included in the session broke the *story*.

(4) He'll be very happy if that *story* holds up.

(5) The Rita Hayworth's *story* is one of the saddest.

(6) What a *story*! I don't believe a word of it.

(7) Last December *The Post* first reported that probes were being made in each of those cities, but officials refused to confirm the *story*.

(8) The *story* about him became smaller and by and by faded out from American TV.

Judging from the context, "story" in the above sentences indicates different senses respectively: (1) event; (2) situation; (3) inside information; (4) statement; (5) experience; (6) lie; (7) news; (8) report. Therefore, the corresponding Chinese versions should be：

(1) 这场战争将成为这一代人所经历的最重大的**事件**。

(2) 现在的**情况**完全不同了。

(3) 有些未获准参加那次会议的记者把**内情**捅出去了。

(4) 如果这一**说法**当真，那他就太高兴了。

(5) 丽泰·海华丝的**遭遇**算最惨的了。

(6) 弥天**大谎**！我只字不信。

(7) 去年12月，《邮报》首先报道调查工作已在那些城市里进行，但官员们拒绝证实这条**消息**。

(8) **报道**中对他的渲染减少了，不久就从美国电视上销声匿迹了。

On the other hand, a Chinese word or phrase may be translated into various English versions in different contexts. Take the Chinese expression "情况" for example:

- 在这种**情况**下 under such *circumstances* (such being the *case*)
- 这种**情况**必须改变。This *state of affairs* must change.
- 现在的**情况**不同了。Now *things* are different.
- 他们的**情况**怎么样？How do *matters* stand with them?
- 前线有什么**情况**？How is the *situation* at the front?
- 我们可能去那儿，那得看**情况**而定。We may go there, but *that depends*.

It is evident that there is no fixed pattern of word-for-word transformation that is available to either E-C or C-E translation.

I. Equivalence Between English and Chinese at Word Level

Generally speaking, the equivalence between English and Chinese at word level may be categorized as follows:

1. Word-for-Word Equivalence

This is most evidently shown in proper nouns and technical terms. For example:

- Marxism：马克思主义
- Internet：因特网
- 计算机：computer
- 白血病：leukemia

2. One Word with Multiple Equivalents of the Same Meaning

This is a common case in translation. For example:

- wife: 妻子、爱人、夫人、老婆、老伴、媳妇、堂客、内人……
- potato: 马铃薯、洋芋、土豆、山药蛋……

- 人：human being, man, people, person...
- 犬：dog, hound, spaniel, mastiff, pointer, setter, retriever, terrier...

3. One Word with Several Equivalents of Different Meanings

This is also very common in translation. For example:
- cousin: 堂兄、堂弟、堂姐、堂妹、表哥、表弟、表姐、表妹、远亲……
- president: 总统、总裁、主席、董事长、议长、会长、社长、校长……
- carry: 搬、运、送、提、拎、挑、担、抬、背、扛、搂、抱、端、举、夹、捧……
- 走：walk, saunter, amble, stride, trudge, traipse, shamble, prance, scamper, clump, tiptoe...
- 机：machine, engine, plane, aircraft...
- 羊：sheep, goat, ram, ewe, lamb...

4. Equivalents Interwoven with One Another

In this case, a certain word may be treated differently according to various circumstances or collocations. For example:

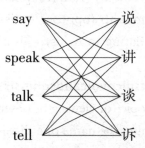

5. Words Without Corresponding Equivalents

In this case, an explanation is given instead of an equivalent. For example：
- teenager: 13 岁至 19 岁的青少年
- cyberslacker: 利用工作时间在公司上网、做与工作无关的事情的雇员
- meatloaf: 朋友、同事之间以群体信件的方式自发传播的电子信件
- 阴：*yin* (in Chinese thought) the soft inactive female principle or force in the world
- 阳：*yang* (in Chinese thought) the strong active male principle or force in the world
- (目不识) 丁：(not know one's) ABC

II. Methods to Make out the Meaning of a Given Word

Since the meaning of English words is unfixed, it is up to the translator to single out the right wording in light of a given context. And the following are some major methods to make out word meaning.

1. Judging by Word Formation

In order to make out the original meaning of an English word, it is necessary for us to have a knowledge of English lexicology, and specifically, a knowledge of word formation, such as compounding, derivation, affixation, blending, acronym formation, clipping, etc. A good command of them will help to shed light on the correct meaning of some difficult words. For example:

indefatigability=in-(not) + de-(reversing the effect of) + fatig(ue)-(tiredness) + -able (capable of) + -lity (the state or condition) 不屈不挠，孜孜不倦

biomicrominiaturization=bio-(of life) + micro-(very small) + miniature (of very small copy) + -ize (to make, cause to become) + -tion (of noun) 生物超小型化

antidisestablishmentarianism=anti-(oppose) + dis-(apart) + establish (to set up) + -ment (of noun) + -arian (of or relating to Arius) + -ism (a distinctive doctrine or theory) 反对教会与国家分开学说

pneumonoultramicroscopicsilicovolcanoconiosis = pneumono-(of lung) + ultra-(beyond) + micro-(very small) + scopic-(of viewing or observing) + silico-(of silicon) + volcano + coni-(koni, of dust) + -osis (forming the name of a disease) 硅酸盐沉着病，肺尘病

2. Judging by References

In many cases the meaning of a pronominal word may be judged from the references, as shown in the following points.

(1) Third person pronouns; indefinite pronouns such as some, any, each, both; and definite pronouns such as much, many, few, little, etc. For example:

- He [father] sent John to the university and was eager to have *him* distinguish *himself*. 他送约翰上大学，巴望能让**儿子**出类拔萃。

(2) Demonstrative pronouns, such as this, that, these, those, and demonstrative adverbs such as here, there, now, then, etc. For example:

- Health is above wealth, for *this* cannot give so much happiness as *that*. 健康比财富更重要，因为**财富**不能像**健康**那样给人那么多幸福。(Or: 因为**后者**不能像**前者**那样给人那么多幸福。)

(3) References of comparison. For example:
- I hate blue shirts; white shirts suit me but gray is *the most preferable*. 我讨厌穿蓝衬衫，喜欢穿白衬衫，而最喜欢穿**灰衬衫**。

Without the referential words "son", "health", "wealth" and "shirt" in the above three sentences, it would be very difficult to make out the real meaning of such words as "him", "himself", "this", "that" and "the most preferable".

3. Judging by Context and Collocation

Context refers to the parts of a text or statement that come before or follow a word or passage and determine its meaning, as in the previous cases of "tension" and "story". Here are some more examples in the case of "develop".

- His plane *developed* engine trouble only seven miles after takeoff. (发生故障)
- The wings must *develop* a lift force in order to sustain the aircraft. (产生升力)
- In 1752 Franklin *developed* a practical lightning rod. (研制避雷针)
- Until a new theory was *developed*, they did not have much success. (提出理论)
- Their skill *developed* until it rivaled their teacher's. (提高技术)
- He revealed the secret of a new type of potato he had *developed*. (培育新品种)
- As young Goddard grew into manhood, he *developed* tuberculosis. (患上结核病)
- We must *develop* all the natural substances in our country. (开发资源)
- Several attempts have been made through the years to *develop* the deposit. (开采矿床)
- He is an instructor who *develops* the capabilities of each student. (激发潜能)
- The boys did exercises that *develop* muscles. (促进肌肉生长)
- She *developed* her thesis in a series of articles. (阐明论点)
- With hard work, she *developed* into a great writer. (成为作家)
- I *developed* a photograph in the nearby shop. (冲洗照片)

Collocation, an arrangement of words that sounds natural, is also an inseparable factor that affects the outcome of diction. As we may see from the following illustrations, the word "delicate" may be rendered into various Chinese expressions to suit different occasions.

- *delicate* difference 讲不大清楚的差别
- *delicate* diplomatic question 微妙的外交问题
- *delicate* ear for music 对音乐有鉴赏力
- *delicate* features 清秀的五官
- *delicate* food 美味的食物
- *delicate* health 虚弱的身体

- *delicate* living 奢侈的生活
- *delicate* porcelain 精致的瓷器
- *delicate* sense of smell 灵敏的嗅觉
- *delicate* skin 娇嫩的皮肤
- *delicate* stomach 容易吃坏的胃
- *delicate* surgical operation 难做的外科手术
- *delicate* touch 生花妙笔
- *delicate* upbringing 娇生惯养
- *delicate* vase 容易碰碎的花瓶

4. Judging by Branches of Learning and Specialties

For example, the word "base" means "词根" in lexicology; "本金" in business; "底涂" in painting; "基线" in survey; "根据地" in military science; and here are some more:

- The lathe should be set on a firm *base*. (machinery) 车床应安装在坚实的**底座**上。
- As we all know, a *base* reacts with an acid to form a salt. (chemistry) 众所周知，**碱**与酸反应生成盐。
- A transistor has three electrodes, the emitter, the *base* and the collector. (electronics) 晶体管有三个电极，即发射极，**基极**和集电极。
- Line AB is the *base* of the triangle ABC. (maths) AB 线是三角形 ABC 的**底边**。
- He is on the second *base*. (sports) 他在二**垒**。
- The weary troops marched back to the *base*. (military science) 疲惫不堪的士兵列队返回**基地**。

III. Techniques of Translating a Given English Word

In their translation practice, Chinese translators have summed up a lot of translation techniques that are available to picking the right meaning of a given English word, as shown in the following cases:

1. Deduction

This is a major means in E-C translation which is used to deduce the original meaning in the light of the explanation of an English dictionary. For example：

- *boomer*—a person born in the marked rise in birthrate (as in the U.S. immediately following the end of World War II) 生育高峰期出生的人

- *cybercafé*—a coffee house that provides patrons with computer terminals for browsing the Internet for a fee 网吧
- *smart card*—electronic card: a small plastic card containing a microchip that can store personal data and bankaccount details 智能卡
- *win-win*—beneficial to each of the two in some way 双赢

2. Transplant

By this technique, we may translate the ingredients of a given English word literally and then combine each part of them.

- *bandwidth* 带宽
- *microwave* 微波
- *splashdown* 溅落
- *blue tooth* 蓝牙
- *supermarket* 超级市场
- *whitecollar* 白领

3. Extension

The extension of meaning may be either from the specific to the general or from the concrete to the abstract, and vice versa.

- *bottleneck* 瓶颈→交通狭口→薄弱环节 (from the concrete to the abstract)
- *brain trust* 脑托拉斯→智囊团 (from the specific to the general)
- *ecstasy* (an illegal drug) 入迷→摇头丸 (from the abstract to the concrete)
- It is more than transient *everydayness*. 这远非一时的**柴米油盐问题**。(from the abstract to the concrete)
- *cry wolf* 叫"狼来了"→发假警报 (from the specific to general)

4. Substitution

This technique is used to replace the words of the original expression with Chinese synonyms or idioms according to different situations.

- to *kill sb. as an example* 杀一儆百（或：**杀鸡给猴看**）
- Please *withhold* the handout. 请**不要发**这些材料。
- He was indeed a good *riddance*. 他还**是不在**的好。
- The same is not true with a *mortal illness*. 如果是得了**不治之症**（或：**绝症**），情况就不一样了。

5. Explanation

This technique is commonly used when there is no corresponding Chinese expression and all the abovementioned techniques fail to make sense.

- *mindlessness* 思想上的混沌状态

- *togetherness*（家庭或社会的）和睦相处
- *redshirt* [美] 红衫运动员（指出色的美国大学生运动员，尤指橄榄球运动员）
- *swan song* 绝唱；天鹅临死时发出的忧伤动听的歌声，（诗人、音乐家等）最后的作品

6. Combination

This technique is used to integrate two words of close meaning into one expression.

- so *subtle* and *careful* an observer 一位如此**精细**的观察者
- his *mendacity* and *dishonesty* 他的**狡诈**
- a *grim* and *tragic* Christmas 一个**惨淡**的圣诞节
- the *body* and *mind* cramped by noxious work 有害工作造成的**身心**困顿

7. Transliteration

This technique is commonly used in dealing with proper nouns (especially the names of people and places, trademarks, etc.). Besides, it is also used in coinage when no existing Chinese expression is available.

- *bungee* 蹦极
- *Citroen* 雪铁龙（轿车）
- *domino* 多米诺骨牌
- *hacker* 黑客
- *pizza* 比萨饼
- *The Times* 《泰晤士报》
- *calorie* 卡路里
- *clone* 克隆
- *euro* 欧元
- *Internet* 因特网
- *quinine* 奎宁（金鸡纳霜）
- *Wall Street* 华尔街

8. Pictographic Translation

By this technique English words are translated according to their actual shapes.

- *H-beam* 工字梁
- *U-steel* 槽钢
- *X-brace* 交叉支撑
- *O-ring* 环形圈
- *V-belt* 三角皮带
- *Y-curve* 叉形曲线

IV. Diction in C-E Translation

Diction in C-E translation is somewhat different from that of E-C translation. If the crux of the latter lies in picking out the right Chinese word from those we know very well, the former then is much more difficult—we have to deal with an English vocabulary that we are not so familiar with. For example, the familiar Chinese adjective "老", so simple and common a word, when used in different contexts, the English equivalents rarely keep to its original meaning "old"—that explains why we are often frustrated when trying to find out an accurate English equivalent for a certain Chinese word.

- 老战士 a *veteran*
- 老师傅 a *master* craftsman
- 老黄牛 a *willing* ox
- 老皇历 *ancient* history, *obsolete* practice
- 老家 *hometown*, *native* place
- 老领导 a *senior* leader
- 老儿子 the *youngest* son
- 老芹菜 *overgrown* celery

Another example, the Chinese noun "书":

- 申请书 *letter* of application
- 成绩通知书 grade *report*
- 家书 a *letter* from home
- 楷书 regular *script*
- 保证书 *guarantee*
- 协议书 *agreement*
- （使用）说明书 *directions*
- 国书 *credential*
- 证书 *certificate*
- 白皮书 White *Book*

A further example, the Chinese expression "运动":

- 运动有益身心。*Exercise* is good for health.
- 足球是我喜欢的运动。Football is my favorite *sport*.
- 他在香港热心推广手球运动。He is a keen promoter of *handball* in Hong Kong.
- 我国每年纪念"五四运动"。The May Fourth *Movement* is commemorated in our country every year.
- 人们热烈响应筹款运动。There was great enthusiasm for the donation *drive*.
- 他们发动了一场戒烟运动。They started a *campaign* against smoking.
- 这属于运动神经疾病。This belongs to *motor* nerve disease.
- 技术革新运动是成功的关键。Technological *renovation* is a key to the success.

Finally, the Chinese character "着":

- 她着凉了。She has *caught* (a) cold.
- 你猜着了。You've guessed *right*.
- 炉子着得很旺。The fire is *burning* briskly in the stove.
- 上不着天，下不着地。Be *suspended in mid air*.
- 老李躺下就着了。Lao Li *fell asleep* as soon as he lay down.
- 他有点着慌。He *got* alarmed.
- 他走错了一着。He has made a false *move*. (or: taken a wrong *step*)
- 屋顶上全都覆盖着积雪。The roofs are all covered *with* snow.
- 这些孩子穿着整齐。These children *are* all neatly *dressed*.
- 再着一把力。*Make* one more effort.

- 我们着眼于未来。We *have* our eyes on the future.
- 他们正在着手制订计划。They are *starting* drawing up the plan.

Evidently, there is no fixed diction pattern for us to follow either in E-C or C-E translation. Therefore, a qualified translator must take all these factors into consideration and make efforts to achieve the best effect in his/her translation.

Reflections and Practice

I. Discuss the following questions.

1. What does "diction" mean? Can we match each Chinese word with a corresponding English word in translation? Why, or why not?
2. What do you know about "context"? How do you understand the statement "each word, when used in a new context, is a new word"?
3. What kinds of correspondence are there between English and Chinese at word level?
4. What are the basic methods to make out the meaning of a given English word? Cite some examples to illustrate them.
5. Summarize the eight techniques employed in translating a given English word, trying to find some examples of your own.

II. Put the following into Chinese, paying attention to the italicized words.

1. Needing some *light* to see by, the burglar crossed the room with a *light* step to *light* the *light* with the *light* green shade.
2. "I *got* on horseback within ten minutes after I *got* your letter. When I *got* to Canterbury, I *got* a chaise for town, but I *got wet through,* and *have got* such a cold that I shall not *get rid of* it in a hurry. I *got* to the Treasury about noon, but first of all *got* shaved and dressed. I soon *got* into the secret of *getting* a memorial before the Board, but I could not *get* an answer then; however I *got* intelligence from a messenger that I should *get* one next morning..."
3. All citizens in this nation are *subject to* the law.
4. Payments are *subject to* change in keeping with inflation.
5. *Subject to* the fulfillment of other formalities, they shall be granted all necessary permits.
6. Before it begins to work, the yeast is *subject to* disruption caused by fluctuations in temperature.

UNIT 2 Diction

7. Accession shall be *subject to* approval of a twothird vote of the Directors of the Governing Body.
8. Samples are *subject to* a series of tests in the lab, the object of which is largely to determine the correct processing methods to be adopted in each case.
9. The *mechanism* of the process, slow and delicate, often escapes our attention.
10. Under capitalism drugs and alcohol are used by some as an escape *mechanism*.
11. But people are apt to marvel at an ingenious *mechanism* and obliterate the man who makes it.
12. Perhaps this is the very *mechanism* of the creators of our nation who hold these truths to be selfevident.
13. And, again as a result of the development of modern technology, *mechanism* in philosophy became an upstart.
14. The two model variants of the socialist economic *mechanism* are to be distinguished from the point of view of market function.
15. Society needs a *mechanism* for sorting out its more intelligent members from its less intelligent ones, just as a track team needs a *mechanism* (such as a stopwatch) for sorting out the faster athletes from the slower ones.

III. Translate the following Chinese words and expressions into English, paying attention to the bold-faced words.

1. 馆：
   博物馆、图书馆、旅馆、宾馆、大使馆、领事馆、茶馆、饭馆、理发馆、体育馆、展览馆、文化馆、美术馆、科技馆、天文馆、照相馆……
2. 酒：
   葡萄酒、白酒、烈酒、啤酒、香槟酒、鸡尾酒、白兰地酒、威士忌酒、杜松子酒……
3. 笔：
   钢笔、铅笔、圆珠笔、蜡笔、粉笔、毛笔、画笔、电笔……
4. 机：
   收音机、电话机、电视机、拖拉机、推土机、搅拌机、起重机……
5. 好：
   a. 他是祖国的**好**儿子。 b. 庄稼长得真**好**。
   c. 他们对我真**好**。   d. 这幢建筑质量不**好**。
   e. 这个问题很**好**回答。   f. 啊，**好**票！
6. 学习：
   a. 学习知识   b. 学习技术
   c. 学习外语   d. 学习成绩

  e. 学习年限   f. 互相学习
  g. 学习雷锋好榜样   h. 学习别人的长处

7. 献：
  a. 献花；b. 献丑；c. 献艺；d. 献计；e. 献媚；f. 献身；g. 捐献财物

8. 送：
  a. 送某人一本书   b. 送礼
  c. 送信   d. 送客
  e. 送行   f. 送雨伞
  g. 送命   h. 送孩子上学
  i. 送某人回家   j. 将卫星送上天
  k. 送葬   l. 送罪犯上法庭审判

Unit 3 Conversion

● 单元要点概述

相关翻译技巧训练英译汉：What Defines a Genius?
相关翻译技巧训练汉译英：泼水节

I. 英译汉的词类转换
 1. 各种词类转换成动词　　　　2. 各种词类转换成名词
 3. 各种词类转换成形容词　　　4. 各种词类转换成副词
 5. 英译汉句子成分的转换

II. 汉译英的词类转换
 1. 动词转换为名词、形容词、介词、副词等
 2. 各种词类之间的相互转换

本单元讲解、归纳了翻译中的词类转换和句子成分的转换问题。

由于英汉两种语言在语法和表达习惯上的差异，我们有时必须改变某些词语的词类或句子成分才能有效地翻译出原文的准确意思。英语一个句子只能有一个谓语动词，而汉语动词的数量不受限制，因此英译汉往往需要我们将英语的各种词类转换成汉语动词。此外，各种词类也可以转换成名词、形容词、副词等。句子成分的转换包括主语与宾语之间的互相转换及主语转换为谓语、状语等。

汉译英的关键是使译文符合英语的表达习惯，必须将汉语中的大量动词转换为名词、形容词、介词、副词等。除动词之外，汉译英也涉及其他一些词类的转换。

Practice of the Relevant Skill

1. E-C Translation

What Defines a Genius?

People attach the label "genius" to such diverse characters as Leonardo da Vinci, Bobby Fischer and Toni Morrison. The varied achievements of such individuals beg the question: what defines a genius? People have long equated genius with intelligence, but it is more aptly characterized by creative productivity. Such exceptional output depends on a combination of genetics, opportunity and effort. Nobody can be called out for outstanding contributions to a field without a lot of hard work, but progress is faster if you are born with the right skills. Personality also plays a role. If you are very open to new experiences and if you have psychopathic traits (yes, as in those shared by serial killers) such as being aggressive and emotionally tough, you are more likely to be considered a genius.

To make the contributions for which they are known, all geniuses depend on the same general process. It starts with an unrestrained search for ideas without foresight into their utility. This hunt takes a creator down many dead-end roads, causing him or her to backtrack and start over. This trial-and-error process eventually leads a solution that works. For anyone who has engaged in a project for which progress is hard to measure or that seems to stall or meander, this theory is heartening. When a problem or endeavor is difficult, we should probably not expect our research to proceed in a linear fashion. The many seemingly wasted hours exploring roads that lead nowhere may really be necessary to find an effective and innovative solution.

Of course, not everyone is equally equipped to come up with such solutions. True creativity and genius depends on an unfiltered view of the world, one that is unconstrained by preconceptions and more open to novelty. In particular, a less conceptual and more literal way of thinking, one more typical of people with autism, can open the mind up to seeing details that most people miss. People with a more open mindset see visual elements in ways that enable them to create strikingly realistic drawings. One boy gained impressive mechanical skills from a brain injury that gave him an unusual eye for the parts of things.

Our schools devote scant resources on nurturing nascent genius, focused as they are on helping those students most likely to be left behind. School-based gifted education receives little state or federal funding. Only four states currently mandate services for gifted students and fully fund those mandates. The failure to develop the talents of our children deprives all of us of a stable of future innovators, creative thinkers, leaders and outstanding performers.

Notes and Explanations

1. Leonardo da Vinci 达·芬奇（1452—1519），意大利文艺复兴时期博学者
2. Bobby Fischer 博比·菲舍尔（1943—2008）美国历史上首位也是唯一一位国际象棋世界冠军
3. Toni Morrison 托尼·莫里森（1931— ）美国黑人女小说家，1993年获诺贝尔文学奖
4. beg the question 回避问题实质，用未经证实的假定来辩论
5. aptly *adv.* 适宜地，适当地
6. psychopathic trait 精神变态特征
7. unrestrained search 无限制的搜索
8. foresight into their utility 预见它们的实用性
9. dead-end road 死胡同
10. trial-and-error process 试错过程；反复试验
11. roads that lead nowhere 没出路的道路
12. unfiltered view 对世界全面的视角
13. unconstrained by preconceptions 不受先入之见限制
14. autism *n.* 自闭症，自我中心主义
15. mindset *n.* 心态，倾向，精神状态
16. nascent *adj.* 初生的，幼稚的
17. mandate *n.* 授权
18. a stable of 一大批

2. C-E Translation

泼 水 节

泼水是傣族新年的主要喜庆活动。人们互相泼水，表示洗去身上一年的尘垢，迎接新一年的到来。泼水有文泼和武泼之分。文泼是对长者的泼法，舀起一勺水，一边说着祝福的话，一边拉开长者的衣领，将水顺着领口往下浇。被泼的人欣然接受对方的祝福。武泼则没有固定的形式，用瓢、用盆、用桶都可以，互相追逐，劈头盖脸地泼。被人泼的水越多，说明受到的祝福越多，被泼的人也越高兴。

Notes and Explanations

1. 泼水 water splashing
2. 新年的主要喜庆活动 the main New Year celebration activity
3. 洗去尘垢 wash off the dust and dirt
4. 文泼/武泼 gentle splashing/fierce splashing
5. 舀水 ladle some water
6. 欣然接受祝福 accept it with good grace
7. 互相追逐 run after each other
8. 劈头盖脸 face to face, head-on

Conversion, one of the commonly adopted translation techniques, means the change of parts of speech in translation. Owing to the syntactical differences between English and Chinese, it is usually impossible for a translator to keep to the original part of speech in the process of translation. Therefore, we have to resort to the technique of conversion. For example:

Original English: This watch never *varies* more than a second in a month.

Chinese Version: 这块表一个月的误差从不超过一秒钟。

The English verb "vary" can hardly be rendered into Chinese by the same part of speech without spoiling the original meaning. In fact, a word belonging to a certain part of speech in one language sometimes has to be converted into a different part of speech, so as to bring forth a readable and coherent sentence. And here are more instances from the above Practice of the Relevant Skill:

- *The varied achievements* of such individuals beg the question: what defines a genius? 他们的成就千差万别，这就引出了这样一个回避问题实质的问题：天才的定义是什么？
- People have long equated genius with intelligence, but it *is more aptly characterized* by creative productivity. 长久以来，人们一直认为天才与才智等同，其实它更**恰当的特征**是创造性生产力。
- Such exceptional output *depends on a combination of* genetics, opportunity and effort. 只有**把**遗传、机遇、努力等因素**结合起来**，才能产生如此超常的结果。
- Nobody can *be called out for outstanding contributions to a field* without a lot of hard work, but progress *is faster* if you are born with the right skills. 不经过艰苦的努力，谁也不能**以杰出贡献问鼎某一领域**。但是如果你天赋异禀，成功会**来得更快**。
- If you are *very open* to new experiences and if you have psychopathic traits (yes, as in those shared by serial killers) such as being aggressive and emotionally tough, *you are more likely to be considered* a genius. 如果你**乐于尝试**新鲜事物，还有一

些精神变态特征（没错，类似某些连环杀手的特征），比如生性好斗、情感强硬，那么别人就更有可能认为你是天才。

- *To make the contributions for which they are known*, all geniuses depend on the same general process. 所有天才**在一鸣惊人之前**，都经历过同一个过程。
- This hunt *takes a creator down many dead-end roads*, causing him or her to backtrack and start over. 在这一过程中，**他们会不断地碰壁，走进死胡同**；这让他们不得不退回去从头再来。
- In particular, *a less conceptual and more literal way of thinking*, one more typical of people with autism, can open the mind up to seeing details that most people miss. 尤其是**思考时多贴近事实，少考虑些概念性的东西**，这种思考方式有助于打开眼界、发现别人错过的细节。
- Our schools *devote scant resources* on nurturing nascent genius, focused as they are on helping those students most likely to be left behind. 我们的学校过于关注帮助潜在后进生，而在培养新生才俊方面**投入不足**。
- *The failure to develop* the talents of our children deprives all of us of a stable of future innovators. **我们未能及时开发**孩子们的天分，使我们所有的人都失去了一大批未来的发明家。

I. Conversion in E-C Translation

Conversion of parts of speech in E-C translation generally takes the following forms.

1. Converting into Verbs

One of the most remarkable differences between English and Chinese syntax is the use of the verb. It is taken for granted that an English sentence contains no more than one predicate verb, while in Chinese it is not unusual to have clusters of verbs in a simple sentence. For example:

Original English: Families upstairs *have* to carry pails to the hydrant downstairs for water.

Chinese Version: **住**在楼上的人家**得提**着水桶**去**楼下的水龙头**打**水。

Five verbs are clustered in the Chinese version of an English simple sentence. This indicates obviously that in E-C translation the conversion of English words of various parts of speech into Chinese verbs is a matter of common occurrence.

(1) Nouns converted into verbs

- The *sight* and *sound* of our jet planes filled me with special longing. **看到**我们的喷气式飞机，**听见**隆隆的机声，我感到心驰神往。
- Rockets have found *application* for the *exploration* of the universe. 火箭已被**用来探索**宇宙。
- I think my little brother is a better *teacher* than I. 我认为我的小弟弟比我**教**得好。

(2) Prepositions converted into verbs

- "Coming!" Away she skimmed *over* the lawn, *up* the path, *up* the steps, *across* the verandah, and *into* the porch. "来啦！"她转身蹦跳着**越**过草地，**跑**上小径，**跨**上台阶，**穿**过凉台，**进**了门廊。
- Party officials worked long hours *on* meager food, *in* cold caves, *by* dim lamps. 党的干部每天长时间工作，**吃**的是粗茶淡饭，**住**的是冰冷的窑洞，**点**的是暗淡的油灯。
- A force is needed to move an object *against* inertia. 为使物体**克服**惯性而运动，就需要一个力。

(3) Adjectives converted into verbs

Many English adjectives after a link verb indicating one's consciousness, feelings, emotions, desires, etc. may always be converted into Chinese verbs. These words include "confident, certain, careful, cautious, angry, sure, ignorant, afraid, doubtful, aware, concerned, glad, delighted, sorry, ashamed, thankful, anxious, grateful, able", etc.

- Doctors have said that they are not *sure* they can save his life. 医生说他们不敢**肯定**能否救得了他的命。
- The fact that she was *able* to send a message was a hint. But I had to be *cautious*. 她**能够**给我带个信儿这件事就是个暗示。但是我必须**小心谨慎**。
- Both of the substances are *soluble* in water. 两种物质都能**溶**于水。

(4) Adverbs converted into verbs

- His poor health forced him *away* from England. 健康不佳迫使他**离开**英国。
- When the switch is *off*, the circuit is open and electricity doesn't go *through*. 当开关**断开**时，电路就形成开路，电流不能**通过**。
- In this case the temperature in the furnace is *up*. 这种情况下，炉温就**升高**。

2. Converting into Nouns

Nouns account for an overwhelming majority of the vocabulary both in Chinese and in English. Conversion between nouns and other parts of speech is also frequently adopted in E-C translation.

(1) Verbs converted into nouns

Some verbs derived from nouns may be translated into Chinese nouns.

- Such materials are *characterized* by good insulation and high resistance to wear. 这些材料的**特点**是：绝缘性好，耐磨性强。
- To them, he *personified* absolute power. 在他们看来，他就是绝对权力的**化身**。
- The design *aims* at automatic operation, easy regulation, simple maintenance and high productivity. 设计的**目的**在于自动操作，调节方便，维护简易，生产率高。

(2) Adjectives converted into nouns

Adjectives with the definite articles to indicate categories of people, things, or adjectives used as predicative to indicate the nature of things may also be converted into nouns.

- They did their best to help *the sick* and *the wounded*. 他们尽了最大的努力帮助**病号**和**伤员**。
- Both the compounds are acids: *the former* is strong, *the latter* weak. 这两种化合物都是酸，**前者**是强酸，**后者**是弱酸。
- In the fission process the fission fragments are very *radioactive*. 在裂变过程中，裂变碎片具有强烈的**放射性**。

(3) Pronouns converted into nouns

Pronouns are more frequently used in English than in Chinese. Sometimes we have to convert them into nouns to avoid confusion.

- Radio waves are similar to light waves except that *their* wavelength is much greater. 无线电波与光波相似，但**无线电波**的波长要长得多。
- The specific resistance of iron is not so small as *that* of copper. 铁的电阻系数不如铜的**电阻系数**那样小。
- The result of this experiment is much better than *those* of previous ones. 这次实验的结果比前几次的**实验结果**都好得多。

3. Converting into Adjectives

Some parts of speech in English can be converted into Chinese adjectives to smooth the translation.

(1) Nouns converted into adjectives

Sometimes it is more preferable to convert an English noun into a Chinese adjective.

- The *pallor* of her face indicated clearly how she was feeling at the moment. 她**苍白**的脸色清楚地表明了她那时的情绪。
- This experiment was a *success*. 这个实验很**成功**。
- Independent thinking is an absolute *necessity* in study. 学习中的独立思考是绝对**必需的**。

(2) Adverbs converted into adjectives

English adverbs are used more extensively than Chinese adverbs; and many of them can be converted into Chinese adjectives.

- Earthquakes are *closely* related to faulting. 地震与地层断裂有**密切**的关系。
- It is demonstrated that gases are *perfectly* elastic. 人们已经证实，气体具有**理想**的可收缩性。
- The pressure *inside* equals the pressure *outside*. **内部的**压力和**外部的**压力相等。

Not only can English adverbs be converted into Chinese adjectives, but also into nouns occasionally.

- He is *physically* weak but *mentally* sound. 他**身体**虽弱，但**心智**健全。

4. Converting into Adverbs

Sometimes, for the sake of convenience, some parts of speech in English may be converted into Chinese adverbs.

(1) Adjectives converted into adverbs

This is the most common case when a noun modified by an adjective is converted into a verb in the Chinese version.

- Below 4℃, water is in *continuous* expansion instead of *continuous* contraction. 水在 4 摄氏度以下就**不断地**膨胀，而不是**不断地**收缩。
- Only when we study their properties can we make *better* use of the materials. 只有研究这些材料的特性才能**更好地**利用它们。
- A helicopter is *free* to go almost anywhere. 直升机几乎可以**自由地**飞到任何地方去。

(2) Nouns and verbs converted into adverbs

This conversion is adopted to make the version conform to the idiomatic Chinese expression.

- I have the *honor* to inform you that your request is granted. 我**荣幸地**通知您，您的请求已得到批准。
- The new mayor earned some appreciation by the *courtesy* of coming to visit the city poor. 新市长**礼节性地**前来看望城市贫民，获得了他们的一些好感。
- As noted earlier, gifted children of all kinds *tend to be strong-willed nonconformists*. 如前所示，具有各种不同天赋的孩子**往往都固执己见，从不墨守成规**。

5. The Conversion of Sentence Elements

"Conversion" in a broader sense includes the change of various elements of a sentence. It may also involve the change of the voices, i.e. from the "active voice" into the "passive", and vice versa. For example:

UNIT **3** Conversion

- As the match burns, *heat and light are given off.* 火柴燃烧时**发出**光和热。(from the subject to the object)
- This sort of stone has *a relative density* of 2.7. 这种石头的**相对密度**是2.7。(from the object to the subject)
- *Care* must be taken at all times to protect the instrument from dust and damp. 应当始终**注意**保护仪器，不使其沾染灰尘和受潮。(from the subject to the predicate)
- *Careful comparison of them* will show *you* the difference. 只要仔细将它们比较一下，你就会发现不同之处。(from the subject to the adverbial, from the object to the subject)
- *The baby* doubled *its weight* in a year. 婴儿的**体重**一年中长了一倍。(from the subject to the attributive)
- She *behaves* as if she were a child. 她的**举止**像是个孩子。(from the predicate to the subject)
- The test *is intended* to reinforce what you have learnt in the past few weeks. 本测验**旨在**强化你们过去几周内所学的知识。(from the predicate to the predicative)
- Mathematics is well taught *at that school.* 那个**学校**的数学教得好。(from the adverbial to the subject)

II. Conversions in C-E Translation

1. Converting Verbs into Other Parts of Speech

Conversion is also a common practice in C-E translation. Unlike that of English, a Chinese sentence may contain more than one verb. When translated into English, many of the Chinese verbs have to be converted into other parts of speech such as nouns, adjectives, prepositions or preposition phrases, etc., so as to comply with English sentence structure. For example:

Original Chinese: "坐山观虎斗""借刀杀人""引风吹火""站干岸儿""推倒油瓶不扶"，都是全挂子的本事。

English Version: "Sitting on a hill to watch tigers fight", "murdering with a borrowed sword", "borrowing wind to fan the fire", "watching people drown from a dry bank" and "not troubling to right an oil bottle that's been knocked over"—

they're all good hands at such tricks.

Here are some more examples:

- 徐悲鸿**画**马画得特别好。Xu Beihong's *drawings* of horses are exceptionally good. (*v.* → *n.*)
- 林则徐认为，要**成功地制止**鸦片买卖，就得首先把鸦片**焚毁**。Lin Zexu believed that *a successful ban* of the trade in opium must be preceded by the *burning* of the drug itself. (*adv.* + *v.* → *adj.* + *n.*; *v.* → *n.*)
- 邓小平说："一定要**少说空话，多做工作**。"Deng Xiaoping said, "There must be *less empty talk and more hard work*." (*adv.* + *v.* + *n.* → *adj.* + *n.*)
- 绝对**不许违反**这个原则。*No violation* of this principle can be tolerated. (*v.* → *adj.* + *n.*)
- 获悉贵国遭受地震，我们极为**关切**。We are deeply *concerned* at the news that your country has been struck by an earthquake. (*v.* → *adj.*)
- 这种人**闹**什么东西呢？**闹**名誉，**闹**地位，**闹**出风头。What are these people *after*? They are *after* fame, position and opportunity to be in the limelight. (*v.* → *prep.*)
- 他们**不顾**一切困难、挫折，坚持战斗。They kept on fighting *in spite of* all the difficulties and setbacks. (*v.* → *prep.* phrase)
- 你**熟悉**这种晶体管放大器的性能吗？Are you *familiar* with the performance of this type of transistor amplifier? (*v.* → *adj.*)

2. Conversions Between Different Parts of Speech

Besides verbs, conversion between other parts of speech is also very common in C-E translation, such as the conversion from nouns into verbs, from adjectives into nouns, and vice versa.

- 该厂产品的**主要特点**是工艺精湛，经久耐用。The products of this factory *are chiefly characterized* by their fine workmanship and durability. (*adj.* + *n.* → *v.*)
- 街中的一切逐渐消失在**灰暗**的暮色里。Everything in the street was gradually disappearing into a pall of *gray*. (*adj.* → *n.*)
- 电导率在选择电气材料时**很重要**。Electrical conductivity has *great importance* in selecting electrical materials. (*adv.* + *adj.* → *adj.* + *n.*)
- 我们的教育方针，应该使受教育者在**德育、智育、体育**几方面都得到发展，成为有社会主义觉悟、有文化的劳动者。Our educational policy must enable everyone who receives an education to develop *morally, intellectually* and *physically* and become a worker with both socialist consciousness and culture. (*n.* → *adv.*)

UNIT 3 Conversion

Reflections and Practice

I. **Discuss the following questions.**
1. When and where is conversion used in translation?
2. Why is it necessary for a translator to convert parts of speech in translation?
3. What are the major forms of conversion in E-C translation?
4. What are the major forms of conversion in C-E translation?
5. What is the similarity or difference in conversion between E-C translation and C-E translation?

II. **Put the following sentences into Chinese, using the technique of conversion. Pay attention to the italicized words.**
1. With the passage of time, my *admiration* for him grew more and more.
2. He has long been an *enemy* of stilted and pretentious English.
3. The audience attending the performance *varied* from tens to thousands.
4. Independent observers have *commented favorably* on the achievement you have made in this direction.
5. No wonder *the sight of it* should send the memories of quite a number of people of the old generation back to 36 years ago.
6. There is a *big increase* in demand for all kinds of consumer goods in every part of our country.
7. *Out of* all the glorious tales written about the U.S. revolution *for* independence *from* Britain the fact is hardly known that a black man was the first to die for American independence.
8. I buried my head under *the miserable sheet and rug,* and cried like a child.
9. The thief made *a trembling confession* of his wrongdoing.
10. The sailors swarmed into *a laughing and cheering ring* around the two men.
11. I enjoy the clean voluptuousness of the warm breeze on my skin and *the cool support* of water.
12. It was a truth of which I had for some time been conscious that *a figure with a good deal of frontage* was, as one might say, almost never a public institution.

III. **Put the following sentences into English, using the technique of conversion.**
1. 他在讲话中特别强调提高产品质量。

2. 采用这种新装置可以大大降低废品率。
3. 社会主义革命的目的是解放生产力。
4. 他们一不会做工，二不会种地，三不会打仗。
5. 语言这个东西不是随便可以学好的，非下苦功不可。
6. 中秋节这天夜晚皓月当空；人们合家团聚，共赏明月。
7. 改革开放以来，首都北京的建设日新月异，发生了巨大的变化。现代化建筑雨后春笋，相继崛起。
8. 中国人民百年以来不屈不挠、再接再厉的英勇斗争，使得帝国主义至今不能灭亡中国，也永远不能灭亡中国。
9. 对外国的科学、技术、文化，不加分析地一概排斥，和不加分析地一概照搬，都不是马克思主义的态度，都对我们的事业不利。
10. 中国已成功地发射了第一颗实验通信卫星。这颗卫星是由三级火箭推动的，一直运转正常。它标志着我国在发展运载工具和电子技术方面进入了一个新阶段。

IV. Put the following sentences into Chinese, paying attention to idiomatical expression.

1. He was a nonsmoker and a teetotaler.
2. Since he lost his job, he's been a loner.
3. These problems defy easy classification.
4. I marveled at the relentless determination of the rain.
5. High blood pressure is a contraindication for this drug.
6. He had surfaced with less visibility in the policy decisions.
7. He spoke with firmness, but his face was very sad and his eyes at times were dim.
8. The actual date of the completion of the purchase should coincide with the availability of the new facilities.
9. This is the day for our two peoples to rise to the heights of greatness which can build a new and a better world.
10. Laser is one of the most sensational developments in the 20th century, because of its applicability to many fields of science and its adaptability to practical uses.

Unit 4 Amplification

单元要点概述

相关翻译技巧训练英译汉：Lincoln and Leadership

相关翻译技巧训练汉译英：梅贻琦

I. 增词法在英汉翻译中的运用

  1. 增添原文所省略的词语   2. 增添必要的连接词语

  3. 表达出复数概念   4. 表现不同的时态或先后顺序

  5. 逻辑性增词   6. 从修辞连贯角度考虑增词

  7. 重复性增词

II. 增词法在汉英翻译中的运用

  1. 增添必要的代词   2. 增添必要的冠词

  3. 增添必要的连接词语   4. 增添必要的介词

  5. 增添必要的背景词语

本单元对英译汉、汉译英的增词法作了探讨、归纳。

    作为翻译的一个普遍准则，译者不应对原文的内容随意增添或缩减。不过，由于英汉两种语言文字之间所存在的悬殊差异，在实际翻译过程中很难做到词字上的完全对应。因此，为了准确地传达出原文的信息，译者往往需要对译文做一些增添或删减，把原文中隐含的一些东西适当增补出来，以便于读者理解。

    英译汉的增词主要是出于汉语表达的需要，用增词法译出原文所省略的词语，增添必要的连接词、量词或复数概念，表现不同的时态或先后顺序，或从修辞连贯等方面考虑，使译文的遣词造句符合汉语的表达习惯。

    汉译英的增词旨在使译文符合英语的语法结构和表达习惯，常增添代词、冠词、连接词语以及介词等词语。

Practice of the Relevant Skill

1. E-C Translation

Lincoln and Leadership

Abraham Lincoln regularly tops historians' lists of the greatest American presidents. But he owes his greatness partly to the fact that he was an outsider on whom no sensible man would have bet. He made a series of bold moves—such as sending ships to supply Fort Sumter, thereby forcing the South to fire the first shot of the civil war—that his more experienced rivals might not have made. And he gave a series of nation-defining speeches that nobody else in the country could have delivered.

It is no surprise that the leadership-cum-management industry has embraced the outsized figure of Lincoln. In his new book, *Indispensable*, Gautam Mukunda, of Harvard Business School, uses Lincoln to examine one of the liveliest debates in modern management—whether insiders or outsiders make better bosses. Before the financial crisis the consensus was strongly in favour of insiders. But it is shifting, partly because so many insiders made a hash of things and partly because companies are casting around for a way to reignite growth.

Mr. Mukunda divides leaders into two types, "filtered" and "unfiltered". The filtered are known quantities: insiders who have been subjected to a succession of tests designed to reveal their strengths and weaknesses. The unfiltered are enigmas: outsiders like Lincoln who have never been tested by high office; insiders like Winston Churchill who have fallen out of favour; or transplants like Mr. Carney who have made their reputations in alien organizations. Filtered leaders tend to make little difference: the other insiders on the shortlist might have done just as well. But unfiltered leaders can make a huge difference, sometimes for the better as Lincoln and Churchill did, but more often for the worse.

Another recent book from the HBS stable, William Thorndike's *The Outsiders*, reinforces Mr. Mukunda's argument about the possible advantages of unfiltered leaders. Mr. Thorndike examines eight bosses whose firms outperformed the S&P average by more than 20 times over their business careers and finds that they were all outsiders who brought fresh perspectives to their industries. Katharine Graham of *The Washington Post* was a widow who had not had a paid job for years, Bill Anders (General Dynamics) was a former astronaut, Tom Murphy (Capital Cities) had never worked in the media before he took over a struggling television station and Warren Buffett (Berkshire Hathaway) is Warren Buffett.

UNIT 4 Amplification

But for every successful outsider there are a dozen failures. Booz points out that in 2009-2011 34.9% of outside bosses were sacked, compared with only 18.5% of insiders. This suggests that it is best to avoid outsiders if things are humming along fine. It is much easier to go from good to bad than it is to go from good to great.

Notes and Explanations

1. bet on 打赌，对……侥幸，碰运气
2. bold move 大胆的举动，大胆举措
3. a series of nation-defining speeches 一连串决定国家命运的演讲
4. the leadership-cum-management industry 领导及管理行业
5. cast around 四处寻找
6. a way to reignite growth 一种重新激起增长的方法
7. "filtered" and "unfiltered" "筛选出的领导"和"未经筛选的领导"
8. known quantities 熟知的人或事，[数] 已知量
9. alien organizations 业外机构
10. fall out of favour 失宠
11. the HBS stable 哈佛商学院的同行；HBS: Harvard Business School
12. S&P (Standard & Poor's) 标准普尔
13. Katharine Graham 凯瑟琳·格雷厄姆
14. Bill Anders 比尔·安德斯，通用动力公司总裁
15. Tom Murphy 汤姆·墨菲
16. Warren Buffett 华伦·巴菲特
17. if things are humming along fine 如果业务一帆风顺

2. C-E Translation

梅贻琦

梅贻琦（1889—1962）教育家、天津人。1909年考取清华第一批"直接留美生"，入吴斯特工业学院学习电机工程。1915年9月应聘来清华大学任物理学教授，1926年出任教务长。1931年出任校长直至1948年年底。他仅用几年时间就使当时的清华大学在许多方面跻身于世界名校之林。作为教育家，梅贻琦有一套完整的教育思想体系，其治校方略可归结为三个组成部分：通才教育（或"自由教育"）、教授治校（或"民主管理"）和学术自由（或"自由探讨之风气"）。其代表作是1941年撰发的《大学一解》。他的"大学者，非谓有大楼之谓也，有大师之谓也"的著名论说，至今在教育界广为传诵。

Notes and Explanations

1. 直接留美生 students who passed the exam of direct studying in USA
2. 吴斯特工业学院 Worcester Polytechnic Institute
3. 电机工程 electrical engineering
4. 应聘 be engaged/be invited to work
5. 教务长 Dean of Studies
6. 跻身于 rank among
7. 完整的教育思想体系 a complete ideological system of education
8. 治校方略 strategy of running the university
9. 通才教育 generalist education
10. 自由探讨之风气 free atmosphere of airing one's views
11. 《大学一解》 An Interpretation of University
12. 教育界 the educational circles

Amplification, also called addition, means supplying necessary words in the translation on the basis of accurate comprehension of the original. As a matter of principle, a translator is not supposed to add in or subtract any meaning from the original work. However, more often than not, a translator has to amplify the connotation of a given word in practical translation, and sometimes even put in more words to explain the original meaning. This is because English and Chinese are two entirely different languages and each has its own historical and cultural background. Besides, many ideas, idiomatic expressions and shorthand words, etc. that are well understood in the country of their origin can hardly make sense to people of different societies. Therefore, we have to resort to "amplification", instead of stiffly sticking to the original wording or sentence patterns. For example, the translation of the word "wash":

- Mary *washes* before meals. 玛丽饭前洗手。
- Mary *washes* before going to bed. 玛丽睡前洗漱。
- Mary *washes* after getting up. 玛丽起床后洗脸。
- Mary *washes* for a living. 玛丽靠洗衣度日。
- Mary *washes* in a restaurant. 玛丽在饭店洗碗碟。

More examples may be found in the above Practice of the Relevant Skill, where amplification is used to make the Chinese version clear and accurate.

UNIT 4 Amplification

- But he owes his greatness partly to the fact that he was an outsider on whom *no sensible man would have bet.* 但林肯将这种伟大部分归因于自己是局外人，因为**任何明智的人当初都不敢打赌他能成功**。
- —that *his more experienced rivals* might not *have made.* 要是换上经验丰富的对手，也许就不会**做出此举了**。
- And he gave a series of nation-defining speeches that *nobody else in the country could have delivered.* 而且他还发表了一连串决定国家命运的演讲——**除他之外美国谁也做不出类似的演讲**。
- But *it* is shifting, partly because so many insiders *made a hash of things* and partly because companies *are casting around for a way to reignite growth.* 但**这种看法现在已经开始转变**，这一方面是因为很多局内人**把公司管得一团糟**，另一方面是因为很多公司**现在正急于寻找一种方法来重新激发业务增长**。
- But unfiltered leaders can make a huge difference, sometimes for the better *as Lincoln and Churchill did*, but more often *for the worse*. 但"未经筛选的领导"的选择则大不一样，偶尔也可能会**碰到像林肯或是丘吉尔那样的人才**，但更常见的情况是会**把局面搞得更糟**。
- Another recent book from the HBS stable, *William Thorndike's The Outsiders*, *reinforces* Mr. Mukunda's argument about the possible advantages of unfiltered leaders. 同样来自哈佛商学院的**威廉姆·索恩戴克**最近也出了一本名为《局外人》的新书。该书**对**穆昆达关于"未经筛选领导"可能存在优势的论据做了进一步补充。
- *Tom Murphy (Capital Cities)* had never worked in the media before he *took over a struggling television station* and *Warren Buffett (Berkshire Hathaway)* is Warren Buffett. 首都通讯公司的总裁汤姆·墨菲在**临危受命**接手电视台之前从未干过媒体这一行；而伯克希尔·哈撒韦公司的老板华伦·巴菲特则是（**大名鼎鼎的股神**）巴菲特。
- But for every successful outsider there *are a dozen failures.* 但每一个局外人的成功都意味着**十几例他人的失败**。
- *Booz points out that in 2009-2011* 34.9% of outside bosses were sacked, compared with only 18.5% of *insiders*. 博斯公司的数据显示，2009 至 2011 年共有 34.9% 的局外人总裁被解职，**而局内人总裁中这个比例**只有 18.5%。
- This suggests that it is best to *avoid outsiders* if things are *humming along fine*. It is much easier to *go from good to bad* than it is to go from good to great. 这表明如果业务一帆风顺，最好还是**避免用局外人**。因为把一个好摊子搞砸要比把它做得更棒要容易得多。

I. Amplification in E-C Translation

1. Putting in Words Omitted in the Original

- "If so grand, why so poor? If so poor, why so grand?" "既然那么阔,干嘛要叫穷?既然那么穷,干嘛摆阔气?"
- Matter can be changed into energy, and energy into matter. 物质可以转化为能量,能量也可以**转化**为物质。
- The best conductor has the least resistance and the poorest the greatest. 最好的导体电阻最小,最差的**导体电阻**最大。
- In the evening, after the banquets, the concerts and the table tennis exhibitions, he would work on the drafting of the final communique. 晚上在**参加**宴会、**出席**音乐会和**观看**乒乓球表演以后,他还得起草最后公报。

2. Putting in Necessary Connectives

- Heated, water will change into vapor. 水如受热,**就会**汽化。
- However carefully boiler casings and steam pipes are sealed, some heat escapes and is lost. 不管锅炉壳与蒸汽管封闭得多么严密,**还是**有一部分热散失损耗掉。
- Since air has weight, it exerts force on any object immersed in it. 因为空气具有重量,**所以**处在空气中的任何物体都会受到空气的作用力。

3. Putting in Words to Convey the Concept of Plurality

- Note that the *words* "velocity" and "speed" require explanation. 请注意,"速度"和"速率"这**两个词**需要解释。
- He stretched his *legs* which were scattered with *scars*. 他伸出**双腿**,露出腿上的**道道**伤痕。
- The *mountains* began to throw their long blue *shadows* over the valley. **群山**开始向山谷投下**一道道**蔚蓝色长影。

4. Putting in Words to Indicate Different Tenses or Sequences

- In Beijing, there *was* a divine scale and a higgledypiggledy scale. 过去的北京**既有**一种神圣的规模,**又有**一种杂乱无章的格局。
- We *won't* retreat; we never *have* and never *will*. 我们**不会**后退,我们从未后退过,**将来**也绝不后退。
- I *had* imagined it to be merely a gesture of affection, but it *seems* it is to smell the lamb and make sure that it is her own. 我**原本**以为这不过是一种亲热的表示,但是

现在看来，这是为了嗅嗅羊羔的气味，以断定它是不是自己的孩子。

5. Amplification by Common Sense

- Air pressure decreases with altitude. 气压随**海拔**高度的**增加**而下降。
- I was taught that two sides of a triangle were greater than the third. 我学过，三角形的两边**之和**大于第三边。
- This shows that the resistance of an electric conductor is inversely proportional to its cross-section area. 这表明，导体电阻的**大小**与导体横切面的**大小**成反比。

6. Amplification for the Purpose of Rhetoric or Coherence

- This printer is indeed cheap and fine. 这部打印机真是**价廉物美**。
- I came to a garden of grottoes, pavilions and shapely rocks and trees. 我来到一个建有人工洞穴的花园前，园中亭阁**玲珑**，山石**嶙峋**，树木**葱郁**。
- A scientist constantly tried to defeat his hypotheses, his theories, and his conclusion. 科学家经常设法**推翻**自己的假设，**否定**自己的理论，**放弃**自己的结论。

7. Amplification by Repetition

- Avoid using this computer in *extreme* cold, heat, dust or humidity. 不要在**过冷**、**过热**、灰尘**过重**、湿度**过大**的情况下使用此电脑。
- I had experienced oxygen or/and engine *trouble*. 我曾经遇到的情况，不是氧气设备**出故障**，就是引擎**出故障**，或两者都**出故障**。
- The world has never seen a nation as big *as China* rise as far and as fast *as China* has in the past 30 years. 过去 30 年里，全世界从未见过哪个崛起的国家**有中国**这样大、崛起的速度**有中国**这样快、影响**有中国**这样广。

II. Amplification in C-E Translation

1. Adding Necessary Pronouns

- 大作收到，十分高兴。*I* was very glad to have received *your* writing.
- 没有调查研究就没有发言权。*He who* makes no investigation and study has no right to speak.
- 交出翻译之前，必须读几遍，看看有没有要修改的地方。Before handing in *your* translation, *you* have to read *it* over and over again and see if there is anything in *it* to be corrected or improved.

2. Adding Necessary Articles

- 去粗取精，去伪存真。Discard *the* dross and select *the* essential, eliminate *the* false and retain *the* true.
- 我们对问题要做全面的分析，才能解决得妥当。We must make *a* comprehensive analysis of *a* problem before it can be properly solved.
- 耳朵是用来听声音的器官，鼻子用来嗅气味，舌头用来尝滋味。*The* ear is the organ which is used for hearing. *The* nose is used for smelling. *The* tongue is used for tasting.

3. Adding Necessary Connectives

- 老师在等我，我得走了。The teacher is expecting me, *so* I must be off now.
- 虚心使人进步，骄傲使人落后。Modesty helps one to go forward, *whereas* conceit makes one lag behind.
- 留得青山在，不怕没柴烧。*So long as* green hills remain, there will never be a shortage of firewood.

4. Adding Necessary Prepositions

- 咱们校门口见吧。Let's meet *at* the school gate.
- 你是白天工作还是夜间工作？Do you work *in* the daytime or *at* night?
- 该地区已没什么城乡差别。There is little difference *between* town and countryside *in* this region.

5. Adding Necessary Background Words

- 三个臭皮匠，赛过诸葛亮。Three cobblers with their wits combined equal Zhuge Liang *the mastermind*.
- 别班门弄斧。Don't try to show off your proficiency with the ax before Lu Ban *the master carpenter*.
- 我们提倡五讲四美。We advocate the culture of "five stresses and four points of beauty", *i.e.* stress on *decorum, manners, hygiene, discipline and morals, beauty of the mind, language, behavior and the environment.*

UNIT 4 Amplification

Reflections and Practice

I. **Discuss the following questions.**
1. What is amplification? What is the function of this technique? And why is it needed in translation?
2. What are the major means of amplification employed in E-C translation?
3. What are the major means of amplification employed in C-E translation?
4. Do you think the application of the technique of amplification in C-E translation is just the same as in E-C translation? Why or why not? Try to explain.

II. **Put the following sentences into Chinese, using the technique of amplification.**
1. Oceans do not so much divide the world as unite it.
2. When she came to, she saw smiling faces around her.
3. The planet we live on is not just a ball of inert material.
4. The pupil of the eye responds to the change of light intensity.
5. Courage in excess becomes foolhardiness, affection weakness, thrift avarice.
6. Reading maketh a full man; conference a ready man; and writing an exact man.
7. Their host carved, poured, served, cut bread, talked, laughed, proposed health.
8. This digital camera is easy to operate, versatile, compact and has a pleasing modern design.
9. A scientific hypothesis can be proven—or, perhaps more importantly, disproven—but a poem, a picture, or a piece of music, cannot.
10. Histories make men wise; poets witty; mathematics subtle; natural philosophy deep; moral grave; logic and rhetoric able to contend.

III. **Put the following sentences into English, using the technique of amplification.**
1. 请把这张表填一下，填完给我。
2. 要提倡顾全大局。
3. 吃饭防噎，走路防跌。
4. 送君千里，终有一别。
5. 一个篱笆三个桩，一个好汉三个帮。
6. 天气寒冷，河水都结冰了。
7. 前途是光明的，道路是曲折的。
8. 理论联系实际，这是我们应当牢记的一条原则。
9. 天气这样闷，十之八九要下雨。
10. 年满18岁的公民，都有选举权和被选举权。

IV. Put the following sentences into Chinese, paying attention to the diction of the words in boldface.

And:

1. The sun came out **and** the grass dried.
2. He read for an hour **and** went to bed.
3. He did the work, **and** he did it very well.
4. One step more, **and** you are a dead man.
5. I went to his house, **and** he came to mine.
6. He is so rich and lives like a beggar.
7. These parts are made of woods or plastics **and** not metals.
8. Rust is abrasive **and** can cause damage to the injection components.
9. The solution was to place many filters in the system **and** hope for the best.
10. Chemical splashes can cause eye irritation **and** permanent eye damage.
11. This means drying the oil before it enters the system **and**, to be sensible, ensuring that the air above the oil is dry.
12. He analyzed the dependence of pressure on temperature **and** concluded that pressure decreased with increasing temperature.

When:

1. I stayed till noon, **when** I went home.
2. **When** you cross the river you are safe.
3. He usually walks **when** he might ride.
4. How can I convince him **when** he won't listen?
5. **When** one is older, one is also more experienced.
6. Why are you here **when** you should be in school?
7. They had only three transistors **when** they needed five.
8. Turn off the switch **when** anything goes wrong with the machine.
9. **When** the teacher had left the classroom, the pupils started talking.
10. **When** that man says "To tell the truth", I suspect that he's about to tell a lie.
11. How could you do it **when** you knew that this might damage the apparatus?
12. We'll go to the countryside at the beginning of June, **when** the summer harvest will start.
13. **When** I am opposed to such actions on general principles, how can I make this case an exception?
14. Insurance companies are obliged to recover the cost of everything insured **when** it is lost or damaged during the valid period of insurance.
15. **When** there is really planned and proportionate development, our national economy will achieve sustained, stable and highspeed growth.

Unit 5 Omission

单元要点概述

相关翻译技巧训练英译汉：Companionship of Books

相关翻译技巧训练汉译英：外语系图书馆

I. 省略法在英汉翻译中的运用

　　1. 代词的省略　　2. 冠词的省略　　3. 介词的省略

　　4. 连词的省略　　5. 动词的省略　　6. 非人称代词"It"的省略

II. 省略法在汉英翻译中的运用

　　1. 省略冗词赘语

　　2. 省略概念范畴类词语

　　3. 省略过详的细节描述

本单元对英译汉、汉译英的省略法做了分析、归纳。

省略法是与增词法相对应的翻译技巧。在同一译例里，要是英译汉用了增词法，那么，回译成英语时自然便是省略法了。

一般来说，汉语比英语简练。英译汉时，许多在原文中必不可少的词语要是原原本本地译成汉语，就会成为不必要的冗词，译文会显得十分累赘。因此省略法在英译汉中使用得非常广泛，其主要作用是删去一些可有可无、不符合译文习惯表达的词语，如实词中的代词、动词的省略；虚词中的冠词、介词和连词的省略等。

汉语中也有重复啰嗦、拖泥带水的语言现象，因此省略法也同样适用于汉译英的某些情况。汉译英的省略主要是省略冗词赘语，以及一些表示概念范畴的词语和过于细枝末节的描述。

Practice of the Relevant Skill

1. E-C Translation

Companionship of Books

A man may usually be known by the books he reads as well as by the company he keeps; for there is a companionship of books as well as of men; and one should always live in the best company, whether it be of books or of men.

A good book may be among the best of friends. It is the same today that it always was, and it will never change. It is the most patient and cheerful of companions. It does not turn its back upon us in times of adversity or distress. It always receives us with the same kindness; amusing and instructing us in youth, and comforting and consoling us in age.

Men often discover their affinity to each other by the love they have each for a book—just as two persons sometimes discover a friend by the admiration which both have for a third. There is an old proverb, "Love me, love my dog." But there is more wisdom in this: "Love me, love my book." The book is a truer and higher bond of union. Men can think, feel, and sympathize with each other through their favorite author. They live in him together and he in them.

"Books," said Hazlitt, "wind in the heart; the poet's verse slides in the current of our blood. We read them when young, we remember them when old. We feel that it has happened to ourselves. They are to be had very cheap and good. We breathe but the air of books."

A good book is often the best urn of a life enshrining the best that life could think out; for the world of a man's life is, for the most part, but the world of his thoughts. Thus the best books are treasuries of good words, the golden thoughts, which, remembered and cherished, become our constant companions and comforters. "They are never alone," said Sir Philip Sidney, "that are accompanied by noble thoughts."

Books introduce us into the best society; they bring us into the presence of the greatest minds that have ever lived. We hear what they said and did; we see them as if they were really alive; we sympathize with them, enjoy with them, grieve with them; their experience becomes ours, and we feel as if we were in a measure actors with them in the scenes which they describe.

The great and good do not die even in this world. Embalmed in books, their spirits walk abroad. The book is a living voice. It is an intellect to which one still listens. Hence we ever remain under the influence of the great men of old. The imperial intellects of the world are as much alive now as they were ages ago.

Notes and Explanations

1. companionship *n.* 伴侣关系，友谊，陪伴
2. turn one's back on (upon) somebody 转过脸去不理某人，背弃，抛弃，违背
3. affinity *n.* 密切关系，强烈的吸引力
4. They live in him together and he in them. 他们一道生活在作者的世界里，作者与他们随时相伴。
5. wind in the heart 沁人心扉；wind *v.* 蜿蜒，萦绕，萦怀
6. Hazlitt 黑兹利特（1778—1830），英国作家、评论家
7. They are to be had very cheap and good. 它们物美价廉、随处可得。
8. We breathe but the air of books. 我们无不呼吸到书本的芬芳气息。
9. the best urn of a life enshrining the best that life could think out 人生精华的缩影
10. They are never alone, that are accompanied by noble thoughts. = They who are accompanied by noble thoughts are never alone.
11. Sir Philip Sidney 菲利普·西德尼爵士(1554—1586)，英国诗人、政治家
12. in a measure 一部分，在一定程度上
13. Embalmed in books, their spirits walk abroad. 他们的精神永驻书中，传遍世界各地。

2. C-E Translation

外语系图书馆

外语系图书馆占地面积 125 平方米，藏书 2.3 万册。整个图书馆包括 3 间书库，1 个阅览室，即英、俄文图书混合库，英文工具书库，日、法、德语混合库和中英文期刊阅览室。所藏图书以英语语言研究及相关文献为主体，兼藏日、俄、德、法语书籍资料。此外，订有各类中外文期刊近 200 种。

外语系图书馆为专业图书馆，着重语言研究与语言教学，是学校图书馆人文分馆的一个重要分支。目前，馆内全部馆藏已实现计算机化管理，并提供网络服务。

Notes and Explanations

1. 占地面积 with a floor space of
2. 藏书 have books in storage

3. 书库 stack room
4. 工具书 dictionaries and reference books
5. 期刊 magazines and periodicals
6. 相关文献 relevant literatures
7. 兼藏 concurrently keep (books)
8. 专业图书馆 a library for special purpose
9. 人文分馆 a sublibrary of the humanities
10. 计算机化管理 computerized management

Omission is a technique opposite to amplification. True, a translator has no right to subtract any meaning from the original work. But it does not follow that he should refrain from omitting any words at all in translation. In fact, one of the marked difference in syntax between English and Chinese is the disparity in wording. What is regarded as a natural or indispensable element in one language may be regarded as superfluous or even "a stumbling block" in the other. Take the following English sentence and its Chinese version for example：

Original English: The timekeeping devices of electronic watches are much more accurate than those of mechanical ones.

Chinese Version: 电子表比机械表准确得多。

A comparison between the Chinese version and the English original shows that many of the "redundant" English words have been omitted in the Chinese translation, otherwise, the Chinese sentence would sound wordy and unnatural. Therefore, a manipulation of the technique "omission" is always called for in E-C translation. And here are some more instances from the above Practice of the Relevant Skill:

- It is the same today that it always was, and it will never change. 它过去始终如此，现在仍是这样，将来也绝不会改变。
- turn one's back on (upon) somebody 背弃某人
- There is an old proverb, "Love me, love my dog." 古谚云："爱屋及乌"。
- They are to be had very cheap and good. 它们价廉物美，随处可得。
- the best urn of a life enshrining the best that life could think out 人生精华的缩影
- as much alive now as they were ages ago 其影响一点不亚于当年

Omission is also used in C-E translation either to get rid of redundant wording or conform to idiomatic English expressions.

UNIT 5 Omission

I. Omission in E-C Translation

Generally speaking, omission in E-C translation is used to achieve the effect of succinctness, especially in the cases of English pronouns and functional words such as the article, the preposition, the conjunction, etc.

1. Omitting the Pronoun

Pronouns are more frequently used in English than in Chinese. Therefore, when translated into Chinese, many English pronouns may be omitted so as to comply with idiomatical Chinese expression.

- He put *his* hands into *his* pockets and then shrugged *his* shoulders. 他将双手放进衣袋，然后耸了耸肩。
- For two weeks, he had been studying the house, looking at *its* rooms, *its* electric wiring, its path and *its* garden. 两周以来，他一直注意观察房子的情况，查看各个房间，留心电线的走向、通道和花园的布局。
- They went in to dinner. *It* was excellent, and the wine was good. *Its* influence presently had *its* effect on them. *They* talked not only without acrimony, but even with friendliness. 他们进入餐室用餐。美酒佳肴，顿受感染，言谈间不但没有恶言恶语，甚至还充满友好之情。

2. Omitting the Article

The article is the hallmark of English nouns. When translated into Chinese, it is usually omitted except that when the definite article is intended to indicate the "this, that, these, those", the indefinite article to indicate the numeral "one", or "a certain".

- *The* moon was slowly rising above *the* sea. 月亮慢慢从海上升起。
- Any substance is made up of atoms whether it is *a* solid, *a* liquid, or *a* gas. 任何物质，不论是固体、液体或气体，都由原子组成。
- The direction of *a* force can be represented by *an* arrow. 力的方向可以用箭头表示。

Exceptions:
- This is *the* book you wanted. 这就是你要的**那本书**。
- *An* apple *a* day keeps the doctor away. **一天一个苹果**，医生没有事做。

3. Omitting the Preposition

Chinese is characterized by its succinctness and the preposition is less frequently used in Chinese than in English, and therefore omission of prepositions is a common practice in

E-C translation.
- Smoking is prohibited *in* public places. 公共场所不许吸烟。
- The difference *between* the two machines consists in power. 这两台机器的差别在于功率不同。
- Hydrogen is the lightest element *with* an atomic weight of 1.008. 氢是最轻的元素，原子量为 1.008。

4. Omitting the Conjunction

Chinese is considered an analytic language and many conjunctions that are indispensable in English may seem redundant in Chinese.
- He looked gloomy *and* troubled. 他看上去有些忧愁不安。
- *If* I had known it, I would not have joined in. 早知如此，我就不参加了。
- Like charges repel each other *while* opposite charges attract. 同性电荷相斥，异性电荷相吸。

5. Omitting the Verb

As Chinese is a language of parataxis（意合联结）, its grammar is not so strict as that of English, and predicative verbs in Chinese sometimes may also be omitted.
- When the pressure *gets* low, the boiling point *becomes* low. 气压低，沸点就低。
- Solids expand and contract as liquids and gases *do*. 如同液体和气体一样，固体也能膨胀和收缩。
- For this reason television signals *have* a short range. 因此，电视信号的传播距离很短。

6. Omitting the Impersonal Pronoun "it"

This often occurs when "it" stands for time, weather, distance, or formal subject/object of a sentence.
- Outside *it* was pitch-dark and *it* was raining cats and dogs. 外面一团漆黑，大雨倾盆。
- This formula makes *it* easy to determine the wavelength of sounds. 这一公式使得测定声音的波长十分简单。
- *It* was not until the middle of the 19th century that the blast furnace came into use. 直到 19 世纪中叶，高炉才开始使用。
- *It* is the people who are really powerful. 真正强大的是人民。

UNIT 5 Omission

II. Omission in C-E Translation

Omission in C-E translation is usually used to avoid unnecessary repetition, usually in three cases, i.e., redundant words in original Chinese, such as unnecessary repetition and wordy expressions; the original meaning that has already been implied in the context of the English version; and the original meaning obviously shown in the English version without further elaboration.

1. Omitting Redundant Words

- 同一个世界，同一个梦想。*One* world, *one* dream.
- 质子带正电，电子带负电，而中子**既不带正电，也不带负电**。A proton has a positive charge and an electron a negative charge, but a neutron *has neither*.
- 我已经提前完成了交给我的工作，他也**提前完成了交给他的工作**。I have fulfilled my assigned work ahead of schedule, *so has he*.
- 我们说，**长征**是历史记录上的第一次，**长征**是宣言书，**长征**是宣传队，**长征**是播种机。We answer that *the Long March* is the first of its kind in the annals of history, that *it is* a manifesto, a propaganda force, a *seeding-machine*.
- 匪军所至，**杀戮**人民，**奸淫**妇女，**焚毁**村庄，**掠夺**财物，无所不用其极。Where the bandit troops went, they *massacred and raped, burned and looted*, and stopped at nothing.

2. Omitting Words of Conceptual Category

Sometimes, omission is used in C-E translation when the original Chinese indicates not a specific case but a conceptual category, especially such nouns as "任务、工作、情况、问题、事业、局面" and so on. For example:

- 我们党结束了那个时期的社会**动荡和纷扰不安的局面**。Our party has put an end to the social *unrest and upheaval* of that time.
- 这些都是**人民内部矛盾问题**。All these are *contradictions among the people.*
- 她的朋友们听到她家中的**困难情况**后，都主动伸出援助之手。After her friends heard about her family *difficulties*, they offered her a helping hand.

3. Omitting Meticulous Descriptions

Occasionally, omission is used to simplify the sentence structure, especially when the original Chinese is too meticulous in description.

- 200千米航道上遍布着无数险滩。险滩上**江流汹涌，回旋激荡，水击礁石，浪花飞溅，**

59

声如雷鸣。Numerous shoals scattered over the 200 km course give rise to many eddies. *Pounding on the midstream rocks, the river roars thunderously.*

- 花园里面是人间的乐园，有的是吃不了的大米白面，穿不完的绫罗绸缎，花不完的金银财宝。The garden was a paradise on earth, *with more food and clothes than could be consumed and more money than could be spent.*

Reflections and Practice

I. **Discuss the following questions.**
1. What is the technique of omission in translation?
2. When and where is omission needed in E-C translation? Cite an example to elaborate your statement.
3. When and where is omission needed in C-E translation? Cite an example to elaborate your statement.
4. What is the similarity or the difference between omission used in E-C translation and C-E translation?

II. **Put the following sentences into Chinese, using the technique of omission.**
1. If you give him an inch, he will take a mile.
2. Never trouble yourself with trouble till trouble troubles you.
3. The true joy of joys is the joy that joys in the joy of others.
4. It is not entirely right to say that if there is food, let everyone share it.
5. There was no haste or restlessness in his manner but a poised friendliness.
6. Radioactivity may cause illness that could be passed on to our children and grandchildren.
7. Bacteria capable of causing disease are known as pathogenic, or disease-producing germs.
8. For generations, coal and oil have been regarded as the chief energy source to transport men from place to place.
9. Patients with influenza must be separated from the well lest the disease should spread from person to person.
10. Among the 18 species of penguins, 8 have chosen the environs of the South Pole as their habitats.
11. These developing countries cover vast territories, encompass a large population and

UNIT 5 Omission

abound in natural resources.

12. In order to survive, to feed, clothe and shelter himself and his children, man is engaged in a constant struggle with nature.

13. Winter is the best time to study the growth of trees. Although the leaves are gone and the branches are bare, the trees themselves are beautiful.

14. Scientific exploration, the search for knowledge, has given man the practical result of being able to shield himself from the calamities of nature and the calamities imposed by others.

III. Put the following sentences into English, using the technique of omission.

1. 他一开口总是三句话不离本行。
2. 每条河流都有上游、中游、下游。
3. 他把事情一五一十地都给父母讲了。
4. 人们利用科学去了解自然，改造自然。
5. 我们必须培养分析问题解决问题的能力。
6. 这些新型汽车速度快，效率高，行动灵活。
7. 多年来那个国家一直存在严重的失业现象。
8. 新老队员要互相学习，互相帮助，取长补短。
9. 中国人民历来是勇于探索，勇于创造，勇于革命的。
10. 生也好，死也好，我们要忠于党，忠于人民，忠于祖国。
11. 我昨天没有进城，一来是因为天气不好，二来是我不舒服。
12. 独立自主，自力更生，无论过去、现在和将来，都是我们的立足点。

IV. Put the following sentences into Chinese, paying attention to the omission of the pronoun.

1. We have seven days in a week.
2. You can never tell!
3. They say it's so.
4. Is it a he or a she?
5. This is Brown speaking.
6. One should do one's duty.
7. It's no use crying over spilt milk.
8. As it is, we got there before it got dark.
9. She found it difficult to make it as a writer.
10. In ancient Rome we have patricians, knights, plebeians, slaves...

V Put the following words and expressions into Chinese, trying to get the correct meaning of the original.

1. apple of the eye
2. a good (bad) sailor
3. flash in the pan
4. dry(wet)nurse
5. pull one's leg
6. turn the tables
7. face the music
8. be out with sb.
9. make water
10. worth one's salt
11. sleep late
12. doesn't hold water
13. blow hot and cold
14. a bull in a china shop
15. pull the string
16. put all one's eggs in one basket
17. eat one's words
18. turn over a new leaf
19. on the rocks
20. a man in good shape

Unit 6 Restructuring

● 单元要点概述

相关翻译技巧训练英译汉：The World Is Going to University
相关翻译技巧训练汉译英：张光斗：与水"相恋"的世纪人生
I. 英汉语言的词序差异
　　1. 不同的思维模式　　　2. 不同的倒装结构
II. 英汉翻译的结构调整
　　1. 保持原文的语序（原序法）
　　2. 颠倒原文的语序（逆序法）
　　3. 按时间先后顺序（时序法）
　　4. 按逻辑关系排序
III. 汉英翻译的结构调整

　　由于英汉不同的造句结构和表达习惯，翻译有时需要打破原文的句式结构，对译文进行结构调整，以符合汉语的表达习惯。本单元通过语句结构的对比，分析了英汉两种语言的词序差异，归纳了英汉翻译的结构调整方法。

　　英汉词序差异表现在不同的思维模式、不同的句式结构上。英语思维模式是由点及面的外展螺旋式，其表达方式是由小到大，由近及远，由轻到重，由弱到强；而汉语恰恰相反，呈内旋式：由面到点，由大到小，由远及近，由重到轻，由强到弱。此外，英语多倒装句，汉语则很少见。英译汉的结构调整大致可采用顺译法、逆序法、时序法和逻辑分析等4种方法。汉译英的结构调整须注意英语的词语组合的独特习惯，尤其须注意用于修饰成分的各类定语、状语的位置。

Practice of the Relevant Skill

1. E-C Translation

The World Is Going to University

"After God had carried us safe to New England, and we had built our houses, provided necessaries for our livelihood, reared convenient places for God's worship and settled Civil Government, one of the next things we longed for and looked for was to advance learning and perpetuate it to posterity." So ran the first university fundraising brochure, sent from Harvard College to England in 1643 to drum up cash.

America's early and lasting enthusiasm for higher education has given it the biggest and best-funded system in the world. Hardly surprising, then, that other countries are emulating its model as they send ever more of their school-leavers to get a university education. But, as our special report argues, just as America's system is spreading, there are growing concerns about whether it is really worth the vast sums spent on it.

The modern research university, a marriage of the Oxbridge college and the German research institute, was invented in America, and has become the gold standard for the world. Mass higher education started in America in the 19th century, spread to Europe and East Asia in the 20th and is now happening pretty much everywhere except sub-Saharan Africa. The global tertiary-enrolment ratio—the share of the student-age population at university—went up from 14% to 32% in the two decades to 2012; in that time, the number of countries with a ratio of more than half rose from five to 54. University enrolment is growing faster even than demand for that ultimate consumer good, the car. The hunger for degrees is understandable: these days they are a requirement for a decent job and an entry ticket to the middle class.

There are, broadly, two ways of satisfying this huge demand. One is the continental European approach of state funding and provision, in which most institutions have equal resources and status. The second is the more market-based American model, of mixed private-public funding and provision, with brilliant, well-funded institutions at the top and poorer ones at the bottom. The world is moving in the American direction. More universities in more countries are charging students tuition fees. And as politicians realise that the "knowledge economy" requires top-flight research, public resources are being focused on a few privileged institutions and the competition to create world-class universities is intensifying.

In some ways, that is excellent. The best universities are responsible for many of the discoveries that have made the world a safer, richer and more interesting place. But costs are rising. OECD countries spend 1.6% of GDP on higher education, compared with 1.3% in 2000. If the American model continues to spread, that share will rise further. America spends 2.7% of its GDP on higher education.

Notes and Explanations

1. convenient places for God's worship 便于敬奉上帝的场所
2. Civil Government 文职政府
3. fundraising brochure 筹资手册
4. drum up cash 招揽资金
5. early and lasting enthusiasm 初期且持续的热情
6. Oxbridge college 牛津—剑桥大学
7. the gold standard 金本位（黄金准则）
8. pretty much everywhere 几乎在世界各地
9. sub-Saharan Africa 撒哈拉以南非洲地区
10. global tertiary-enrolment ratio 全球大学入学率
11. ultimate consumer good 最终消费品
12. state funding and provision 国家拨款提供资金
13. top-flight *adj.* 第一流的，最高的
14. in some ways 在某种程度上
15. be responsible for 对……负责，是……的原因
16. OECD countries 世界经合组织国家 (Organization for Economic Cooperation and Development)

2. C-E Translation

张光斗：与水"相恋"的世纪人生

95岁的清华大学水利系教授、工程教育家张光斗用自己的学识与人生参与和见证了我国20世纪水利建设历史的波澜壮阔。他创建了国内的水工结构和水电工程学科，编写了国内第一本《水工结构》中文教材，建立了国内最早的水工结构实验室，培养了国内首批水工结构专业研究生……

56年风起雨落，他一直走在与水为伍这条小路上；56年花开花谢，他在小路那头的讲台上倾注了满腔热忱。16位两院院士、5名国家级设计大师，以及为数众多的高级工程师、教授，桃李满天下的张光斗也将他那句"做一个好的工程师，一定要先做人——正直，爱国，为人民做事"的座右铭在一代代弟子中传承下去。

Notes and Explanations

1. 水利系 Department of Hydraulic Engineering
2. 水工结构 hydraulic engineering structure
3. 用自己的学识与人生 devote one's wisdom and whole life to
4. 参与和见证 witness and participate in
5. 波澜壮阔 grand surge of/the great development of
6. 培养 supervise/bring up/cultivate/foster
7. 56年风起雨落 in the past fifty-six years of ups and downs
8. 与水为伍这条小路上 along the path of hydraulics
9. 倾注满腔热忱 pour all one's enthusiasm on sb./into sth.
10. 桃李满天下 have students all over the world

Restructuring, also called rearrangement or inversion, refers to altering the structure or sentence pattern in translation so as to achieve idiomatic effects of the target language. Here are some instances of restructuring from Practice of the Relevant Skill:

- "After God had carried us safe to New England, and we had built our houses, provided necessaries for our livelihood, reared convenient places for God's worship and settled Civil Government, one of the next things we longed for and looked for was to advance learning and perpetuate it to posterity." 上帝把我们安全地带到了新英格兰，在那里我们建造了房屋，为自己提供了生活必需品，修建了敬奉上帝的便利场所，设立了文职政府。在完成所有这些之后，我们渴望的下一件事就是推进教育，并延泽子孙万代。"
- So ran the first university fundraising brochure, sent from Harvard College to England in 1643 to drum up cash. 1643年从哈佛学院寄往英国筹措资金的第一本大学筹款宣传册中这样写道。
- America's early and lasting enthusiasm for higher education has given it the biggest and best-funded system in the world. 美国很早就热衷于高等教育，其热情持续至今，因此形成了目前世界最大、财力支持最雄厚的高等教育体系。
- Hardly surprising, then, that other countries are emulating its model as they send ever more of their school-leavers to get a university education. 于是其他国家也模仿美国的教育模式，让更多的高中毕业生接受大学教育，这就不足为奇了。
- The modern research university, a marriage of the Oxbridge college and the German research institute, was invented in America, and has become the gold standard for the world. 美国创造的现代研究型大学是一种牛剑大学与德国研究机构的合体，已成为全球的金本位（黄金准则）。

UNIT 6 Restructuring

- The best universities are responsible for many of the discoveries that have made the world a safer, richer and more interesting place. 由于这些顶尖大学的许多发现，才使我们这个世界更安全、更富裕、更有趣。

I. Different Word Orders in English and Chinese

1. Different Modes of Thinking

In the process of translation, we often have to adjust or rearrange the word order owing to the different syntaxes of English and Chinese languages. Generally speaking, English sentence patterns tend to put the near distance, the minor and specific first, in a weak-strong sequence, while the Chinese sentence patterns are on the contrary, putting the far distance, the major and general first, in a strongweak sequence, as shown in the following illustration.

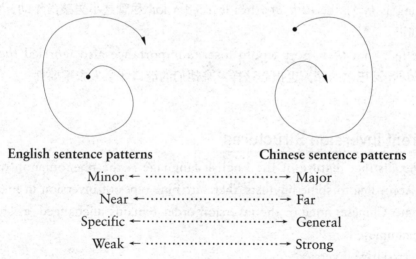

English sentence patterns   Chinese sentence patterns

Minor ←·····················→ Major
Near ←·····················→ Far
Specific ←·····················→ General
Weak ←·····················→ Strong

Here are some examples:

- His address is *3612 Market Street, Philadelphia, PA. 19104, USA.* 他的地址是**美国宾夕法尼亚州费城市场街** 3612 号，邮政编码 19104。
- Mr. Gates built a huge mansion *on the shores of Lake Washington not far from Microsoft's headquarters in Redmond, a suburb of Seattle.* 盖茨先生在**西雅图市郊距微软总部不远的雷德蒙附近的华盛顿湖畔**建造了一座庞大的豪宅。
- 一定要分清**敌我**。We must draw a clear distinction between *ourselves* and *the enemy*.
- 因此，我们并不认为，他们**必须**或者应当采取中国的做法。Therefore, we do not

67

maintain that they *should* or *must* adopt the Chinese way.

Besides, English attributive phrases and clauses usually follow the words being modified (the antecedent), whereas in Chinese such phrases and clauses always precede the words being modified. For example:

- Most of the information *we have got* is through that channel. **我们得到的**大部分消息是通过那个渠道获得的。

Furthermore, adverbials of time and place in English are usually placed at the end of a sentence, with the adverbials of place preceding those of time, whereas Chinese is just the opposite. For example:

- My uncle passed away *in hospital at* 2:30 *a.m. on September 12, 1999*. 我的伯父于1999年9月12日凌晨2点30分在医院逝世。

In English sentences, the possessive pronoun often precedes the noun it stands for, and a subordinate clause containing a personal pronoun precedes the main clause. However, in Chinese it is quite the opposite, and sometimes the nouns and pronouns are simply omitted. For example:

- Young as *he* is, the *little boy* has learned a lot. 尽管这**小男孩**尚年幼，可已学了不少知识。
- The fear that *their* port would lose its importance also worried *the people of Baltimore*. 巴尔的摩人也担心这样一来他们的港口就会失去重要性。

2. Different Inversion Structures

Another distinct feature of the English language is the phenomenon of inversion structures. According to some linguists, there are nine types of inversion in English. When translated into Chinese, none of the inversion order remains unchanged, as shown in the following examples:

(1) Interrogative inversion

What did you do yesterday? 你昨天干什么来着？

(2) Imperative inversion

"Speak you," said Mr. Black, "Speak you, good fellow!" 布莱克先生叫道："说，说吧，伙计！"

(3) Exclamatory inversion

How dreadful this place is! 这地方好可怕啊！

(4) Hypothetical inversion

Had you come yesterday, you could have seen him here. 要是你昨天来了，你就会

在这里看到他的。

(5) Balance inversion

Through a gap came an elaborately described ray. 从一个空洞透出一束精心描绘的光线。

(6) Link inversion

On this depends the whole argument. 整个争论都以此为论据。

(7) Signpost inversion

By strategy is meant something wider. 这里用"战略"一词，其含义较广。

(8) Negative inversion

Not a word did he say. 他只字未说。

(9) Metrical inversion

As pants the hart for cooling streams. (Normal order: As the hart pants for cooling streams.) 像公鹿渴望清凉的小溪一样。

II. Restructuring in E-C Translation

The technique of restructuring in English-Chinese translation may usually be used in the following cases.

1. Keeping the Original Sequence

- Laid out in the early 15th century, the Forbidden City unfolds powerfully in courtyard after courtyard, as if the power of the emperor himself could never quite be reached. 早在15世纪初，紫禁城就形成了现在的格局：重重庭院错落有致，威严无比，犹如皇帝的龙威，可望而不可即。
- In order to survive, to feed, clothe and shelter himself and his children, man is engaged in a constant struggle with nature. 为了生存，为了自己和子孙后代的衣食住行，人类和大自然不断进行斗争。
- Rocket research has confirmed a strange fact which had already been suspected: there is a "high-temperature belt" in the atmosphere, with it center roughly thirty miles above the ground. 火箭研究证实了早先人们就怀疑的这样一个奇异的事实：大气层中有一个"高温带"，其中心在距地面约30英里高的地方。

2. Reversing the Original Sequence

- *It is easy* to see what weight can be overcome and what thrust is necessary to maintain flight. 要知道应该抵消多大重力并需要多大推力才能保持飞行,**这很容易**。
- *The confusion is compounded* by the anniversary's observance on a date rather than a day of the week. ("9·11") 周年纪念日是一个固定日期而不是星期几,这就**使得纪念活动更为混乱**。
- In reality, the lines of division between sciences are becoming blurred, and science again approaching the "unity" that it had two centuries ago—*although the accumulated knowledge is enormously greater now, and no one person can hope to comprehend more than a fraction of it.* 虽然现在积累起来的知识要多得多,而且任何个人也只可能了解其中的一小部分,但实际上,各学科之间的界线却变得模糊不清,科学将再次近似于两百年前那样的"大一统"状态。

3. Restructuring by Time Sequence

- *As was cleared up some time later,* news came from a distance that an earthquake was felt the very day the little copper ball fell. 过了一些时候,从远方传来了消息:在小铜球坠落的当天,确实发生了地震。**这一切终于得到了澄清**。
- *Dr. Smith resumed the activities of anti-cancer experiment* begun in 1985 and financed by the Federal government as soon as he snapped from his original disappointment at repeated failures, which had resulted in its forced suspension. 史密斯医生于1985年开始着手由联邦政府资助的抗癌实验。他由于屡遭失败而感到沮丧,被迫终止了实验工作。现在他一重新振作起来,**便立即恢复了抗癌实验活动**。
- *And I take heart from the fact* that the enemy, which boasts that it can occupy the strategic point in a couple of hours, has not yet been able to take even the outlying regions, because of the stiff resistance that gets in the way. 敌人吹嘘说能在几小时内就占领该战略要地,可是由于沿途一路受到顽强抵抗,结果甚至连外围地带也没能占领。**这一事实使我增强了信心**。

4. Restructuring by Logical Sequence

- With the fear of *largely imaginary* plots against his leadership, his selfconfidence seemed totally to desert him. 由于害怕有人阴谋推翻他的领导,他似乎完全丧失了自信。但所谓的阴谋**在很大程度上是他自己假想出来的**。
- Interest in historical methods has arisen *less through* external to the validity of history as an intellectual discipline *and more from* internal quarrels among historians themselves. 人们关注历史研究的方法,**主要是因为**史学界内部意见不统

一，其次是因为外界怀疑历史是不是一门学科。
- In practice, the selected interval thickness *is usually a compromise between* the need for a thin interval to maximize the resolution and a thick interval to minimize the error. 为保证最大分辨率必须选用薄层，为使误差最小却须选用厚层，实际上通常选择介于两者之间的最佳厚度。

III. Restructuring in C-E Translation

1. Different Sequences in Customary Word Combinations

Every language has its own peculiar ways of combining words, and so do English and Chinese. Generally speaking, Chinese word-combination is in a strong-weak sequence, as shown in the following examples:
- 华东 *East China*
- 东南西北 *north* and *south, east* and *west*
- 你、我、他 *you, he* and *I*
- 衣食住行 *food, clothing,* shelter and transportation
- 祸福与共 share the *weal* and *woe*
- 无论晴雨 *rain* or *shine*
- 言行不一 inconsistency of *deeds* with *words*
- 钢铁工业 the *iron* and *steel* industry
- 救死扶伤 heal the *wounded* and rescue the *dying*
- 血肉相连 as close as *flesh* and *blood*
- 水火不容 be incompatible as *fire* and *water*
- 水陆并进 advance by both *land* and *water*
- 前前后后，来来去去 *back* and *forth, to* and *fro*
- 父母 *mom* and *dad*
- 左顾右盼 glance *right* and *left*

2. Cases of Restructuring in C-E Translation

The cases include translating attributive elements, some adverbials or negative sentences, etc. Sometimes, it is used for the purpose of avoiding anticlimax effects. The following are some typical instances.
- 社会主义的现代化强国 *a modern, powerful socialist* country
- 一位美国当代优秀作家 *an outstanding contemporary American* writer

- 各条战线上的先进工作者们 *advanced workers from* various fronts
- 这是能**想象得出**的最好解决办法。This is the best solution *imaginable*.
- 仅公寓房租一项就要 1 000 美元。The rent of the flat *alone* is $1,000.
- 许多代表激动地说："我们从来没有看见过这样光明的前途。" A great number of deputies said excitedly, "*Never have we seen* so bright a future before us!"
- 院士此刻正在实验室和他的两个新助手一道工作。The academician is working *with his two new assistants in the laboratory at the moment*.
- 中国人民正在中国共产党的领导下，团结一致地进行着伟大的社会主义建设。*Led by the Chinese Communist Party*, the Chinese people, *united as one*, are engaged in the great task of building socialism.
- 救死扶伤，实行革命的人道主义。*Heal the wounded, rescue the dying*, and practice revolutionary humanitarianism.
- 我们以热爱祖国、贡献全部力量建设社会主义祖国为**最大光荣**，以损害社会主义祖国利益、尊严和荣誉为**最大耻辱**。We deem it *the highest honour* to love our socialist motherland and contribute our all to her socialist construction. We deem it *the deepest disgrace* to impair her interests, dignity and honour.

Reflections and Practice

I. Discuss the following questions.

1. What are the different modes of thinking between English and Chinese?
2. What are the differences between inversion structures in English and Chinese sentences?
3. What is restructuring? How is it used in E-C translation?
4. How is the technique of restructuring used in C-E translation?

II. Put the following sentences into Chinese, using the technique of restructuring.

1. It is easy to see what weight can be overcome and what thrust is necessary to maintain flight.
2. He was dumbfounded at her insistence that he explain where every cent of his allowance had gone.
3. That our environment has little, if anything, to do with our abilities, characteristics and behavior is central to this theory.

4. Behaviorists, in contrast, say that differences in scores are due to the fact that blacks are often deprived of many of the educational and other vantages that whites enjoy.
5. He would be a rash man who should venture to defy world public opinion and act arbitrarily.
6. I was all the more delighted when, as a result of the initiative of your government, it proved possible to reinstate the visit so quickly.
7. Accounts are given of huge mountains sinking, of former plains seen heaved aloft, of fires flashing out amid the ruin.
8. The president has also called for an annual moment of silence at 8∶46 a.m. Eastern time, when the first plane hit the first tower.
9. Nowadays it is understood that a diet which contains nothing harmful may result in serious disease if certain important elements are missing.
10. Can you forge against these enemies in a grand and global alliance, north and south, east and west, that can assure a more fruitful life for all mankind? Will you join in that historic effort?
11. Many more visitors than it can comfortably accommodate poured into it, off the regular steamers, off chartered motorboats and off yachts; all day they ambled up the towpath, looking for what?
12. I believe that I speak for every sincere and serious representative in the United Nations—so I am encouraged to believe by the speeches to which we have already listened this morning—when I say that the anniversary must be an occasion for an honest assessment of our failures in the past, matched by an equally determined will to do better in the future, so that we can escape from frustration and turn the anniversary into an inspiration and an achievement.

III. Put the following sentences into English, using the technique of restructuring.

1. 直到昨天我才知道他住院了。
2. 我们必须清楚地了解所有牵涉到的问题。
3. 他们的部队水陆并进，及时抵达前线。
4. 这次大会充分发扬了民主；大家心情舒畅，生动活泼。
5. 他穿过马路时，左顾右盼，害怕撞到过路的车上。
6. 只有听党中央指挥，调动一切积极因素，才能顺利实现四个现代化。
7. 丰收年多积累一点，灾荒年或者半灾荒年就不积累或者少积累一点。
8. 所有这些成就，标志着我国在全面建设小康社会道路上又迈出坚实的一步。

9. 这所大学现有计算机科学、高能物理、激光、地球物理、遥感技术、遗传工程六个新建的专业。
10. 中国内地周围有470多万平方千米的广大的海域，渤海、黄海、东海、南海四海相连，环绕着中国的东部和东南部海岸。

IV. Put the following sentences into Chinese, paying attention to the italicized words.

1. I *challenge* my own conclusion.
2. I *challenge* you to answer the question.
3. China *challenges* the world in discipline.
4. Recent discoveries have *challenged* the old notions.
5. His question *challenges* us to think.
6. Survival in enemy-occupied territory *challenged* skill.
7. He is not *committed* to an early election.
8. I am *committed* to improving relations with China.
9. I can't *commit* myself by telling you that.
10. I wish to know more before I *commit* myself.
11. I have no wish to *commit* you to anything.
12. The boss *committed* him to do it.
13. He is the *last* man to accept a bribe.
14. He is the *last* man for such a job.
15. A bikini was the *last* thing she'd like to wear.
16. This is the *last* place where I expected to meet you.

Unit 7 Affirmative vs. Negative

单元要点概述

相关翻译技巧训练英译汉：The Legend of Valentine Chocolates

相关翻译技巧训练汉译英：谦虚与诚恳

I. 英译汉的正反调换
 1. 英语为肯定，汉语译作否定
 2. 英语为否定，汉语译作肯定
 3. 译作肯定否定均可
 4. 强调性双重否定
 5. 间接式肯定
 6. 否定的陷阱

II. 汉译英的正反调换
 1. 根据英语惯用法确定肯定或否定
 2. 从强调或修辞角度考虑肯定或否定
 3. 用正反调换传达出原文的确切意思

　　本单元探讨了英语中的肯定与否定结构，介绍分析了各类否定结构的翻译方法技巧。

　　英语的否定类型大致可分为四类：完全否定、半否定、部分否定及带否定含义的词语。一般情况下采用对号入座即可，必要时可以"正说反译"或"反说正译"。对英语中的双重否定和貌似否定的迂回式肯定结构需小心翼翼，对于几类句型所造成的"否定的陷阱"尤其需要提防注意。

　　本单元的后部分对汉译英的肯定、否定结构作了扼要的归纳，进而提出根据英语的习惯表达、从强调或修辞角度考虑以及视具体情况采用肯定或否定，以准确地表达出原文的精神风貌。

Practice of the Relevant Skill

1. E-C Translation

The Legend of Valentine Chocolates

None of the popular hagiographies of St. Valentine give any hint of him liking chocolate, or even being vaguely associated with the confection. For good reason: it would be another millennium before descendants of the patricians and plebeians of Ancient Rome would learn of Mesoamerica, let alone sample the delights of *xocolatl* (a linguistic blend of Mayan and Nahuatl for "hot drink").

Europeans only started importing the seeds of Theobroma cacao, a tree native to the Andes foothills between the Amazon and Orinoco rivers, after Christopher Columbus's fourth and final mission to the Americas in 1502. But once the Spanish started adding honey or sugar to the bitter drink, Europeans embraced chocolate as a refreshing beverage to sip throughout the day. So much so that the Dutch, the Belgians, the French and the British would eventually plant swathes of cacao trees in their newly acquired colonies in the tropics—and thereby established the foundations of their chocolate industries of today. West Africa accounts for two thirds of the world's current cocoa production.

To return briefly to Roman times, legend has it that, of the several martyrs named Valentinus who were persecuted for ministering to Christians, one in particular is venerated above all others. As the story goes, Valentine of Rome healed the blind daughter of his jailer during his imprisonment, and wrote a note to her signed "Your Valentine" prior to being thrown to the lions. Whether his unhappy end happened on the day the Gregorian calendar now calls February 14th is unknown.

The martyrdom myth aside, there is no association between St. Valentine's Day and romantic love until *Parlement of Foules*, written by Geoffrey Chaucer in the late 1300s, to celebrate the first anniversary of Richard II's engagement to Anne of Bohemia. Chaucer's lines in colourful Middle English (pronounced like modern-day Geordie) read: "For this was on seynt Volantynes day/When euery bryd comyth there to chese his mate." ("For this was on St. Valentine's Day, when every bird comes there to choose his mate.") As a point of interest, both Richard and Anne were 15 at the time.

However, it was not until the late 18th century that young couples in England started using the occasion to express their love for one another, by offering gifts of flowers, greetings cards (known as Valentines) and confectionery. Today, the weeks prior to St. Valentine's Day are among the chocolatiers' busiest of the year. Meanwhile, the tradition

UNIT **7** Affirmative vs. Negative

of exchanging Valentine cards anonymously commenced when the penny post spread uniformly across the British Isles in 1840, and saved shy admirers from having to deliver their tokens of affection in person.

Notes and Explanations

1. confection *n.* 糖果，蜜饯
2. hagiography *n.* 圣徒传记，圣徒言行录
3. St. Valentine 圣瓦伦丁
4. millennium *n.* 千年期，千禧年
5. patrician *n.* 贵族，有教养的人
6. plebeian *n.* 平民
7. Mesoamerica *n.* 中美洲
8. Mayan and Nahuatl 玛雅和纳瓦特尔语
9. Theobroma *n.* 可可属，梧桐科植物
10. the Andes foothills 安第斯山山麓
11. the Amazon and Orinoco rivers 亚马孙河与奥里诺科河
12. Christopher Columbus 克里斯多弗·哥伦布（意大利航海家）
13. swath *n.* 长而宽的一条（或地带）
14. venerate *v.* 崇敬，尊敬
15. the Gregorian calendar 公历，格里高里历
16. *Parlement of Foules* 《百鸟议会》
17. Geoffrey Chaucer 杰弗里·乔叟
18. Richard II 理查二世
19. Anne of Bohemia 波西米亚公主安妮
20. save from 免于，使免遭

2. C-E Translation

谦虚与诚恳

一位中国人到美国朋友家做客。"你的房子不错，真宽敞，"客人赞美道。主人听了十分高兴，按美国习惯笑着回答说"谢谢"。这令客人感到意外。

"你的英语讲得真棒，很流利，"主人夸道。"不！不！我的英语说得很不好，"客人回答道。主人没想到客人会这样回答，很是迷惑不解。

主人的回答是否"不谦虚"？客人的回答是否"不诚恳"？显然都不是。讲英语的人

听到别人赞扬，一般说"谢谢"，表示接受，认为对方的赞扬是诚心诚意的，不应故作谦虚。但对中国人来说，听到别人赞扬时，通常要表示受之有愧，做得很不够，接受赞扬则意味着骄傲自满或缺乏教养。两种回答引起不同反应表明各自不同的语言习惯。

Notes and Explanations

1. 赞美 compliment
2. 按美国习惯 in good American fashion
3. 迷惑不解 be perplexed
4. 故作谦虚 show of pretended modesty
5. 受之有愧 not worthy of the praise
6. 缺乏教养 lack of manners

As some linguists point out, every language has its peculiarities in negation. And there is indeed an important, though often neglected, difference between English and Chinese in negation. For example:

A: Are you not going tomorrow?

B: *No*, I'm not going.

In Chinese, the above "no" should be rendered as "是的"，otherwise, it would cause confusion. Similarly, it is idiomatic to say "我认为他不对", "我想他不会来了" in Chinese. In English, however, these ideas would be expressed as "I don't think he is correct", "I don't think he will come", with the negative put immediately after "I".

Look at the following dialogue between an American landlady and her tenant, a Chinese international student who came back after school.

A: Did you eat anything yet?

B: No.

A: So you didn't eat anything.

B: Yes.

A : (hesitated) Did you eat?

B: No.

A: (puzzled) So you didn't eat.

B: Yes.

A (at a loss for words): ...

And here are some more instances from Practice of the Relevant Skill:

- *None of* the popular hagiographies of St. Valentine give any hint of him liking chocolate, or even being *vaguely* associated with the confection. 流行的关于圣瓦伦

UNIT 7 Affirmative vs. Negative

丁的圣徒传记中**没有一星半点**提及他喜欢吃巧克力或者与巧克力有**任何**关系。
- For good reason: it would be another millennium before descendants of the patricians and plebeians of Ancient Rome would learn of Mesoamerica, *let alone* sample the delights of xocolatl (a linguistic blend of Mayan and Nahuatl for "hot drink"). 这样说是有充分的理由的：古罗马时代上至贵族、下至平民百姓还要过一千年才能知道有那么个中美洲，**更不要说**品尝什么"遭古力"的美味了。
- But once the Spanish started adding honey or sugar to the bitter drink, Europeans embraced chocolate as a refreshing beverage to sip *throughout the day*. 然而一旦西班牙人开始向这种苦涩的饮料中加入蜂蜜或糖之后，巧克力就成了欧洲人提神的饮品，**一天之中有事没事都喜欢喝上两口**。
- Whether his unhappy end happened on the day the Gregorian calendar now calls February 14th *is unknown*. 他的不幸结局是否发生在公历的 2 月 14 日我们**不得而知**。
- The martyrdom myth *aside*, there is *no association* between St. Valentine's Day and romantic love... **且不论**这位殉道罹难的传说，就连"圣瓦伦丁"这个节日也和浪漫的爱情**毫无关联**……
- However, it was *not until* the late 18th century that young couples in England started using the occasion. 然而，**直到** 18 世纪末，英国年轻的情侣们**才**开始利用这个机会。
- ...and *saved* shy admirers *from* having to deliver their tokens of affection in person. ……使害羞的爱慕者再**也不用**亲自登门来表达爱意了。

I. Negation in E-C Translation

From the above illustrations we may find what is affirmative in form in English may be translated into negative and vice versa. Generally speaking, English negative words and expressions fall into the following categories:

(1) **Full negatives:** no, not, none, never, nothing, nobody, nowhere, neither, nor;

(2) **Semi negatives:** hardly, scarcely, seldom, barely, few, little, etc.;

(3) **Partial negatives:** not every, not all, not both, not much, not many, not always, etc.;

(4) **Words with negative implication:** fail, without, beyond, until, unless, lest, ignorant, refrain, refuse, neglect, absence, instead of, other than, except, rather than, etc.

In most cases, we may translate these negative expressions literally; otherwise convert them into affirmatives so as to guarantee idiomatical Chinese version.

1. Affirmative in English, but Negative in Chinese

Such cases are found in a wide range of scope: words of different parts of speech, various phrases, or sentence structures.

- He *denied* it to be the case. (*v.*) 他说事实**不是**这样。
- Time is what we want most, but what, alas, many use *worst*. (*adv.*) 时间是我们最缺少的，但可叹之至，偏偏许多人最**不**善于利用。
- I have read your article. I expected to meet an *older* man. (*adj.*) 拜读了你的大作，**没**想到你这样年轻。
- It was *beyond* his power to sign such a contract. (*prep.*) 他**无**权签订这种合同。
- The guerrillas would fight to death *before* they surrender. (*conj.*) 游击队员们宁愿战死也**绝不**投降。
- They feel great *anxiety* about his sickness. (*n.*) 他们对他的病情感到焦虑**不**安。
- The lecturer spoke *above* the heads of his audience. (*prep.*) 讲演者讲得太深奥，听众听**不**懂。
- I'm *at my wit's end* to keep this child quiet. (phrase) 我实在是**没办法**让这孩子安静下来。
- The mother said she would *let* her son *off* washing the dishes if he could finish his assignment before supper. (phrase) 母亲说，如果儿子晚饭前能做完作业，就**不让**他洗碗了。
- If it worked once, *it can work twice*. (sentence) 一次得手，**再次不**愁。

2. Negative in English, but Affirmative in Chinese

This case is just opposite to the above-mentioned cases.

- The doubt was still *unresolved* after his repeated explanation. (*adj.*) 经他一再解释，疑团仍然**存在**。
- He *carelessly* glanced through the note and then left. (*adv.*) 他**马马虎虎**地看了看那张便条就走了。
- All the articles in the museum are *untouchable*. (*adj.*) 博物馆内一切展品**禁止触摸**。
- He manifested a strong *dislike* for his father's business. (*n.*) 他对他父亲的行业表示强烈的**厌恶感**。
- *Don't lose time* in posting this letter. (phrase) **赶快**把这封信寄出去。
- Such flight *couldn't long escape* notice. (sentence) 这类飞行**迟早会**被人发觉的。

3. Same English Wording, Either Affirmative or Negative in Chinese

In this case, we have to pick out a right one to adapt to the context.

- I'm *new* to the work. 这工作我是**生手**。/ 这工作我**不熟悉**。

UNIT 7 Affirmative vs. Negative

- He is *free* with his money. 他花钱**大手大脚**。/ 他花钱从**不吝啬**。
- He realized that he was *in trouble*. 他意识到**遇到麻烦**了。/ 他感到自己的**处境不妙**。
- The station is *no distance* at all. 车站**近在咫尺**。/ 车站一点儿也**不远**。
- It's *no less than* a fraud. 这简直是一场骗局。/ 这无异于一场骗局。
- The works of art were left *intact*, the money gone. 艺术品**还在**，钱却不翼而飞。/ 艺术品**原封未动**，钱却不翼而飞。
- The criminal is still *at large*. 罪犯还**未捉拿归案**。/ 罪犯仍旧**逍遥法外**。

4. Double Negative for Emphasis

Double negative in English, as in Chinese, is used for emphasis. In translating such a structure we may either drop both the negative words, or keep the original structure, depending on which is more idiomatic in Chinese.

- There is *no* rule that has *no* exception. 任何规则**都不无例外**。
- There is *not any* advantage *without* disadvantage. 有一利**必有一弊**。
- It *never* rains *but* it pours. 不雨则已，雨**必倾盆**。
- It is *impossible but* that a man will make some mistakes. 人**不会不犯错误**。
- Today, there's *scarcely* an aspect of our life that *isn't being affected* by the Internet. 今天，我们生活中的方方面面**无不受到因特网的影响**。
- *Hardly* a month goes by *without* word of another survey revealing new depths of scientific illiteracy among U.S. citizens. 美国公民科学知识匮乏的现象日益严重，这种调查报告几乎月月**屡见不鲜**。

5. Roundabout Affirmative

This is an indirect way of expressing a strong affirmative. When translated into Chinese, the original emotion should be properly kept.

- He *didn't half* like the girl. 他非常喜欢那姑娘。
- I *couldn't* feel *better*. 我觉得身体**好极了**。
- I *couldn't agree* with you *more*. 我**太赞成**你的看法了。
- If that *isn't what I want*! 我所要的就是这个呀！
- He *can't see* you *quick enough*. 他很想**尽快**和你见面。

6. Some Traps in Negative Structures

Occasionally we may encounter some negative structures with elusive connotation, i.e., "translation traps". The following are some typical patterns that call for attention.

(1) not...because

- The engine *didn't* stop *because* the fuel was finished. 引擎并**不是因为**燃料耗尽而停

止运转。

- *Don't* scamp your work *because* you are pressed for time. 不要因为时间紧而敷衍塞责。
- In that city, we had *never* suffered discrimination *because* we were Jews. 我们在那个城市从未因为是犹太人而遭受歧视。
- Gates *didn't* drop out *because* he wanted to avoid work but to start his company. 盖茨辍学**不是**想逃避学业，而是为了开办自己的公司。

(2) *cannot...too/never...too*

- The importance of this conference *cannot* be *overestimated*. 这次会议的重要性**无论怎么强调也不过分**。
- I shall *never* be able to stress *too* much your kindness. 对您的好意我真是感激**不尽**。
- You *cannot* be *too* careful in proofreading. 校对时，**越仔细越好**。

(3) *all/every...not*

- *All* that glitters is *not* gold. 发光的**不一定都**是金子。
- *All* cities did *not* look like they do today. 在过去，城市**并不都**像今天这样个个千篇一律。
- No, *everything* is *not* straightened out. 不，**并非每一个**问题都弄清楚了。

(4) *both...not*

- But you see, we *both cannot* go. 但是我告诉你，我们俩**不能**同时**都**走。
- *Both* the instruments are *not* precision ones. 这两件东西**不都**是精密仪器。
- Both read the same Bible, and pray to the same God; and each invokes His aid against the other. The prayers of *both* could *not* be answered. 双方念的是同一本圣经，拜的是同一个上帝，但各方都要求上帝帮助去打倒对方。所以，双方的祈求**不可能都**得到满足。

(5) *for all one care/know*

- You may leave at once *for all I care*. 你尽可立即离开，**我才不管呢**。
- *For all we knew*, the files we were supposed to photograph were already on their way. **说不定**那些该由我们去拍摄的文件已在途中。

(6) *It be + adj. + noun + that...*

- It is a good workman that never blunders. 智者千虑，必有一失。
- It is a long lane that has no end. 路必有弯。（凡事总有变化，不会永远不变。）
- It is an ill wind that blows nobody good. 坏事未必对人人都有害处。
- It's a good horse that never stumbles. 好马也有失蹄时。

UNIT 7 Affirmative vs. Negative

II. Negation in C-E Translation

Negation is also a linguistic phenomenon in Chinese language. The conversion between the negative and the affirmative in C-E translation is generally based on the following three considerations.

1. Negation According to English Usage

- 在他还没来得及阻拦我之前，我已经跑出教室。*Before he could stop me*, I had rushed out of the classroom.
- 俗话说，"男儿有泪不轻弹，只因未到伤心处"嘛。As the saying goes, "Men *only weep when* deeply hurt."
- 白茫茫的大地，除了呼呼的北风外，没有一点儿声响。Except for the howl of the north wind, *all was still* in the snowmantled ground.

2. Negation for Emphasis or Rhetorical Effect

- 这个惨痛的历史教训，我们全党同志一定要永远记取，引以为鉴。*No comrade* in the Party *must ever forget* this bitter lesson and we must all take warning from it.
- 我们讨论问题时，不能忘记这些基本点。These basic concepts *must be kept in mind* in our discussion.
- 党的十九大充分表明我们党兴旺发达，后继有人。The 19th Party Congress fully demonstrates that our Party is flourishing and *has no lack of successors*.

3. Negation to Convey Exactly the Original Meaning

- 到目前为止，该组织辜负了世界人民所寄予的希望。This organization *has not*, so far, *justified* the hopes which the people of the world place in it.
- 正如没经历过大事的人一样，他经不起成功也经不起失败。Like those of little experience, he *was easily elated by success and deflated by failure*.
- "我找老王说句话，马上就回来。""Just to have a word with Wang. It *won't be long!*"

Reflections and Practice

I. Discuss the following questions.

1. How are English negatives generally classified?

2. What are the general patterns in translating English negatives?
3. What are the traps in English negative structures?
4. When and where are negatives used in C-E translation?

II. Put the following sentences into Chinese, using the technique of negation.
1. One could not be too careful in a new neighborhood.
2. I'm wiser than to believe what you call money talks.
3. Nothing is so beautiful but it betrays some defect on close inspection.
4. I know it is a square peg in a round hole; still, it serves after a fashion.
5. Africa is not kicking out western imperialism in order to invite other new masters.
6. Both sides thought that the peace proposal was one they could accept with dignity.
7. All the chemical energy of the fuel is not converted into heat.
8. All graduates from the Foreign Languages Institute will not be appointed to do translation work.
9. All these various losses, great as they are, do not in any way contradict the law of conservation of energy.
10. All other sources of heat besides the sun would not raise the temperature of the earth 1/4 degree F.
11. Not all sounds made by animals serve as language, and we have only to turn to that extraordinary discovery of echolocation in bats to see a case in which the voice plays a strictly utilitarian role.
12. The target is wrong, for in attacking the tests, critics divert attention from the fault that lies with ill-informed or incompetent users.
13. One may as well be asleep to read for anything but to improve his mind and morals, and regulate his conduct.
14. Few things are impossible in themselves: and it is often for want of will, rather than of means, that men fail of success.

III. Put the following sentences into English, using the technique of negation.
1. 他开车时心不在焉，几乎闯祸。
2. 工作没有经验，出点差错，在所难免。
3. 会议开得冷冷清清，有时甚至开不下去了。
4. 那城市及周围的地方是不冻港和无核区。
5. 他只顾自己，不顾别人，使得大家都很生气。
6. 日子很快过去了，她做工却丝毫没有放松。

UNIT 7 Affirmative vs. Negative

7. 她没有同伴，独自一人坐在车厢一角动也不动。
8. 任何事物都有两点，说只有一点叫"知其一不知其二"。
9. 即使没有新的主意也可以，就是不要变，不要使人们感到政策变了。
10. 中国政府一直提倡"以人为本"的发展理念，强调人们以公交而不是私家车出行。
11. 在中国，父母总是竭力帮助孩子，甚至为孩子做重要决定，而不管孩子想要什么，因为他们相信这样做是为孩子好。
12. 如果分析不当，造成误解，就会变得谨小慎微，不敢解放思想，不敢放开手脚，结果是丧失时机，犹如逆水行舟，不进则退。

IV. Point out mistakes in the following translation, and then correct them.

1. They often talk horse. * 他们常常谈论马。
2. That woman walks the streets. * 那个妇女常在那些街上走。
3. I'll report that official. * 我要向那位官员报告。
4. The machine is in repair. * 那台机器正在修理之中。
5. We'll stand up to the project. * 我们都赞成这个工程。
6. Don't make a fuss of them! * 别对那些事大惊小怪！
7. She is in the dock. * 她在码头上。
8. The boss gave her the sack. * 老板给了她一个麻袋。
9. That girl student is in the green. * 那个女学生身着绿装。
10. The old lady has gone to her rest. * 那个老太太休息去了。
11. That young man lost his heart to the girl. * 那个青年人失去了信心。
12. The old man often takes his medicine. * 那老人常服药。
13. That fellow did hard labor for 3 years. * 那人干过三年艰苦的劳动。
14. The woman in labor is his wife. * 那个劳动的妇女是他的妻子。
15. I'm not a little afraid of snakes. * 我一点也不怕蛇。
16. We charged him to do it. * 我们指控他干了那个事。
17. They surprised him doing it. * 他们惊吓得他做那个事。
18. I have seen him through. * 我看透了他。
19. He is the Speaker. * 他是讲演者。
20. Where is the Book? * 那本书在哪？
21. Do you know anything about japan? * 你了解日本吗？
22. I bought some salts yesterday. * 我昨天买了一些食盐。
23. The man is in the dumps. * 那个人在垃圾堆里。
24. Don't call him names! * 别叫他的名字！
25. The little boy is a love child. * 那个小男孩是个可爱的孩子。

26. He is a confidence man.* 他是个有信心的人。
27. He is a medicine man.* 他是一个医务工作者。
28. What he bought is invaluable.* 他买的东西毫无价值。
29. This is a disused machine.* 这是一台没有用过的机器。
30. He is disinterested in the affairs.* 他对此事不感兴趣。

Unit 8 The Passive Voice

> ● 单元要点概述
>
> 相关翻译技巧训练英译汉：Vanishing Twins
> 相关翻译技巧训练汉译英：基因工程
> I. 英汉翻译的被动语态
>   1. 被动语态转为主动
>   2. 被动语态转为无主句
>   3. 被动语态保持不变
>   4. 被动语态用其他手段代替
> II. 汉英翻译的被动结构
>   1. 带有被动标签的汉语句子
>   2. 不带被动标签的汉语句子
>   3. 汉语主动转为英语被动
>   4. 汉语中一些源于英语的习惯表达

本单元讲解、归纳了英语被动语态和汉语被动结构的一般翻译方法。

被动语态在英语中广泛使用，尤其以科技英语为甚。而汉语的被动结构却并不常见，因为汉语的"被""遭""受""挨"等字眼往往带有负面含义。因此在英汉翻译时，我们应尽量将被动语态转化为主动。英译汉被动语态的常用方法有：1. 将英语被动语态转为主动（包括保持原主语不变、转换主语、宾语位置、增添适当主语等）；2. 将英语被动语态转为汉语的无主句；3. 英语被动语态保持不变；4. 英语被动语态用汉语其他手段代替。

汉语的被动结构一般有三种情况：一是带有"被""遭""受""挨"等被动标签的句子；二是不带这些被动标签的汉语句子，而后者更为常见；三是原文本身是主动句，但根据句式重心或表达的需要，在翻译成英语时需译作被动语态。

Practice of the Relevant Skill

1. E-C Translation

Vanishing Twins

Humans do not normally produce litters. Nevertheless, it is estimated that one person in 20 who was born alone has a lost twin who was conceived at the same time, but failed to reach term.

It has been known for many years that the loss of one twin in this way late in a pregnancy is bad for the other. That other is more likely to be born prematurely, to have cerebral palsy, or even to die as well. What has not been known until now is whether such a loss in the first few months has any effect on the survivor. But a paper just published in *Human Reproduction* by Peter Pharoah of the University of Liverpool, in Britain, suggests that it does.

There are several ways that a "vanished twin" can come to light. Most gruesomely, fully formed body parts of the dead twin may be found embedded in the body of its surviving sibling. More commonly, lost twins are discovered as tiny mummified attachments to the placenta of the live twin, after it is born. And the widespread use of ultrasonic scanning means that, increasingly often, twins are spotted in early scans and subsequently vanish. Neither early ultrasonic "sightings" nor papery mummified corpses are always officially registered. They may not even be mentioned to the mother, so it is hard to know just how often a twin goes missing.

Dr. Pharoah, however, made a stab at finding out. He examined three sets of data from northern England. One collated information about infant deaths. A second recorded congenital abnormalities. The third was a register of all pregnancies of twins, triplets or other multiple births.

What made this last register so useful was that it recorded multiple pregnancies as soon as they were recognized ultrasonically, rather than at birth. He found 138 instances in which one twin died before 16 weeks' gestation and the other was born and survived. Eleven of these survivors had a congenital anomaly such as a malformation of the heart or a facial cleft. From these figures Dr. Pharoah calculates that the risk of congenital anomaly in a surviving twin following the early loss of its sibling is 2.4 times higher than if the sibling survives—and almost four times higher than that of true singletons, who had the womb all to themselves from day one. He thinks the harm is done if the blood supply is shared between the two individuals, something more common in twins who share a chorion.

Whether this knowledge can be used to help surviving twins is moot. But identifying a problem is the first step to remedying it. Dr. Pharoah seems to have done that.

Notes and Explanations

1. litter *n.* (一)窝

UNIT 8 The Passive Voice

2. term *n.* 足月，正常妊娠期的终结
3. cerebral palsy 〈医〉大脑性麻痹，脑瘫
4. come to light 显露，暴露出来，成为人所共知
5. body parts 身体部位/器官
6. embed *v.* 使……嵌入，使……牢牢地安置在包围物中
7. mummify *v.* 成木乃伊状，干瘪
8. made a stab at 尝试
9. moot *adj.* 有待讨论的，未决的

2. C-E Translation

基因工程

"基因工程"这一术语1951年由美国科幻小说家杰克·威廉森杜撰，半个世纪以来这一技术已广泛应用到各个行业，主要在医药和农业领域取得了一些成功。

但是国外也有些科学家反对搞基因工程。他们害怕由此会产生引起癌症的病毒或细菌，使癌症广泛流行；还害怕扰乱和破坏了正常细胞的功能，造成奇怪的疾病……

众所周知，一门新科学给人类带来的是祸还是福，其实并不取决于这门科学本身，就像原子能那样，既可以用来造福于人类，也可以用来做杀人武器。我们相信，如果加以合理运用，基因工程一定能成为人类征服自然、改造自然的有力工具。

Notes and Explanations

1. 科幻小说家 science fiction writer
2. 杰克·威廉森 Jack Williamson (1908–2006)
3. 杜撰 coin
4. 广泛应用到 be extensively applied to
5. 害怕 for fear that
6. 引起癌症的病毒 cancerogenic virus
7. 扰乱和破坏 disrupt and damage
8. 祸还是福 weal or woe
9. 取决于 be decided by
10. 造福于人类 benefit human beings

The wide use of the passive is considered to be one of the outstanding features of the English language, especially in its scientific works, as shown in the following example: in a short section with 14 predicate verbs, the passive accounts for 13.

Original English: As oil *is found* deep in the ground its presence cannot *be determined* by a study of the surface. Consequently, a geological survey of the underground rock structure must *be carried* out. If it *is thought* that the rocks in a certain area contain oil, a "drilling rig" *is assembled*. The most obvious part of a drilling rig *is called* "a derrick". It *is used* to lift sections of pipe, which *are lowered* into the hole made by the drill. As the hole *is being drilled*, a steel pipe *is pushed* down to prevent the sides from falling in. If oil *is struck*, a cover *is firmly fixed* to the top of the pipe and the oil *is allowed* to escape through a series of valves.

Chinese Version: 由于石油深埋地下，靠研究地表不能确定石油的有无。因此对地下岩层结构必须进行地质探测。如果认为某地区的岩层含石油，则在该处安装"钻机"。钻机中最显眼的部件叫"井架"。井架用来吊升分节油管，把油管放入由钻头打出的孔中。当孔钻成时，放入钢管防止孔壁坍塌。如发现石油，则在油管顶部紧固地加盖，让石油通过一系列阀门流出。

More instances of the passive voice may be found from Practice of the Relevant Skill:

- Nevertheless, it *is estimated* that one person in 20 who *was born* alone has a lost twin who *was conceived* at the same time. 然而**据估计**，每 20 个单胞胎**呱呱坠地**之前，就有一个**在母体怀孕期**其实是双胞胎。
- It *has been known* for many years that... 很早之前，**人们就知道**……
- That other is more likely to *be born prematurely*. 另一个胎儿很可能会**早产**。
- What *has not been known* until now is... 人们至今也**不知道**的是……
- ...body parts of the dead twin may *be found embedded* in the body of its surviving sibling. 可能会**发现死尸**的身体部位**牢牢嵌在**存活的胎儿体内。
- ...lost twins *are discovered* as tiny mummified attachments to the placenta of the live twin, after it *is born*. 在胎儿**降生**后，会发现死去的胎儿变成了极小的干尸附在胎盘上。
- ...increasingly often, twins *are spotted* in early scans. 越来越多地在妊娠早期扫描**发现孪生胎**。
- ...nor papery mummified corpses *are* always officially *registered*. 通常也没有纸状干尸的正式**记载**。
- They may not even *be mentioned* to the mother. 甚至不会向产妇**提及**。
- He thinks the harm *is done* if the blood supply *is shared* between the two individuals. 他认为当一份血液同时供给两个胎儿的时候，危害就**产生**了。
- Whether this knowledge can *be used* to help surviving twins is moot. 这一认识是否可以**用来**帮助存活下来的多胞胎，问题还有待讨论。

As we have learned from English grammar, the passive voice in English is used to indicate an unknown subject, for the purpose of emphasis, or for the sake of stylistic device, as shown in the following cases:

(1) When the active subject is unknown or cannot be readily stated, for example:
- We *are kept* strong and well by clean air. 洁净的空气使我们身体健康。

(2) When the actor (doer of the action) is known but need not be mentioned, for example:
- Visitors *are requested* not to touch the exhibits. 观众请勿触摸展品。

(3) When the actor is emphasized for some special purpose, for example:
- The three machines can *be controlled* by a single operator. 这三台机器可以由一人单独操纵。

(4) When the passive structure is used as a stylistic device to avoid the incoherence of structure shifting, for example:
- John was a lawyer's son and *was destined* to the bar. 约翰是律师的儿子，注定要当律师。

I. The Passive Voice in E-C Translation

The passive voice is seldom used in Chinese. Therefore, in E-C Translation, we should try to convert the passive into various "active" patterns instead of sticking to the English patterns. And the following are usual methods of translating English sentences in the passive voice.

1. Converting the Passive Voice into the Active

(1) Keeping the original subject unchanged
- The whole country *was armed* in a few days. 几天之内全国就**武装起来了**。
- The sense of inferiority that he acquired in his youth *has never been totally eradicated*. 他在青少年时期留下的自卑感**还远远没有完全消除**。
- Every moment of every day, energy *is being transformed* from one form into another. 每时每刻，能量都在由一种形式**变为**另一种形式。

(2) Changing original object into subject
- By the end of the war 800 people had been saved *by the organization*. 到大战结束时，**这个组织拯救了** 800 人。
- A new way of displaying time has been given *by electronics*. **电子技术提供了**一种新的显示时间的方法。

- Communications satellites are used for international live transmission *throughout the world*. 全世界都将通信卫星用于国际实况转播。

(3) Changing the passive into the predicative verb "是"

- The picture *was painted* by Professor Smith. 这幅画**是**史密斯教授画的。
- The house *was built* of wood in 1985. 这座房子**是**1985年用木头修建的。
- The volume *is not measured* in square millimeters. It *is measured* in cubic millimeters. 体积**不是**以平方毫米计量的，而**是**以立方毫米计量的。

(4) Adding a subject to make the Chinese version smooth

- To explore the moon's surface, rockets *were launched* again and again. 为了探测月球的表面，**人们**一次又一次地发射火箭。
- Salt *is known* to have a very strong corroding effect on metals. **大家**知道，盐对金属有很强的腐蚀作用。
- It *is well known* that smoking is harmful to the health. **众所周知**，吸烟有害健康。

2. Converting the Passive Voice into a Subjectless Sentence

Omission of the subject is one of the typical features of Chinese syntax. Therefore, in the practice of E-C translation, we may translate the passive voice into a subjectless sentence.

- The unpleasant noise *must be immediately put to an end*. 必须立即**终止**这种讨厌的噪声。
- *Attention has been paid to* the new measures to prevent corrosion. **已经注意到**采取防腐新措施。
- Best surface finish *is provided* by machining methods, especially by grinding. 用机械加工方法，特别是磨削，可以**获得**最佳表面光洁度。

3. Keeping the Passive Structure Unchanged

Sometimes, we may keep the passive voice unchanged, especially when it comes to something unpleasant.

(1) Rendering into Chinese by using "被……" "给……" "遭……" "受……"

- If the scheme *is disapproved*, work on the project will stop immediately. 如果方案**被否决**，这项工程将立即停工。
- At the end of the month he *was fired* for incompetence. 月底，他因不胜任工作而**被解雇了**。
- He *was set upon* by two masked men. 他**遭到**两个蒙面男子的**袭击**。
- Everyone *was fed up with* her gossip. 人人都**受够了**她的流言蜚语。

(2) Rendering into Chinese by using "为……所" "予以……" "由……加以"

- Such conduct will *be looked down upon by* all with a sense of decency. 这种行为将会**为**一切有良知的人**所蔑视**。
- As soon as all the facts *have been found out,* we can begin to formulate a theory. 一旦所有的事实**为**人们**所发现**，理论即可形成。
- All the buildings *were destroyed* in a big fire. 所有的建筑物均为一场大火所焚毁。
- Objections to the plan will *be taken* into consideration. 对本计划的异议将**予以考虑**。
- Excise tax, value added tax, customs duties and payroll tax *are stipulated by law*. 消费税、增值税、进口税以及就业税均**由法律加以规定**。

4. Replacing the Passive Voice with Other Means

In some cases, however, the passive voice in English cannot be rendered into good Chinese by any of the above means. Therefore, it is up to the translator to adjust or remold the whole structure, trying to find a readable and smooth Chinese version. For example:

- The village *is populated* by about 13,000 farmers. 这个村子里**住着**大约 13 000 个农民。
- Most trees *are denuded of* leaves in winter. 大多数树木冬天要**落叶**。
- The news *was passed on* by word of mouth. 众口相传，消息**不胫而走**。
- She *was delivered of* a boy. 她**生了**一个男孩。
- He *was told* that two of them seemed unlikely to make the grade. 他已**得知**他们中有两个人好像不能及格。
- She and her husband *have been asked* out for the banquet. 她和丈夫**应邀**赴宴去了。
- He *has been wedded* to translation. 他与翻译**结下不解之缘**。
- She did not wish to *be troubled.* 她不愿**别人麻烦她**。

II. Passive Structures in C-E Translation

Owing to its unpleasant connotation, the passive is less commonly used in Chinese than in English, and usually the passive implication of a Chinese sentence is covered up by its object-first structure. For example, "作业做完了""任务完成了""路修好了", etc. These Chinese sentences, seemingly without passive labels, actually should be treated as passive structures, which may roughly be classified into two categories, i.e. sentences with or without the passive labels.When translated into English, both of them should be rendered into passive structures. Besides, some Chinese "active" structures also should be converted into the passive voice for the purpose of emphasis.

1. Chinese Sentences with Passive Labels

This category includes such Chinese expressions as "被、受、遭、给、让、挨、叫、为……所、加以、予以", and so on. We may simply copy the Chinese passive structures and translate them into corresponding English sentences.

- 他**被选**为校学生会主席。He *was elected* Chairman of the Students' Union of this university.
- 她**深受**大家的尊敬。She *is greatly respected* by everyone.
- 窗上的玻璃**叫**那个孩子**打破了**，他一定要**挨骂**的。The windowpane *was broken* by the child; he will certainly *be scolded*.
- 社会主义思想体系已**为**全国人民**所接受**。Socialist ideology *has been accepted* by all the people of the country.
- 该计划将由一个特别委员会**加以审查**。The plan will *be examined* by a special committee.

However, not all Chinese sentences with passive labels should be translated into English passive voice, especially when it comes to an intransitive verb.

- 老太太**被**风**吹病了**。The old lady *fell ill* because of the draught.
- 天太冷，水管都**给冻住了**。It was so cold that the water pipes *froze*.

2. Chinese Sentences Without Passive Labels

Sentences of this category seem to be active in structure, but actually passive in meaning, with their subjects being logical objects of the predicate verbs.

- 这座桥将在今年年底**建成**。The construction of the bridge will *be completed* by the end of this year.
- 知识分子的问题就是在这样的基础上**提出来**的。On such a basis *has* the question of the intellectuals *been raised*.
- 这个问题正**在研究**。The problem *is now being studied*.
- 来宾**请**出示入场券。Visitors *are requested* to show their tickets.

3. Converting the Active Structure into the Passive Voice

This is the usual case when the object of the action is emphasized, or for the sake of coherence.

- 我国各族人民每年都要**热烈庆祝**"十一"国庆节。National Day *is enthusiastically celebrated* on Oct. 1st by the Chinese people of all nationalities every year.
- 中美已经**建立了**外交关系。Diplomatic relations *have been established* between

China and the United States of America.
- 一群人立刻把他**围住**了，向他**提出**一个又一个的问题。Very soon he *was surrounded* by a crowd and *was snowed* under with questions.
- 他出现在舞台上，观众**给予**热烈的掌声。He appeared on the stage and *was warmly applauded* by the audience.
- 口试时，问了 10 个问题，她全都答对了。She *was asked* ten questions in the oral examination and answered every one of them correctly.

4. The Translation of Some Idiomatic Chinese Expressions

Some Chinese sentence patterns drawn from English may be conveniently converted into the passive voice.
- 众所周知，火药是中国古代的四大发明之一。*It is well-known that* gunpowder is one of the four great inventions of the ancient Chinese people.
- 据谣传，那场事故是由于玩忽职守而造成的。*It is rumored that* the accident was due to negligence.
- 应该说，情况基本上是健康的。*It should be said that* the situation is basically sound.
- 必须指出，有些问题还需要澄清。*It must be pointed out that* some questions have yet to be clarified.

Reflections and Practice

I. Discuss the following questions.
1. When and where is the passive voice generally used in English?
2. What are the usual methods of translating English passive voice?
3. Is there any passive voice in Chinese? Cite examples to support your argument.
4. How are Chinese passive structures categorized? How is the technique of voice conversion used in C-E translation?

II. Put the following sentences into Chinese, paying attention to the conversion of the voice.
1. The oil of the world will have been used up, and man will be using the more convenient power obtained from the splitting of the atom.
2. There are some radioactive isotopes which are produced artificially by bombardment

of nuclei with neutrons.

3. Care should be taken to decrease the length of time that one is subjected to loud continuous noise.
4. Much has been said about the complexity of embryonic stem-cell research.
5. Goodyear, an American, had been trying for years to find a way in which rubber could be made hard, non-stick, and yet elastic.
6. We are taught that business letters should be written in a formal style rather than a personal one.
7. She told me that her master had dismissed her. No reason had been given; no objection had been made to her conduct. She had been forbidden to appeal to her mistress.
8. The increasing speed of scientific development will be obvious if one considers that TV, space craft, and nuclearpowered ships, which are taken for granted now, would have seemed fantastic to people whose lives ended as recently as 1920.
9. The rusting of iron is one example of corrosion, which may be described as the destructive chemical attack on a metal by media with which it comes in contact, such as moisture, air and water.
10. Pure science has been subdivided into physical science, which deals with the facts and relations of the physical world, and biological science, which investigates the history and makings of life on the planet.
11. It has been noted with concern that the stock of books in the library has been declining alarmingly. Students are asked to remind themselves of the rules for the borrowing and return of books, and to bear in mind the needs of other students. Penalties for overdue books will in the future be strictly enforced.
12. A current search of the files indicates that the letter is no longer in this bureau's possession. It is noted that the letter was received two months ago, and after study, returned to your office. In view of the foregoing, it is regretted that your office has no record of its receipt. If the letter is found, it would be appreciated if this bureau was notified at once.

III. Put the following sentences into English, paying attention to the conversion of the voice.

1. 旅客请在此填写"报关表"。
2. 刚才有人在这里讲了一些不该讲的话。
3. 他准备给我一份工作，这使我大吃一惊。

UNIT 8 The Passive Voice

4. 那个男孩受了重伤，医院立即把他收下了。
5. 采取"一国两制"适合中国国情，并非权宜之计。
6. 有朝一日家庭将由安装在地下室的小型反应堆供热。
7. 很抱歉，因为雨太大，参观博物馆得推迟到明天了。
8. 请全系师生于星期三下午二时在会议室集合，听报告。
9. 如果连锁反应不受控制，一直进行下去，就会引起一场大爆炸。
10. 利用一架显微镜，就可以看到集成电路被分离和被测试的情况。
11. 如果资本主义在港台地区得不到保障，那里的繁荣与稳定就不能维持，和平解决问题也就不可能了。
12. 还设计了另外一些设备，能将噪声分解成构成该噪声的各种不同的音响频率，并能记录不同频率的音响度。

IV. Compare the following pairs of sentences carefully and try to find their differences.

1. She bought a red and a yellow dress.
   She bought a red and yellow dress.
2. She was with a child.
   She was with child.
3. This tool is no more useful than that one.
   This tool is not more useful than that one.
4. He hurled the bone to the dog.
   He hurled the bone at the dog.
5. Quite properly, he was punished.
   He was punished quite properly.
6. Although he is busy, Henry is in high spirits.
   He is busy, but Henry is in high spirits.
7. They say David is mad, and so he is.
   He says Jane is mad, and so is he.
8. This cup of tea is fairly hot.
   This cup of tea is rather hot.
9. He is anything but a teacher.
   He is nothing but a teacher.
10. You may as well say so.
    You might as well say so.
11. You have offended the girl as deeply as I.

97

You have offended the girl as deeply as me.
12. His success is out of question.
    His success is out of the question.
13. It has been raining continually for two hours.
    It has been raining continuously for two hours.
14. I regret to say he was wrong.
    I regret saying he was wrong.
15. She spoke to the boy as a mother.
    She spoke to the boy like a mother.
16. He stood there to watch the train come in.
    He stood there watching the train come in.
17. I, as well as you, shall not do this test.
    I shall not do this test as well as you.
18. The children who wanted to play soccer ran to an open field.
    The children, who wanted to play soccer, ran to an open field.

Unit 9 Nominal Clauses

单元要点概述

相关翻译技巧训练英译汉：Crime and Poverty
相关翻译技巧训练汉译英：消除极端贫困

I. 英语名词性从句的翻译
  1. 主语从句   2. 宾语从句
  3. 表语从句   4. 同位语从句

II. 汉语复句的翻译
  1. 句子的合并   2. 句序

    本单元分析探讨了英语名词性从句及汉语复合句的一般翻译方法。
    英语名词性从句可分为主语从句、宾语从句、表语从句、同位语从句4大类。这些从句的翻译相对较为容易，一般按原文的语序处理即可，不过在翻译以"it"为形式主语、形式宾语的主语从句、宾语从句时，语序需要作适当调整。
    本单元重点介绍了同位语从句的四种翻译方法：1. 保持原文语序；2. 译为"这一"，"这种"（事实、情况……）等字眼；3. 加入冒号、破折号或"即"字眼；4. 译作汉语无主句。
    汉语没有类似的英语名词性从句。汉语的复合句大致分为联合复句和偏正复句两类。在翻译汉语复句时，关键在于抓住句子的重心，将主要信息译为英语主谓结构，其余部分视情况可分别用分词、动名词、不定式、介词短语等来处理。与英语相比，汉语句子较为简短、零散，词序也较为固定，翻译时应注意合并句子、调整语序。

Practice of the Relevant Skill

1. E-C Translation

Crime and Poverty

"Poverty", wrote Aristotle, "is the parent of crime." But was he right? Certainly, poverty and crime are associated. And the idea that a lack of income might drive someone to misdeeds sounds plausible. But research by Amir Sariaslan of the Karolinska Institute, in Stockholm, and his colleagues, just published in the *British Journal of Psychiatry*, casts doubt on the chain of causation—at least as far as violent crime and the misuse of drugs are concerned.

Using the rich troves of personal data which Scandinavian governments collect about their citizens, Mr. Sariaslan and his team were able to study more than half a million children born in Sweden between 1989 and 1993. The records they consulted contained information about these people's educational attainments, annual family incomes and criminal convictions. They also enabled the researchers to identify everybody's siblings.

In Sweden the age of criminal responsibility is 15, so Mr. Sariaslan tracked his subjects from the dates of their 15th birthdays onwards, for an average of three-and-a-half years. He found, to no one's surprise, that teenagers who had grown up in families whose earnings were among the bottom fifth were seven times more likely to be convicted of violent crimes, and twice as likely to be convicted of drug offences, as those whose family incomes were in the top fifth.

What did surprise him was that when he looked at families which had started poor and got richer, the younger children—those born into relative affluence—were just as likely to misbehave when they were teenagers as their elder siblings had been. Family income was not, per se, the determining factor.

That suggests two, not mutually exclusive, possibilities. One is that a family's culture, once established, is "sticky"—that you can, to put it crudely, take the kid out of the neighbourhood, but not the neighbourhood out of the kid. Given, for example, children's propensity to emulate elder siblings whom they admire, that sounds perfectly plausible. The other possibility is that genes which predispose to criminal behaviour are more common at the bottom of society than at the top, perhaps because the lack of impulse-control they engender also tends to reduce someone's earning capacity.

Neither of these conclusions is likely to be welcome to social reformers. The first suggests that merely topping up people's incomes, though it may well be a good idea for other reasons, will not by itself address questions of bad behaviour. The second raises the possibility that the problem of intergenerational poverty may be self-reinforcing, particularly in rich countries like Sweden where the winnowing effects of education and the need for high levels of skill in many jobs will favour those who can control their behaviour, and not those who rely on too many chemical crutches to get them through the day.

UNIT **9** Nominal Clauses

Notes and Explanations

1. misdeed *n.* 不端行为
2. plausible *adj.* 貌似可信的，貌似有理的
3. psychiatry *n.* 精神病学
4. cast doubt on 对……产生怀疑
5. causation *n.* 因果关系
6. trove *n.* 收藏的东西
7. educational attainments 受教育程度
8. criminal conviction 刑事定罪
9. siblings *n.* 兄弟姐妹
10. be convicted of 宣判有罪
11. drug offences 贩卖毒品罪
12. per se 本身，自身
13. propensity *n.* 倾向，习性
14. emulate *v.* 仿真，模仿
15. predispose *v.* 预先处置，使……偏向于
16. engender *v.* 使产生，造成
17. top up 加满，充值
18. intergenerational *adj.* 两代间的
19. self-reinforcing *adj.* 自我强化的
20. winnowing effects 筛选作用
21. chemical crutches 化学药品支撑

2. C-E Translation

消除极端贫困

在帮助国际社会于 2030 年前消除极端贫困过程中，中国正扮演着越来越重要的角色。自 20 世纪 70 年代末实施改革开放以来，中国已使多达四亿人摆脱了贫困。在未来五年中，中国将向其他发展中国家在减少贫困、发展教育、农业现代化、环境保护和医疗保健等方面提供援助。

中国在减少贫困方面取得了显著进步，并在促进经济增长方面做出了不懈努力，这将鼓励其他贫困国家应对自身发展中的挑战。在寻具有自身特色的发展道路时，这些国家可以借鉴中国的经验。

Notes and Explanations

1. 消除极端贫困 eradicate extreme poverty
2. 扮演着越来越重要的角色 play an increasingly important role
3. 实施改革开放 the implementation of reform and opening up
4. 使摆脱贫困 help...out of poverty
5. 减少贫困 poverty reduction/poverty alleviation
6. 农业现代化 agricultural modernization
7. 环境保护、医疗保健 environmental protection, health care
8. 促进经济增长 promote economic growth
9. 不懈努力 unremitting efforts
10. 应对挑战 cope with challenges
11. 有自身特色的发展道路 the path of development with their own characteristics

English subordinate clauses fall into six categories, i.e. subject clauses, object clauses, predicative clauses, appositive clauses, attributive clauses, and adverbial clauses. Since the first four of them function as nouns in a complex sentence, they are generally called nominal clauses. And here are some nominal clauses from the above Practice of the Relevant Skill:

- And *the idea that a lack of income might drive someone to misdeeds* sounds plausible. (appositive clause) 而收入拮据或许会导致行为不端的说法听起来也合情合理。
- He found, to no one's surprise, *that teenagers who had grown up in families whose earnings were among the bottom fifth were seven times more likely to be convicted of violent crimes.*（object clause, predicative clause）他发现，不出所料，成长在收入最低的1/5家庭的孩子与收入最高的1/5家庭的孩子相比，暴力犯罪的概率很可能为后者的7倍。
- *What did surprise him was that*...the younger children...were just as likely to misbehave. (subject clause) 真正令他感到惊讶的是，……那些年龄较小的弟妹……也容易产生不良行为。
- One is *that a family's culture, once established, is "sticky"— that you can, to put it crudely, take the kid out of the neighbourhood,* but not the neighbourhood out of the kid. (object clause, predicative clause) 一种可能性是，家庭文化（家风）一旦形成，便具有"附着性"。说得难听点，孩子可以离开四邻，但身上的邻里印迹却难以磨灭。
- The other possibility is *that genes which predispose to criminal behaviour are more common at the bottom of society than at the top.*（object clause, predicative

clause）另一种可能性就是下层社会的孩子比上层社会的孩子身上有更多的容易犯罪的基因。

- The first suggests *that merely topping up people's incomes... will not by itself address questions of bad behaviour.* (object clause) 第一种可能表明，仅仅提高人们的收入……是无法解决犯罪问题的。
- The second raises the *possibility that the problem of intergenerational poverty may be self-reinforcing.* (appositive clause) 第二种提出了这样一种可能性：代际贫困问题可能会自我强化。

I. The Translation of English Nominal Clauses

1. Subject Clauses

(1) Subject clauses introduced by pronouns

These clauses are usually introduced by such pronouns as "what, whatever, whoever"..., etc. When we translate them into Chinese, we may generally keep their original sentence order.

- *What he told me* was only halftruth. 他告诉我的只是半真半假的东西而已。
- *Whatever he saw and heard on his trip* gave him a very deep impression. 他此行所见所闻都给他留下了深刻的印象。
- *Whoever comes to our public reference library* will be welcome. 什么人到我们公共参考图书馆来都受欢迎。

(2) "It" functions as a formal subject

In this case, we may put the subject clause either at the beginning or at the end of the Chinese version.

- It doesn't make much difference *whether he attends the meeting or not.* 他参不参加会议都没多大关系。
- It seemed inconceivable *that the pilot could have survived the crash.* 驾驶员在飞机坠毁之后竟然还能活着，这看来是不可想象的事。
- It is strange *that she should have failed to see her own shortcomings.* 真奇怪，她竟然没有看出自己的缺点。
- It is rumored *that the meeting will be held in June.* 据传闻，这次会议将在六月举行。

2. Object Clauses

Generally speaking, object clauses may be translated in their original sentence order.

However, in some cases, when "it" functions as the formal object of a complex sentence, or sometimes, when the object is preceded by a preposition, a change of order is necessary.

- I understand *that he is well qualified,* but I feel *that he needs more experience.* 我知道他完全够条件，但我觉得他需要更多的经验。
- I take it for granted *that you will come and talk the matter over with him.* 我理所当然地认为，你会来跟他谈这件事的。
- I regard it as an honor *that I am chosen to attend the meeting.* 能当选参加会议，我感到十分荣幸。
- We have no definite information yet as to *which route he will take.* 关于他将走哪条路线，我们还没有确切的消息。

3. Predicative Clauses

English predicative clauses, like object clauses, are generally translated without changing their original sentence order.

- This is *where the shoe pinches.* 这就是问题的症结所在了。
- Things are not always *as they seem to be.* 事物并不总是如其表象。
- His view of the press was *that the reporters were either for him or against him.* 他对新闻界的看法是，记者们不是支持他，就是反对他。

4. Appositive Clauses

Appositive clauses are used in English to describe words or phrases that refer to the same person or thing and have the same relationship to other sentence elements. The following are usual methods of translating English appositive clauses.

(1) Keeping the sentence order

- He expressed the hope *that he would come over to visit China again.* 他表示希望能再来中国访问。
- We are not investigating the question *whether he is trustworthy.* 我们不是在调查他是否可以信任的问题。
- She had no idea *why she thought of him suddenly.* 她不明白自己为什么突然想到了他。

(2) Translating into such expressions as "这一""这种" plus a noun

- Yet, from the beginning, the fact *that I was alive* was ignored. 然而，从一开始，我仍活着这一事实却偏偏被忽视了。
- They were very suspicious of the assumption *that he would rather kill himself than surrender.* 对于他宁愿自杀也不投降这种假设，他们是很怀疑的。
- The fact *that the gravity of the earth pulls everything towards the center of the*

earth explains many things. 地球引力把一切东西都吸向地心这一事实解释了许多现象。

(3) Using punctuation marks and specific word "即"

Punctuation marks such as colon(：), dash (——), and specific word "即", etc. are usually used to introduce appositive clauses.

- But considering realistically, we had to face the fact *that our prospects were less than good*. 但是现实地考虑一下，我们不得不正视**这样一个事实**：我们的前景并不妙。(using a colon)
- And there was the possibility *that a small electrical spark might accidentally bypass the most carefully planned circuit*. 而且总有**这种**可能性——一个小小的电火花，可能会意外地绕过了最为精心设计的电路。(using a dash)
- Not long ago the scientists made an exciting discovery *that this "waste" material could be turned into plastics*. 不久以前，科学家们有了一个令人振奋的发现，**即可以把这种废物变为塑料**。(using the expression "即")

(4) Changing it into a subjectless sentence

- An order has been given *that the researchers who are now in the skylab should be sent back*. **已下命令**将目前在太空实验室里的研究人员送回来。
- Even the most precisely conducted experiments offer no hope *that the result can be obtained without any error*. 即使是最精确的实验，也**没有希望**获得无任何误差的实验结果。
- However, the writing of chemical symbols in the form of an equation does not give any assurance *that the reaction shown will actually occur*. 但是，将化学符号写成反应式，并**不意味着**所表示的反应确实会发生。

II. The Translation of Chinese Complex Sentences

There are no such categories as subordinate clauses or nominal clauses in Chinese. Instead, Chinese complex sentences fall into two categories: coordinate complex sentences（联合复句）and subordinate complex sentences（偏正复句）. When we translate them into English, the most important is to discern their subject-predicate structures and comply with idiomatic English sentence patterns.

1. Sentence Combination

Syntactically, English complex sentences tend to be long with clauses embedded in one another; while Chinese sentences are short and brief. Therefore, in C-E translation, we may combine clusters of short, loose Chinese sentences into long and compact English sentences. For examples:

- 门口放着一堆雨伞，少说也有12把，五颜六色，大小不一。In the doorway lay at least twelve umbrellas of all sizes and colors.
- 我访问了一些地方，遇到了不少人，要谈起来，奇妙的事儿可多着呢。There are many wonderful stories to tell about the places I visited and the people I met.
- 我有一个问题弄不懂，想请教你，你能回答吗？Could you kindly answer a question which is puzzling me?
- 西湖的湖面波光闪闪，湖边茂林修竹，景色四季宜人。With glistening water and luxuriant trees and bamboo groves along its bank, the West Lake has attractive landscape all the year round.
- 因为距离远，又缺乏交通工具，农村社会是与外界隔绝的。这种隔绝状态，由于通信工具不足，就变得更加严重了。The isolation of the rural world because of distance and the lack of transport facilities is compounded by the paucity of the information media.
- 他这时已是将近六旬的人，一表人才，高个儿，眉清目秀，头发又多又黑，略带花白，恰好衬出他那堂堂的仪表。He was at this time in his late fifties, a tall, elegant man with good features and thick dark hair only sufficiently graying to add to the distinction of his appearance.

2. Sentence Sequence

Sentence sequence is another point for attention in C-E translating of Chinese complex sentences. Different sentence sequences may indicate the focus of stress in translation. For instance:

Original Chinese 1: 黑龙江省林业厅顾问赵树森在《人民日报》上撰文指出，中国的森林是丰富的再生能源，在农村地区应当大力开发，用作烧柴。

English Version A: In an article carried in *The People's Daily*, Zhao Shusen, consultant to Heilongjiang Forestry Bureau, says that, "China's forests are a vast source of renewable energy and should be largely developed for firewood in the rural areas."

English Version B: Heilongjiang Forestry Bureau consultant Zhao Shusen says in an article carried in *The People's Daily* that "China's forests are a vast source of renewable energy and should be largely developed for firewood in the rural areas."

English Version C: China's forests are a vast source of renewable energy and should be largely developed for firewood in the rural areas, says Zhao Shusen, Heilongjiang Forestry Bureau consultant, in an article carried in *The People's Daily*.

Original Chinese 2: 只要一发现有可能反对他的人，他就本能地要用他的魅力和风趣将这个人争取过来。

English Version A: When he catches a glimpse of a potential antagonist, his instinct is to win him over with charm and humor.

English Version B: As soon as he finds any possible opponent, he is, by instinct, to have an inclination for winning him over with charm and humor.

English Version C: The sight of any potential antagonist arouses his innate impulse for winning him over with charm and humor.

Reflections and Practice

I. Discuss the following questions.

1. How are English subordinate clauses classified?
2. What are nominal clauses in English?
3. What are the approaches of translating nominal clauses in E-C Translation?
4. What is the syntactical difference between English complex sentences and Chinese ones?

II. Put the following sentences into Chinese, paying attention to the subordinate clauses.

1. Whatever form is used by the majority of educated speakers or writers is correct; or as Sweet puts it, "Whatever is in general use in a language is, for that reason, grammatically, correct."
2. He boasts that a slave is free the moment his feet touch British soil and he sells the children of the poor at six years of age to work under the lash in the factories for sixteen hours a day.
3. It is flattering to believe that they (ideas) are too profound to be expressed so clearly that all who run may read, and very naturally it does not occur to such writers that the fault is with their own minds which have not the faculty of precise reflection.
4. It is not that the scale in the one case, and the balance in the other, differ in the

principles of their construction or manner of working; but that the latter is a much finer apparatus and of course much more accurate in its measurement than the former.

5. Allen's contribution was to take an assumption we all share—that because we are not robots we therefore control our thoughts—and reveal its erroneous nature.

6. ...but since what used to seem to the great majority of civilized humanity the assurance of another life beyond the grave has come to seem to more and more people less certain, a feeling for the value of human life has become deeper and more widespread.

7. He was puzzled that I did not want what was obviously a "step" toward what all Americans are taught to want when they grow up: money and power.

8. He poured into his writing all the pains of his life and the conviction it had brought to him that the world could be made a better place to live in if the exploited would rise up.

9. There has long been a superstition among mariners that porpoises will save drowning men by pushing them to the surface, or protect them from sharks by surrounding them in defensive formation.

10. Furthermore, it is obvious that the strength of a country's economy is directly bound up with the efficiency of its agriculture and industry, and that this in turn rests upon the efforts of scientists and technologists of all kinds.

11. For example, tests do not compensate for gross social inequality, and thus do not tell how able an underprivileged youngster might have been had he grown up under more favourable circumstances.

12. It leads the discussion to extremes at the outset: it invites you to think that animals should be treated either with the consideration humans extend to other humans, or with no consideration at all.

III. Put the following sentences into English, paying attention to subordination.

1. 恐怕这台旧收音机没法修了。
2. 我不在家时请你把房间收拾干净好吗？
3. 众所周知，火药是中国古代的四大发明之一。
4. 7%的经济年增长目标表明政府是在重视生活质量而不是增长速度。
5. 中国宴席上典型的菜单包括开席的一套凉菜及其后的热菜，如肉类、鸡鸭、蔬菜等。
6. 正是通过丝绸之路，中国的造纸、火药、指南针、印刷四大发明才被引介到世界各地。
7. 教育部还决定改善欠发达地区学生的营养，并为外来务工人员的子女提供在城市接受教育的同等机会。

8. 新公布的计划旨在减少四种主要污染源，包括500万辆机动车的尾气排放、周边地区燃煤、来自北方的沙尘暴和本地的建筑灰尘。

9. 中国在减少贫困方面取得了显著进步，并在促进经济增长方面做出了不懈努力，这将鼓励其他贫困国家应对自身发展中的挑战。

10. 公元100年中国第一部字典编撰完成，收入9 000个字，提供释义并列举不同的写法。其间，科技方面也取得了很大进步，发明了纸张、水钟、日晷以及测量地震的仪器。

IV. **Translate the following sentences, paying attention to the essence of each sentence instead of their formal structure.**

1. He acts a lot older than his years.
2. He always lives ahead of his salary.
3. Life here is as cheap as taxies are expensive.
4. The minimal cost far outweighs the inconvenience of being immobile in this vast urban area.
5. Hardly a day passes without him getting scratched or bruised as he scrambles for a place on a bus.
6. The company's top executives all are refugees from the country's bureaucratic and underfinanced state research sector.
7. It's one of Asia's most traditional cities, rich with a Chinese culture that is gracious and lively, and boasts an amazing archive of Chinese art and artifacts.
8. All told China has roughly 380 million women between the age of 15 and 55, and few of them—particularly in the cities—want to look any less than their budgets allow.
9. Eager to trust but determined to verify, many single women in an age of risky romance are hiring private detectives to check the background of their suitors.
10. The first shiploads of immigrants bound for the territory which is now the United States crossed the Atlantic more than a hundred years after the 15th-and-16th-century explorations of North America.
11. In the space of three decades Lee Kuan Yew built a poor island of tin-roofed shacks and chicken coops into a clockwork city of gleaming office towers.
12. Battered by an almost daily terror of worrisome reports about the hazards of what they eat and how they live, Americans have become engulfed in an epidemic, not of cancer but of fear.
13. But, the force of geographic conditions peculiar to America, the interplay of the varied national groups upon one another, and the sheer difficulty of maintaining old-world ways in a raw, new continent caused significant changes.

Unit 10 Attributive Clauses

> ● **单元要点概述**
>
> 相关翻译技巧训练英译汉：Give Part of Yourself Away
> 相关翻译技巧训练汉译英：施一公：以天下事为己任
> I. 英汉定语结构的对比
> II. 限制性定语从句
>   1. 合并法　　　　　　　2. 分译法　　　　　　　3. 混合法
> III. 非限制性定语从句
>   1. 分译法　　　　　　　2. 合并法
> IV. 兼有状语功能的定语从句
>   1. 译作汉语原因句　　　2. 译作汉语结果句
>   3. 译作汉语让步句　　　4. 译作汉语条件句
>   5. 译作汉语目的句

本单元详细介绍了英语定语从句的性质及其翻译方法。

英语的定语从句呈右开放状，可以向右无限扩展；而汉语没有定语从句之说，作为修饰成分的定语习惯上放在被修饰词之前（左边），呈左封闭状，不能像英语那样随意地扩展。因此，我们在翻译较为复杂的英语定语长句时，最有效的方法就是将其切分为一个个短句再分别处理。

英语限制性定语从句的翻译方法一般分为 3 种，即：合并法、分译法、混合法。英语非限制性定语从句的翻译方法与限制性定语从句的译法相似，只不过使用分译法的情况更为常见，有时也可视情况译成汉语的并列句、复合句或独立句。

英语定语从句有时候兼有状语的功能，可视情况将其译作汉语表原因、结果、目的、时间、条件、让步的分句。

UNIT 10 Attributive Clauses

Practice of the Relevant Skill

1. E-C Translation

Give Part of Yourself Away

We are living in one of those periods in human history which are marked by revolutionary changes in all of man's ideas and values. It is a time when every one of us must look within himself to find what ideas, what beliefs, and what ideals each of us will live by. And unless we find these ideals, and unless we stand by them firmly, we have no power to overcome the crisis in which we in our world find ourselves.

I believe in people, in sheer, unadulterated humanity. I believe in listening to what people have to say, in helping them to achieve the things which they want and the things which they need. Naturally, there are people who behave like beasts, who kill, who cheat, who lie and who destroy. But without a belief in man and a faith in his possibilities for the future, there can be no hope for the future, but only bitterness that the past has gone. I believe we must, each of us, make a philosophy by which we can live. There are people who make a philosophy out of believing in nothing. They say there is no truth, that goodness is simply cleverness in disguising your own selfishness. They say that life is simply the short gap in between an unpleasant birth and an inevitable death. There are others who say that man is born into evil and sinfulness and that life is a process of purification through suffering and that death is the reward for having suffered.

I believe these philosophies are false. The most important thing in life is the way it is lived, and there is no such thing as an abstract happiness, an abstract goodness or morality, or an abstract anything, except in terms of the person who believes and who acts. There is only the single human being who lives and who, through every moment of his own personal living experience, is being happy or unhappy, noble or base, wise or unwise, or simply existing.

The question is: How can these individual moments of human experience be filled with the richness of a philosophy which can sustain the individual in his own life? Unless we give part of ourselves away, unless we can live with other people and understand them and help them, we are missing the most essential part of our own human lives.

There are as many roads to the attainment of wisdom and goodness as there are people who undertake to walk them. There are as many solid truths on which we can stand as there are people who can search them out and who will stand on them. There are as many ideas and ideals as there are men of good will who will hold them in their minds and act them in their lives.

Notes and Explanations

1. ideals each of us will live by 我们每个人必须遵循的理念
2. people who behave like beasts, who kill, who cheat, who lie and who destroy 行同禽兽、杀人、行骗撒谎、搞破坏的人
3. make a philosophy out of believing in nothing 持怀疑一切的人生哲学
4. the short gap in between an unpleasant birth and an inevitable death 痛苦出生与必然死亡之间的短暂间隙
5. born into evil and sinfulness 生性邪恶有罪
6. give part of ourselves away 放弃部分自我
7. There are as many... as there are... 有多少……就有多少……
8. people who undertake to walk them 践行真理的人
9. solid truths on which we can stand 我们能够依赖的可靠的真理

2. C-E Translation

施一公：以天下事为己任

2008年2月，40岁的国际著名结构生物学家、美国普林斯顿大学终身教授施一公，全职回到祖国，受聘为清华大学终身教授，并出任清华大学生命科学与医学研究院副院长。他说："普林斯顿大学是美国最适合做研究的地方，从条件上讲，如果只从科研角度出发的话，我确实没有必要回清华，我回清华的目的不只是为了做科研。我回来的根本目的是为了育人，教育一批人。育人在育心，做科研是育人的一个重要环节。我觉得现在的大学生缺乏理想，缺乏一种无论出现什么情况都不会放弃的东西。我想，如果引导正确的话，清华大学一定会有这样的一批学生，他们在为自己奋斗的同时，心里还装着一些自己之外的东西，以天下事为己任，驱使他们往前走，一定会有一批人这样做。如果这样，20或30年后，当我从清华退休时，我会很满意的。"

Notes and Explanations

1. 以天下事为己任 regard the future of one's country as one's own responsibilities
2. 结构生物学家 structural biologist
3. 终身教授 tenured professor
4. 生命科学与医学研究院 Institute of Life Science and Medicine
5. 只从科研角度出发 in terms of academic research alone
6. 育人在育心 The key to education lies in cultivating the minds.
7. 什么情况都不会放弃 never give up under any circumstance

UNIT 10 Attributive Clauses

8. 装着一些自己之外的东西 bear in mind something beyond one's personal interests

Of various English subordinate clauses, the attributive clause is perhaps the most complicated one. This is either because of the disparity between English and Chinese syntax or because of their habitual modes of expressing the same idea in different ways. And here are some instances from the above Practice of the Relevant Skill:

- ...periods in human history *which are marked by*... 人类历史上的一个特殊时代，其标志是……
- It is a time *when every one of us must*... 这是一个我们每个人都必须……的时代。
- the crisis in *which we in our world find ourselves* 这个世界中我们每个人所面临的危机
- achieve the things *which they want and the things which they need* 实现他们的愿望、获取他们所需的东西
- people *who behave like beasts, who kill, who cheat, who lie and who destroy* 那些行同禽兽、杀戮破坏、坑蒙拐骗的人
- bitterness *that the past has gone* 昔日已逝的痛苦
- a philosophy *by which we can live* 一种我们赖以生存的哲学
- people *who make a philosophy out of believing in nothing* 持怀疑一切的人生哲学的人
- others *who say that man is born into evil and sinfulness* 宣称人生性罪恶的人
- the person *who believes and who acts* 相信，并付诸行动的人
- the richness of a philosophy *which can sustain the individual in his own life* 能贯穿到人生每一瞬间的丰富的人生哲学
- people *who undertake to walk them* 践行真理的人
- solid truths *on which we can stand* 我们能够依赖的可靠的真理
- people *who can search them out and who will stand on them* 探求和坚持真理的人
- men of good will *who will hold them in their minds* 将这些东西保存在心中的具有良好意愿的人

I. A Comparative Study of English and Chinese Attributive Structures

Placed adjacent to the noun it modifies without a linking verb, English attributive clause is quite different from that of its Chinese counterpart in structure. And a comparative study of them may help us shed light on this disparity.

1. This is the cat. 这就是那只猫。

2. This is the cat that killed the rat. 这就是那只捕杀了老鼠的猫。

3. This is the cat that killed the rat that ate the cake. * 这就是那只捕杀了偷吃了蛋糕的老鼠的猫。

4. This is the cat that killed the rat that ate the cake that was put in the house. * 这就是那只捕杀了偷吃了放在房间里的蛋糕的老鼠的猫。

5. This is the cat that killed the rat that ate the cake that was put in the house that Jack built. * 这就是那只捕杀了偷吃了放在杰克修建的房间里的蛋糕的老鼠的猫。

As we may see from the above 5 illustrations, English attributive clauses may run on in unlimited number, which is impossible for Chinese to follow suit. Apparently, readable Chinese versions of the above illustration 3, 4 and 5 should be translated as follows:

3. 这就是那只捕杀了老鼠的猫。老鼠偷吃了蛋糕。

4. 这就是那只捕杀了老鼠的猫。老鼠偷吃了放在屋里的蛋糕。

5. 这就是那只捕杀了老鼠的猫。老鼠偷吃了放在屋里的蛋糕。屋子是杰克盖的。

II. Restrictive Attributive Clauses

Attributive clauses fall into two categories, i.e. restrictive attributive clauses and non-restrictive attributive clauses. Restrictive attributive clauses, which are characterized by the absence of a comma between the subordinate clauses and the principal clauses, are very closely related to the antecedents that they are modifying. In translation, we may use three major methods to translate restrictive attributive clauses, i.e. combination, division and mixture.

1. Combination

This is the most common practice of translating English attributive clause that is not too long. In this case, an English restrictive attributive clause is converted into Chinese "……的……" structure, preceding the antecedent. By combination, we have actually converted an English complex sentence into a Chinese simple sentence.

- The people *who worked for him* lived in mortal fear of him. **在他手下工作的人**对他怕得要死。
- Pollution is a pressing problem *which we must deal with*. 污染**是我们必须解决的一个迫切问题**。
- July and August are the months *when the weather is hot*. 七八月是**天气很热的月份**。

UNIT 10 Attributive Clauses

- In the room *where the electronic computer is kept,* there must be no dust at all. 在存放电子计算机的房间里，不能有一点儿灰尘。

2. Division

Sometimes, an English sentence with a restrictive attributive clause is too long or too complicated, and then we may divide it into two or several parts, placing the attributive clause after the principal clause to conform to the Chinese usage, repeating the antecedent being modified.

- They are striving for the ideal *which is close to the heart of every Chinese and for which, in the past, many Chinese have laid down their lives.* 他们正在为实现一个理想而努力，**这个理想是每个中国人所珍爱的，在过去，许多中国人为了这个理想而牺牲了自己的生命**。
- Between these two tiny particles, the proton and the electron, there is a powerful attraction *that is always present between negative and positive electric charges.* 在质子和电子这两种微粒之间有一个很大的吸引力，**而这个吸引力总是存在于正、负电荷之间**。
- Newton invented a paper lantern illuminated by a candle *which he carried with him to light his way* to school on dark winter mornings. 牛顿发明了一只点蜡烛的纸灯笼，在昏暗朦胧的冬天早晨上学时**带着灯笼照路**。

Occasionally, we may translate a restrictive attributive clause without repeating the antecedent.

- He managed to raise a crop of 200 miracle tomatoes *that weighed up to two pounds each.* 他种出了200个大得惊人的西红柿，**每个重达两磅**。
- A fuel is a material *which will burn at a reasonable temperature and produce heat.* 燃料是一种物质，**在适当温度下能够燃烧并放出热量**。
- They worked out a new method *by which production has now been rapidly increased.* 他们创造出一种新方法，**采用之后已迅速提高了生产**。

3. Mixture

This method is usually adopted in translating English "there be…" structure when we combine the principal clause and the attributive clause into a single Chinese sentence without any distinction.

- There were men in that crowd *who had stood there every day for a month.* 在那群人中，**有些人每天站在那里，站了一个月**。
- There is a man downstairs *who wants to see you.* 楼下有人要见你。
- Fortunately, there are some chemical fuels *that are clean and smokeless.* 幸好有些

化学燃料是洁净无烟的。
- There are some metals *which possess the power to conduct electricity and the ability to be magnetized*. 某些金属**既能导电，又能被磁化**。

Besides, there are some English complex sentences with a very simple principal clause, laying their emphasis on the attributive clauses. In this case, the principal clause may be condensed into the subject of a simple sentence, with the attributive clause as its predicate.

- "We are a nation *that must beg to stay alive*," said a foreign economist. 一位外国经济学家曾说过，"我们**这个国家不讨饭就活不下去**。"
- We used a plane of *which almost every part carried some identification of national identity*. 我们驾驶的飞机几乎每一个部件都有国籍的某些标志。
- Good clocks have pendulums *which are automatically compensated for temperature changes*. 好的钟摆可以自动补偿温度变化造成的误差。

III. Non-Restrictive Attributive Clauses

A non-restrictive attributive clause is characterized by a comma between the principal and the attributive clause. It holds a loose relationship with the antecedent, functioning as a supplementary part in the sentence. In terms of translation techniques, division is used more frequently in translating non-restrictive attributive clauses, while the method of combination is less adopted.

1. Division

Division in translating non-restrictive attributive clauses may be conducted in several methods.

(1) Translating into compound sentences by repeating the antecedents

- I told the story to John, *who told it to his brother*. 我把这件事告诉了约翰，约翰又告诉了他的兄弟。
- The process of combining with oxygen is oxidation, *of which burning is one type*. 与氧结合的过程就是氧化，燃烧就是其中的一种。
- This is a college of science and technology, *the students of which are trained to be engineers or scientists*. 这是一所科技大学，该校学生将被培养成工程师或科学工作者。

(2) Translating into compound sentences by omitting the antecedents

- After dinner, the four key negotiators resumed their talks, *which continued well*

UNIT 10 Attributive Clauses

into the night. 饭后，四个主要谈判人物继续进行会谈，一直谈到深夜。
- He saw in front that haggard white-haired old man, *whose eyes flashed red with fury.* 他看见前面那个憔悴的白发老人眼里闪耀着愤怒的目光。
- Electrons also flow in a television, *where they are made to hit the screen, causing a flash of light.* 电子也涌入电视显像管，撞击荧光屏，产生闪光。

(3) Translating into independent sentences
- One time there was a violent thunderstorm, the worst I had ever seen, *which obscured my objective.* 有一次是暴风骤雨，猛烈的程度实为我平生所仅见。这场暴风雨遮住了我的目标。
- Nevertheless the problem was solved successfully, *which showed that the computations were accurate.* 不过，问题还是圆满地解决了。这说明计算很准确。
- One of the greatest promoters of structural organic chemistry around the turn of the century was Emil Fisher, *who, as early as 1893, had already considered the structure of cellulose as a polysaccharide in mind.* 在 19 世纪末和 20 世纪初之间，埃米尔·费希尔是结构有机化学方面最伟大的推动者之一。早在 1893 年，他就认为纤维素的结构是聚糖。

2. Combination

The method of combination in translating non-restrictive attributive clauses is mainly used to avoid a loose structure or for the sake of coherence. This is the usual case when we try to avoid a loose structure and take coherence into consideration.
- The sun, *which had hidden all day,* now came out in all its splendor. 整天躲在云层里的太阳，现在又光芒四射地露面了。
- He liked his sister, *who was warm and pleasant,* but he did not like his brother, *who was aloof and arrogant.* 他喜欢热情洋溢的妹妹，而不喜欢冷漠高傲的哥哥。
- Prisms, *which are made of glass,* may be used to break up a beam of incoherent light. 用玻璃制的棱镜就可以分离非相干光束。
- Transistors, *which are small in size,* can make previously large and bulky radios light and small. 采用体积较小的晶体管可以使先前那种大而笨重的收音机变得又轻又小。

IV. Attributive Clauses Functioning as Adverbials

Some attributive clauses function as the adverbial in the complex sentence, keeping a very close logic relationship with the principal clause. In this case, we may translate them into corresponding adverbial clauses of cause, result, purpose, time, condition, concession, etc.

1. Translating into Adverbial Clauses of Cause

- You must grasp the concept of "work" *which is very important in physics*. 你必须掌握"功"的概念，**因为它在物理学中很重要**。
- A solid fuel, like coal or wood, can only burn at the surface, *where it comes into contact with the air*. 煤或木材之类的固体燃料只能在外层表面燃烧，**因为表面可以接触空气**。
- We know that a cat, *whose eyes can take in many more rays than our eyes*, can see clearly in the night. 我们知道，**由于猫的眼睛比人眼能吸收更多的光线**，所以猫在黑夜也能看得很清楚。

2. Translating into Adverbial Clauses of Result

- Copper, *which is used so widely for carrying electricity*, offers very little resistance. 铜的电阻很小，**所以被广泛地用来传输电力**。
- There was something original, independent, and heroic about the plan *that pleased all of them*. 这个方案富于创造性，独具一格，且很有魄力，**因此他们都很喜欢**。
- The diode is coated with a thin layer of hard glass *which eliminates the need for a hermetically sealed package*. 二极管的表面有一层薄薄的硬玻璃，**故无须使用密封的管壳**。

3. Translating into Adverbial Clauses of Concession

- He insisted on building another house, *which he had no use for*. 他坚持要再造一幢房子，**尽管他并无此需要**。
- The scientist, *who was dogtired*, went on with the experiment. 那位科学家虽已筋疲力尽，但还是继续进行实验。
- Electronic computers, *which have many advantages*, cannot carry out creative work and replace man. **尽管电子计算机有许多优点**，但是它们不能进行创造性工作，也不能代替人。

4. Translating into Adverbial Clauses of Condition

- Men become desperate for work, any work, *which will help them to keep alive their families*. 人们拼命想得到工作，不管什么工作，只要能维持一家人的生活就行。
- A body *that contains only atoms with the same general properties* is called an

element. 物质如果包含的原子性质都相同，则称之为元素。
- For any machine *whose input and output forces are known*, its mechanical advantage can be calculated. 对于任何机器来说，如果知其输入功率和输出功率，就能求出其机械效率。

5. Translating into Adverbial Clauses of Purpose

- They have built up a new college here, *where students will be trained to be engineers and scientists*. 他们在这里建了一所学院，以培养工程师和科学家。
- I'll try to get an illustrated dictionary dealing with technical terms, *which will enable me to translate scientific literature more exactly*. 我要设法弄一本有插图的技术名词词典，以便把科学文献译得更准确。
- We have to oil the moving parts of the machine, *the friction of which may thus be greatly reduced*. 我们必须给机器的运动部件加润滑油，以使摩擦大大减少。

Reflections and Practice

I. Discuss the following questions.

1. What is the difference in structure between English and Chinese attributive structures?
2. What are the major methods of translating English restrictive attributive clauses?
3. What are the major methods of translating English nonrestrictive attributive clauses?
4. What are the usual ways of translating English restrictive attributive clauses which function as the adverbials?

II. Put the following sentences into Chinese, paying attention to the attributive clauses.

1. Each day we make choices that affect our lives and sometimes the lives of others.
2. Americans have a great range of customs and habits that at first may seem puzzling to a visitor.
3. Late 19th century saw all the universities in the United States adopt the credit system, which benefited student a great deal.
4. Private schools in the U.S. have a wide range of programs that are offered to meet the needs of certain students.
5. The fire season takes care of the property that managed to survive the deluge.
6. In fact, many Americans who could afford to hire a cook or driver do not employ

them.

7. While at a museum, one can frequently rent a small recording machine that will explain the objects on display as you move through the museum.
8. Gates, who came of age in the 1970s, has a Watergate-year detachment from politics, a mind-set more me-generation than "love-in", and a passion for the great revolutionary force of his own decade: the personal computer.
9. This reflects a different theory of college, a theory that runs like this: In a society that encourages its members to pursue the career paths that promise the greatest personal or financial rewards, people will, given a choice, learn only what they need to know for success.
10. There is nothing more disappointing to a hostess who has gone to a lot of trouble or expense than to have her guest so interested in talking politics or business with her husband that he fails to notice the flavor of the coffee, the lightness of the cake, or the attractiveness of the house, which may be her chief interest and pride.

III. Put the following into English, paying attention to the attributive structures.

1. 全世界的科学家都在寻找净化空气、防止空气受到各种有害工业废气污染的有效方法。
2. 在我们肉眼看来似乎静止不动的一杯水中，却有数不清的水分子正在进行着大量的无规则的热运动。
3. 在中华民族的几千年的历史中，产生了很多的民族英雄和革命领袖。所以，中华民族又是一个有光荣的革命传统和优秀的历史遗产的民族。
4. 我们不但要有一个农林牧副渔布局合理，全面发展，能够满足人民生活和工业发展需要的发达的农业，还要有一个门类齐全，结构合理，能够满足社会消费和整个国民经济发展需要的先进的工业。
5. 在未来五年中，中国将向其他发展中国家在减少贫困、发展教育、农业现代化、环境保护和医疗保健等方面提供援助。
6. 中国在减少贫困方面取得了显著进步，并在促进经济增长方面做出了不懈努力，这将鼓励其他贫困国家应对自身发展中的挑战。
7. 不久前，中国获得了在印度尼西亚建造一条高铁的合同；中国还与马来西亚签署了为其提供高速列车的合同。这证明人们信赖中国制造的产品。
8. 清华大学是中国著名的高等学府，是中国培养高级科学技术人才和发展科学技术的重要基地之一。清华大学创建于1911年，其前身清华学堂是一所留美预备学校。辛亥革命后更名为清华学校，1925年开始办大学部，1928年改建成国立清华大学。抗日战争爆发后，清华大学南迁长沙，后又迁至昆明，与北京大学、南开大学联合组成西南联合大学。经 1952 年院系调整，清华大学成为一所多学科性工业大学，重点为国家培养工程技术人才，被誉为红色工程师的摇篮。

IV. **Put the following sentences into Chinese, paying attention to the idiomatic expressions.**

1. We cleaned the room against your coming.
2. They are preparing a substantial meal against his return.
3. If we want your two cents, we'll ask for it.
4. Last night I heard him driving his pigs to market.
5. When John was talking about the affair, we smelled a rat.
6. Modern linguistics gets its charter from Leonard Bloomfield's *Language* published in 1933.
7. A revolution of declining expectations vaporizes the hopes and dreams of only yesterday.
8. On flat ground you plow disgustedly through the mud, often getting well over your ankles. But on a climb you do worse.
9. We all developed "Dunkirk throat", a sore hoarseness that was the hallmark of those who had been there.
10. A little after midnight the pilot landed narrowly averting a crackup.
11. The ship turned just in time, narrowly missing the immense wall of ice which rose over 100 feet out of the water beside her.
12. When they find who killed that kid and its mother, they'll throw the book, and never mind who it hits.
13. Hoover was proud of his wife. She spoke five languages fluently and set what was considered to be the finest table in White House history.
14. Miss Crawley admitted her as a dear, artless, tenderhearted, affectionate, incomprehensible creature.

Unit 11　Adverbial Clauses

单元要点概述

相关翻译技巧训练英译汉：Why Measure Life in Heartbeats
相关翻译技巧训练汉译英：艾滋病

I. 英语状语从句的翻译
   1. 时间状语从句　　　　　　2. 地点状语从句
   3. 原因状语从句　　　　　　4. 条件状语从句
   5. 让步状语从句　　　　　　6. 目的状语从句

II. 汉语复句中的状语分句
   1. 分清主次关系　　　　　　2. 使用无灵主语

   本单元就英语状语从句的翻译问题做了归纳，并对汉语复句中的类似结构做了简介。英语状语从句根据功能的不同可分为时间、地点、原因、条件、让步、目的等状语从句，在英汉翻译时一般比较容易处理，不会造成理解表达障碍，关键在于怎样将其放入恰当的位置，怎样处理好句与句之间的连接关系。

   汉语复句分为联合复句和偏正复句两类，前者类似英语的并列句，后者类似英语带状语从句的复合句。汉语复句的翻译需注意两点：一是分清轻重主次；二是学会使用无灵主语。英语喜欢用无灵名词充当役使主语，汉译英学会这种造句法有助于简化译文的结构，将汉语的某些复合结构翻译成英语简单句。

Practice of the Relevant Skill

1.　E-C Translation

Why Measure Life in Heartbeats

When I became aware of my imminent mortality, my attitudes changed. There was

UNIT 11 Adverbial Clauses

real meaning to the words, "This is the first day of the rest of your life." There was a heightened awareness of each sunny day, the beauty of flowers, and the song of a bird. How often do we reflect on the joy of breathing easily, of swallowing without effort and discomfort, of walking without pain, of a complete and peaceful night's sleep?

After I became ill, I embarked upon many things I had been putting off before. I read the books I had set aside for retirement and wrote one myself, entitled *The Art of Surgery*. My wife Madeleine and I took more holidays. We played tennis regularly and curled avidly; we took the boys fishing. When I review these past few years, it seems in many ways that I have lived a lifetime since I acquired cancer. On my last holiday in the Bahamas, as I walked along the beach feeling the gentle waves wash over my feet, I felt part of universe, even if only a minuscule one, like a grain of sand on the beach.

Although I had to restrict the size of my practice, I felt a closer empathy with my patients. When I walked into the Intensive Care Unit there was an awesome feeling knowing I, too, had been a patient there. It was a special satisfaction to comfort my patients with cancer, knowing that it is possible to enjoy life after the anguish of that diagnosis. It gave me a feeling to see the sparkle in one patient's eyes—a man with a total laryngectomy—when I asked if he would enjoy a cold beer and went to get him one.

If one realizes that our time on this earth is but a tiny fraction of that within the cosmos, then life calculated in years may not be as important as we think. Why measure life in heartbeats? When life is dependent on such an unreliable function as the beating of the heart, then it is fragile indeed. The only thing that one can depend upon with absolute certainty is death.

Notes and Explanations

1. imminent mortality 即将来临的死亡，大限
2. a heightened awareness 提高（加强）了的意识
3. reflect on 仔细考虑（注意此句中the joy 后面的四个of 之间的并列关系的译法）
4. embark on (upon) 着手，从事
5. curl v.（苏格兰的）玩冰上溜石游戏（在冰上滑送圆形石板curling stone的游戏）
6. Bahamas n. [拉丁美洲]巴哈马群岛
7. minuscule adj. 小写的，微小的，微不足道的
8. empathy n. 同情，同感
9. the Intensive Care Unit 特别护理室
10. that diagnosis 此处指"确诊为癌症"（注意此句It作形式主语的逆序翻译法）
11. laryngectomy n. [医]喉头切除术（注意此句语序、状语的位置和形式主语It的翻译法）

2. C-E Translation

艾滋病

世界各地有 3 600 万人染上了艾滋病——这比整个澳大利亚的人口还多。目前，艾滋病是全球第 4 大死因，而在非洲则是头号罪魁。在非洲，艾滋病使工人丧失工作，使家庭丧失经济来源，使父母丧失孩子。在 7 个非洲国家中，15 岁至 49 岁的艾滋病病毒携带者占 20% 以上：南非为 20%，博茨瓦纳为 36%。赞比亚培训教师的速度，赶不上教师患艾滋病而死亡的速度。据估计，在未来 10 年非洲将有 4 000 万名艾滋病孤儿。

亚洲受艾滋病的影响相对较小。只有柬埔寨、泰国和缅甸的艾滋病病毒感染率超过 1%。但这种流行病就像台风一样，总是在意想不到的海岸积聚力量。印度的艾滋病病毒感染率虽然"仅有" 0.70%，但按这个比例，也有 370 万人。到 2005 年，估计中国艾滋病病毒携带者达 500 万 ~ 600 万人。

Notes and Explanations

1. 感染上艾滋病 suffer from/be infected with/come down with AIDS
2. 头号罪魁 the chief culprit
3. 艾滋病病毒 HIV human immunodeficiency virus(即人体免疫缺损病毒)
4. 博茨瓦纳、赞比亚 Botswana, Zambia
5. 赶不上 not fast enough to replace
6. 影响相对较小 comparatively untouched/less affected
7. 柬埔寨、泰国和缅甸 Cambodia, Thailand and Burma
8. 感染率 infection rate
9. 艾滋病病毒携带者 HIV-positives (注意英语的简略表达法)

I. The Translation of English Adverbial Clauses

English adverbial clauses include adverbials of time, place, cause, condition, concession, purpose, result, etc. These adverbial clauses generally do not pose any obstacle to either comprehending or translating, and the crux of the matter is how to make the translation conform to Chinese usage, i.e. how to arrange them properly. Another point for attention is how to deal with the redundant conjunctives that frequently arise in English adverbial clauses. And here are some instances from Practice of the Relevant Skill:

UNIT 11 Adverbial Clauses

- *When I review these past few years*, it seems in many ways that I have lived a lifetime *since I acquired cancer.* (adverbial clause of time) 回顾我得癌症后这几年，从许多方面来看，我似乎已经活了一辈子。
- *Although I had to restrict the size of my practice,* I felt a closer empathy with my patients. (adverbial clause of concession) 虽然我不得不限制自己的医务工作量，但我感到与病人更加心灵相通。
- *If one realizes that our time on this earth is but a tiny fraction of that within the cosmos,* then life calculated in years may not be as important as we think. (adverbial clause of condition) 倘若人们意识到人的一生只不过是宇宙的时间长河中转瞬即逝的一刹那，那么以岁月计算的生命就不会像我们所想象的那样重要了。
- *When life is dependent on such an unreliable function as the beating of the heart,* then it is fragile indeed. (adverbial clause of supposition) 要是生命依赖于心跳这样一种不可靠的功能，那么它的确脆弱不堪。

1. Adverbial Clauses of Time

When translated into Chinese, English adverbial clauses of time may usually be translated into corresponding Chinese sentences. Occasionally, they may be translated into compound sentence or adverbial of condition.

- *While she spoke*, the tears were running down. 她说话时，泪水直流。(adverbial of time)
- She sang *as* she prepared the experiment. 她一边唱着歌，一边准备实验。(compound sentence)
- I was about to speak, *when* Mr. Smith cut in. 我正想讲，史密斯先生就插嘴了。(compound sentence)
- Turn off the switch *when anything goes wrong with the machine.* 如果机器发生故障，就把电门关上。(adverbial of condition)
- A body at rest will not move *till a force is exerted on it.* 若无外力的作用，静止的物体则不会移动。(adverbial of condition)

2. Adverbial Clauses of Place

English adverbial clauses of place may often be translated into adverbial clauses of condition in Chinese.

- Make a mark *where you have any doubts or questions.* 在有疑问的地方做个记号。
- The materials are excellent for use *where the value of the workpieces is not high.* 如果零件价值不高，使用这些材料是最好不过的了。
- *Where water resources are plentiful,* hydroelectric power stations are being built in

large numbers. 哪里水源充足，就在哪里修建大批的水电站。

3. Adverbial Clauses of Cause

This kind of clauses can be translate into corresponding Chinese adverbial clauses preceded with "因""由于", etc.

- The crops failed *because the season was dry*. 因为气候干燥，所以作物歉收。
- *As the moon's gravity is only about 1/6 the gravity of the earth*, a 200-pound man weights only 33 pounds on the moon. 由于月球的引力只有地球引力的六分之一，所以一个体重200磅的人在月球上仅重33磅。

Sometimes, we may omit such conjunctives as "because", "since", etc.

- Pure iron is not used in industry *because it is too soft*. 纯铁太软，所以不用在工业上。

4. Adverbial Clauses of Condition

This kind of clauses can be translated into corresponding clauses of condition or supposition.

- *If something has the ability to adjust itself to the environment*, we say it has intelligence. 如果某物具有适应环境的能力，我们就说它具有智力。
- *Should there be an urgent situation*, press the red button to switch off the electricity. 万一有紧急情况，请按红色按钮以切断电源。

Sometimes, they may also be translated into supplementary clauses.

- You can drive tonight *if you are ready*. 你今晚就可以出车，如果你愿意的话。
- Any body above the earth will fall *unless it is supported by an upward force equal to its weight*. 地球上的任何物体都会落下来，除非它受到一个大小与其重量相等的力的支持。

5. Adverbial Clauses of Concession

This kind of clauses can be translated into corresponding adverbial clause of concession.

- *While this is true of some*, it is not true of all. 虽然有一部分是真的，但不见得全部都如此。
- I still think that you made a mistake *while I admit what you say*. 就算我承认你所说的那番话，但我还是认为你犯了个错误。

Besides corresponding adverbial clause of concession, they may also be translated into "unconditional" clauses such as "不管""不论", etc.

- He got the same result *whichever way he did the experiment*. 不论用什么方法做实验，他所得到的结果都相同。
- All living things, *whether they are animals or plants*, are made up of cells. 一切生物，

不管是动物还是植物，都是由细胞组成的。

6. Adverbial Clauses of Purpose

Adverbial clauses of purpose may either precede or follow the principal clause when translated into Chinese.

- We should start early *so that we might get there before noon.* 为了正午以前赶到那里，我们应当早点动身。/ 我们应当早点动身，以便能在正午之前赶到那里。
- Steel parts are usually covered with grease *for fear that they should rust.* 钢制零件通常涂上润滑脂，以防生锈。/ 为了防锈，钢制零件通常需涂上润滑脂。
- A rocket must attain a speed of about five miles per second *so that it may put a satellite in orbit.* 火箭必须获得每秒大约 5 英里的速度，以便把卫星送入轨道。/ 为了能把卫星送入轨道，火箭必须获得每秒大约 5 英里的速度。

II. Adverbial Clauses in Chinese Complex Sentences

Adverbial clauses generally do not pose obvious barriers in C-E translation. What we should keep in mind is that English is a hypotactic（形合）language, while Chinese tends to be paratactic（意合）. The disparity of their structures now and then may hinder the mode of thinking and thus interfere with our translation.

1. Discerning Subordination

It is generally acknowledged that English syntax strictly abides by grammar rules, whereas Chinese syntax seems simple and compact, free of functional words in many cases. Therefore, it is up to the translator to discerning subordination and put in necessary connectives. For example：

- 她不老实，我不能信任她。*Since* she is not honest, I cannot trust her.
- 人不犯我，我不犯人。We won't attack others *unless* we are attacked.
- 打肿脸充胖子，吃亏的是自己。*If* you get beyond your depth, you'll suffer.
- 种瓜得瓜，种豆得豆。*As* you sow, so will you reap.
- 有饭大家吃。Let everybody share the food *if* there is any.
- 不到黄河心不死。*Until* all is over, ambition never dies.

2. Using Inanimate Subjects

Another distinctive feature of English syntax is that inanimate nouns may function as agents of a sentence. Therefore, it is advisable to use this feature in C-E translation.

- 一看到那棵大树，我就会想起童年的情景。*The sight of the big tree* always reminds me of my childhood.
- 恕我孤陋寡闻，对此关系一无所知。*My total ignorance* of the connection must plead my apology.
- 凭良心讲，你待我礼貌有加，我却受之有愧。*My conscience* told me that I deserved no extraordinary politeness.
- 小梅心地善良，性情温和，对她朋友这种没有心肝的行为实在看不顺眼。Xiaomei's *kindly and gentle nature* could not but revolt at her friend's callous behavior.

Reflections and Practice

I. Discuss the following questions.

1. How many types of adverbial clauses are there in English? And what are they?
2. Is it all right for a translator to render English adverbial clauses exactly into corresponding Chinese adverbials? Why or why not?
3. What are the points for attention in the translation of adverbial clauses in Chinese complex sentences?
4. Compare English adverbial clauses with Chinese ones and try to find the similarity and disparity between their structures.

II. Put the following sentences into Chinese, paying attention to the adverbial clauses.

1. It is that time of year again, when the cherry trees are blooming and Americans are stuck indoors wrestling with their taxes.
2. When Chou Enlai's door opened they saw a slender man of more than average height with gleaming eyes and a face so striking that it bordered on the beautiful.
3. It had been a fine, golden autumn, a lovely farewell to those who would lose their youth, and some of them their lives, before the leaves turned again in a peacetime fall.
4. The hunting of deer has been largely supported by local governments because the huge deer population in the U.S. has doubled, even tripled in some states, in just the last decade.
5. When I try to understand what it is that prevents so many Americans from being as

happy as one might expect, it seems to me that there are two causes, of which one goes much deeper than the other.

6. The assertion that it was difficult, if not impossible, for a people to enjoy its basic rights unless it was able to determine freely its political status and to ensure freely its economic, social and cultural development was now scarcely contested.
7. Aluminum remained unknown until the 19th century, because nowhere in nature is it found free, owing to its always being combined with elements, most commonly with oxygen, for which it has a strong affinity.
8. The scientist believed that by linking directly to our nervous system, computers could pick up what we feel and, hopefully, simulate feeling too, so that we can start to develop full sensory environments just like the holidays in science fiction films.
9. Napoleon is famously said to have declared, "When China wakes, it will shake the world." That is becoming true even in spheres that China historically has had little connection with, like chess, basketball, rare earth minerals, cyber warfare, space exploration and nuclear research.
10. It was a day as fresh as grass growing up and clouds going over and butterflies coming down can make it. It was a day compounded from silences of bee and flower and ocean and land, which were not silences at all, but motions, stirs, flutters, rising, each in its own time and matchless rhythm.

III. Put the following sentences into English, paying attention to the sentences without subjects or adverbial clauses.

1. 活到老，学到老。
2. 不入虎穴，焉得虎子。
3. 留得青山在，不怕没柴烧。
4. 屋内悄无一人，只听见钟在滴答滴答地走。
5. 突然钻出一只狗，追着她咬，几乎把她吓糊涂了。
6. 一有问题就去解决，不要等问题成了堆才去作一次总解决。
7. 识落后，才能改变落后。学习先进，才有可能赶超先进。
8. 港内水域宽阔，水深浪静，万吨轮船通行无阻，五万吨轮船可以乘潮自由进出。
9. "两千年历史看西安，一千年历史看北京，一百年历史看上海"——上海是近现代中国的缩影。
10. 1978年以来，为适应我国社会主义建设的需要，清华大学先后于1984年和1985年成立了研究生院和继续教育学院。为了适应世界范围内兴起的新技术革命，适应现代科学技术发展和社会进步出现的不同学科间交叉综合的新趋势，学校对系科设置和结构不断进行调整，创立了一批高技术及新兴系科专业，增设了理科、经济管理学科和文科，恢复了理学院、法学院，成立了经济管理学院、人文学院和信息科学技术学院，并入了美术学院，新建了医学院。清华大学现有本科专业65个，第二学士学位专业7个；有硕士学位授权点271个；博士学位授权点252个，其中38个一级学科，还有37个博士后科研流动站。清华大学校园面积392.4公顷，建筑面积249.6万平方米，图书馆藏书372万册。学校现有教职工7 186人，其中教授1 262人，副教授1 814人，中国科学院院士37人，中国工程院院士34人；在校学生31 643人，其中本科生14 608人，硕士生9 783人，博士生7 252人。

IV. Put the following sentences into Chinese, paying attention to the idiomatic expressions.

1. I was not one to let my heart rule my head.
2. Application of laser in medicine is still in its infancy.
3. I hope this concession of ours will set the ball rolling.
4. Bitterness fed on the man who had made the world laugh.
5. He had left a note of welcome for me, as sunny as his face.
6. A nice enough young fellow, you understand, nothing upstairs.
7. Why are you rushing around like a chicken with its head cut off?
8. I'd love to go out to lunch, but you know I'm living on a shoestring.
9. During the war, he was an embryo surgeon, and joined the mobile medical team.
10. The man was as strong as a horse, and his temper was as fierce as he was strong.
11. He gets up very early and sits up very late and is burning the candle at both ends.
12. His success in this field has pushed his forerunners' point into the background.
13. There are three steps which must be taken before we graduate from the integrated circuit technology.
14. The country was shockingly beautiful, and just as shockingly difficult to capture from the enemy.
15. Sometimes, walking the street at night, I've been that desperate I've made up my mind to win the horse or lose the saddle.
16. The competing interest groups confront each other with a show of passion and drama, sometimes over inconsequential matters or over a mere linguistic difference.
17. The murder was foul and unnatural and for a long time even Gryce, veteran solver of police mysteries, was confounded by the simplicity of the crime.
18. The gap between industrialized and developing countries, or between rich and poor continents is going to widen. Underdevelopment is still winning the battle.

Unit 12　Long Sentences

● 单元要点概述

相关翻译技巧训练英译汉：The Three New Yorks
相关翻译技巧训练汉译英：上海

I. 英汉翻译的长句处理
   1. 长句翻译的两个阶段和五个步骤
   2. 长句分析示例
II. 英译汉长句的翻译方法
   1. 内嵌法　　　　2. 切分法　　　　3. 拆分法
   4. 插入法　　　　5. 重组法
III. 汉译英的长句处理

本单元对英文长句的翻译进行了讲解、分析，归纳了英译汉、汉译英长句翻译的一般方法。

英译汉的长句处理一般可分为理解和表达两个阶段和五个具体的翻译步骤。英语长句的翻译方法包括"内嵌法""切分法""拆分法""插入法""重组法"等，其中"切分法"和"拆分法"最为常见，也即是化整为零，分散解决；"嵌入法"多用于定语从句的翻译；"插入法"涉及标点符号的灵活运用；"重组法"难度最大，需要完全打乱原文的框架结构，这对译者的外语和母语驾驭能力是一个严峻的考验。

汉译英长句的一般处理方法是长句化短。对于译者来说，至关重要的是如何把握好译文的要点，安排好译文的框架结构，分清句子的主次轻重及层次，使译文符合英语的表达习惯。

Practice of the Relevant Skill

1. E-C Translation

The Three New Yorks

There are roughly three New Yorks. There is, first, the New York of the man or woman who was born here, who takes the city for granted and accepts its size and its turbulence as natural and inevitable. Second, there is the New York of the commuter—the city that is devoured by locusts each day and spat out each night. Third, there is the New York of the person who was born somewhere else and came to New York in quest of something. Of these three trembling cities the greatest is the last—the city of final destination, the city that is a goal. It is this third city that accounts for New York's high-strung disposition, its poetical deportment, its dedication to the arts, and its incomparable achievements. Commuters give the city its tidal restlessness; natives give it solidity and continuity; but the settlers give it passion. And whether it is a farmer arriving from Italy to set up a small grocery store in a slum, or a young girl arriving from a small town in Mississippi to escape the indignity of being observed by her neighbors, or a boy arriving from the Corn Belt with a manuscript in his suitcase and a pain in his heart, it makes no difference; each embraces New York with the intense excitement of first love, each absorbs New York with the fresh eyes of an adventurer, each generates heat and light to dwarf the Consolidated Edison Company.

The commuter is the queerest bird of all. The suburb he inhabits has no essential vitality of its own and is a mere roost where he comes at day's end to go to sleep. Except in rare cases, the man who lives in Mamaroneck or Little Neck or Teaneck, and works in New York, discovers nothing much about the city except the time of arrival and departure of trains and buses, and the path to a quick lunch. He is deskbound, and has never, idly roaming in the gloaming, stumbled suddenly on Belvedere Tower in the park, seen the ramparts rise sheer from the water of the pond, and the boys along the shore fishing for minnows, girls stretched out negligently on the shelves of the rocks; he has never come suddenly on anything at all in New York as a loiterer, because he had no time between trains. He has fished in Manhattan's wallet and dug out coins, but has never listened to Manhattan's breathing, never awakened to its morning, never dropped off to sleep in its night.

UNIT 12 Long Sentences

Notes and Explanations

1. commuter *n.* 经常（乘火车）往返者，使用月（季）票乘车者
2. high-strung disposition 高度紧张的禀性
3. The Corn Belt （a region extending from Ohio through Iowa, with rich soil, good climate, and sufficient rainfall for excellent farming）玉米地带（从俄亥俄州延伸至爱荷华州的地区，土地肥沃、气候适宜、雨水充沛，非常适合耕作）
4. Consolidated Edison Company 爱迪生联合电气公司
5. Mamaroneck, Little Neck, Teaneck 马马罗内克、利特尔内克、蒂内克（分别为纽约和泽西城附近的3个小镇）
6. Belvedere Tower 观景塔，公园中俯视风景的一种建筑
7. shelves of the rocks 岩石的狭长突出部分
8. fish in Manhattan's wallet 将手伸进曼哈顿的钱包摸索

2. C-E Translation

上 海

上海位于长江入海口，是一座历史文化名城和著名的旅游城市，全国最大的经济中心和贸易、金融、文化中心。新中国成立前上海被称为"冒险家的乐园"，是一个工商业畸形发展的城市。今日的上海，交通四通八达，成为中国最大港口、华东地区最大的交通枢纽，沪宁、沪杭两条铁路干线的起点，又是中国重要航空中心和国际航空港之一。这里有发达的商业，是中国特大型综合性贸易中心和国际经济、金融、贸易中心之一。2010年上海世博会的成功举办，吸引了全球近200个国家和国际组织参展，海内外7 000余万名游客前来参观。"城市，让生活更美好"这一主题为全世界留下一份丰厚的精神遗产。

Notes and Explanations

1. 入海口 estuary
2. 畸形发展 lopsided development
3. 缩影 epitome
4. 特大型 super large
5. 2010年上海世博会 World Expo 2010 Shanghai
6. "城市，让生活更美好" "Better City, Better Life"
7. 丰厚的精神遗产 rich spiritual heritage

I. Long Sentences in E-C Translation

The translation of the long sentence is perhaps the most difficult of all in the process of E-C translation. The prerequisites for the correct handling of long and complex sentences in E-C translation lie in the translator's correct comprehension of the original, and in his/her capability for adequate representation of the thought of the author in the target language. And here is an example from Practice of the Relevant Skill:

And whether it is a farmer arriving from Italy to set up a small grocery store in a slum, or a young girl arriving from a small town in Mississippi to escape the indignity of being observed by her neighbors, or a boy arriving from the Corn Belt with a manuscript in his suitcase and a pain in his heart, it makes no difference; each embraces New York with the intense excitement of first love, each absorbs New York with the fresh eyes of an adventurer, each generates heat and light to dwarf the Consolidated Edison Company. 无论是从意大利来到贫民窟开小杂货店的农夫，还是为了躲避邻居的淫秽目光，从密西西比州某小镇跑出来的年轻姑娘，或是从玉米地带满怀酸楚，拎着手稿来纽约的小伙子，情况都没有什么两样：每个人都怀着初恋的激情拥抱纽约，每个人都以冒险家的新目光来审视纽约，每个人散发出的光和热都足以令爱迪生联合电气公司相形见绌。

1. Two Stages and Five Steps

The process of translating a typical English long sentence generally consists of two stages which may be subdivided into five steps.

Stage I Comprehension

Step 1: presenting the long sentence in a skeleton form

Step 2: inferring the main idea from the context and the whole text

Step 3: distinguishing between the principal and subordinate elements and find out the interrelations between principal and subordinate clauses

Stage II Presentation

Step 4: entering on a tentative translation of each sentence division

Step 5: rearrangement and finishing touches

2. Sample Analysis

Original English: It is nothing else than impurities prenatally inherent in ore that seriously affect the quality of the latter, which is formed as a result of geological vicissitudes including diastrophic movement, eruption of volcano, sedimentation, glaciation and weathering, etc., under the action of which pyrogenic rocks, volcanic complex, aqueous rocks, sedimentary rocks, etc., come into being, some of which exist in a stage of symbiosis, the main cause of the absence of pure rocks in nature, wherein lies the reason for the need of separation technology and apparatus, namely, oredressing devices and equipment, (which have been) so far impotent to meet the requirements of metallurgical industry; the scientists make every endeavor to elevate to a new high by laser separation.

Step 1 Presenting the long sentence in a skeleton form by grasping the major structure of the long sentence. The skeleton may be drawn as follows:

It is nothing else than impurities... that seriously affect the quality of..., which is formed as..., under the action of which... rocks, etc., come into being..., some of which exist in..., wherein lies the reason for the need of..., (which have been) so far impotent to meet the requirements of...

Step 2 Inferring the main idea from the context and the whole text:

(1) Impurities prenatally inherent in ore seriously affect its quality.

(2) Ore is formed as a result of geological vicissitudes.

(3) Separation technology and apparatus are needed.

(4) The scientists endeavor to elevate it to a new high by laser separation.

Step 3 Distinguishing between the principal and subordinate elements:

The principal element lies in the latter part of the long sentence, and the subordinate element is in the first part which accounts for the scientists' endeavor: since natural ore is impure, the scientists endeavor to purify it by means of advanced technology and apparatus.

The principal clause: It is... in ore;

Subordinate clause: that seriously affect... by laser separation;

Attributive clauses in the subject clauses: which is formed..., under the action of which... come into being, wherein (= in which), (which have been) so far impotent to..., metallurgical industry (which) the scientists make every endeavor to...

Step 4 Entering on a tentative translation of each sentence division:

(1) 影响矿石质量的不是别的东西而是矿石中天然固有的杂质。

(2) 这些矿石的形成是由于地壳变迁运动、火山爆发、沉积作用、冰川作用和风化作用等造成的结果。

(3) 在上述地质变化的作用下，生成了火成岩、火山杂岩、水成岩和沉积岩等。

(4) 上述岩石中有些处于共生状态，这是自然界没有纯净矿石的主要原因。

(5) 人们之所以需要分离技术与器械——即选矿装置与设备，其原因就在于此。

(6) 迄今为止，分离技术和器械尚不足以适应冶金工业的需要，科学家们力图利用激光分离机把冶金工业提高到一个新水平。

Step 5 Rearrangement and finishing touches：

The above separate Chinese sentences offer a global idea of the original. However, they are loose and incoherent. Therefore rearrangement and synthesis are needed to turn them into a coherent Chinese text. With all the five steps completed, we may come to the polished Chinese version：

矿石是由地质变化形成的，这些地质变化包括地壳变迁运动、火山爆发、沉积作用、冰川作用和风化作用等。在上述地质变化的作用下，形成了火成岩、火山杂岩、水成岩和沉积岩等。正是岩石中的天然固有杂质影响了矿石的质量。上述这些岩石中，有些处于共生状态——这也是自然界没有天然纯矿石的主要原因。人们之所以需要矿石分离技术与器械，即选矿装置与设备，其原因盖出于此。迄今为止，分离技术和器械尚远不能满足冶金工业的需要，科学家们正全力以赴，利用激光分离机把冶金工业提高到一个新水平。

The abovementioned five steps are generally interwoven throughout the process of translation and we should learn to make use of them according to different circumstances. On the other hand, the layout of a good piece of translation, to a great extent, comes from the creative work of the translator, whose flexibility and adaptability are tested whenever long and complex sentences occur. In this sense, there is no reason for us to stick to the above sequence mechanically.

II. Methods of Translating Long English Sentences

In the practice of translation, numerous methods or approaches have been devised to tackle long and complex English sentences.

1. Embedding

With modifiers being embedded between the predicate verb and the object to be modified, embedding is often adopted in the translation of attributive and appositive clauses to make the Chinese version compact and coherent.

- In the meantime, a growing China has started to help solve *global problems, from support for the government of Afghanistan to the fight against AIDS.* 同时，日益强大的中国已经开始帮助解决**从支持阿富汗政府到抗击艾滋病之类的全球性问题**。

- This is no class war, but a war in *which the whole British Empire and Commonwealth of Nations is engaged, without distinction of race, creed, or party.* 这不是一场阶级之间的战争，而是一场**不分种族、不分信仰、不分党派，整个大英帝国及英联邦全体成员国无不参加的**战争。

- Congress has made laws requiring most pressure groups to give information *about how much they spend and how they spend it, the amount and sources of funds, membership, and names and salaries of their representatives.* 国会已制定法律，要求大部分压力集团呈报他们花费了多少钱，怎样花的，以及款项的总额和来源、成员人数、代表的姓名和薪金等情况。

Occasionally, clauses functioning as adverbials of cause, condition, premise, etc. may also be translated by means of embedding：

- In 1970, he was placed under house arrest *when he refused to use massive force in suppressing worker riots on the seacoast.* 1970年他因拒绝使用武力大规模镇压沿海城市的工人骚乱而被软禁。
- A bar of iron *placed in a coil, through which a current is flowing*, becomes magnetized. 铁棒置于通电的线圈中就会被磁化。

2. Dividing

The most effective method to tackle long and complicated sentences, dividing is usually used to break up a long English sentence into different parts according to its sense groups, and then translate each part one by one.

- Human beings have distinguished themselves from other animals, and in doing so ensured their survival, by the ability to observe and understand their environment and then either to adapt to that environment or to control and adapt it to their own needs. 人类把自己和其他动物区别开来。与此同时，人类还具有观察和了解周围环境的能力。他们要么适应环境，要么控制环境，或根据自身的需要改造环境。人类就这样一代代地生存下来。
- Plastics are made from water which is a natural resource inexhaustible and available everywhere, coal which can be mined through automatic and mechanical processes at less cost and lime which can be obtained from the calcination of limestone widely present in nature. 塑料是由水、煤和石灰制成的。水是取之不尽到处可以获得的天然资源；煤是用自动化和机械化的方法开采的，成本较低；石灰是由煅烧自然界中广泛存在的石灰石得来的。
- Steel is usually made where the iron ore is smelted, so that the modern steelworks forms a complete unity, taking in raw materials and producing all types of cast iron and steel, both for sending to other works for further treatment, and as finished products such as joists and other consumer goods. 通常炼铁的地方也炼钢。因此，现代炼钢厂是一个配套的整体，运进原料，生产各种类型的铸铁与钢材；有的送往其他工厂进一步加工处理，有的就地制成成品，如工字钢及其他一些成材。

3. Splitting

By splitting we mean separating certain elements (clause, phrase, or word) from a sentence and treating them as parenthesis. This technique is usually employed when it comes to describing the subjective opinion of the original author.

(1) Splitting a single word

- An outsider's success could even *curiously* help two parties to get the agreement they want. 说来奇怪，一个局外人取得的成功竟然能够促使双方达成一项他们希望取得的协议。
- The number of the young people in the United States who cannot read is *incredible*—about one in four. 大约有 1/4 的美国青年人没有阅读能力，**这简直令人难以置信！**

(2) Splitting phrases

- The foreign visitors watched *in a fascinated manner* the tournament held in Beijing, which exhibited a superb performance in smash service, twist service, steady service, high drop and killing and ended in a draw. 外宾观看了在北京举行的这场锦标赛。这场比赛在发扣球、转球、保险球、吊球和扣杀方面技术都十分精湛，最后打成平局。**他们看得简直入迷了。**
- My mother, Jane Lampton Clements, died in her 88th year, *a mighty age* for one who at 40 was so delicate of body as to be accounted a confirmed invalid destined to pass soon away. 我的母亲简·兰普顿·克莱门斯是在她 88 岁那年去世的。这对于一位四十岁时就身体纤弱、被公认有痼疾缠身、注定不久于人世的人来说，**是难得的高龄。**

(3) Splitting clauses or absolute construction

- This land, *which once barred the way of weary travelers,* now has become a land for winter and summer vacations, a land of magic and wonder. 这个地方现在已经成了冬夏两季的休假胜地，风光景物，蔚为奇观；**而从前，精疲力竭的旅游者只能到此止步。**
- A few days later, with appeals to the Supreme Court and Governor Arnold Schwarzenegger both rejected, Clarence Ray Allen, a blind, diabetic 76-year-old *convicted of having three people killed, including his son's girlfriend,* was helped from his wheelchair and put to death by lethal injection in California. 几天之后，提交到最高法院和阿诺·施瓦辛格州长的两个上诉都被驳回。76 岁的糖尿病患者、盲人克拉伦斯·雷·艾伦被判定有罪，在加州被抱下轮椅，注入毒剂处死。**他的罪名是杀害了三个人，其中包括他儿子的女友。**

4. Inserting

By putting in additional punctuation marks such as dash, parenthesis, colon, etc., inserting is usually used to translate long and complex sentences so as to make the Chinese version both clear and smooth.

- The second aspect is the application by all members of society from the government official to the ordinary citizen, of the special methods of thought and action that scientists use in their work. 第二个方面是全体社会成员（从政府官员到普通公民）都使用科学家们在他们工作中所采用的那种特殊的思考方法和行为方法。(inserting parentheses)

- Only through the intellectual activities of logical thinking such as judgment, inference, deduction, induction, synthesis and sublimation, etc., namely a process of discarding the dross and selecting the essential and eliminating the false and retaining the true, can perceptual cognition be elevated to the level of conceptual cognition. 只有通过逻辑思维的智力活动，如判断、推理、演绎、归纳、综合、升华等——去粗取精、去伪存真的过程，感性认识才能上升到理性认识的水平。(inserting a dash)

- If you go to visit Nobel's old residence, the house in which the great chemist remained a bachelor throughout his life, you will catch sight of a shelf laden with experimental records. 如果你参观诺贝尔的故居——在那座房子里，这位伟大的化学家过了一辈子的独身生活——你将会看到一个堆满实验记录的书架。(inserting two dashes)

- As far as sight could reach, I feasted my eyes on a vastness of infinite charm, which presents itself in a profusion of color, in verdant luxuriance, in dulcet warbling, in pervading perfume, in rippling undulation, in cataract sprays, in hilly waves, in field crisscross and verily in vitality and variety. 纵目眺望，我饱览了一片无限娇艳的风光：万紫千红，郁郁葱葱，鸟语悦耳，花香袭人，涟漪荡漾，瀑布飞流，层峦起伏，阡陌纵横。真可谓生机勃勃，气象万千。(inserting a colon)

5. Recasting

Recasting, also called synthesis, is reckoned as the most difficult translation technique of all. For it entails a skillful control over both English and Chinese languages on the part of the translator, who, based on an accurate comprehension of the original, should flexibly adjust or rearrange it without considering the original wording and structure. In other words, the translator should creatively put the English original into Chinese in his/her own words.

- The saga of the White Star Liner Titanic, which struck an iceberg and sank on its maiden voyage in 1912, carrying more than 1,500 passengers to their death, has been celebrated in print and on film, in poetry and song. 白星公司班轮"泰坦尼克"号在1912年的处女航中因撞上冰山而沉没，致使船上1 500多名乘客罹难。此后关于它的轶事传闻就一直成为各种刊物、电影以及诗歌、歌曲的内容而广为流传。

- But without Adolf Hitler, who was possessed of a demoniac personality, a granite will, uncanny instincts, a cold ruthlessness, a remarkable intellect, a soaring imagination and—until toward the end, when drunk with power and success, he overreached himself—an amazing capacity to size up people and situations, there almost certainly would never have been a Third Reich. 然而，如果没有阿道夫·希特勒，那就几乎可以肯定不会有第三帝国。因为阿道夫·希特勒有着恶魔般的性格，花岗石般的意志，不可思议的本能，无情的冷酷，杰出的智力，深远的想象力以及对人和时局惊人的判断力。这种判断力最后由于权力和胜利冲昏了头脑而自不量力，终于弄巧成拙。

- What the New Yorker would find missing is what many outsiders find oppressive and distasteful about New York—its rawness, tension, urgency; its bracing competitiveness; the rigor of its judgment; and the congested, democratic presence of so many other New Yorkers encased in their own world. 纽约的粗犷、紧张，那种急迫感和催人奋发的竞争性，它的是非观念之严酷无情，纽约市的那种各色人等熙熙攘攘，兼容并蓄于各自天地之中的格局，这一切都使那些非纽约人感到厌恶和窒息；而这一切，又正是纽约人所眷恋的。

III. Long Sentences in C-E Translation

Long sentence translation is also a headache for the translator in C-E translation. Since there is an obvious disparity between Chinese and English sentence structures, we should learn to tackle them discriminatingly. One case for example is the translation of Chinese four-character expressions. Sometimes, when the original Chinese is too meticulous, we may simplify the structure by using simple sentences, laying stress on the subject and the predicate verb.

- 这种床垫**工艺先进**，结构新颖，造型美观，款式多样，舒适大方，携带方便。*The technological design* of this bed cushion *is advanced* with novel structure, beautiful shape and various patterns. They are comfortable and convenient to carry.

- 由于这台仪器性能稳定、操作可靠、维修方便，因此**受到用户的好评**。This

instrument *has been well received by the customers* because of its stability in service, reliability in operation and simplicity in maintenance.

The usual method of translating Chinese long sentences into English is dividing, i.e. cutting them into several segments regardless of the punctuation marks. And the key to guaranteeing a good translation is to discern the main idea and the subordinate ones, taking the structure of the whole sentence into consideration. We may find layers of meaning from the overlapped structure and then cut the sentence into two, three, or even more segments before tackling them one by one. The following are some examples.

- 一定要言行一致，理论与实践密切结合，反对华而不实和任何虚夸，少说空话，多做工作，扎扎实实，埋头苦干。Deed and word must match and theory and practice must be closely integrated. We must reject flashiness without substance and every sort of boasting. There must be less empty talk and more hard work. We must be steadfast and dedicated. (dividing into 4 sentences)
- 历来只有真正老实的劳动者，才懂得劳动生产财富的道理，才能排除一切想入非非的发财思想，而踏踏实实地用自己的辛劳劳动，为社会也为自己创造财富和积累财富。Throughout the ages only honest laboring people see the truth that wealth is created through labor. Only they can free their minds of any fantastic ideas of getting rich. And only they create and accumulate wealth for both society and themselves through practical work. (dividing into 3 sentences)
- 年岁不好，柴米又贵；这几件旧衣服和旧家伙，当的当了，卖的卖了；只靠着我替人家做些针黹生活寻来的钱，如何供得你读书？Times are hard, and fuel and rice are expensive. Our old clothes and our few sticks of furniture have been pawned or sold. We have nothing to live on but what I make by my sewing. How can I pay for your schooling? (dividing into 4 sentences)
- 接着，他继续设想，鸡又生鸡，用鸡卖钱，钱买母牛，母牛繁殖，卖牛得钱，用钱放债，这么一连串的发财计划，当然也不能算是生产的计划。He went on indulging in wishful thinking. Chickens would breed more chickens. Selling them would bring him more money. With this he could buy cows. The cows would breed too and selling oxen would make more money for him. With the money, he could become a moneylender. Such a succession of steps for getting rich, of course, had nothing at all to do with production. (dividing into 7 sentences)
- 我们已经明确了21世纪头20年的奋斗目标，这就是全面建设惠及十几亿人口的更高水平的小康社会，到2020年实现国内生产总值比2000年翻两番，达到4万亿美元，人均国内生产总值达到3 000美元，使经济更加发展、民主更加健全、科教更加进步、文化更加繁荣、社会更加和谐、人民生活更加殷实。We have already set our vision for the first 20 years of this century, which involves the

building of a moderately prosperous society of a higher standard in an all-round way for the benefit of well over one billion Chinese people. By 2020 the GDP will be quadrupled from the figure of 2000 to 4 trillion U.S. dollars, with the per capita level averaging at 3,000 U.S. dollars. By then the nation will be immersed in an ambience of greater social harmony with an improved quality of life for the people, featuring a more developed economy, more sound democracy, more thriving culture and more advanced science and education. (dividing into 3 sentences)

Reflections and Practice

I. Discuss the following questions.

1. What are the two stages and five steps in handling a long English sentence?
2. What is embedding? And when is it used to translate long English sentences?
3. What is the technique of "dividing"? Why is it often used to translate long English sentences?
4. What is the technique of "splitting"? What are the usual methods of splitting?
5. What is the technique of "inserting"? And when is this technique usually adopted in translation?
6. What is the technique of "recasting"? Why is it considered the most difficult of all translation techniques?
7. What is the usual method of translating long Chinese sentences?

II. Put the following long sentences into Chinese, paying attention to their structures.

1. There are swift flowing rivers, slow, sluggish rivers, mighty rivers with several mouths, rivers that carry vast loads of alluvium to the sea, clear, limpid rivers, rivers that at some seasons of the year have very much more water than at others, rivers that are made to generate vast quantities of electricity by their power, and rivers that carry great volumes of traffic. (dividing)
2. Is the claim of the G&C Merriam Company, probably the world's greatest dictionary maker, that the preparation of the work cost $3.5 million, that it required the efforts of three hundred scholars over a period of twenty-seven years, working on the largest collection of citations ever assembled in any language—is all this a fraud, a hoax? (dividing/recasting)

UNIT 12   Long Sentences

3. The secret of the moon remained veiled until the latter half of the 20th century due to the lack of a lunar space carrier, for a series of questions concerning fuel, material, safe landing, propelling mechanism and particularly electronic computation, etc. were too intricate to solve under the technical conditions early in this century, which have since been undergoing profound change and greatly improving. (reversing/inserting)

4. All members, in order to ensure to all of them the rights and benefits resulting from membership, shall fulfill in good faith the obligations assumed by them in accordance with the present Charter. (splitting)

5. Americans who would be patriots must try to learn what it is that they have in common, what it is in the republic that is worth cherishing and preserving; until they know that, their patriotism will have no more content than a bright, loud afternoon parade. (dividing/splitting)

6. Computer language may range from detailed low level close to that immediately understood by the particular computer, to the sophisticated high level which can be rendered automatically acceptable to a wide range of computers. (recasting)

7. A complex bureaucracy favors the status quo, because short of an unambiguous catastrophe, the status quo has advantage of familiarity, and it is never possible to prove that another course would yield superior results. It seemed no accident that most great statesmen had been locked in permanent struggle with the experts in their foreign offices, for the scope of the statesman's conception challenges the inclination of the expert toward minimum risk. (dividing/reversing/embedding)

8. He ranged the summer woods now, green with gloom, if anything actually dimmer than they had been in November's gray dissolution, where even at noon the sun fell only in the windless dappling upon the earth which never completely dried and which crawled with snakes—moccasins and water-snakes and rattlers, themselves the color of the dappled gloom so that he would not always see them until they moved; returning to camp later and later, first day, second day, passing in the twilight of the third evening the little log pen enclosing the log barn where Sam was putting up the stock for the night. (dividing/embedding/recasting/splitting)

9. This spirit of fairplay, which in the public schools, at any rate, is absorbed as the most inviolable of traditions, has stood our race in good stead in the professions, and especially in the administration of dependencies, where the obvious desire of the officials to deal justly and see fair-play in disputes between natives and Europeans has partly compensated for a grant of sympathetic understanding, which has kept the English strangers in lands of alien culture. (dividing/recasting)

10. As a last resort, conditions permitting, we may seek at home medical service, namely,

diagnosis and treatment from abroad, to use professional terminology, telesatdiag, as compared with vis-a-vis consultation, say, in an ill-equipped, poorly staffed hospital, particularly on an acute, severe or, in physician's view, unidentified case, undoubtedly a most effective therapeutic device available. (dividing/embedding/inserting)

III. Put the following long sentences into English, paying attention to their structures.

1. 我厂生产的 112 升和 145 升电冰箱，造型美观，质量可靠，噪音小，耗电少，使用方便安全。

2. 当前我们迫切需要有一个装备优良、人员齐备、按照安全保护原则、本着一丝不苟的精神建立起来的先进核能实验室。

3. 本厂已有 50 年生产丝绸服装的历史，其产品远销全球 50 多个国家和地区。完全真丝，质量上乘，做工精细，款式新颖，光滑柔和，耐洗耐晒，永不褪色，舒适高雅，女士必备。如欲购买，尽快联系。

4. "书山有路勤为径，学海无涯苦作舟。"这句话意在告诉人们，在读书、学习的道路上，没有捷径可走，没有顺风船可驶，想要在广博的书山、学海中汲取更多、更广的知识，"勤奋"和"潜心"是两个必不可少的重要条件。

5. 历史业已证明，人类对资源的认识、开发和利用，以及制造生产工具利用资源的能力，是社会生产力发展水平的重要标志，也在一定的程度上决定了一定的社会基本结构和发展形态。

6. 从 1978 年开始，中国开启了新的征程，从计划转向市场，从封闭转向开放，从自成一体转向融入经济全球化，走独立自主地建设中国特色社会主义的道路，取得了举世瞩目的辉煌成就。

7. 从 19 世纪 40 年代之后的鸦片战争、甲午战争，到庚子之乱乃至 20 世纪 30 年代的日本侵华战争，中国惨遭东西方列强的屠戮和极其野蛮的经济掠夺；再加上封建腐败和连年内乱，中国主权沦丧、生灵涂炭、国力衰弱、民不聊生。

8. 信息技术是在微电子、计算机和现代通信技术基础上发展起来的一门高科技，具有信息采集、传输、处理和信息服务等一系列功能。现今已能在一片 8 英寸的芯片上集成 5 亿个电子元件，其宽度仅为 0.2503 微米；微机的信息处理速度已达每秒近亿次以上；计算机虚拟技术将大大拓宽信息技术应用的范围。

IV. Put the following into Chinese, paying attention to their wording and implications.

1. "It's from President Bush." "I don't care if it is from bush, tree, or grass."

2. If my mother had known of it she'd have died a second time.

UNIT 12 Long Sentences

3. Speaker Jim Wright brushes tear away as he throws in towel yesterday in D. C.
4. Every gain in the fight against AIDS raises hope that a magic bullet can be fashioned to cure the disease.
5. This paper is our passport to the gallows. But there's no backing off now. If we don't hang together, we shall most certainly be hanged separately.
6. Of me my mother would say, with characteristic restraint, "This bandit. He doesn't even have to open a book—'A' in everything. Albert Einstein the second."
7. Mr. Brown is a very white man. He was looking rather green the other day. He has been feeling blue lately. When I saw him he was in a brown study. I hope he'll soon be in the pink again.
8. OK, fellas, this is it! D-Day! Let's get out there and blitz the competition. Give'em hell! Now we've planned our strategy down to the last T. No Maginot Line here! And oh, we want no Quislings on our team. The last thing we want in this outfit is a Fifth Column. On the other hand, give yourselves room to maneuver. Don't get into any Catch-22 situation. Promise them anything: a New Deal, a Fair Deal, and a Square Deal. Make the first sale and the rest will follow like the domino effect. The bottom line is sale, sell, sell!

Unit 13 English for Science and Technology and Its Translation

● 单元要点概述

相关翻译技巧训练英译汉：Making Artificial Cells

相关翻译技巧训练汉译英：科技英语

I. 英语科技词语的构成

II. 科技英语的句法特点

III. 科技英语的翻译方法

本单元从科技英语的词汇和句法特点两个方面介绍了科技英语的翻译方法。

英语科技词语一般以 3 种形式存在，即单词式、复合式和短语式，其构词法与普通英语构词法无异。本单元分析了英语技术词语的 5 种构成模式，即缀合式、复合式科、缩合式、首字母缩略式、专有名词式。

科技英语的句法特点主要表现在 6 个方面：1. 使用结构复杂的长句；2. 频繁使用名词短语；3. 广泛使用被动语态；4. 多用非限定动词；5. 用不同的时态表示先后状况；6. 大量使用后置定语。

科技英语的翻译方法包括：1. 将名词性短语扩展成汉语分句；2. 将名词性短语译成动宾结构；3. 将定语成分转为独立句、状语分句等；4. 将被动转为主动；5. 补充适当的词语表示特定的时间。

Practice of the Relevant Skill

1. E-C Translation

Making Artificial Cells

Many biologists—and Dr. Szostak is one of them—think that life had a simpler early stage in which the varied tasks now carried out by DNA, RNA and proteins were all achieved by RNA alone. Even today, RNA molecules are not only messengers; they are also fetchers and carriers of amino acids, the building blocks of proteins. And they can catalyse reactions, as proteins do, too. In principle, then, RNA could act as both a cell's genetic material and its self-assembly mechanism.

If this idea is true, it should be possible to make a cell using just a membrane to hold things in place, some RNA, ingredients for more RNA, and an energy source. This comes in the form of an energy-rich molecule, ATP, which is what modern cells use to move energy from where it is generated to where it is used. Dr. Szostak has already made a range of "ribozymes", as catalytic pieces of RNA are known in the trade, and some of them are ATP-powered. He does not, yet, have a system that is capable of replicating itself. But that is his goal.

Dr. Szostak's cell, if it does come to pass, will be quite different from the protein-and-DNA-based life familiar to biologists. It would in some ways be a greater achievement than Dr. Venter's, in that it would create something truly from scratch; but it would be of less practical importance, since that something would be very primitive compared even with a bacterium.

George Church, a colleague of Dr. Szostak's at Harvard, dreams instead of making something intensely practical that Dr. Venter has left out: a ribosome. The Venter shortcut—booting up a bacterial cadaver—means that the newminted bug has to rely on ribosomes from its dead host to make the proteins its genome describes. It has the genes with which to make its own ribosomes, though, and as time goes by it will do so, diluting out the legacy that got it started. Dr. Venter calculates that once JCVI-syn 1.0 has undergone 30 divisions, all trace of the original cell will have disappeared. But that does not address the point that the new cells have relied on the output of genes from the old one to get going in the first place.

Dr. Church is working on making ribosomes—complex contraptions with dozens of protein and RNA components—from scratch. He has managed to synthesise all the RNA components in such a way that, when they are mixed with natural ribosome proteins, they form working ribosomes. Making the proteins from scratch is more difficult, because their shape is crucial to their function, so it is not clear whether he will bother to do so.

Notes and Explanations

1. DNA deoxyribonucleic acid 脱氧核糖核酸
2. RNA Ribonucleic Acid 核糖核酸
3. Adenosine Triphosphate 三磷酸腺苷（生化药物）
4. a range of "ribozymes" 一系列的"核酶"

5. from scratch 从零开始，白手起家
6. boot up 启动
7. JCVI-syn 1.0 首个基于人工合成基因组的支原体细菌

2. C-E Translation

科技英语

科技英语是指在自然科学和工程技术方面的科学著作、论文、教科书、科技报告和学术讲演中所使用的英语。科技英语不像普通英语那样具有感性思维和感情色彩，通常也不运用比喻、夸张等修辞手段，而是按逻辑思维准确、清晰地描述客观世界、揭示自然规律。科技英语是一种书面语，它要求行文严谨、简洁，不堆砌辞藻，也不需考虑朗读效果。科技英语的词汇意义比较专一、稳定，具有国际性。据统计，70%以上的科技英语词汇来自拉丁语、希腊语。随着科技的发展与全球经济一体化的逐步深入，科技英语将会在国际交流中发挥越来越重要的作用。

Notes and Explanations

1. 感性思维 perceptual thinking
2. 感情色彩 emotional coloring
3. 比喻、夸张 metaphor, hyperbole
4. 修辞手段 rhetoric means
5. 行文严谨、简洁 rigorous, simple writing style
6. 堆砌辞藻 string together ornate phrases
7. 揭示客观世界 reveal the objective world
8. 专一、稳定 constant and stable
9. 全球经济一体化 the integration of global economy
10. 发挥重要作用 play an important role

With rapid and remarkable advances in modern science and technology, an increasingly large number of English technical terms have arisen in our daily life, giving rise to a new genre—English for science and technology (EST). More and more people tend to accept EST, for the modern methods of scientific research, investigation and operation have led to numerous new concepts, materials and processes. In brief, scientific and technical registers provide a swift, economical, efficient, impersonal, sometimes international, means of exposition and discussion of specialized issues.

UNIT 13 English for Science and Technology and Its Translation

The translation of EST is somewhat different from that of general English, especially in its peculiar wording and characteristic syntax. And here are some examples from Practice of the Relevant Skill of this unit:

DNA 脱氧核糖核酸、RNA 核糖核酸、catalyse 催化、genetic material 基因材料、self-assembly mechanism 自组装机理、membrane 膜、energy-rich molecule 富能量分子、ATP 三磷酸腺苷、ribozymes 核酶、the protein-and-DNA-based life 基于蛋白质和DNA 的生命、ribosome 核糖体、JCVI-syn 1.0 首个基于人工合成基因组的支原体细菌、synthesise 合成，etc.

I. Formation of English Technical Terms

One of the most distinctive features of EST is its technical terms, which not only account for a large part of English vocabulary, but also are the most important source of newly coined words in modern English, ranging over an extensive area of various fields. A mastery of them will benefit us a great deal in the translation of EST.

In terms of formation, English technical terms may be classified into three categories, i.e. single words (e. g. robot 机器人, Internet 因特网, etc.), compound forms (e. g. feedback 反馈, splashdown 溅落, etc.) and phrases (e. g. on-and-off-the-road 路面越野两用的, anti-armored-fight-vehicle-missile 反装甲车导弹, power transmission relay system 送电中继系统, etc.). Most of the technical terms come out of the basic rules of word-formation, such as affixation, compounding, blending, acronym, etc.

1. Affixation

Affixation is an important means of coining new English words and technical terms, with prefix and suffix as inseparable elements of the words being coined. It is the most flexible means of word-formation which is extensively used in EST. Besides prefix and suffix of English origin, there are some foreign borrowings, noticeably the Latin ones, e.g. bio- (生命、生物), thermo- (热), electro- (电), aero- (空气) carbo- (碳), hydro- (水), -ite (矿物), -mania (热、狂), etc. The following are some typical examples:

- miniultrasonicprober=mini + ultra + sonic + prober 微型超声波探伤仪
- macrospacetransship=macro + space + trans + ship 巨型空间转运飞船
- teletypesetter=tele + type + setter 电传排字机
- bathythermograph=bathy + thermo + graph 海水测温仪
- barothermograph=baro + thermo + graph 气压温度记录器

- deoxyribonucleic=de + oxy + ribo + nucleic 脱氧核糖核酸的
- photomorphogenesis=photo + morpho + genesis 光形态发生

2. Compounding

Combining two or more words to form a new word is called compounding such as loudspeaker, baby-sit, highschool, etc. English technical terms formed by compounding generally assume three forms: combining with a hyphen (e.g. dew-point 露点，pulse-scaler 脉冲定标器) or without it (e.g. fallout 放射性尘埃，hovercraft 气垫船，waterlock 水闸，thunderstorm 雷暴), or two or more separate words forming a word combination (e.g. stem cell 干细胞，optical drive 光驱，satellite antimissile observation system 卫星反导弹观察系统).

Most of such compound words may be translated literally. But sometimes there are exceptions—literal translation may lead astray. For example, bull's eye（靶心），cat-and-mouse（航向与指挥的），dog house（高频高压电源屏蔽罩），etc. Therefore whenever we are confronted with unfamiliar terms and are not sure of their meaning, we should consult dictionaries of relevant specialties. In many cases some additional explanations are needed to make the original meaning clear and accurate.

3. Blending

Blending, also called portmanteau, is a variant of compounding by omitting the latter part of the first word and clipping off the first part of the second word, as the formation of smog from smoke and fog, motel from motorist and hotel. This blending of words generally holds the combined meaning of both; therefore, literal translation is usually used in translation, with one element modifying the other.

- bit=binary + digit（二进制）位，比特
- blog=web + log 博客
- copytron=copy + electron 电子复写技术
- gravisphere=gravity + sphere 引力范围
- maglev=magnetic + levitation 磁悬浮
- medicare=medical + care 医疗保健
- nanotech=nanometer + technology 纳米技术

4. Acronyms

An acronym is a word formed from the initial letters of a name, such as WAC for Women's Army Corps, or by combining initial letters or parts of a series of words, such as radar for radio detection and ranging. Simple and concise, acronyms sometimes tend to be ambiguous in meaning. Therefore, it is up to the translator to discern their actual meaning

in different contexts.
- ADP　Automatic Data Processing 自动数据处理
- AIDS　Acquired Immune Deficiency Syndrome 艾滋病
- CAD　Computer-Aided Design 计算机辅助设计
- EDPM　Electronic Data Processing Machine 电子数据处理机
- IEEE　Institute of Electrical and Electronic Engineers 电气和电子工程师协会
- LASER　Light Amplification by Stimulated Emission of Radiation 激光
- LED　Light-Emitting Diode 发光二极管
- RAM　Random Access Memory 随机存取存储器
- SCI　Science Citation Index 科学引文索引
- UFO　Unidentified Flying Object 不明飞行物

Sometimes, an acronym happens to be an actual English word, or it may hold more than one meaning. In this case, special attention should be paid to pick out the right Chinese equivalent.
- CAT　Computer-Aided Translation 计算机辅助翻译
- MOUSE　Minimum Orbital Unmanned Satellite of the Earth（仪表载重50公斤以下的）不载人的最小人造地球卫星
- SALT　Strategic Arms Limitation Talks 限制战略武器会谈
- WHO　World Health Organization（联合国）世界卫生组织
- SNAP　Subsystem for Nuclear Auxiliary Power 辅助（原子）核动力子系统
  Space Nuclear Auxiliary Power 空间核辅助能源
  Systems for Nuclear Auxiliary Power 辅助核动力系统
- AS　air scoop 空气收集器
  air seasoned 风干的（木材）
  air speed 空速，气流速率
  air station 航空站，飞机场
  American Standard 美国标准
  atmosphere and space 大气层与宇宙空间
  automatic sprinkler 自动洒水车
  automatic synchronizer 自动同步器

5. Proper Nouns

Many of the technical terms in English are borrowed from proper nouns such as names, places, firms, trade marks, organizations, etc., normally beginning with a capital letter. In such cases, consulting relevant dictionaries or reference books will be of great help. The usual way in translating proper nouns is transliteration. Sometimes, adding a label to the corresponding translation is necessary to indicate the nature of the given words.

- Xerox 静电复制 (derived from a trademark used for a photo copying process)
- Petri dish 培养皿 (named after the German bacteriologist Julius R. Petri)
- Chevrolet 雪弗兰牌汽车 (derived from an American automobile company)
- Marathon 马拉松长跑 (derived from the village and plain of ancient Greece northeast of Athens)
- pasteurize 对……进行消毒或灭菌 (derived from the French biologist Louis Pasteur)

Of course, there are some other forms of technical terms in English. For instance, clipping (e.g. "lab" comes from "laboratory"), back-formation (e.g. "to lase" comes from "laser"), coinage (e.g. "quark" in physics), functional shift (e.g. in the phrase "to contract the terminal", the word "contract" is converted from a noun to a verb), borrowing (e.g. "gene" is borrowed from German), and so on. In any case, a discrimination of the original meaning and a contextual analysis are of vital importance. Only when we get an accurate understanding of them, can we put them into Chinese exactly as they actually mean.

II. Characteristic Syntax of EST

1. Long and Complicated Sentences

EST as a formal style of writing tends to use long and complicated sentences. When translated into Chinese, a long sentence may be cut into several parts. For example：

- The efforts that have been made to explain optical phenomena by means of the hypothesis of a medium having the same physical character as an elastic solid body led, in the first instance, to the understanding of a concrete example of a medium which can transmit transverse vibration but later to the definite conclusion that there is no luminiferous medium having the physical character assumed in the hypothesis. 为了解释光学现象，人们曾试图假定有一种具有与弹性固体相同的物理性的介质。这种尝试的结果，最初曾使人们以为存在一种有形的能传输横向振动的介质的具体实例，但后来却使人得出了这样一个明确的结论：并不存在任何具有上述假定所认为的那种物理性质的发光介质。
- One of the most important things which the economic theories can contribute to management science is building analytical models which help in recognizing the structure of managerial problems, eliminating the minor details which might obstruct decision making, and in concentrating on the main issues. 经济理论对于管

理科学可作的最重要贡献之一,就是建立分析模型。这种模型有助于认清管理问题的结构,排除可能妨碍决策的次要细节,从而有助于集中精力于主要问题。

2. High Frequency of Noun Phrases

Different from general English, EST tends to use more noun phrases. This is because scientific literature contains more abstract concepts such as definitions, principles, laws, conclusions, etc.

- All substances will permit *the passage of some electric current,* provided the potential difference is high enough.
  Poor translation: 只要有足够的电位差,所有的物体都允许一些电流通过。
  Proper translation: 只要有足够的电位差,**电流便可通过任何物体**。
- The heat loss can be considerably reduced *by the use of firebricks* round the walls of the boiler.
  Poor translation: 通过在炉壁周围使用耐火砖,热损失可以被大大降低。
  Proper translation: 炉壁**采用耐火砖**可大大降低热耗。
- Television is *the transmission and reception of images of moving objects* by radio waves.
  Poor translation: 电视是通过无线电波的活动物体的图像的传播和接收。
  Proper translation: 电视通过无线电波**发射和接收**各种活动物体的图像。

3. Extensive Use of the Passive Voice

The passive voice is extensively used in EST to achieve objectivity, as shown in the following illustrations.

General English: People get natural rubber from rubber trees as a white, milky liquid, which is called latex. They mix it with acid, and dry it, and then they send it to countries all over the world.

Chinese Version: 人们从橡胶树中获得天然橡胶。这是一种叫作"乳胶"的白色乳状液体。人们先将橡胶与酸混合在一起,将其烘干,然后再运往世界各国。

Scientific English: Natural rubber *is obtained* from rubber trees as a white, milky liquid known as latex. This *is treated* with acid and dried, before *being dispatched* to countries all over the world.

Chinese Version: 天然橡胶**取自**橡胶树——在取出时是一种**叫作**"乳胶"的白色乳状液体。**在**运往世界各国之前,橡胶**要经过酸处理**和烘干。

4. More Non-Finite Forms of the Verb

Non-finite forms of the verb, i.e. the infinitive, the gerund, the present and the past participles are frequently used in EST than in general English. For example:

- Today the electronic computer is widely used in *solving* mathematical problems *having to do with* weather *forecasting* and *putting* satellites *into* orbit. 今天，电子计算机广泛地运用于**解决**一些数学问题，这些问题与天气**预报**和**把**卫星**送入**轨道**有关**。
- Numerical control machines are most useful when quantities of products *to be produced* are low or medium; the tape *containing* the information *required to produce* the part can *be stored, reused or modified when required*. 少量或中量**生产产品时**，数控机床是极为有用的。**录有生产零件资料的磁带可以被存储、重用，或在需要时加以修改**。

5. Different Uses of the Tense

In general English, the past tense is used to indicate things of the past that no longer exist now. But in scientific English, the past tense may just indicate time sequences. For example:

- When steam is condensed again to water, the same amount of heat is given out as *was taken* in when the steam *was formed*. 当蒸汽重新冷却为水时，所释放出的热量与其原来形成蒸汽时所**吸收**的热量相等。

If we invert the sequence, there is no need for the past tense.

- When water is evaporated into steam, heat is taken in. When it is condensed again to water, the same amount of heat is given out. 当水蒸发为蒸汽时，吸收热量。当蒸汽重新冷却为水时，释放出相等的热量。

6. The Post-Position of the Attributive

The post-position of the attributive is a common phenomenon in EST. But in Chinese the attributive usually precedes the noun it modifies.

- Non-mobile robots, *capable of learning to perform an industrial task and then of being left to perform it tirelessly*, are even now in use in industrial plants all over the world. 非移动性机器人**能学会执行生产任务，然后就可以置之一旁不倦地工作**，这样的机器人甚至在今天也广泛用于世界各地的工厂。
- In radiation, thermal energy is transformed into radiant energy, *similar in nature to light*. 热能在辐射时转换成**性质与光相似的**辐射能。
- The force *upward* equals the force *downward* so that the balloon stays at the same height. 向上的力与向下的力相等，所以气球就保持在这一高度。

UNIT 13 English for Science and Technology and Its Translation

III. Methods of Translating EST

1. Expanding Noun Phrases into Separate Clauses

- *The slightly porous nature of the surface of the oxide film* allows it to be colored with either organic or inorganic dyes. 氧化膜表面具有轻微的渗透性，因此可以用有机或无机染料着色。
- This position was completely reversed by *Haber's development of the utilization of nitrogen from the air*. 由于哈伯发明了利用空气中的氮气的方法，这种局面就完全改观了。

2. Converting Noun Phrases into Verb-Object Structures

- *The building of these giant iron and steel works* will greatly accelerate the development of the iron and steel industry of our country. 建立这些大型钢铁厂会大大加速我国钢铁工业的发展。
- Two-eyed, present-day man has no need of such microscopic delicacy *in his vision*. 普通的现代人**看物体时**不需要达到这种显微镜般的精密程度。

3. Converting Attributive Elements into Independent Sentences, Adverbial Clauses, etc.

- This is an electrical method, *which is most promising* when the water is brackish. 这是一种电气方法。当水含盐时，**它最有希望**。
- Nowadays it is understood that a diet *which contains nothing harmful* may result in serious disease if certain important elements are missing. 现在人们已经懂得，如果饮食中缺少了某些重要成分，即使食物不含有任何有害物质，也会引起严重疾病。

4. Converting the Passive into the Active

- In the 16 months since the first graft, *the ersatz skin has not yet been rejected by any of the patients*. 第一次植皮后的 16 个月，人造皮肤在每个病人身上都还没有排异现象。
- Thin layers of other impermeable materials *are found* in nature, too. 在自然界中也**发现**有其他非渗透性薄层物质。
- Plants and trees *are provided by nature* with four means of dispersing their seeds. **大自然赋予**草木 4 种传播种子的方法。

5. Supplementing Necessary Words to Indicate Given Time

- It *was understood* that atoms were the smallest elements. It is known now that atoms are further divided into nuclei and electrons, neutrons and protons. 以前人们认为原子是最小的结构单元，现在才知道原子还可以分为原子核与电子、中子与质子。

- Although no one *has yet set* foot on Vesta, and no spacecraft *has been near*, planetary scientists *have obtained* conclusive evidence during the last decade that cold, silent Vesta *was once* the scene of volcanic activity. 尽管从未有人登上过灶神星，也从未有太空飞船飞近过灶神星，但是研究行星的科学工作者在最近10年中已经获得了可靠的证据证明寒冷而宁静的灶神星曾经是火山活动的场所。

Reflections and Practice

I. Discuss the following questions.

1. What are the reasons for the rapid growth of English technical terms?
2. What are the major forms and categories of English technical terms?
3. What are the sources of English proper nouns? Cite more examples to explain.
4. What is the characteristic syntax of English for science and technology?
5. What are the usual methods employed in the translation of EST?

II. Translate the following terms.

1. ball bearing, test bed, carrier rocket, pneumatic cushion, tractor shoe, monkey driver, ball cock, die plate, automatic pecker, worm auger, decay daughter, sister metal, foreign tissue, getter pump, ghost image, heel block, Chinese wood oil, rubber policeman, plastic surgery, nose cap, first aid, fire engine, skid chain, sweet water, drug-fast, vital capacity
2. I-bar, O-ring, T-square, zigzag rule, set square, octahedron, gable roof, cross stitch, arch dam, cam shaft, cone buoy, U-bar, U-bolt

III. Put the following English passages into Chinese, paying attention to technical terms.

1. Biochemistry is the study of the chemical processes in living organisms that deals with the structures and functions of cellular components such as proteins, carbohydrates,

UNIT 13 English for Science and Technology and Its Translation

lipids, nucleic acids and other biomolecules.

2. Early developments of the integrated circuit go back to 1949, when the German engineer Werner Jacobi (Siemens AG) filed a patent for an integrated-circuit-like semiconductor amplifying device showing five transistors on a common substrate arranged in a 2-stage amplifier arrangement.

3. The term clone is derived from a Greek word for "trunk, branch", referring to the process whereby a new plant can be created from a twig. In horticulture, the spelling clon was used until the 20th century; the final e came into use to indicate the vowel is a "long o" instead of a "short o".

4. Electrical engineering is a very broad area that may encompass the design and study of various electrical & electronic systems, such as electrical circuits, generators, motors, electromagnetic/electromechanical devices, electronic devices, electronic circuits, optical fibers, optoelectronic devices, computer systems, telecommunications and electronics.

5. The most well known implementation of high-speed maglev technology currently operating commercially is the IOS (initial operating segment) demonstration line of the German-built Transrapid train in Shanghai, China that transports people 30 km (18.6 miles) to the airport in just 7 minutes 20 seconds, achieving a top speed of 431 km/h (268 mph), averaging 250 km/h (160 mph).

6. The Science Citation Index (SCI) is a citation index originally produced by the Institute for Scientific Information (ISI) and created by Eugene Garfield in 1960, which is now owned by Thomson Reuters, covering more than 6,500 notable, and significant journals, across 150 disciplines such as life sciences, clinical medicine, physics, chemistry, agriculture, biology, veterinary science, engineering and technology, etc., from 1900 to the present.

7. Optical fibers are widely used in fiber-optic communications, which permits transmission over longer distances and at higher bandwidths (data rates) than other forms of communications. Fibers are used instead of metal wires because signals travel along them with less loss and are also immune to electromagnetic interference. Fibers are also used for illumination, and are wrapped in bundles so they can be used to carry images, thus allowing viewing in tight spaces.

8. Nanotechnology may be able to create many new materials and devices with a vast range of applications, such as in medicine, electronics, biomaterials and energy production. On the other hand, nanotechnology raises many of the same issues as with any introduction of new technology, including concerns about the toxicity and environmental impact of nanomaterials, and their potential effects on global

economics, as well as speculation about various doomsday scenarios.

IV. Point out mistakes in the following translation and correct them.

1. In 1827, he published the results in a paper titled *The Galvanic Chain, Mathematically Treated*. * 在1827年，他用《电流的链、数学化处理》为标题在报纸上出版了这个结果。

2. Great was his joyous pride when he proved to his own satisfaction, by patient experiments of his own, the explanations given in the lectures. * 当他由于自己勤奋的试验和讲课中所得到的解释显得满意时，他是兴高采烈的。

3. Scientific discoveries and inventions do not always influence the language in proportion to their importance. * 科学的发现与发明，就其重要性的比例而言，并不一定对语言有什么影响。

4. How wild his white hair looked—as if it had been electrified. * 他满头白发，十分凌乱——简直像刚电烫过一般。

5. The importance of superconductors in the uses of electricity cannot be overestimated. * 超导体在电器应用上的重要性不能被估计过高。

6. All your moods are created by your thoughts, or "cognitions". "You feel the way you do right now because of the thoughts you have at this moment." * 所有的情绪都是由思维产生的，或者说来源于"认识"。"你之所以感到这么做是对的，那是因为你的大脑就是这么想的。"

7. Afterwards he found a sunspot which lived long enough to disappear from view on the western limb of the sun, to reappear on its eastern limb, and finally to regain its old position. * 后来，他发现有一个停留在太阳西部的边缘上的黑子过了很长一段时间才消失在太阳的东部边缘上，最后再次获得了原位。

8. The new method reduced the use of solvent by fourfold. * 新方法将溶剂用量减少了四倍。

9. The pilot lamp stopped to represent the termination of the operation. * 指示灯停止显示操作终止。

10. If a designer were to design a bracket to support 100 lb. when it should have been figured for 1,000 lb., failure would be forthcoming. * 如果设计者所设计的托架能支撑100磅，当它被设计为1 000磅时，事故一定会出现。

Unit 14 The Translation of Documentation

单元要点概述

相关翻译技巧训练英译汉：Copyright

相关翻译技巧训练汉译英：文献

I. 合同与协议的翻译

II. 建议、报告与评论的翻译

III. 专利与商标的翻译

IV. 版权文献的翻译

V. 招标文献的翻译

VI. 摘要、索引与文献目录的翻译

本单元介绍、归纳了几种常见文献的语言特点及一般翻译方法。

文献资料包括的范围极广，从一般评论报告到商务合同、版权专利、招标竞标，等等。不同的文献有不同的语言特点，翻译时应有所区别。译者除自身的外语水平之外，最重要的是具有广博的综合知识和必要的专业知识。本单元用 6 个小标题分别介绍了 10 余种常见文献的特点和翻译要点。

1. 合同与协议：译者应熟悉合同、协议的内容，注意常规格式，规范译文措辞；2. 建议、报告与评论：此类文献内容繁杂，译者应了解原文的目的，熟悉题材内容，搞清撰写者与审阅者之间的关系，把握原文的口气；3. 专利与商标：专利文献有其严格的措辞和格式，译文应尽量与原文保持一致，商标翻译多用音译法，应注意保持原本的独特效果；4. 版权文献：翻译版权文献除了应注意其正式文体风格之外，亦应注意其客观的就事论事的态度；5. 招标文献：招标文献的文体极为正式，译文的风格应尽量与原文保持一致；6. 摘要、索引与文献目录：这类文献应尽量文字简洁，注意术语、专有名称的大小写、译名的约定俗成。

Practice of the Relevant Skill

1. E-C Translation

Copyright

Copyright, a body of legal rights that protect creative works from being reproduced, performed, displayed, or disseminated by others without permission. The owner of copyright has the exclusive right to reproduce a protected work; to prepare other works based on the protected work; to sell, rent, or lend copies of the protected work to the public; to perform protected works in public; and to display copyrighted works publicly. These basic exclusive rights of copyright owners are subject to exceptions depending on the type of work and the type of use made by others.

The term *work* used in copyright law refers to any original creation of authorship fixed in a tangible medium. Thus, works that can be protected by copyright include literary pieces, musical compositions, dramatic selections, dances, photographs, drawings, paintings, sculpture, diagrams, advertisements, maps, motion pictures, radio and television programs, sound recordings, and computer software programs.

Copyright does not protect an idea or concept; it only protects the way in which an author has expressed an idea or concept. If, for example, a scientist publishes an article explaining a new process for making a medicine, the copyright prevents others from copying the article, but it does not prevent anyone from using the process described to prepare the medicine. In order to protect the process, the scientist must obtain a patent.

Copyright is a legal protection extended to those who produce creative works. Originally only for books, copyright now extends to magazines, newspapers, maps, plays, motion pictures, television programs, computer program software, paintings, photographs, sculpture, musical compositions, choreographed dances, and similar works. Essentially a copyright protects an intellectual or artistic property.

This type of property is unusual because it is normally intended for public use or enjoyment. If an individual buys a copyrighted book, it belongs to him as an object. But making copies of it to sell or give away is illegal. This right belongs to the publisher, author, or whoever holds the copyright.

Notes and Explanations

1. body of legal rights 合法权利的体现
2. disseminate *v.* 散播，传播，宣传（注意翻译此句时需对定语从句进行灵活处理）

UNIT 14 The Translation of Documentation

3. exclusive right 专有权
4. reproduce v. 再生，复制（注意right后面5个并列不定式结构的翻译，可以考虑将其分别译作句子）
5. subject to 受……支配的，由……决定的
6. original creation of authorship 原作者的创作物
7. tangible medium 有形媒介
8. literary pieces 文学作品
9. musical compositions 音乐作品
10. motion pictures 电影片
11. prevent others from copying 阻止他人抄袭
12. choreographed dances 经设计的舞蹈动作
13. intend for 打算供……使用

2. C-E Translation

文 献

　　文献是指各类非书籍、非刊物类印刷材料，其覆盖面很广。根据学科专业，可细分为医学文献、技术文献(如软件文档、产品规格、数据表或专利)、法律文献、管理文献、历史文献等。也可指用于解释某一物体、系统或程序属性的任何可传授材料(如文本、视频、音频等)。文献也常常用来指工程文献或软件文献，通常为纸质册子或电脑可读文件(如超文本标记语言页面)，用以描述某一系统或产品的结构、成分，或描述其运作。常见的计算机软件、硬件的文献类型包括在线帮助、常见问题、操作方式和用户指南。

Notes and Explanations

1. 非书籍、非刊物类材料 the printed non-book or non-periodical materials
2. 根据学科专业 in terms of branches of learning
3. 细分 subdivide/fall into subfields
4. 管理文献 administrative documentation
5. 可传授材料 communicable material
6. 超文本标记语言 HTML (Hyper Text Mark-up Language)
7. 常见问题 FAQ (Frequently Asked Questions)
8. 操作方式 How-tos

　　Documentation refers to all the printed materials that are non-books or non-periodicals. This special field mainly includes: contracts/agreements, proposals, reports, patents, trademarks, copyrights, conference papers, product specifications, etc. This unit is going to present some major methods of translating English documentation.

Different documentary works may have different linguistic features although documentation of various kinds does have some similar characteristics in common. Therefore, we should treat the translation of each kind of documentary work discriminatingly. For example, when translating the patent documents, we should keep the stereotyped expressions and formal patterns, while trademarks should preserve their novelty and uniqueness so as to maintain their original emotions. Copyright works usually call for rigid grammar; whereas legal documents, contracts and agreements are characterized by their strict syntax, as well as their formal styles. And in the translation of proposals and reports, the matter-of-fact attitude is of chief concern.

Furthermore, as is mentioned in Unit 1, general knowledge and knowledge of the subject matter are also of vital importance. For there is always the problem of the subject matter involved in translation and we can hardly fulfill a given task of document translation without having adequate knowledge of the subject matter and the relevant background information.

I. The Translation of Contracts and Agreements

A contract is an agreement between two or more parties which is enforceable by law or by binding arbitration. Generally speaking, the form of contracts and agreements is usually fixed and some specific terms are frequently used in the texts. For example: preamble（序言）, clauses（条款）, exclusive（专有的、独家的）, licensed（许可的）, agency（代理权）, arbitration（仲裁）, product（产品）, knowhow（专有技术）, royalty（提成费）, force majeure（不可抗力）, party（一方、当事人）, hereinafter（以下）, whereas（因此）, hereby（以此）, whereof（以此）, wherein（其中）, etc. When translating document of contracts and agreements, due attention should be paid to the modal word "shall", which, when used in legal documents, no longer possesses the ordinary meaning of future tense used in the first persons, but "a command or what must be done", or "the responsibility and obligation that should be undertaken". For example:

- Neither party *shall* terminate this contract without reasonable cause prior to the agreed date of expiration. 双方均**不得**无故提前终止合同。

The following is a sample translation of the preamble of a contract between two corporations.

UNIT 14 **The Translation of Documentation**

English Version:

This CONTRACT is made this _____ day of _____, 20_____, in (place of signature) by and between (name of one party), a corporation duly organized and existing under the laws of (name of the country) with its domicile at (address) (hereinafter referred to as Party A) and (name of the other party) a corporation duly organized and existing under the laws of (name of the country) with its domicile at (address) (hereinafter referred to as Party B).

Whereas Party A has been engaged in the manufacture and marketing of (name of products), and possesses valuable up-to-date technology, relating to the manufacture, assembly and marketing of the said products; whereas Party B has been a leading trading company in the field of the said products and is willing to arrange for the manufacture, assembly and marketing of the said products, and whereas both parties are desirous to establish a joint venture company to manufacture, assemble and market the said products.

Therefore, in consideration of the premises and conventions herein contained and other good and valuable considerations flowing from either party to the other, the receipt whereof both parties by their execution of this Contract do hereby acknowledge, the parties hereby agree as follows:

…

Chinese Version:

本合同于20××年×月×日在（签订地点）签订。合同一方为（一方名称），是一家依照（国家名称）法律组织而存在的公司，其所在地为（地址）（以下简称甲方）；合同另一方为（另一方名称），是一家依照（国家名称）法律组织而存在的公司，其所在地为（地址）（以下简称乙方）。

鉴于甲方长期从事（产品名称）的制造和销售，并拥有制造、装配、销售上述产品的有价值的先进技术；鉴于乙方长期以来是一家经营上述产品的主要贸易公司，愿意安排上述产品的制造、装配和销售；鉴于双方都希望建立一家合资公司以便制造、装配和销售上述产品。

考虑到上述各点和本合同所载各项条款，以及双方通过签署本合同而确认收到的彼此间其他有效的有价报酬，双方特定此协议如下：

……

II. The Translation of Proposals, Reports and Reviews

Since proposals and reports fall into a variety of categories which concern a vast range of subjects, it is impossible to elaborate the ways of their translation. However, a summary of the gist and an illustration of the specific subject would be of some help. It is desirable to keep in mind the following tips:

1. The purpose of the subject matter

    Make sure if it is a suggestion or a request, or an offer to solve a particular problem, or something else.

2. The contents of the proposal or report

    Try your best to be familiar with the contents of the proposal, the technical terms, the specific means, measures and solutions, all in detail.

3. The relationship between or the identity of the writer and the receiver

    This is the guarantee for the faithful representation of the original writing.

4. The original tone and attitude

    Find out whether it is in a formal style, a semiformal style or an informal style and then reflect the original tone and attitude of the proposal in the Chinese version.

The following is an extract from "Proposal for Formal Report Project", a research proposal from a student to his professor, and the corresponding Chinese version.

English Version:

Dear Professor Doe,

    For my formal research report assignment, I propose to research the problem of computer security and produce a formal report that would be of value to office managers who have an interest in maintaining the confidentiality of electronically stored records.

    Since I am completing the requirement for a major in computer science and am contemplating graduate work in Business Administration, I have a strong academic interest in knowing just how secure computerized information is and how secure it can be. I also have an occupational interest in the subject because computer security has become a much-discussed subject in the office where I hold a part-time job as a Data Processor...

    Rather than spend a great deal of time trying to show the seriousness of the problem of insufficient security, I only want to assure a reader who already is of the opinion that lack of adequate security can be financially dangerous. Thus I would like to devote only the introduction of the report to showing how serious the problem is.

UNIT 14　**The Translation of Documentation**

The main body of the report would be divided into just two sections—one for the controls that are already widely practiced and one for those that are too new, too expensive, or too complicated to have become widely adopted. In the first section, I will investigate the reason why the established methods aren't as successful as they should be. In the second, I will evaluate the relative merits of the more exotic controls. This is my present plan of organization…

Chinese Version:

尊敬的 Doe 教授：

关于我的正式研究报告任务，我提议着手计算机的安全性问题，并提交一份对行政管理人员有价值的正式报告。这些人员对怎样维护电子存储记录的机密问题颇感兴趣。

我目前正在攻读计算机科学专业的必修课，并考虑做商务管理研究生，因此对目前计算机处理信息的安全性以及可能会达到什么样的安全程度产生了浓厚的专业兴趣。我也对这一课题产生了职业兴趣，因为在我打工的这家公司里（我担任公司的数据处理员），计算机的安全性已成为大家讨论最多的一个热门话题……

我不打算花大量的时间来说明计算机缺乏安全性这一问题的严重性。我只想让已有这种看法的读者确信：缺乏足够的安全防范，可能会导致经济危险。因此，我打算仅用报告的引言部分来说明该问题的严重性。报告的正文只分为两部分———一部分讨论已经广泛用于实践的操作控制，另一部分探讨不宜广泛地采用的一些太新、太昂贵或者太复杂的操作控制。在报告的第一部分，我将调查为什么现有的方法不像我们所期待的那样成功。在报告的第二部分，我将对一些更新奇的操作控制的相对优点做出评估。以下是我目前所计划的报告结构……

Reviews cover a vast range of various fields and miscellaneous categories. What we can advise the reader to do is to accumulate experience from constant practice. The following is a sample of review extracted from *Encarta 2005 Encyclopedia*.

English Version:

The history of computing began with an analog machine. In 1623 German scientist Wilhelm Schikard invented a machine that used 11 complete and 6 incomplete sprocketed wheels that could add and, with the aid of logarithm tables, multiply and divide.

French philosopher, mathematician, and physicist Blaise Pascal invented a machine in 1642 that added and subtracted, automatically carrying and borrowing digits from column to column. Pascal built 50 copies of his machine, but most served as curiosities in parlors of the wealthy. 17th century German mathematician Gottfried Leibniz designed a special gearing system to enable multiplication on Pascal's machine.

In the early 19th century French inventor Joseph-Marie Jacquard devised a specialized type of computer: a loom. Jacquard's loom used punched cards to program patterns that were output as woven fabrics by the loom. Though Jacquard was rewarded and admired by French emperor Napoleon I for his work, he fled for his life from the city of Lyon pursued by weavers who feared their jobs were in jeopardy due to Jacquard's invention. The loom prevailed, however, when Jacquard passed away, more than 30,000 of his looms existed in Lyon. The looms are still used today, especially in the manufacture of fine furniture fabrics.

Chinese Version:

机器计算的历史起始于一台模拟机。1623 年德国科学家 W. 施卡尔首创了一台模拟机，该机器利用 11 个完整的与 6 个不完整的链轮进行加法运算，并能借助对数表进行乘除运算。

法国哲学家、数学家和物理学家 B. 帕斯卡于 1642 年发明了可进行加减运算的机器，该机器可以自动进行竖式借位运算。帕斯卡将机器复制了 50 部，但其中的大多数成了富人客厅中引人好奇的摆设。17 世纪德国数学家 G. 莱布尼茨设计了一种特殊齿轮传动装置，能在帕斯卡的机器上进行乘法运算。

19 世纪初，法国发明家 J. M. 雅卡尔设计出一种专用计算机：织机。雅卡尔的织机利用打了孔的卡片为图样编制程序，而输出的是织好的布匹。尽管雅卡尔的发明受到法国皇帝拿破仑一世的奖赏和赞许，但他为了躲避织布工匠的追捕逃离了里昂城，亡命他乡——因为工匠们害怕他的发明会砸了大家的饭碗。然而，织机最终还是越来越流行。雅卡尔逝世时，里昂市的织机总量已超过 30 000 台。织机沿用至今，在精美家具布帘（垫）制造业尤甚。

III.　The Translation of Patents and Trademarks

Patent is an exclusive right to market an invention, an exclusive right officially granted by a government to an inventor to make or sell an invention. There are some stereotyped expressions and patterns in patent documents. A mastery of them would be of great help in translating them into Chinese. For instance, the various expressions with the word "claim" (What is claimed is... What I claim is... What we claim is... We claim... I claim...) may generally be translated as "请求权项""要求承认某人的所有权""专利权要求范围""本专利的权项范围是""我们（我）申请的专利是" and so on. Expressions such as "make reference to"（参考，提及），"copending"（与此有关的，尚待批准的）and so on, are frequently used in patent documents. Some expressions may have similar meanings or the same meaning in a patent document. For instance, such words and expressions as "relate to", "be concerned with", "pertain to", "deal with", etc., may either be translated as "有关""关于""涉及" or "相关", etc. in accordance with the context. On the other hand, some words in patent documents are very subtle and abstract. For instance, "embodiment" may be translated into a variety of Chinese expressions, such as "例子，实例，方案，试样，方法，装置，元件，器件，电路", and so on. Therefore, we should be cautious about wording in its translation.

The following are some more examples:

- Reference is made to our copending application No.38658/97 file 31 May, 1997. 请参阅我们在1997年5月31日登记的与此有关的申请书，其申请号为38658/97。
- This invention relates to methods for audio signal amplification and to audio amplifier circuitry and power supplies therefor. 本发明介绍的是音频信号放大的方法、音频放大电路及其电源。
- Figures 2 to 5 are schematic diagrams illustrating different embodiments of the inventive concept. 图2至图5为本发明具体机构的电路图。
- The operation of the embodiment of Figure 2 is identical to that of Figure 1. 图2的工作原理与图1相同。
- Figures 6 to 8 are perspective views of three alternative embodiments (keyholder) of the invention. 图6至图8是本发明三种不同形式的钥匙套的透视图。

Trademark is a name or symbol used to show that a product is made by a particular company and legally registered so that no other manufacturer can use it. The translation of trademarks is a very serious job which allows no arbitrary assumption. Since trademarks are exclusively monopolized, the coinage of their marks is generally characterized by novelty and uniqueness, defying existing words and expressions in the dictionary. There are usually three ways to create a trademark, namely, full coinage, such as Mack (the trademark of a truck made in the United States), Microsoft, Pentium, etc.; naming after the founder of an enterprise or the inventor of a new product, such as Ford, Bell, Marconi; names with abbreviations, such as the case is when the name of a company is used for a trademark. For instance, Kobelco（神钢，Kobe Steel Company Limited，神户钢铁有限公司），Siemens AG（西门子股份公司），Bayer HealthCare（拜耳医药保健有限公司），etc.

The most common method of translating trademarks is transliteration. For example: Coca-Cola 可口可乐，Canon 佳能，Xerox 施乐，Sharp 夏普，Sony 索尼，Kodak 柯达，etc.

Sometimes, a trademark happens to coincide with the name of the company, or its product. In this case, we should make a clear distinction between them before putting

them into Chinese. For instance:
- At IBM, developing information systems is just a part of our job.

"IBM" here refers to the company instead of a trademark, thus, the corresponding Chinese version should be: 在国际商用机器公司，开发信息系统仅是我们的部分工作。

IV. The Translation of Copyright Documents

Copyright document is an official document setting out the terms of a patent. In the translation of copyright regulations, due attention should be paid to the following points.

1. The formal style

   The language of copyrights is usually very formal and sometimes seems rigorous. When translated into Chinese, the original wording, style and form should be kept.

2. The matter-of-fact attitude

   As a kind of objective description, copyright document usually refrains from using pronouns. Instead, specific names for persons or things are given. More often than not, some key words and expressions are frequently repeated so as to avoid ambiguity.

3. Rigid grammar and frequent use of passive voice

   As a rule, copyright document keeps to a very strict English grammar. In accordance with the demand for objectivity, passive voice is frequently used.

The following paragraph is an excerpt from the introduction to Transfer of Copyright Agreement from American Association of Physics Teachers.

English Version:

Under U.S. copyright law, the transfer of copyright from the author(s) should be explicitly stated to enable the publisher to disseminate the work to the fullest extent. The following transfer must be signed and returned to the Editor's Office before the manuscript can be accepted for publication. Please note that if the manuscript has been prepared as a Work Made For Hire, the transfer should be signed by both employer and employee. Address requests for further information or exceptions to the Editor, *American Journal of Physics*, 222 Merrill Science Building. Box 2262 Amherst College, Amherst. MA 01002.

Chinese Version:

根据美国的版权法，作者的版权转让应当尽量陈述清楚，以便出版商能将作品在最大范围内传播。在原稿被接受出版之前，必须在以下的转让书上签名，并送交编辑部。请注意，如果原稿是"雇人之作"，转让书则应由雇主和被雇者同时签署。欲知有关进一步的信息，或有异议，请与《美国物理学报》编辑联系。联系地址：马萨诸塞州（邮编 01002）阿默斯特，阿默斯特学院 2262 信箱，梅里尔科学大楼 222 号。

V.   The Translation of Bid-Documents

Bid-documents as a highly specialized language genre use a strict syntax and their wording is very formal, free of any colloquial words, dialect, slang or ambiguous expressions. For instance, "commence" is used instead of "begin", "inform" is used for "tell", "purchase" for "buy", "revise" for "change", "augment" for "increase", "as per" for "based on", etc. And here is a typical sentence：

- The successful tenderer may be required to revise or augment his Program and Method Statements as set out in the Contract. 可以要求中标者对合同中的方案和方法说明加以修正和补充。

There are also some special terms used in tender documents which entail accurate wording in their translation. For instance:

bill of quantities（工程量清单）, prequalification（资格预审）, postqualification（资格后审）, eligible source country（合格来源国）, alternative offer（备选方案）, pretender meeting（标前会议）, performance security（履约保证）, notice to proceed（开工令）, award criteria（授标依据）.

The modal word "shall" is frequently used to indicate the obligation or responsibility on the parties concerned and compound adverbs such as "therefrom, thereto, thereof, hereinafter...", etc. are repeatedly used in tender documents so as to solemnize the style. For instance:

- The tenderer *shall* submit a basic tender which complies fully with the requirements of the tender documents. 投标者应提交一份完全符合招标文件要求的基本投标书。
- The Shanghai Sewerage Project Construction Company (*hereinafter* referred to as the Employer) will in no case be responsible for those costs. 上海市污水治理工程建设公司（以下称业主）在任何情况下将不承担这些费用。

The sentence structure of bid-documents is always complicated, with more passive voice structures and long sentences than other documents, as shown in the following illustration:

English Version:

International Tender

1. In order to be considered further by the Employer in the process of tender evaluation, each alternative shall be accompanied by a detailed price breakdown indicating the tender's estimate of the additional or reduced cost in present (discounted) value to the Employer compared with the basic Tender Sum, if the alternative offer were to be accepted by the Employer and incorporated into the Contract.

2. The tender shall submit a basic tender which complies fully with the requirements of the tender documents. The original and duplicates of the tender shall be typed or written in indelible ink and shall be signed by a person or persons duly authorized. Proof of authorization shall be furnished in the form of a written Power of Attorney which shall accompany the tender.

3. The employer will respond in writing to any request for clarification which is received more than 28 days prior to the deadline for submission of tenders. Written copies of the response will be sent to all tenders who have picked up the tender documents.

4. Any consequence of the tender's omission to notify SFECO that pages are missing or information is illegible will be considered the fault of the tender and any claim arising therefrom will be rejected.

Chinese Version:

国 际 招 标

1. 为了让业主在评标过程中做进一步的考虑，每一项备选方案应附有详细的标价细目分项，指出如果备选方案被业主接受并列入合同后，投标者关于备选方案价格与基本投标金额相比对业主按现值计算增加或减少的估计费用。

2. 投标者应提交一份完全符合招标文件要求的基本投标书。投标书的正本与副本应使用不褪色的墨水打印或书写，并应由正式授权过的一个或几个人签字。授权证明应按书面委托书的格式提交，并应附于投标书中。

3. 业主在截标 28 天前收到投标者提出的澄清要求后，将以书面形式予以答复。该答复的书面复印件将送至所有已获得招标文件的投标者。

4. 如果投标者不按上述要求通知 SFECO 文件有遗漏，或材料意义不清，由此造成的后果，应视为投标者的过失，由此引起的申诉不予受理。

UNIT 14 The Translation of Documentation

VI. The Translation of Abstracts, Indexes and Bibliographies

Since abstracts cover a vast range of categories, we can hardly summarize the translation methods in a few words. Nevertheless, a few points for attention may be of some help.

1. Be aware of the purpose of the abstract

   You should understand the purpose of the abstract to be translated, making sure whether a brief summary of the document is helpful to the reader.

2. Be familiar with the entire document

   Before settling down to translation work, try to have a global survey of the document, grasping its main idea, major sections and some key words.

3. Be succinct in wording

   As abstracts are characterized by their brief and concise nature, you should be succinct in wording and keep the same writing style in Chinese.

The following is an abstract of a dissertation from *Dissertation Abstracts International* (DAI) and its Chinese version.

English Version:

Environmental tobacco smoke (ETS) is a major source of indoor air pollution. A major point stressed in both the Surgeon General's Report and the National Academy of Science's Report is that methods used to determine the exposure of the nonsmoking population to ETS must be improved. In this dissertation, a semi-real time system for monitoring ETS is proposed and compared with other systems. Several new tracers for ETS are proposed. The generalization and decay of ETS in an indoor environmental laboratory is studied. A new technique for analyzing microgram and submicrogram amount of nicotine and cotinine biological fluids is developed. A unique study of exposure to ETS is to be carried out wherein neversmokers are exposed to ETS.

Much evidence has accumulated that fine particulate matter in the atmosphere affects human health and atmospheric properties. To monitor airborne particles, it is necessary to separate various particle sizes in the atmosphere and to determine the chemical compositions of the particles. A new high flow rate, multichannel parallel plate denuder sampling system has been developed which is capable of determining the particle size distributions and the semi-volatile organic compounds which can be lost from particles during sampling.

Chinese Version:

周围烟草烟(ETS)是造成室内空气污染的主要污染源。来自(美国)军医局局长和国家科学院的报告都着重强调了这一点：传统的用以确定有多少非吸烟者受到ETS危害的方法必须加以改进。本文提出了一种监控ETS的半实时系统，并将该系统与其他系统进行了比较。作者建议使用一些新的跟踪器对ETS进行监控，并对ETS在室内环境实验室的一般情况及衰减问题做了研究。作者研制了一项新技术分析尼古丁和可铁宁的生物液微克和亚微克量。并将对ETS进行一项独特的暴露研究，即将非吸烟者置于ETS环境里进行试验。

现今业已积累的大量证据表明，大气层中的微粒会影响人类健康和大气的性质。为了监控空气中的微粒，很有必要将大气层中各种微粒的大小分开，并确定其化学成分。已研制出一种新的高流速率，多通道平行盘溶蚀器取样系统，它能确定微粒大小的分布，以及在取样期间微粒失去的具有半挥发性的有机混合物。

The key to the translation of indexes lies in tackling proper names and paying due attention to the translation of professional terms of different branches of learning. For a certain word of common use in English may have different meanings according to different specialties and professions. For instance, "vector" is translated as "向量" in mathematics, but "矢量" in physics; "electric potential" is called "电势" in physics, but "电位" in electronics; "macromolecule" is called "大分子" in biology, but "高分子" in chemistry. The word "matrix", which originated from Latin with the original meaning of "womb" or "breeding animal", means "基质" in geology, "字模" "纸型" in printing, "基片" in medical science, "矩阵" in mathematics, "浮雕片" in photography, "矩阵变换电路" in communications, "主句" in linguistics, etc. Some words may even have more than a dozen Chinese equivalents. For instance, "load" may be translated as "负荷、负载、载荷、荷载、载重、荷重、加荷、加载、装载、充填、输入、存入", etc.; "ergonomics" may be translated as "人机学、工作环境改造学、工效学、功力学、功效学、劳作卫生学、劳动经济学、人体规律学、生物工艺学、人类环境改造学、人机功效学、人类工程学、人体工程学、人与机器控制、人机工程学", etc. Sometimes, the same English term may find several Chinese equivalents of the same meaning. For instance, "laser" may be translated as "激射光辐射放大、光受辐射放大、受激光辐射放大、光量子放大、收发激光、莱塞、激光", etc. "Internet" may be translated as "互联网、交互网、国际网、国际联网、国际互联网、国际交互网、国际网络、英特网、因特网", etc. In such cases, the standard established version should be preferable. Thus we pick "激光" for "laser", and "因特网" for "Internet".

Generally speaking, the translation of bibliographies is unnecessary. However, sometimes we do have to translate them in order to facilitate international communication. The problem that occurs most frequently in such translation is the proper rendering of the bibliographic titles.

UNIT 14 The Translation of Documentation

The translation of English bibliographic titles may be either literal or free translation, depending on different circumstances. Occasionally transliteration may be adopted to keep the original sounds.

- *The Adventures of Tom Sawyer* 《汤姆·索亚历险记》(literal translation)
- *Waterloo Bridge* 《魂断蓝桥》(free translation)
- *Gone with the Wind* 《飘》(literal translation),《乱世佳人》(free translation)
- *Uncle Tom's Cabin* 《汤姆叔叔的小屋》(literal translation),《黑奴吁天录》(free translation)
- *Oliver Twist* 《雾都孤儿》(free translation),《奥列佛·退斯特》(transliteration)

However, if there is an established Chinese version, we should follow suit, instead of making up one's own version. For example:

- *Genesis* 《创世记》
- *Chronicles* 《历代志》
- *Romans* 《罗马书》
- *Song of Solomon* 《雅歌》
- *Carve Her Name with Pride* 《女英烈传》
- *Wuthering Heights* 《呼啸山庄》
- *Red Star Over China* 《西行漫记》

Bibliographic titles in Chinese can be classified into five types: A. titles made up of phrases; B. titles of verbobject structure; C. titles containing a statement; D.titles with a question mark; E. titles plus a subtitle. Of all the five types A, C, E are the most prevalent. However, when these Chinese bibliographic titles are translated into English, they should be adapted to English usage by omission, amplification, conversion or rearrangement, as shown in the following illustrations.

- 《马恩早期著作中关于科学技术的思想》(a title made up of phrases) *Marx's and Engels' Views on Science and Technology as Reflected in Their Earlier Works*
- 《论蔡锷》(a title of verbobject structure) *On Cai E, a Leader of the Revolt Against the Restoration of Monarchy in 1915*
- 《试论我国建设社会主义时期反封建残余的斗争》(a title with a verb plus a compound object) *The Struggle Against Vestiges of Feudalism in Socialist China*
- 《章太炎是什么派？》(a title with a question mark) *The Political Stand of Zhang Taiyan*
- 《再现人物神韵的典范——王佐良译〈雷雨〉欣赏》(a title plus a subtitle) *On Wang Zuoliang's English Version of the Chinese Play Thunderstorm*
- 《农业现代化是扩大就业的物质基础》(a title containing a statement) *Modernization of Agriculture as the Material Basis for Enlarged Employment*

Reflections and Practice

I. Discuss the following questions.

1. What is documentation? What does it mainly include?
2. What are the linguistic features of contracts and agreements? Cite an example to explain.
3. What do you know about proposals, reports, patents and trademarks?
4. What are the linguistic features of copyright documents and bid-documents?
5. What should we do in translating abstracts, bibliographies and indexes?
6. What are the points for attention in translating bid-documents?
7. Is it necessary for us to translate abstracts, bibliographies and indexes in usual cases? What should we do if we do need to translate them?

II. Put the following documentation into Chinese.

1. Contract

Contract, in law, is an agreement that creates an obligation binding upon the parties thereto. The essentials of a contract are as follows: (1) mutual assent; (2) a legal consideration, which in most instances need not be pecuniary; (3) parties who have legal capacity to make a contract; (4) absence of fraud or duress; and (5) a subject matter that is not illegal or against public policy.

In general, contracts may be either oral or written. Certain classes of contracts, however, in order to be enforceable, must be written and signed. These include contracts involving the sale and transfer of real estate; contracts to guarantee or to answer for the miscarriage, debt, or default of another person, etc.

2. Report

The General Manager,
Acme Electronics Ltd.,
Canberra, ACT2600.

Dear Sir,

UNIT 14 The Translation of Documentation

RENOVATIONS, 153 HILLCREST

You instructed me on 20th June, 1998 to report on the repairs and renovation needed at the Company's premises at 153 Hillcrest. I accordingly visited the premises on 25th June and made the following observations:

(1) That the walls of the Branch Office Manager's office need to be repainted.

(2) That the air-conditioning plant needs to be serviced in the near future.

(3) That the carpet in the reception hall is very worn and needs to be replaced by a new one.

(4) That the lock on the rear door of the premises can very easily be forced and needs to be replaced by a stronger "dead lock".

(5) That an additional telephone is needed in the General Office.

I therefore recommend that the Maintenance Office be instructed to carry out the renovations 1-4 above and that the Telephone Company be requested to install an additional receiver in the General Office on the same line as the existing receivers.

Yours faithfully,
(Signature)
C. S. Spencer
Maintenance Engineer

3. Instruction

Selection of papers for presentation and inclusion in the digest will be made on the basis of abstracts submitted by intending authors. Abstracts and any supporting figures must be confined to a single A4 or 210×297mm page.

The letter accompanying the abstract must include the principal author's complete mailing address and fax number. All abstracts must be received by 6 December, 1992.

Forward abstracts to the Technical Program Chairman: (omitted)

Following review of abstracts by the Technical Committee authors will be advised by 6 March, 1993 whether or not their papers have been accepted. All papers must be in English.

Complete papers, of length up to 4 pages, will be sought at that stage and must be received by 8 May, 1993. The digest will be prepared directly from photo-ready materials submitted by authors and be provided to conference attendees.

4. Trademarks

Trademarks are federally registered in the U.S. Patent and Trademark Office of the Department of Commerce. When a trademark owner applies for registration, the office will examine the application to see if the mark meets the conditions of federal law. One important condition is that the trademark is not confusingly similar to a mark previously registered or used in the United States. Under a 1996 revision to the law, the owners of famous trademarks may seek to prevent use of similar marks, even if used by unrelated products. On approval of the application, the trademark is published in the official gazette to enable any objections to be heard in an opposition proceeding. If a registration is granted, it lasts for ten years and may be renewed at tenyear intervals for as long as the trademark is still in use. Once a federal registration has been obtained, the owner may give notice by using the symbol ® next to the trademark.

Anyone who uses a mark so similar to a registered trademark that it is likely to cause customers confusion is an infringer and can be sued in a state or federal court. In deciding whether there is infringement, the court compares the conflicting trademarks as to similarity in sound, appearance, and meaning, and compares the similarity of the goods and services. Other relevant factors include whether the competing parties' goods are sold to similar customers, through similar channels of trade, and the fame of the marks. Unlike patent or copyright infringement, trademark infringement is defined solely by the likely confusion of customers. The usual remedy after a court trial finding trademark infringement is an injunction prohibiting the infringer from using its mark.

5. Bibliography

Bibliography (Greek *bibliographia*, "the writing of books"), originally, the writing or copying of books; since the mid-18th century, the word has come to mean a list of books or other forms of written material, or the technique of compiling such a list. Certain kinds of information are supplied in a bibliography: authors, titles, editions, and dates and places of publication; style of type, book size, and other physical characteristics may also be included. Frequently, bibliographies are annotated, that is, brief notes indicating the subject treated or commenting on the usefulness of a book are appended. Bibliographies, essential to scholars and those involved professionally with book-collectors, librarians, and dealers, can be useful sources of information for all serious readers.

Bibliography may be divided into two broad types: analytic (sometimes called critical) and descriptive. Analytic bibliography is concerned with books as objects; it uses the evidence of physical features (for example, the kind of paper and printing idiosyncrasies) to establish authorship or judge the reliability of variant texts. Descriptive bibliography, with which this article is concerned, is the systematic enumeration of publications; it is, in turn, divided into universal, or general, bibliography and selective bibliography. General bibliographies may list works on several subjects, published in various countries and at different times. Selective bibliographies are limited, perhaps, to a particular subject, to the country of origin, to works of one author, or to books for a particular purpose or audience.

III. Put the following passages into English.

1. 合同

……

中途终止合同。双方均不得提前终止合同。受聘方如中断合同，必须在离华前一个月向聘方提出书面申请，未经聘方同意，受聘方仍需照常工作。聘方自同意之日起的两周后，停发工资，并停止提供受聘方及其家属的有关待遇。回国的一切费用自理。

受聘方违反中国法令，聘方有权提出解聘。自提出解聘之日起一个月内工资照发，但受聘方应在此期间安排回国。聘方负担受聘方及其家属在中国境内的旅费。国际旅费自理。

对渎职的受聘方，聘方有权提出解聘。自提出解聘之日起一个月内，安排受聘方回国。受聘方及其家属回国的旅费，由聘方负担，其他费用自理……

受聘方因健康原因，经医生证明连续病休两个月后仍不能继续工作，聘方有权提前终止合同。聘方提供受聘方及其家属回国的飞机票。

本合同用中、英两种文字写成，两种文字具有同等效力。

2. 专利

美洲的第一批发明专利是于 1642 年由殖民政府发布的。1790 年美国的首部专利法根据《宪法》第一条第八款在国会获得通过，该项法令由一个三人委员会监督实施，这三人分别为美国国务卿、陆军部长和司法总长。美国现行专利体系是在 1836 年 7 月 4 日通过的法令的基础上建立起来的。很多立法条例修改了最早的专利法，其中最重要的有 1870 年 7 月 8 日通过的法令，以及后来的 1952 年 7 月 19 日法令。后者修订和整理了专利法，和修正案一起，构成了现行专利法。1849 年专利局成为内政部的一部分，1925 年总统颁布行政命令，将专利局转属商业部管辖。1975 年 1 月 2 日，更名为专利商标局。

3. 索引与文摘

索引与文摘这两种文献包括原材料目录和文献目录。索引包括任何当前出版材料中的无数文献目录，通常为期刊文章的文献目录。有时候，一些图书馆会主动提供材料，帮助读者查找期刊文章。例如，美国国家医学图书馆已出版了名为 Medicus 的索引，每月列出全世界 3 500 家生物医学期刊中的文章索引。在其他一些情况下，各科学团体也主动采取了相应的措施。早在 20 世纪初，美国化学学会就开始为化学工作者准备索引和文摘，以帮助他们在自己的领域获得相关的文献信息。同时，英国物理研究院在物理领域也采取了类似的步骤。由纽约市 H. W. Wilson 公司出版的长卷索引目录系列尽管主要限于美国出版界，却涵盖了众多的学术领域，因而蜚声世界，为各国学者所广泛使用。这种以某个国家为重点的索引目录引起了别国的仿效，如《现行技术索引目录》(英国)和《英国教育索引目录》等。

Unit 15 Application Documents for Studying Abroad

> ● 单元要点概述
>
> 相关翻译技巧训练汉译英：自我陈述
> I. 留学目标定位
> II. 个人简历的翻译
> III. 推荐信的翻译
> IV. 自我陈述的翻译

出国留学申请的翻译属于实用文体类，需要翻译的主要内容包括成绩报告单、各类证明书、推荐信、申请书、个人简历、自我陈述等。

一般来说，留学申请应当用英语进行写作，但对于大多数中国学生来说，往往不能一步到位，需将精心准备的个人资料翻译成英语。相对而言，成绩报告单、各类证明书、申请书之类的翻译都有比较固定的格式，翻译起来较为容易。个人简历、推荐信、自我陈述等因人而异。尤其是个人陈述，自成一体，独具个性，因此翻译起来难度较大。本单元从汉译英的角度，对几种常见出国申请文件的翻译做了介绍，包括个人简历、成绩单、推荐信、自我陈述等，并用英汉对照的方式为大家提供了几个成功出国申请的完整案例。

Practice of the Relevant Skill

C-E Translation

个人陈述（人文专业）

打记事起近 20 年来，我就从没见父亲上过医院。这并不是因为他身强体壮，而是因为根本就上不起医院。作为一个在中国农村贫困家庭中长大的女孩，我深知乡下人对付小病最好的办法就是硬扛着。而一场大病对全家来说往往无异于灭顶之灾。

所以，一听说 EM 项目，我便马上想到了父亲。每次假期回家，我都见到日渐苍老、疾病缠身的父亲。他年迈体衰，成天咳嗽不止，徒劳地与命运抗争。每次见面，除了安慰他保重身体之外，别无他法。我感到心如刀绞，一股自责和内疚感涌上心头。事实上，这并不仅仅是我一个家庭的遭遇，上亿中国农民，都没有享受到任何的医疗保障。

美国社会学家C.赖特·米尔斯曾经说过，一项好的社会科学研究计划，应该是源于民众个人烦恼的公众问题研究。如果说以前我只能把这种个人烦恼埋藏在心里的话，那么现在，这个项目则为我提供了一个机会，将它与更广泛的公众问题联系起来。我开始感觉到，也许我可以为我的父辈们做些什么。

EM项目在中国的启动具有深远的现实意义。自1978年中国改革开放以来，中国政府事实上一直在坚持一种以市场化为取向的医疗改革，公共卫生福利在很大程度上被忽略了，由此带来了许多不公平的现象。农村居民无法享受最基本的医疗保障，就是明显的表现。因此，如何从世界先进国家的成功模式中吸取经验，并结合中国的实际情况，创造出一种能给全体中国人，尤其是占人口大多数的农民带来福利的公共健康制度，是广大民众的迫切希望，也是我们这一代青年的职责。欧洲的福利制度在世界上独树一帜，正是我们必须关注和学习的对象。反过来，中国的探索和经验，也会给欧洲带来启迪。

EM项目为我提供了一个了解欧洲卫生福利制度的机会，而我在国内四年的本科学习，则为我赢得这个机会奠定了基础。在大学生活的头两年里，我接受了包括社会学、政治学、经济学、历史和哲学在内的人文社科的通识教育。这使我获得了大多数中国学生所不具备的广阔的知识面。大三时，我选择哲学作为自己的专业，迅速培养并提高了我的反思和批判精神。与此同时，正如我的CV所展现的那样，我还积极参加了一些学术实地调查研究，这让我对社会科学的研究方法有了亲身的实践。

"万事俱备，只欠东风。"我已为此次航行做好了准备，现在所需要的只是一个机会。我希望能有幸加入EM项目。这样我就能在若干年后，作为一个使者，将欧罗巴先进的卫生福利理念带回祖国。届时，我将和千千万万志同道合的朋友们一道，致力于中国的卫生福利事业，让全国人民，无论在城市还是乡村，都能享受到公平、健全、高效的医疗卫生福利。

Notes and Explanations

1. 硬扛着 put up with it
2. 无异于一场灭顶之灾 no less than a disaster
3. EM卫生福利项目 Erasmus-Mundus of Health and Welfare，由欧盟提供各类奖学金，全奖为42 000欧元
4. 年迈体弱，成天咳嗽不止 coughing ceaselessly all day in senile weakness
5. 感到内疚，心如刀绞 so conscience-stricken and painful that my heart ached as if it was stabbed with a knife
6. C.赖特·米尔斯 Charles Wright Mills（1916-1962）美国社会学家

UNIT 15 Application Documents for Studying Abroad

7. 以市场化为导向的 market-oriented
8. 反思和批判的精神 reflective spirits and critical thinking
9. "万事俱备，只欠东风" All is ready except for the east wind to raise the sail.
10. 公平、健全、高效的卫生福利制度 a fair, sound, efficient health welfare system

Application documents for studying abroad usually include school report, graduation certification, application letter, letters of recommendation, résumé(curriculum vitae), personal statement, etc. Strictly speaking, all these documents should be written in English without any translation. However, owing to their limitations of English, many of the applicants have to translate them from the elaborate Chinese version—a roundabout way to success.

I. Orienting Your Target

Before starting your application, you should set your goal: studying in U.S. or U.K.? And how about universities in Canada or Australia? Top 10 universities or top 50, top 100? Studying for master degree or doctor degree? On scholarship or paying tuition? With a clear idea about your target, you may then browse the websites of relevant universities to find the right university and proper program that suits your purpose well. For instance, if you are a top student of a Chinese key university and wish to study at Harvard University in the United States, you may access the following website:

http: //www.harvard.edu/admissions/index.php

Under the home page you may see

1. Undergraduate Admissions & Aid

2. Graduate & Professional Schools

Doctoral Program

Harvard Graduate School of Arts and Sciences

Harvard Graduate School of Education

Harvard Law School

Harvard Medical School

Advanced Graduate Education

Harvard School of Engineering and Applied Sciences

3. Continuing Education

Harvard Extension School

…

And then, you may download related forms to be filled out and prepare your application documents in light of the requirement of schools or departments concerned.

II. Résumé (Curriculum Vitae)

A résumé (also known as curriculum vitae, personnel vita, or autobiographical statement) is a document used by individuals to present their background and qualifications. A typical résumé contains a summary of relevant personal experience and education. One of the first items of application documents for studying abroad, a typical résumé usually covers 4 parts: a. personal data, such as the name, sex, date of birth, address, postcode, telephone number, email address, hobbies, etc.; b. education background or experience; c. scholastic honors; d. reference. And the following is a sample of original Chinese résumé and its English translation.

个 人 简 历

个人基本情况

姓名：刘××

出生日期：1994 年 9 月 28 日

通信地址：北京清华大学紫荆公寓 1 号楼 705A

邮编：100084

手机：＋86 1512000××××

E-mail：liuy-08@mails.tsinghua.edu.cn

教育背景

2007.8—2010.6	就读于天津市南开实验中学
2010.8—2013.6	就读于天津市第一中学
2013.8—今	就读于清华大学化学系

社会工作

2014.4	马约翰杯羽毛球赛志愿者
2014.9—2015.9	清华大学学生会外联部干事

2015.10	紫荆志愿服务队校园导游
2015.10—今	基科班副班长

科研工作

2014.9—2015.7	在梁××教授实验室研究微流控芯片管道及阀门设计
2015.9—今	在李××教授实验室研究生物传感以及化学发光检测

主要奖励

2014.9	获清华大学化学系系内奖学金
2015.9	获全国大学生数学建模大赛北京赛区二等奖

计算机应用技能

正在攻读计算机技术与应用第二学位

精通 MATLAB 以及 Origin 等工程以及统计软件使用

熟练掌握 C++，C 以及 Pascal 等编程语言

熟练使用 Windows 操作系统，以及 Microsoft Office 系列办公软件

英语技能

擅长英语口语以及英文写作，已完成 GRE 的写作测试部分，正在准备 6 月份的笔试

CET-6: 553/710 (2014.12)

清华大学英语水平 I 考试：80/100（口语：13.2/15，笔试：66.8/85; 2016.3）

TOEFL IBT: 102/120（写作：29/30，口语：23/30，阅读：25/30，听力：25/30; 2016.3）

个人爱好

电影、纪录片、阅读（历史、地理以及人文类）、音乐

推荐人

周××	清华大学化学系学生工作处老师
电话	010-6277××××
卢××	天津市第一中学校长
电话	022-2413××××

Résumé

Personal Details

Name: Liu ××

Date of birth: Sept. 28, 1994

Address: Room 705A, Zijing Building No.1, Tsinghua University, Beijing, P. R. China

Post Code: 100084

Cell phone number: + 86 1512000××××

E-mail: liu-y08@mails.tsinghua.edu.cn

Education

Aug. 2013-present	Department of Chemistry, Tsinghua University, P. R. China
Aug. 2010-June 2013	No.1 Senior High School, Tianjin, P. R. China
Aug. 2007-June 2010	Nankai Experimental Middle School, Tianjin, P. R. China

Social Services

Oct. 2015-present	Co-Monitor of Class Fundamental Science
Oct. 2015	Campus tour guide of the Zijing Volunteer Team
Sept. 2014-June 2015	Member of the Student Union in charge of liaison, Tsinghua University
Apr. 2014	Volunteer for the Ma Yuehan Cup badminton contest

Research Experience

Sept. 2015-present	Participant in biosensing and chemiluminescent detecting in Prof. Li ××'s research group
Sept. 2014-July 2015	Participant in designing valves and tubes of microfluidic chips in Prof. Liang ××'s research group

Honors & Awards

Sept. 2015	Second prize in National Mathematical Contest in Modeling, held in Beijing
Sept. 2014	Academic Scholarship of Dept. of Chemistry, Tsinghua University

Computer Skills

Candidate for a second degree in Application of Computer Technology

Skilled in engineering and statistical software including MATLAB and Origin

Experienced in programming languages of C ++, C and Pascal

Proficient in Windows operating system, skilled application of Microsoft Office series of Office software

English Proficiency

Skilled in writing and oral English, having taken the analytical writing of GRE test and now preparing for the general test to be held in the coming June

College English Test Band 6: 553/710 (Dec. 2014)

English Proficiency Test I of Tsinghua University: 80/100 (Speaking 13.2/15, Written Test 66.8/85; Mar. 2016)

TOEFL IBT: 102/120 (Writing 29/30, Speaking 23/30, Reading 25/30, Listening 25/30; Mar. 2016)

Hobbies & Interests

movies, documentaries, reading (history, geography and humanities) and music

Reference

Zhou ××	Teacher of Student Service Office, Department of Chemistry, Tsinghua University
Tel	010-6277××××
Lu××	Headmaster of Tianjin No.1 Senior High School
Tel	022-2413××××

III. School Transcript (Academic Record)

School transcript refers to an official college document that shows a list of a student's classes and the results they received. Besides the original Chinese transcript, an equivalent English version is required, as can be seen from the following sample.

The original Chinese transcript (1: 1.5 scale)

清华大学学生历年学习成绩表

第 1 页/共 1 页

姓名	许可	学号	2000012392	性别	男	系所名	化学系	专业名	化学
班级	化学01	入学日期	2000年09月07日	毕业日期		2004年07月08日	学制		4年

课程名	学分	成绩	考试时间	课程名	学分	成绩	考试时间
体育(1)	1	73	2001-01	可持续发展与环境保护概论	1	通过	2001-01
计算机文化基础	2	优秀	2001-01	思想道德修养	2	85	2001-01
无机化学A(1)	4	83	2001-01	微积分(1)	5	86	2001-01
无机化学实验A(1)	1.5	85	2001-01	几何与代数(1)	3	74	2001-01
军事理论	2	91	2001-06	计算机图形学	3	95	2001-06
分析化学A	3	93	2001-06	微积分(2)	5	84	2001-06
体育(2)	1	83	2001-06	科技英语(1)	2	通过	2001-06
大学物理(1)	5	91	2001-06	科技英语视听说	2	81	2001-06
数理逻辑基础	1	88	2001-06	无机化学A(2)	2	85	2001-06
法律基础	2	75	2001-06	无机化学实验A(2)	2	90	2001-06
<<老子>>与<<庄子>>	2	90	2001-06	毛泽东思想概论	3	83	2001-06
化学现状与未来	1	通过	2001-06	集中军训	2	84	2001-09
西方文学选读	2	87	2002-01	分析化学实验A	3	91	2002-01
随机数学方法	3	86	2002-01	马克思主义政治经济学原理	3	93	2002-01
有机化学A(1)	4	81	2002-01	面向对象与可视化程序设计	4	优秀	2002-01
物理实验(1)	2	91	2002-01	法律文化概论	2	90	2002-01
体育(3)	1	88	2002-01	大学物理(2)	4	100	2002-01
几何与代数B(2)	2	95	2002-01	物理学前沿讲座	1	通过	2002-01
量子力学	2	98	2002-06	英语高级口语	2	95	2002-06
交响音乐赏析	1	通过	2002-06	邓小平理论概论	3	83	2002-06
物理化学A(1)	3	95	2002-06	有机化学实验A(1)	2	86	2002-06
有机化学A(2)	3	95	2002-06	物理实验(2)	2	94	2002-06
电工与电子技术	4	100	2002-06	计算机软件技术基础	3	优秀	2002-06
体育(4)	1	80	2002-06	数理方程引论	2	68	2002-06
数据结构	3	100	2002-06	大学生研究训练项目(SRT)	2	96	2002-09
电子工艺实习(集中)	2	87	2002-09	有机化学实验A(2)	2	86	2002-11
工程经济学	2	92	2003-01	物理化学实验A(1)	3	90	2003-01
物理化学A(2)	4	94	2003-01	物理学史和物理学方法	2	94	2003-01
影视欣赏	2	88	2003-01	体育专项(1)	1	91	2003-01
近代物理实验B(1)	3	94	2003-01	专业英语(1)	2	优秀	2003-01
结构化学	4	97	2003-01	天体物理前沿讲座	2	100	2003-01
英语水平考试I	12	96	2003-04	文献检索与利用(化工类)	1	97	2003-07
物理化学实验A(2)	3	95	2003-07	马克思主义哲学原理	3	96	2003-07
计算机硬件技术基础	4	98	2003-07	天然产物化学	2	95	2003-07
有机电子学的发展及其应用	2	91	2003-07	体育专项(2)	1	90	2003-07
仪器分析A	4	88	2003-07	高等无机化学	2	94	2003-07
高分子化学导论	4	96	2003-07	专业英语(2)	2	优秀	2003-07
中级化学实验	4	优秀	2003-09	配位化学	2	98	2004-01
体育专项(3)	1	80	2004-01	仪器分析实验A	2	87	2004-01
催化动力学	2	95	2004-01	统计热力学	3	92	2004-01
高等有机化学	3	89	2004-01	生物化学原理	4	90	2004-01
体育专项(4)	1	90	2004-06	综合论文训练	15	96	2004-06

已获总学分数:	227.5	获得学位:	理学学士	系主任签字:	(盖章)
第二学位专业:	————	获得学位:	————		成绩单专用章
备注:					

注: 重-重修课　　　制表人: 姜玲　　　制表日期: 2004-07-01

UNIT 15 Application Documents for Studying Abroad

The English version (1: 3 scale)

TSINGHUA UNIVERSITY STUDENT ACADEMIC RECORD (ENGLISH TRANSLATION)

Page 1 of 1

Name	Xu Ke	Date of Birth	1982/12	Date of Admission	2000/09	Department	Department of Chemistry
Sex	Male	Student Number	20000123392	Schooling	4 years	Date of Graduation	2004/07	Specialty	Chemistry

Course	Credits	Record	Exam Date	Course	Credits	Record	Exam Date
Physical Culture(1)	1	73	2001-01	Introduction to Sustainable Development	1	Pass	2001-01
Fundamentals of Computer Literacy	2	Excellence	2001-01	Ideological and Moral Education	2	85	2001-01
Inorganic Chemistry A(1)	4	83	2001-01	Calculus(1)	5	86	2001-01
Lab. of Inorganic Chemistry A(1)	1.5	85	2001-01	Geometry and Algebra(1)	3	74	2001-01
Military Course(1)	2	91	2001-06	Computer Graphics	3	95	2001-06
Analytical Chemistry A	3	93	2001-06	Calculus(2)	5	84	2001-06
Physical Culture(2)	1	83	2001-06	English of Science and Technology(1)(Reading)	2	Pass	2001-06
Physics(1)	5	91	2001-06	English for Science and Technology(Video)	2	81	2001-06
Mathematical Logic	1	88	2001-06	Inorganic Chemistry A(2)	2	85	2001-06
Fundamentals of Law	2	75	2001-06	Lab. of Inorganic Chemistry A(2)	2	90	2001-06
"Lao zi" and "Zhuang zi"	2	90	2001-06	Introduction to Mao Zedong's Thought	3	83	2001-06
Chemistry's Today and Tomorrow	1	Pass	2001-09	Military Course(2)	3	84	2001-09
Selected Readings in Western Literature	2	87	2002-01	Lab. of Analytical Chemistry A	3	91	2002-01
Stochastic Mathematical Methods	3	86	2002-01	Principle of Marxist Political Economics	3	93	2002-01
Organic Chemistry A(1)	4	81	2002-01	Object Oriented and Visual Programming	4	Excellence	2002-01
Lab. of Physics(1)	2	91	2002-01	An Introduction to Legal Culture	2	90	2002-01
Physical Culture(3)	1	88	2002-01	Physics(2)	4	100	2002-01
Geometry and Algebra B(2)	2	95	2002-01	Current Research Topics of Physics	1	Pass	2002-01
Quantum Mechanics	2	98	2002-06	Advanced English Speaking	2	95	2002-06
Appreciation of Symphony Music	1	Pass	2002-06	A Survey of Deng Xiaoping's Theory	3	83	2002-06
Physical Chemistry A(1)	3	95	2002-06	Lab. of Organic Chemistry A(1)	2	86	2002-06
Organic Chemistry A (2)	3	95	2002-06	Lab. of Physics(2)	2	94	2002-06
Electrical Engineering and Applied Electronics	4	100	2002-06	Fundamentals of Computer Software Technique	3	Excellence	2002-06
Physical Culture(4)	1	80	2002-06	Introduction to Methods of Mathematics and Physics	2	68	2002-06
Data Structure	3	100	2002-06	Students Research Training	2	96	2002-09
Electronic Working Technology Practice	2	87	2002-09	Lab. of Organic Chemistry A(2)	2	86	2002-11
Engineering Economics	2	92	2003-01	Lab. of Physical Chemistry A(1)	3	90	2003-01
Physical Chemistry A(2)	4	94	2003-01	Physics History and Physical Methods	2	94	2003-01
From the Silver Screen: English Films Appreciation	2	88	2003-01	Physical Culture	1	91	2003-01
Lab. of Modern Physics B(1)	3	94	2003-01	Speciality-reading in English(1)	2	Excellence	2003-01
Structural Chemistry	4	97	2003-01	Seminars on Frontiers of Astrophysics	2	100	2003-01
English Level Test I	12	96	2003-04	Literature Searching and Utilization(Chem.Eng.)	1	97	2003-07
Lab. of Physical Chemistry A(2)	3	95	2003-07	The Principle of Marxist Philosophy	3	96	2003-07
Fundamentals of Computer Hardware Technology	4	98	2003-07	Natural Product Chemistry	2	95	2003-07
The Development and Application of Organic Electronics	2	91	2003-07	Physical Culture	1	90	2003-07
Instrumental Analysis A	4	88	2003-07	Advanced Inorganic Chemistry	2	94	2003-07
Introduction to Polymer Chemistry	4	96	2003-07	Speciality-reading in English(2)	2	Excellence	2003-07
Intermediate Chemical Experiments	4	Excellence	2003-09	Coordination Chemistry	2	98	2004-01
Physical Culture	1	80	2004-01	Lab. of Instrumental Analysis(A)	2	87	2004-01
Catalytic Kinetics	2	95	2004-01	Statistical Thermodynamics	3	98	2004-01
Advanced Organic Chemistry	3	89	2004-01	Principles of Biochemistry	4	98	2004-01
Physical Culture	1	90	2004-06	Diploma Project(Thesis)	15	98	2004-06

Total Credits in All Academic Years	227.5	Academic Degree	Bachelor of Science
Minor in		Academic Degree	

Note: R: Repeat
System I (examination): One Hundred Scores (Less Than 60 Fail) System II (non-examination): Pass, Fail, Excellence

Table Maker: Jiang Ling   Date: 2004-07-01

Official Seal

IV. Letter of Recommendation

Letter of recommendation, also called recommendation letter, letter of reference, or reference letter, is a letter in which the writer makes a general assessment of the qualities, characteristics, and capabilities of a person, or confirms details about that individual's situation or circumstances. Two or three such letters are needed to apply for entrance to a foreign university. When translating such documents we should be careful in meticulous wording, keeping the original formal writing style. And the following is a sample of a letter of recommendation and its English translation.

尊敬的女士 / 先生：

我很高兴地向贵校推荐我的学生聂 ×× 女士。聂 ×× 在大三时上过我在清华大学开设的"广义相对论"，是当时班上最优秀的学生之一。她的优秀不仅表现在学习态度勤奋，而且还表现在思维方式活跃，这两点都给我留下了深刻印象。

聂 ×× 具有扎实的物理数学基础。她经常在课下和我就广义相对论的一些物理概念进行讨论，由此可见她对理论思路清晰，理解透彻。同时她还主动完成课上省略的推导，仔细进行复杂的计算。广义相对论这门课本是为大四学生而设，但聂 ×× 同学取得了考试满分的成绩，名列全班第一。

聂 ×× 善于积极思考、独立钻研。在不知道前人工作的前提下，她把广义相对论知识和已学过的热力学统计物理知识相联系，由此产生了对弯曲时空中的热平衡条件的兴趣。她从引力红移理论猜测，热平衡时两点的固有温度可能不同，进而导致弯曲时空中的一个物体内部存在温度梯度但没有热流。在和我讨论这一有趣现象的过程中，她敏锐地指出问题的关键在于测量的局域性。之后她用黑体辐射理论做了进一步探讨，得出热平衡时坐标温度相同、但实际测量的固有温度不同的结论，得到的公式与 Peter. T. Landsberg 教授在《热力学与统计力学》一书中用其他方法得到的结论一致。她这篇论文已在中国物理学会主办的重要期刊《大学物理》上发表。

总而言之，聂 ×× 是一个专业基础扎实、思想活跃、富于创新的优才生。我完全相信她具备物理学研究的潜力，十分愿意推荐她攻读贵校博士学位。如果有问题，请随时与我联系。

清华大学物理系副教授

徐 ×× 博士

2016.10.2

UNIT 15 Application Documents for Studying Abroad

Physics Department of Tsinghua University
Beijing, P. R. China
Oct. 2, 2016

Dear Madam/Sir,

It's my pleasure to recommend Miss Nie ×× for graduate study of physics at your university. I came to know her when she took my course "General Relativity" in Tsinghua University. She was one of the excellent students in my class, and deeply impressed me with her diligence and independent thinking.

My first impression of Miss Nie is her solid foundation of physics and mathematics. She often discussed with me some physical concepts in General Relativity, from which I knew she had established a very good and clear understanding of the theory. At the same time, she voluntarily accomplished the derivations abbreviated at class, which entailed much patience and carefulness. As a junior student, Miss Nie got a full score of 100 in the course which was designed for senior students, ranking first in my class.

Miss Nie is an active thinker endowed with independent abilities. Without knowing relevant work of others, she combined what she had learned from General Relativity and Statistical Mechanics, and became interested in the conditions for thermal equilibrium in curved spacetime. Starting from gravitational redshift, she conjectured that the proper temperatures of two systems are not equal, which means no heat flow exists in an object with temperature gradient. When discussing this interesting phenomenon with me, she keenly pointed out that the crux lies in locality of measurement. Then she adopted blackbody radiation theory to further study the problem, and arrived at a conclusion that coordinate temperatures are equal but proper temperatures differ in thermal equilibrium. Her formula coincides with that of Professor Peter. T. Landsberg, author of *Thermodynamics and Statistical Mechanics,* who used an alternative way. Miss Nie then summarized her finding in a thesis and got it published in *College Physics,* a major journal by Chinese Physical Society.

In sum, Miss Nie is an excellent student endowed with independent thinking and original ideas, and a solid foundation in physics and mathematics as well. I am convinced that she has great potential in doing research of physics and would like to strongly recommend her to the Physics PhD program at your university. Please feel free to contact me in case you need further information about her.

Sincerely yours,
Dr. XU ××
Associate Professor of Physics Department, Tsinghua University

V. Personal Statement (Statement of Purpose)

A personal statement (PS), or statement of purpose, is a required document when applying for admission to universities, graduate schools in the United States and other countries. It is a brief and focused essay about one's career or research goals, identified means to achieve them and accomplishments so far towards those goals. It is generally regarded as a yardstick to assess the capabilities of a prospective student in terms of critical thinking, analytical abilities, interests, aims and aspirations. Most admissions committees look for a short, crisp and ideologically clear PS that runs for 23 pages. Therefore, a good PS should be written in an easy and fluent style, full of emotions and true feelings. Only in this way can it affect the reader, and eventually get its purpose fulfilled.

Known as a Graduate School Essay, PS is also called "Letter of Intention", "Statement of Intent", "Statement of Intention", "Statement of Interest", "Goals Statement", "Personal Statement", "Personal Narrative" or "Application Essay" according to regulations of different universities. The translation of PS entails great efforts in careful wording, as well as other translation skills, as shown in the PS translation in Practice of the Relevant Skill. And the following is another case of PS in Chinese and its English version.

个人陈述

"如果选择物理，你必须能够耐得住寂寞，做好迎接困难的准备。" 我至今仍记得6年前清华大学招生组组长告诫我的这番话。当时很多亲朋好友都竭力劝我选一个热门专业，但我仍然坚持选择了物理。因为我心中有一个梦想，并且一直为实现这一梦想而不懈努力——当一名优秀的物理学家。清华大学6年广博的学习和研究，帮我打下了扎实的基础。而今，我正向成功迈出更加关键的步伐——加入贵校研究生的队伍。我自信拥有取得成功的潜力和特质。

我神定专注、勤奋好学，有很强的独立思考能力。上中学时，我常常对作业的标准答案提出质疑，总会找到自己新的解题方法。高中时，我自学参加了全国高中物理、数学、英语竞赛，取得了物理、英语全国一等奖，数学二等奖的优异成绩。高考时，我以山东省第九名的成绩，被中国最负盛名的大学——清华大学录取。进入清华大学后，我成绩同样突出并两次获得清华大学学业优秀奖学金。2011年，由于成绩优异，我被免试推荐在物理系攻读硕士学位，并获得研究生奖学金。经过在清华大学数年的勤奋学习和训练，我的学习能力得到进一步提升，同时也展示了强大的潜力。

我善于动脑，勤于思考，具有深刻的理解能力和创新思维，研究和解决实际问题的能力强。这种能力已在我的科研经历中得到证实。大学三年级时，我在超导物理与超导器件实验室学习高温超导滤波器的研制。我在很短的时间内学习并掌握了相关的理论知识和实验手段，同时设计一种大功率高温超导滤波器，并讨论了其性能和可行性。这段研究经历使我对科学研究工作有了一个更加直观的认识和切身的体会。

大学四年级，我加入了龙××教授的研究组，开始了量子干涉效应的学习和研究。我总结和阐述了龙××教授提出的关于量子干涉的5条基本原理，并且利用这些原理来解释一些实验现象。随着学习研究的深入，我开始关注量子信息中另一个关键问题——量子纠缠。我和另一位同学合作，基于纠缠交换的原理提出了一种新的产生多光子W态的方法。我分别计算了我们的新方案和传统的利用参量下转换的方法的效率，从而证明了我们的方案更加有效。这一研究激起了我对这一领域的兴趣，激发我进一步研究量子纠缠标准和度量。

研一时，我和合作者提出用一种新的纠缠度量(MEMS)来度量多粒子纠缠态。我们用MEMS计算了几种态的纠缠度并得到几种最大纠缠态。最近，为了进一步检验我们的结论，我计算了多体约化密度矩阵的平均共点的乘积。我认为这个问题还有很多值得研究的问题，比如MEMS与Bell不等式的关系等。我的另一项工作是基于PPT判据提出了一种新的纠缠判据。这个判据通过部分厄米共轭来实现。我们遇到的主要难题是如何定义部分厄米共轭操作，使其对任何量子态都适用。通过查阅文献和深入思考、不断尝试，我成功地找到了一种有效的定义，并证明了我们的判据是纯态可分的充分必要条件。我正在尝试将此判据推广到混合态的情况。

除了以上的研究，我对量子信息的其他领域也非常感兴趣，比如超导和量子点量子计算。我阅读了很多文献并且经常与我们组从事该方面研究的同学进行讨论。此外，我还参与了一些光学实验工作。通过这些理论和实验研究的工作，我对量子信息领域有了一个较为全面和深入的了解和认识。并且具备了很好的基础和能力从事本领域的研究工作。

我团队精神强，具有领导团队的经历和能力。尽管我有很强的独立思考和解决问题的能力，但我并不一味单干。多年来，丰富的学生工作经历，使我具备了很强的领导、交流和组织能力。高中时我就担任班长工作，一入清华大学就担任班级的学习委员，加入了物理系学生科协，担任联络部部长。读研究生期间，我作为物理系分管学术工作的副主席，组织和举办了很多大型活动。例如，我以组委会主席的身份，成功组织举办了清华大学博士生学术论坛。由于工作成绩突出，2012年我被评为清华大学校优秀学生干部。

我的上述个人特点和优势，最重要的是我对量子信息领域的浓厚兴趣使我相信，我能够在未来几年的研究生学习中取得成功。××大学研究成果卓著，在学术界享有崇高的声誉，在量子信息科学，尤其是在固体量子计算领域有非常强大的研究实力。所有这些对我都极具吸引力。××大学有很多世界著名的科研人员，比如××教授、××教授等。能在这些名师的指导下从事科研，对我来说将是一种莫大的荣誉和无比兴奋的事。有鉴于此，我选择××大学攻读博士学位。我相信这将是我一生中为实现自己的梦想所做出的最重要的选择。我深信自己能像在清华大学那样，在××大学获得成功，并且会做得更好。

Statement of Purpose

"If choosing physics, you must prepare yourself for difficulties and loneliness", this was what the head of the Tsinghua University Admissions Team warned me when I tried to get enrolled into Tsinghua 6 years ago. I still remember that in spite of persuasions from many relatives and friends who strongly advised me to choose a more popular profession, I stuck to my decision and chose physics as my major. For what I dreamed to be was a great physicist, a goal which I would spare no effort to attain. Having studied and researched at Tsinghua University for 6 years I have now laid a solid foundation. Armed with adequate knowledge and burgeoning achievements, I am eager to take a most critical step towards my goal—applying to be a graduate student at your esteemed university. I am confident that I have the potential and capabilities for my success.

As an inquisitive and attentive student, I have strong capabilities of independent thinking. When at high school, I often challenged the standard keys to the questions by finding new ways to solve them. At senior high school I participated in various National Contests and won the first prizes in Physics and English, second prize in maths. In the national college entrance exam, I ranked No.9 in Shandong Province and consequently was admitted into Tsinghua University, the most prestigious university in China. During my undergraduate study, I continued to keep an outstanding academic record. I obtained the Scholarship for Academic Excellence for two successive years. In 2011, I was granted the honor of pursuing my master's degree in the Department of Physics exempt from admission exam. Through diligent study and training in university, I have greatly improved my self-study ability and manifested my potential in study.

I am good at original thinking and possess the ability to solve problem independently, which have been manifested through my research work. My first research was in my junior year in the Superconducting Physics and Device Laboratory. I learned to design and manufacture High Temperature Superconductive Filters (HTSF). After quickly mastering the theory and experimental skills, I designed a possible structure of HTSF with great power handling capability and discussed its feasibility. This experience gave me a clear idea about what scientific research is and how to do it.

Later in the senior year's seminar, I began to study quantum information which I had heard about since high school. I joined in the quantum information group led by Professor Long ××. In the process of the project, I summarized and illuminated five principles proposed by Professor Long concerning quantum interference. Through this work, I gained a better understanding of quantum theory which greatly benefited my following research. Then I turned to quantum entanglement. Together with one of my fellow students I proposed a new method to generate multiphoton W state using entanglement swapping.

I compared the efficiency of our scheme to that of the common ones involving high order spontaneous down conversion process, and proved that our scheme is much more efficient. This research intrigued me into this field and encouraged me to do further research in quantum entanglement criteria and measures.

In the first year of my graduate study, I proposed a new entanglement measure with my colleague, the multiple entropy measures (MEMS), to quantify entanglement of multi-partite state. We analyzed the entanglement properties of some quantum states under MEMS and found some external entangled 4-qubit pure states. In order to further develop our conclusion, I calculated the average concurrence instead of the average entropy of multi-partite state. I think further research can be done in this field such as the relationship between the MEMS and Bell's inequalities. Another work of mine is to put forward a new criterion of quantum entanglement through partial hermitian conjugate (PHC) operation, which is based on PPT criterion. The main difficulty in this criterion is how to define the PHC operation. After perusing some references and massive calculation, I successfully found a general definition of the operation and proved this criterion to be a necessary and sufficient condition of reparability for pure states. I am now trying to generalize the PHC criterion to mixed state.

Apart from my researches in quantum entanglement, I am also interested in some other topics in quantum information, such as quantum computation based on super-conducting Josephson junction, quantum dots and ion trap, etc. I had participated in some optical experiments of my research group. Through these theoretical and experimental research experiences, I've gained a general understanding of quantum information science. I am confident that I have the ability to do research in most fields of quantum information.

Besides strong ability to solve problems independently, I also have a strong sense of team spirit and the camaraderie of group participation. Rich experiences of extracurricular activity and community work have endowed me with deft skills in leadership and communication as well as the capability to organize group work. I was class monitor at high school and was class commissary in charge of studies at university. I also hold some important posts in student associations such as the Student Association of Science and Technology and Graduate Student Union. I successfully organized Doctoral Forum of Tsinghua University as the chairman of organization committee. I was awarded Excellent Graduate Student Leader of Tsinghua University for my meritorious service in 2012.

With all the above qualities of mine, and above all, keen interests in quantum information, I am convinced that I can succeed in my graduate study in the coming years. ×× University enjoys high reputation for its great research achievements and excellent research team in quantum information, especially in solid quantum computation, which attracts me a lot at present. There are many world famous researchers here, such as professors ×××, ×××, etc. It would be a great honor and exciting experience for me to work together with them. Therefore I choose ×× University to pursue my Ph.D. I deem it the most significant decision in my life on the way to fulfill my dream. I am confident that I'll make it at ×× University as I have distinguished myself in Tsinghua University, and even better.

Reflections and Practice

I. **Discuss the following questions.**

1. What do application documents for studying abroad include?
2. What are points for attention when orienting your target?
3. What are the essentials of translating résumés or curriculum vitae?
4. What are points for attention when translating letters of recommendation?
5. What is the importance of personal statements? What are points for attention in translating them?

II. **Put the following résumé into English.**

个人简历

个人基本情况

姓名：王 ××

通信地址：北京清华大学紫荆公寓 5 号楼 212A

手机：+86 15101146×××

电子邮件地址：prongs@gmail.com

教育背景

2007 年 9 月—2010 年 7 月　　武汉实验外国语学校（初中）

2010 年 9 月—2013 年 7 月　　武汉外国语学校（高中）

2013 年 8 月—今　　　　　　清华大学土木水利学院

　　　　　　　　　　　　　　（成绩：88.5/100；名次：12/68）

社会服务工作和课余活动

2013 年 9 月—今　　　　　　清华大学学生艺术团民乐队队员

2014 年 3 月—6 月	清华大学水利水电工程系学生会宣传部干事
2014 年 9 月—2015 年 6 月	清华大学学生科协星火论坛部干事
2015 年 4 月	北京肖家河小学支教
2015 年 9 月—2016 年 6 月	清华大学水利水电工程系学生科协内外联副主席
2016 年 4 月	任清华大学百年校庆志愿者

科研和实习情况

2014 年 10 月—2015 年 6 月	离心场填筑设备的开发与改进
2016 年 3 月—6 月	"交通运输系统概论"课程助教
2016 年 8 月	MVA 宏达交通咨询（深圳）有限公司暑期实习

获奖情况

清华大学暑期社会实践铜奖（2014）
清华大学第二届水利创新大赛二等奖（2015）
辉固特等奖学金（2015）

语言能力

托福：109/120（2016 年 3 月）
大学英语六级：583/710（2014 年 12 月）

III. Put the following letter of recommendation into English.

尊敬的先生/女士：

  我在此向你们郑重推荐我的学生李红同学到贵校深造。李红于 2009 年因学习成绩优异，被保送到清华大学中文系，考入了我校首次创办的文科实验班。文科实验班旨在为培养中西贯通、古今贯通的大师奠定基础。这个班的学生不仅要学习中国的传统文化和各个时期的语言文学，还要学习西方有代表性的文学作品和理论。李红同学在极具挑战性的学业上取得了卓越的成绩，每学期都获得了校级学业奖学金。与此同时，她勤奋创作，在繁重的学习之余发表了许多文学作品，并于 2012 年正式出版了两部长篇小说，在文学的道路上跨出了一大步。

  此外，李红同学还积极参加社会工作，曾担任清华大学学生会的干部，并长期担任文科实验班的班委工作。2010 年年底和 2011 年 3 月，李红同学分别担任了香港浸会大学和日本成城大学学生的中文辅导员。

  我期待李红同学今后能在贵校取得更大成绩，特此推荐！

清华大学人文学院中文系教授
徐 ××

IV. Put the following personal statements into English.

自 我 陈 述

梦想打开了未来之门，毅力使梦想成真。

从孩提时代起我就一直有过很多梦想。第一个梦想来自我的父母。他们教给我很多知识，引我进入一个奇妙的科学世界。

我强烈的学习兴趣是土木工程。这是一个将工程学与建筑技术和社会价值相结合的学科。它为我提供了一个表达思想、展现创造力的良机，我也从中获得成功的喜悦和极大的满足。我希望有朝一日我将成为这一领域中的杰出教授或学者。我也正在尽力为此做好准备。

在过去几年里，在老师的教诲下，我在学业和科研方面都取得了稳步的进展。我学习了土木工程专业的各种课程，包括力学、混凝土结构、钢材结构、高层建筑、抗震结构、实验方法等。这些课程给我打下了坚实的理论基础。我最喜欢的是各种实验课，因为它们为我揭示了大自然的秘密，教会我严谨、科学地思维。我想，要学好土木工程，最重要的是了解相关的领域，譬如建筑学、工程管理和环境等。我选学了一些相关领域的核心课程，受到了良好的训练。

当今世界计算机广泛地用于科研，因此，我学习了FORTRAN语言和C++语言。我编写了许多程序用于设计和实验工作。有了这些程序，我的研究便捷多了。

土木工程的特点是以运用为导向。我常常利用周末或节假日在各种建筑工地、建筑公司和建筑设计院实习。我从这些地方所获得的经验对领会理论知识和建筑设计有很大的帮助。去年，我参与了中国—意大利环境和能源大楼(SIEEB)的建设工程。这一大楼的外形设计与众不同，布满了各种不同材料构成的接合面。在这期间我学会了怎样将理论知识与工程建设相结合。

为了获得更多的实践经验，我设计了自己的作品。在混凝土结构和钢材结构作品设计方面我是最佳设计者之一。在清华大学的第10届结构设计大赛中我荣获了最高综合表现奖和最佳结构分析奖。在第二届北京结构设计大赛中我荣获了综合表现一等奖和最佳结构分析奖。我还作为清华大学代表队的成员之一参加过第二届全国建筑设计竞赛。

我还参加了土木工程和其他的学科发展项目。我聆听过许多中国工程院院士和国外著名教授的讲座。通过这些讲座我得知了当今世界工程学的最新成果和发展趋势。

我认为未来的土木工程有两个主要方向。一是材料的微观理论，这一理论会促进分析方法和结构材料的发展。二是设计和建筑大型建筑物，譬如超高层建筑和超长跨距桥梁。就我看来，两者中的任何一个都极具挑战性，都需要为之付出艰辛的努力。

我非常高兴能在土木工程和其他的相关学科继续从事自己的研究。NUS大学的土木工程的博士课程享誉全世界，也是我长期以来所追求的目标。如果我的申请得到批准，我将努力在学业上取得更大进步。我相信自己在土木工程领域将会非常优秀。

Unit 16 Developing Comprehensive Abilities Through Comparative Studies and Practice

> ● 单元要点概述
>
> 相关翻译技巧训练英译汉：Which Tongues Work Best for Microblogs?
> 相关翻译技巧训练汉译英：中国的创新
> I. 英汉语言宏观对比
>   1. 综合性与分析性　　　　2. 紧凑与松散　　　　3. 形合与意合
>   4. 繁复与简单　　　　　　5. 物称与人称　　　　6. 被动与主动
>   7. 静态与动态　　　　　　8. 抽象与具体　　　　9. 间接与直接
>   10. 替换与重复
> II. 通过比较研究培养翻译综合能力
>   1. 语感能力　　　　　　　2. 语境分析能力　　　3. 逻辑思维能力

　　本单元为全书的末章，旨在通过英汉语言文字的宏观比较，找出两种语言转换的普遍规律，改进学习方法，提高翻译综合能力。

　　如语言学家所示，英汉语言有十大差异：1. 英语属综合性语言，汉语为分析性语言；2. 英语句式紧凑，汉语句式流散；3. 英语重形合，汉语重意合；4. 英语句式繁复，汉语句式简单；5. 英语多用物称，汉语多人称；6. 英语多用被动，汉语习惯主动；7. 英语是静态，汉语为动态；8. 英语抽象，汉语具体；9. 英语间接，汉语直接；10. 英语多用代词，汉语喜欢重复。

　　本单元后部分提出培养翻译综合能力的三要素：语感能力、语境分析能力和逻辑思维能力。

Practice of the Relevant Skill

1. E-C Translation

Which Tongues Work Best for Microblogs?

This 78-character tweet in English would be only 24 characters long in Chinese. That makes Chinese ideal for microblogs, which typically restrict messages to 140 symbols. Though Twitter, with 140m active users the world's best-known microblogging service, is blocked in China, and Sina Weibo, a local variant, has over 250m users. Chinese is so succinct that most messages never reach that limit, says Shuo Tang, who studies social media at the University of Indiana.

Japanese is concise too: fans of haiku, poems in 17 syllables, can tweet them readily. Though Korean and Arabic require a little more space, tweeters routinely omit syllables in Korean words; written Arabic routinely omits vowels anyway. Arabic tweets mushroomed last year, though thanks to the uprisings across the Middle East rather than any linguistic features. It is now the eighth most-used language on Twitter with over 2m public tweets every day, according to Semiocast, a Paris-based company that analyses social-media trends.

Romance tongues, among others, generally tend to be more verbose. So Spanish and Portuguese, the two most frequent European languages in the Twitterverse after English, have tricks to reduce the number of characters. Brazilians use "abs" for abraços (hugs) and "bjs" for beijos (kisses); Spanish speakers need never use personal pronouns ("I go" is denoted by the verb alone: voy). But informal English is even handier. It allows personal pronouns to be dropped, has no fiddly accents and enjoys a well-developed culture of abbreviation. "English is unmatched in its acronyms, such as DoD for department of defence," says Mohammed al-Basha, a spokesman for the Yemeni government, who tweets in English and Arabic.

Twitter's growth around the world has reduced the proportion of total global tweets in English to 39% from two-thirds in 2009, but polyglot tweeters still often favour the language because of its ubiquity. Many Arabic-speaking revolutionaries used it to get their messages to a larger audience during the Arab spring, sometimes using automatic translation services. Until a recent upgrade, users of Arabic, Farsi and Urdu had trouble using hashtags (words prefixed with the # sign to mark a tweet's subject). Some people use English to avoid censorship.

Though ubiquity and flexibility may give English hegemony, Twitter is also helping

UNIT 16 Developing Comprehensive Abilities Through Comparative Studies and Practice

smaller and struggling languages. Basque-and-Gaelic-speakers tweet to connect with other far-flung speakers. Kevin Scannell, a professor at St. Louis University, Missouri, has found 500 languages in use on Twitter and has set up a website to track them. Gamilaraay, an indigenous Australian language, is thought to have only three living speakers. One of them is tweeting—handy for revivalists.

Notes and Explanations

1. 78-character tweet 七十八字符的微博
2. Sina Weibo 新浪微博
3. haiku *n.* 俳句，日本的一种古典短诗
4. Romance tongues 罗曼诸语言
5. verbose *adj.* 冗长的，啰嗦的
6. fiddly accents 准确的发音
7. acronym *n.* 首字母缩写
8. ubiquity *n.* 普遍存在，到处存在
9. hashtag *n.* 标签
10. hegemony *n.* 霸权
11. Basque-and-Gaelic-speakers 巴斯克语和盖立克语使用者
12. far-flung *adj.* 遥远的，广泛的

2. C-E Translation

中国的创新

中国的创新正以前所未有的速度蓬勃发展。为了在科学技术上尽快赶超世界发达国家，中国近年来大幅度增加了研究开发资金。中国的大学和研究所正在积极开展创新研究。这些研究覆盖了从大数据到生物化学、从新能源到机器人等高科技领域。它们还与各地的科技园合作，使创新成果商业化。与此同时，无论在产品还是商业模式上，中国企业家也在努力争做创新的先锋，以适应国内外消费市场不断变化和增长的需求。

Notes and Explanations

1. 前所未有的速度 unprecedented speed
2. 蓬勃发展 flourish
3. 研究开发资金 research and development fund

4. 积极开展创新研究 actively do innovative researches
5. 从大数据到生物化学 from big data to biochemistry
6. 高科技领域 fields of high technology
7. 科技园 technology parks
8. 创新成果商业化 commercialize fruits of innovation
9. 商业模式 business models
10. 创新的先锋 pioneering efforts
11. 国内外消费市场 foreign and domestic market

So far we have covered all the translation techniques and skills. But techniques and skills alone are of little avail unless they are applied to practice. To a great extent, one's translation abilities hinge on a two-way proceeding, i.e. a good command of one's mother tongue on the one hand, and deft handling the foreign language on the other hand. Therefore, a comparative study of the syntax and the basic structure of English and Chinese languages would be of great help to us.

I. A Comparative Study of English and Chinese Languages

According to some linguists, noticeably Mr. Lian Shuneng in his *Contrastive Studies on English and Chinese,* the disparity between English and Chinese languages may be summarized as follows.

1. Synthetic vs. Analytic

English is a synthetic language marked with inflexions, while Chinese is an analytic language, with the inflection implied in the context, or by using auxiliary words such as "的、地、得""着、了、过", etc. For example:
- During the wartime, years like these *would have meant* certain death for many people. Many *would have become* beggars and others *would have been compelled* to sell their children. 战争期间碰到这样的年景，很多人**肯定会**死去，很多人**会**逃荒要饭，很多人**会被迫**卖儿卖女。
- *Thus encouraged*, they made a still bolder plan for the next year. 由于受到这样的**鼓励**，他们为第二年制订了一个更大胆的计划。
- But for many, the fact that poor people *are* able to support themselves almost as

UNIT 16 Developing Comprehensive Abilities Through Comparative Studies and Practice

well without government aid as they *did* with it is in itself a huge victory. 但在许多人看来，穷人**现在**能不靠政府救济养活自己，而且生活得几乎和**过去**依靠政府救济时生活得一样好，这件事本身就是一个巨大的胜利。

2. Compact vs. Diffusive

English sentences are compact, i.e. tightly combined with connectives or prepositions, while Chinese is diffused, i.e. loose in structure.

- Now the integrated circuit has reduced by many times the size of the computer of which it forms a part, thus creating a new generation of portable minicomputer. 现在集成电路成了计算机的组成部分，使计算机的体积大大缩小，从而产生了新一代的便携式微型计算机。
- A notion has taken hold in the U.S. to the effect that the only people who should be encouraged to bring children into the world are those who can afford them. 在美国有一个根深蒂固的观点，即只有对那些抚养得起子女的人，才应鼓励其生育。
- Although lonely in a new land, he was described by his fellow workers and students as cheerful, of a friendly nature, honest, and modest. 虽然他单身一人，又处在异乡客地，但正如他的同事和学生描述的那样，他为人愉快开朗，温文尔雅，诚实谦虚。

3. Hypotactic vs. Paratactic

In English, clauses or phrases are coordinated with or subordinated to one another syntactically while in Chinese they are placed one after another without coordinating connectives.

- The many colors of a rainbow range from red on the outside to violet on the inside. 彩虹有多种颜色，外圈红，内圈紫。
- He had a disconcerting habit of expressing contradictory ideas in rapid succession. 他有一种令人难堪的习惯：一会儿一个看法，自相矛盾，变化无常。
- The present onslaught of vehicles poses a serious threat to urban life and pedestrian peace of mind. 车辆横冲直撞，严重地威胁着城市生活，路上行人无不提心吊胆。

4. Complex vs. Simplex

English sentences are long and complex, while Chinese sentences are short and simple. For example:

- Many man-made substances are replacing certain natural materials because either the quality of the natural product cannot meet our ever-increasing requirement, or, more often, because the physical properties of the synthetic substance, which is the common name for man-made materials, have been chosen, and even emphasized, so that it would be of the greatest use in the fields in which it is to be applied. 人造材料通称为合成材料。许多人造材料正在代替某些天然材料，这或者是由于天然材料的数量不能满足日益增长的需要，或者是由于人们选择了合成材料的一些物理性质并加以突出而造成的。因此，合成材料在其应用领域将具有极大的用途。

5. Impersonal vs. Personal

More impersonal expressions are used as the subject in English than in Chinese, as shown in the following examples:

- *What* has happened to you? 你出了什么事儿啦?
- *An idea* suddenly struck me. 我突然想到一个主意。
- *Not a sound* reached our ears. 我们没有听到任何声音。
- *A great elation* overcame them. 他们欣喜若狂。
- *The truth* finally dawned on her. 她最终明白了真相。
- *Alarm* began to take entire possession of him. 他开始变得惊恐万状。
- *Excitement* deprived me of all power of utterance. 我兴奋得说不出话来。
- *A strange peace* came over her when she was alone. 她独处时感到一种特别的安宁。
- *The thick carpet* killed the sound of my footsteps. 我走在厚厚的地毯上，一点儿脚步声也没有。
- From the moment we stepped into the People's Republic of China, *care and kindness* surrounded us on every side. 一踏上中华人民共和国国土，**我们**就随时随地受到关怀与照顾。

6. Passive vs. Active

As we have mentioned in previous units, the passive voice is extensively used in English, while Chinese is prone to active structures.

- A few years ago it *was thought* unusual that programs could ever *be called* up by viewers to *be displayed* on their TV screens at home. 几年前人们**还以为**，观众居然能够**打电话**要求在自己家里的电视屏幕上**播出**节目是一种稀罕的事情。
- Electrical energy can *be stored* in two metal plates separated by an insulating medium. Such a device *is called* a capacitor, or a condenser, and its ability to store energy *is termed* capacitance. It *is measured* in farads. 电能可**储存**在由一绝缘介质隔开的两块金属极板内。这样的装置**称为**电容器，其储存电能的能力**称为**电容。电容的**测量单位是**法拉。

UNIT 16 Developing Comprehensive Abilities Through Comparative Studies and Practice

7. Static vs. Dynamic

English is static, with agent nouns being repeatedly used, while Chinese is dynamic, with more verbs being used in a single sentence.

- He is a *good eater* and a *good sleeper*. 他能吃又能睡。/ 他吃得饱睡得香。
- You must be a very *bad learner;* or else you must be going to a very *bad teacher*. 你一定很**不善于学习**，要不然就是教你的人很**不会教**。
- The computer is a far more careful and industrious *inspector* than human beings. 计算机比人**检查**得更细心、更勤快。

8. Abstract vs. Concrete

When it comes to indicating the state of affairs, English is very abstract while Chinese is more concrete.

- *The absence of* intelligence is an indication of satisfactory developments. **没有消息**即表明有令人满意的进展。
- *A high degree of carelessness,* preoperative and postoperative, on the part of some of the hospital staff, took place. 医院某些医护人员在手术前后都**非常粗心**。

9. Roundabout vs. Straightforward

English expressions tend to be roundabout in affirmation while Chinese sentences are straightforward, especially when it comes to personal opinions.

- I *couldn't* feel *better*. 我觉得身体**好极**了。
- I *couldn't agree* with you *more*. 我**太赞成**你的看法了。
- He *can't see* you *quick enough*. 他很想**尽快**和你**见面**。
- This book is quite *beyond me*. 这本书我实在**看不懂**。
- Every person has the right to *be free from* hunger. 人人有**不挨饿**的权利。
- If you have a car, you are *independent of* trains and buses. 如果你有小汽车，就**不用去**坐火车或挤公共汽车。

10. Substitutive vs. Repetitive

Pronouns are frequently used in English to substitute the persons or things that are mentioned previously, whereas in Chinese we use repetition instead.

- You should *help her* since you have promised to *do so*. 你既然答应了要**帮助她**就应当帮助她。
- He hated failure; he had conquered *it* all his life, risen above *it,* and despised *it* in others. 他讨厌**失败**，他一生中曾战胜**失败**，超越**失败**，并且藐视别人的**失败**。

- *Men and nations* working apart created these problems; men and nations working together must solve them. 人与人之间、国与国之间离心离德，便产生这些问题，人与人之间、国与国之间齐心协力，定能解决这些问题。

II. Developing Practical Abilities Through Comparative Studies and Practice

The mastery of a foreign language is a long-term task that entails constant efforts. And so is translation. A conscientious translator should learn to develop and enhance various practical abilities all the time. And one of the effective ways is to compare the translated versions with the originals with a critical eye. By doing so, we could not only develop a good translation habit, but also a keen sense of distinguishing right from wrong.

1. Language Sensibility

Language sensibility means the good capacity to perceive or understand a given language phenomenon intuitively. Take the commonly used word "time" for example. It's all right for us to translate the phrase "increase... by (to) X times" into "增加了（增加到）X 倍"，as shown in the following cases：

Sample 1: The output of coal has been increased 3.5 times since 1992. 煤产量自 1992 年以来增长了两倍半。

Sample 2: The annual total of telephone calls between the U.K. and Canada has increased seven times. 英国和加拿大之间的年通话总量增长了 6 倍。

However, when it comes to "reduce... by (to) X times"，quite a lot of people copy this English pattern, rendering it as "降低了（降低到）X 倍". For example：

Sample 3: The new equipment will reduce the error probability by seven times. * 新设备的误差概率将减小 7 倍。

Sample 4: By adopting the new process of production the loss of metal was reduced 8.2 times. * 由于采用了新生产工艺，金属耗损量比原来下降了 8.2 倍。

Comment: Actually, "times" here does not mean "something multiplied", but "equal fractional parts of which an indicated number equal a comparatively great quantity (e.g. seven times smaller)", or rather, "something divided by". Therefore, sensible Chinese versions for the above samples should be:

- 新设备的误差概率将减小到原来的 1/7（或：降低了 6/7）。
- 由于采用了新生产工艺，金属耗损量仅为原来的 12.2%（或：下降了 87.8%）。

UNIT 16 Developing Comprehensive Abilities Through Comparative Studies and Practice

Some more improper translations are illustrated as follows, mostly owing to the lack of language sensibility on the part of the translator.

Sample 5: There are no places left on the earth that the foot of man has not trodden.

Chinese Version A: 地球上所有地方都有人去过。

Chinese Version B: 地球上绝无人迹的地方是没有的。

Both versions A and B fail to convey the emphasis of the original double negative; besides, the original "trodden"（踩、踏）is not accurately expressed in the Chinese versions, furthermore, "man" here refers to human beings, instead of an individual person.

Improved Version: 地球上的任何地方无不留下人类的足迹。

Sample 6: A little fly dropped on her knee, on her white dress. She watched it, as if it had fallen on a rose. She was not herself.

Improper Chinese Version: 一只苍蝇落在她的膝上，落在她的白衣服上，她盯着苍蝇看，仿佛苍蝇落在一朵玫瑰花上似的。她不是她自己了。

The translator blundered in the phrase "not oneself". Actually, it means "not conducting oneself in a usual or fitting manner". e.g., She is not quite herself today.（她今天身体有些不舒服。）

Improved Version: 一只小苍蝇落到她膝上，爬上了白衣裙。她盯着苍蝇看，感到就像虫子落在玫瑰花上一样，心中很不舒服。

Sample 7: Gardens are not made by singing "Oh, how beautiful" and sitting in the shade. (R. Kipling)

Improper Chinese Version: 花园并不是为了哼哼曲子而建造的优哉游哉的庇荫之地。

The translator mistook the passive voice of "to make sth by doing..."（通过做……完成某事）for predicative structure, thus causing the error.

Improved Version: 花园并不是悠闲地赞叹一句"啊，多美啊"，坐在树荫下就能轻轻松松建造好的。

Sample 8: When a woman dresses to kill, the victim is apt to be time.

Improper Chinese Version: 当女人梳妆打扮的时候，时间就成了她的牺牲品。

The translator overlooked the phrase "be dressed to kill"（穿着过分考究的）, which is adroitly linked with another phrase "kill time"（消磨时间）, to create the effect of a pun.

Improved Version: 当女人力图把自己打扮得花枝招展的时候，时间往往就成了牺牲品。

2. Contextual Analysis

As we have mentioned in Unit 2, context plays an indispensable role in translation. Contextual analysis includes both the words, phrases, or passages that come before and after a particular word or passage in the writing and the circumstances in which an event occurs, as shown in the translation of the following paragraph.

Sample 9: The big question is, just how progressive has China become, especially in the villages? Obviously, development occurs on many different levels and phases. A powerful nation without Western ethics or socialist ethics would confront the rest of the world with difficult problems, especially in the nuclear age. It is very much in the future interest of the rest of the world, and especially of the people of the United States, that China should continue on the road to socialism and its historical high ethics as progressively as possible. There is no alternative—none but the unthinkable. (Helen Snow: *My China Years*)

Improper Chinese Version: 一个重大的问题是，中国，特别是中国的广大农村，现在究竟先进到什么程度？显而易见，发展的水平和阶段是多层次的，大不相同的。一个没有西方伦理规范或社会主义伦理规范的大国，是会带着种种难题面对外部世界的，尤其是在原子时代更是这样。中国在通往社会主义，前往自己高尚的历史伦理规范的道路上，应当尽可能地继续前进，这对于世界的未来，特别是对于美国人民的未来，都是非常有利的。别无挑选的余地，否则，那就不可思议了。

The above Chinese version is not faithful to the original in meaning. With the help of contextual analysis of the original English we may do the translation better:

progressive: moving forward or onward "前进，进展" instead of "先进"

different levels and phases 不同层次和方面

confront the rest of the world with difficult problems: to cause to meet, bring face-to-face 使世界面对难题，instead of "带着难题面对外部世界"

the nuclear age 核时代，instead of "原子时代"

It is... that China should: emphatic sentence 正是为了……中国应当

in the interest of "为了……利益"，instead of "非常有利"

none but the unthinkable: no other way except the unthinkable way 除此道路外，别无出路

Improved Version: 一个重要问题是：中国现在发展得怎么样了？尤其是乡村变得怎样了？显而易见，全国上上下下在各方面都有了发展变化。一个泱泱大国要是既没有西方的道德标准，又没有社会主义伦理规范，会给世界带来种种棘手的问题，尤其是在当前这样的核时代。从很大程度上讲，正是为了整个世界的未来，尤其是为了美国人民的未来，中国应当继续沿着社会主义道路走下去，应当在其具有历史意义的高度的伦理道德道路上尽快阔步前进。他们再没有别的路可走——除了这条令人不可思议的道路外，别无他途。

Contextual analysis is needed not only in E-C translation, but also in C-E Translation. Sometimes, a seemingly trivial error may spoil the whole effort, as is shown in the following example.

UNIT 16 Developing Comprehensive Abilities Through Comparative Studies and Practice

Sample 10: ……我从北京到徐州，打算跟着父亲奔丧回家。到徐州见着父亲，看见满院狼藉的东西，又想起祖母，不禁簌簌地流下眼泪。父亲说："事已至此，不必难过，好在天无绝人之路！"

回家变卖典质，父亲还了亏空；又借钱办了丧事。……丧事完毕，父亲要到南京谋事，我也要回北京念书，我们便同行。（朱自清《背影》）

English Version: ...I left Beijing for Xuzhou to join father in hastening home to attend grandma's funeral. When I met father in Xuzhou, the sight of the disorderly mess in *our* courtyard and the thought of grandma started tears trickling down my cheeks. Father said, "Now that things've come to such a pass, it's no use crying. Fortunately, Heaven always leaves one a way out." Father paid off debts by selling or pawning things. He also borrowed money to meet the funeral expenses. ...After the funeral was over, father was to go to Nanjing to look for a job and I was to return to Beijing to study, so we started out together.

A careful reader with some contextual knowledge cannot help wondering at the end of the English version: since father was to go to Nanjing and "I" was to return to Beijing, how could it be that "we started out together"? Evidently, the phrase "*our* courtyard" leads to the confusion. In the light of the Chinese context "回家变卖典质", we may find that the courtyard was not in their hometown but in Xuzhou, where father was making a living. So, instead of "*our* courtyard", "院" here should be translated as "*the* courtyard".

3. Logical Thinking

Logical thinking is also a valuable ability for a translator. In many cases when we focus our attention on literal meaning of some given words and try to copy existing sentence patterns, we are prone to commit logical fallacies, as shown in the following illustrations.

Sample 11: Very wonderful changes in matter take place before our eyes to which we pay little attention.

Improper Version: 我们很少注意的物质中那些奇异的变化都经常在我们眼前发生。

The original English is very explicit, but the Chinese version seems very ambiguous—it may be explained either as "很少注意的物质", or "很少注意的奇异变化". Through logical analysis we may find that "which" in this context refers to "changes".

Improved Version: 物质中那些奇异的变化常常就发生在我们眼前，尽管我们很少注意到这一点。

Sample 12: The most powerful traveling telephones are the ones used on ships. Here there is no problem of weight, as there is on airplanes.

Improper Version: 功率最大的旅行电话是在船上使用的。这里没有重量的问题，像在飞机上那样。

This version fails to grasp the essence of comparison between ships and airplanes, thus leading to a logical fallacy.

Improved Version: 功率最大的旅行电话在船上使用，因为船上没有飞机上那样的严格的超重问题。

Sample 13: The atom as we know is built on scientific investigations and theories.

Improper Version: 原子，正如我们所知，是建立在科学的理论和探索上的。

This Chinese version lacks logical thinking, or to be specific, lacks common sense. In fact, "the atom" here refers to the theory of atom, instead of a specific atom.

Improved Version: 我们知道，原子学说是根据科研理论而建立的。

Sample 14: Epitaph: a belated advertisement for a line of good that has permanently discontinued.

Improper Version: 墓志铭只不过是为断档的商品而做的过时的广告罢了。

As we may see from the wording, there is no logical connection between "epitaph" and "a line of good" in the Chinese version. Obviously, the translator has mistaken "good"(善行) for "goods"(商品).

Improved Version: 墓志铭：为一系列永不复存的善行打出的过时广告。

Sample 15: He was full of enthusiasm and said, "Put 50 in a *plane naked*. It's only three hours!"

Improper Version: 他充满激情地说："光着膀子，一架飞机可以装50人。反正空中时间只有3个小时。"

The Chinese version is against common sense—it is ridiculous to board a plane in naked armies. Actually, "naked" here does not mean "nude", nor "without clothing", but "lacking furnishing or decoration". For example, a naked room（空荡荡的房间）, be naked of weapon（不带武器）, etc.

Improved Version: 他充满激情地说："空舱不带座椅装备，一架飞机塞50人没问题。好歹空中就那么3个小时。"

Sample 16: For more than two years two unyielding men, equally determined, mutually hostile, supposedly allies, *wrestled over* the fate of China.

Improper Version: 在长达两年多时间里，他们（蒋介石和史迪威）为中国的命运搏斗着，他们两人的意志一样坚定，互相敌视，不肯屈服，与此同时却又是名义上的盟友。

If we read the Chinese version without consulting the original sentence, we may feel puzzled at the author's attitude towards these two unyielding men：they seemed to be Chinese people's great saviors who "为中国的命运搏斗着". The fact is just the opposite：

UNIT 16 Developing Comprehensive Abilities Through Comparative Studies and Practice

the very meaning of the phrase "wrestle over" is "to struggle for the control over".

Improved Version: 两年多来，他们俩为争夺中国命运的主宰权而殊死较量。两人都下定决心，都视对方为仇敌，而名义上却是公认的盟友。

Language sensibility, contextual analysis and logical thinking are three inseparable abilities linked with one another, which cannot be acquired until we make constant efforts in translation practice. And once these abilities have been developed they may benefit us all the time. They may help us, consciously or unconsciously, rid our translation of errors, and eventually gain the freedom of accurate and idiomatic expression.

Reflections and Practice

I. Discuss the following questions.

1. How are translation theories and techniques related to practical abilities?
2. What are the major contrasts that indicate the disparity between the English and the Chinese languages? Which of them are you familiar with?
3. What are the three practical abilities proposed by the author? Do you agree or disagree with the author? Why or why not?
4. What is your idea of the best way of acquiring translation abilities? Express your idea with your own experience.

II. Compare the different Chinese versions with the original English and then comment on them.

1. Their accent couldn't fool a native speaker.
   Version A: 他们的口音不能愚弄本地人。
   Version B: 本地人是不会听不出他们是外乡人的。
   Version C: 他们的口音本地人一听便知道是外乡人。
2. John is tall like I am the Queen of Sheba.
   Version A: 约翰高得像我是示巴皇后。
   Version B: 约翰高的话，我就是示巴皇后。
   Version C: 要说约翰个头高，没那回事。
3. He bent solely upon profit.
   Version A: 他只屈身于利润之前。
   Version B: 只有利润才使他低头。
   Version C: 他唯利是图。

4. Would there be any possibility of having breakfast on the train before we are decanted at Munich?
   Version A: 当我们在慕尼黑被腾出车厢之前有任何在火车上吃到早餐的可能性吗？
   Version B: 我们在慕尼黑转车之前，有任何可能性在火车上吃到早餐吗？
   Version C：我们在慕尼黑下车之前，能在车上吃到早点吗？

5. She then uncrossed her legs.
   Version A: 于是她使她的腿不交叉。
   Version B: 于是她把交叉搁着的腿放平。
   Version C: 于是她收起二郎腿。

6. "Did you say 'pig' or 'fig'?" said the Cat. (Lewis Carroll, *Alice's Adventures in Wonderland*)
   Version A："你刚才说的是'猪'还是'无花果'？"猫问。
   Version B："你刚才说的是'pig'还是'fig'？"猫问。
   Version C："你刚才说的是'猪'还是'书'？"猫问。

7. We had plenty of company in the way of wagonloads and muleloads of tourists—and dust. (Mark Twain, *A Tramp Abroad*)
   Version A: 我们有很多以马车装载和骡子负载的旅游者这种方式的同伴——尘土。
   Version B: 跟我们做伴的人真不少，有乘马车的，有骑骡子的——一路尘土飞扬。
   Version C: 我们的伴侣可真不少：马车载，骡子驮——还有滚滚的尘土呢。

8. ("It's an order from President Bush.") （"这是布什总统的命令。"）
   "I don't care if it is from bush, tree, or grass."
   Version A："我不在意它来自灌木、树木还是草。"
   Version B："我不在乎它来自布什、树木还是草。"
   Version C："管它什么布什、布头、布片呢，与我无关。"／"老子不管它什么布什、布八、布九。"

9. Money is the last thing he wants, and you won't succeed by offering it.
   Version A：钱是他想要的最后一件东西，你提供给他钱也不会成功。
   Version B：钱是他最不想要的东西，你给他钱也不会成功。
   Version C：他绝不想要你的钱，你给他钱也白搭。

10. He was not the eldest son of his father for nothing.
    Version A：他不是爸爸的长子，因为什么也不是。
    Version B：他作为他爸爸的长子并不是毫无收获的。
    Version C：他作为父亲的长子，自然不会白当的。

UNIT 16 Developing Comprehensive Abilities Through Comparative Studies and Practice

III. Compare the English versions with the original Chinese and try to find out the problems.

1. 这里又是典故之城……"黄粱美梦""毛遂自荐""负荆请罪""完璧归赵"等众多成语典故，脍炙人口，给人启迪。

   Being a town of allusions, it certainly has numerous greatly inspired allusions, such as "Golden Millet Dream (Pipe Dream)", "Mao Sui Recommending Himself (Volunteering One's Service)", "Bearing the Rod for Punishment", "Returning the Jade Intact to Zhao", etc., which are widely loved and quoted by people.

2. 自十一届三中全会以来，我地区广大干部和群众坚持四项基本原则，坚持改革开放，把工作重点转移到社会主义现代化建设上来，团结奋斗，在物质文明和精神文明建设上都取得了巨大成就。

   Since the Third Plenary Session of the 11th Central Committee, the broad masses of cadres and people in our prefecture, adhering to the Four Cardinal Principles and persisting in reform and opening, have shifted the emphasis of work to socialist modernization construction, united in struggle and achieved great successes in building both material and spiritual civilization.

3. 　　中华大地，江河纵横；华夏文化，源远流长……

   轻快的龙舟如银河流星，瑰丽的彩船似海市蜃楼，两岸那金碧辉煌的彩楼连成一片水晶宫，是仙境？是梦境？仰视彩鸽纷飞，低眸漂灯留霓，焰火怒放，火树银花，灯舞回旋，千姿百态。气垫船腾起一江春潮，射击手点破满天彩球；跳伞健儿绽空中花蕾，抢鸭勇士谱水上凯歌……啊，春江城是不夜城，龙舟会是群英会！

   The divine land of China has its rivers flowing across; the brilliant culture of China has its root tracing back long...

   The lightsome dragon-boats appear on the river as though the stars twinkle in the Milky Way. The richly decorated pleasure boats look like a scene of mirage. The splendid awnings in green and gold chain into a palace of crystal. Is this a fairyland or a mere dream? Looking above, you can see the beautiful doves flying about. Looking below, you can see the sailing lamps glittering. Cracking are the fireworks, which present you with a picture of fiery trees and silver flowers. Circling are the lantern-dancers, who present you with a variation of exquisite manners. Over there the motorboats are plowing the water, thus a tide stirs up. Over there, the marksmen are shooting to their targets; thus colorful beads whirl around. Besides, the bird's chirping, the potted landscape's charm, the exhibition of arts and painting, all claim a strong appeal to you. Therefore, we should say: Chunjiang is a city of no night; its Dragon-boat Festival a gathering of heroes.

Appendix A: Translation Exercises for Independent Work

I. E-C Translation

1. Of Studies

Studies serve for delight, for ornament and, for ability. Their chief use for delight is in privateness and retiring; for ornament, is in discourse; and for ability, is in the judgment and disposition of business. For expert men can execute, and perhaps judge of particulars, one by one; but the general counsels and the plots and marshaling of affairs, come best from those that are learned. To spend too much time in studies is sloth; to use them too much for ornament is affection; to make judgment wholly by their rules is the humour of a scholar. They perfect nature, and are perfected by experience; for natural abilities are like natural plants: that need pruning by study; and studies themselves do give forth directions too much at large, except they be bounded in by experience. Crafty men condemn studies, simple men admire them, and wise men use them; for they teach not their own use; but that there is a wisdom without them, and above them, won by observation. Read not to contradict and confute; nor to believe and take for granted; nor to find talks and discourse; but to weigh and consider. Some books are to be tasted, others to be swallowed, and some few to be chewed and digested; that is, some books are to be read only in parts; others to be read, but not curiously; and some few to be read wholly, and with diligence and attention. Some books also may be read by deputy, and extracts made of them by others, but that would be only in the less important arguments, and the meaner sort of books; else distilled books are like common distilled waters, flashy things. Reading maketh a full man; conference a ready man; and writing an exact man. And therefore, if a man write little, he had need have a great memory; if he confer little, he had need have a present wit; and if he read little, he had need have much cunning, to seem to know that he doth not. Histories make men wise; poets witty; the mathematics subtle; natural philosophy deep; moral grave; logic and rhetoric able to contend. Abeunt studia* in mores. Nay, there is no stand

---

* Abeunt studia: (Latin) studies pass into the character

APPENDIX A Translation Exercises for Independent Work

of impediment in the wit but may be wrought out by fit studies; like as diseases of the body may have appropriate exercises. Bowling is good for the stone and reins; shooting for the lungs and breast; gentle walking for stomach; riding for the head; and the like. So if a man's wit be wandering, let him study the mathematics; for in demonstrations, if his wit be called away never so little, he must begin again. If his wit be not apt to distinguish or find differences, let him study the Schoolmen; for they are cyminisectores*. If he be not apt to beat over matters, and to call up one thing to prove and illustrate another, let him study the lawyers' cases. So every defect of the mind may have a special receipt. (502 words)(直译与意译、遣词用字、增词、省略)

2. Abraham Lincoln's Gettysburg Address

Four score and seven years ago our fathers brought forth on this continent, a new nation, conceived in Liberty, and dedicated to the proposition that all men are created equal.

Now we are engaged in a great civil war, testing whether that nation or any nation so conceived and so dedicated, can long endure. We are met on a great battlefield of that war. We have come to dedicate a portion of the field, as a final resting-place for those who here gave their lives that nation might live. It is altogether fitting and proper that we should do this.

But, in a large sense, we cannot dedicate—we cannot consecrate—we cannot hallow—this ground. The brave men, living and dead, who struggled here, have consecrated it, far above our poor power to add or detract. The world will little note, nor long remember what we say here, but it can never forget what they did here. It is for us the living, rather, to be dedicated here to the unfinished work which they who fought here have thus far so nobly advanced. It is rather for us to be here dedicated to the great task remaining before us—that from these honored dead we take increased devotion to that cause for which they gave the last full measure of devotion—that we here highly resolve that these dead shall not have died in vain—that this nation, under God, shall have a new birth of freedom—and that government of the people, by the people, for the people, shall not perish from the earth. (269 words) (遣词用字、增词、省略、长句)

3. The Significance of Lincoln's Gettysburg Address

The Gettysburg Address is, in both senses of the word, memorable. It is one to

---

* cyminisectores: (Latin) hair-splitters

remember, and easy to. In just 270 words, Abraham Lincoln delivered a prose poem unrivalled in political oratory. His "brief remarks" in dedication of the Soldiers' National Cemetery at the site of the Battle of Gettysburg never strayed from consecrating the sacrifice of America's war dead. And yet, in just under three minutes, his speech soared to capture the meaning of the civil war, the nature of freedom and the promise of a nation. And Lincoln was not even the main speaker: he followed Edward Everett, a politician and famous orator of the day, who spoke for just over two hours. At the time, Everett got the more favourable reviews.

"Four score and seven years ago," Lincoln began, "our Fathers brought forth on this continent a new nation, conceived in Liberty, and dedicated to the proposition that all men are created equal." This whiff of biblical grandeur disguised what was, in the throes of war, a radical assertion. For Lincoln was standing on a battlefield where, just a few months earlier, the army of the Union had scored a bloody victory over the Confederates of the South. Both sides had lost many thousands of men. It was hard to see that Thursday afternoon in November 1863 what the Battle of Gettysburg had been for. Lincoln's answer was clear: it was for more than just the principles of the Constitution, it was for the ideals—equality, as well as life, liberty and the pursuit of happiness—enshrined in *The Declaration of Independence* of 1776. The Confederates clung to the Constitution, claiming to have legal right on their side. In a single sentence, Lincoln made the moral case for the Union.

What is so affecting, however, is that the Gettysburg Address is much more than a political argument. It is an expression of humility. The speech recognizes the inadequacy of speeches. Yet Lincoln does manage to add to those lost lives. He calls on the living to dedicate themselves to the higher purpose of the fallen, "that from these honoured dead we take increased devotion to that cause for which they gave the last full measure of devotion." Lincoln had tried out a similar line a couple of years earlier, but he never nailed it quite so pithily as he did that day.

Not everyone got it. Lincoln's delivery, some said, was shrill, even a little squeaky. *The Times* correspondent deemed it "ludicrous", commenting that "anything more dull and commonplace it would not be easy to produce". Lincoln himself prefaced his dedication by saying "the world will little note, nor long remember what we say here." He was wrong about that. (454 words)（遣词用字、增添省略、专有名词）

4.　History of Western Philosophy

During the 15th century, various other causes were added to the decline of the Papacy

APPENDIX A Translation Exercises for Independent Work

to produce a very rapid change, both political and cultural. Gunpowder strengthened central government at the expense of feudal nobility. In France and England, Louis XI and Edward IV allied themselves with the rich middle class, who helped them to quell aristocratic anarchy. Italy, until the last years of the century, was fairly free from Northern armies, and advanced rapidly both in wealth and culture. The new culture was essentially pagan, admiring Greece and Rome, and despising the Middle Ages. Architecture and literary style were adapted to ancient models. When Constantinople, the last survival of antiquity, was captured by the Turks, Greek refugees in Italy were welcomed by humanists. Vasco da Gama and Columbus enlarged the world, and Copernicus enlarged the heavens. The Donation Constantine was rejected as a fable, and overwhelmed with scholarly derision. By the help of the Byzantines, Plato came to be known, not only in Neoplatonic and Augustinian versions, but at first hand. This sublunary sphere appeared no longer as a vale of tears, a place of painful pilgrimage to another world, but as affording opportunity for pagan delights, for fame and beauty and adventure. The long centuries of asceticism were forgotten in a riot of art and poetry and pleasure. Even in Italy, it is true, the Middle ages did not die without a struggle; Savonarola and Leonard were born in the same year. But in the main the old terrors had ceased to be terrifying, and the new liberty of the spirit was found to be intoxicating. The intoxication could not last, but for the moment it shut out fear. In this moment of joyful liberation the modern world was born. (292 words)(遣词用字、增词、结构调整)

5.　Words! Words! Words!

"It works." These words may be the final judgment on a missile project or a plan to increase the efficiency of a labor group or could be the happy answer to the project that proved too complicated for father to assemble. They also may describe what goes on when the right mixture is put away in sealed bottles or jugs. Some earn their living at a boiler "works" and it is the "works" that make a watch tick. Most people work for a living, but what teenager hasn't "worked" on his dad for the use of the car. And a boat will work its way through an ice field or an army work through a swamp or heavy going.

　　The physicist has a precise meaning for the word "work", but the metallurgist uses the word in relation to a wide variety of processes. Cogging of ingots, rolling of bars or sheets, forging of bars, blocks, or semi-finished parts, piercing of bars to form tubing, drawing of wire through dies or the drawing of sheet into cups, swaging, hammering, extruding, all are operations involving the "working" of materials and produce parts that are classed as "worked" metals. "Work" to the metallurgist is any operation that changes the shape of a metal part without changing its volume. A nail bent by a hammer is "worked" and the straightening that follows is further working. The making of an automobile fender, of a tube for toothpaste, or of an aluminum safety are common examples which involve severe working of metals. Of all parts made of metals, castings and sintered products are the only classes of final product which do not, at some stage or other in their manufacture, go through one or more operations which are classed as "working." (295 words)(遣词用字)

6. The Most Important Speech of the 20th Century

We learned how far up he's come on New Year's Day when every Chinese newspaper heralded a 6,000-word speech in which Deng signaled the end of thousands of years of Chinese xenophobia.

It may eventually come to be regarded the most important speech of the century. For in it, the Maximum Leader of the nation that comprises one-fourth of mankind served notice that China is joining the rest of the world (save Albania) in the 20th century.

"No country can develop by closing its door," said Deng. "We suffered from this, and our forefathers suffered from this." Reversing thousands of years of official hostility to the world outside the Great Wall, Deng said simply: "Isolation landed China in poverty, backwardness and ignorance."

This startling admission contradicts thousands of years of Chinese policy, going back beyond the Ming Dynasty to the Chin Dynasty, when the wall was erected to keep barbarians on horseback out in the wilds where they belonged.

Deng's message: Do not renounce Marxism, but adopt capitalist ideas where they make sense—"it cannot harm us". Economic reform, spearheaded by younger leaders, is the single most important bulwark for the nation's security, for only with economic strength can bombs, missiles and planes be purchased.

If China is trying to catch up to the rest of the world in the 20th century, maybe the 21st century will belong to them. They have people, brains and they can be impressively disciplined. And their industrial potential is awesome.

It may come to be commonly accepted in the next century that the most significant speech ever given by a fellow with a cowboy hat came not from Ronald Reagan but from an 80-year-old Chinese man. (284 words)(遣词用字、语气措辞)

APPENDIX A Translation Exercises for Independent Work

7. How Should One Read a Book?

It is simple enough to say that since books have classes—fiction, biography, poetry—we should separate them and take from each what it is right that each should give us. Yet few people ask from books what books can give us. Most commonly we come to books with blurred and divided minds, asking of fiction that it shall be true, of poetry that it shall be false, of biography that it shall be flattering, of history that it shall enforce our prejudices. If we could banish all such preconceptions when we read, that would be an admirable beginning. Do not dictate to your author: try to become him. Be his fellow-worker and accomplice. If you hang back, and reserve and criticise at first, you are preventing yourself from getting the fullest possible value from what you read. But if you open your mind as widely as possible, then signs and hints of almost imperceptible fineness, from the twist and turn of the first sentences, will bring you into a presence of human being unlike any other. Steep yourself in this, acquaint yourself with this, and soon you will find that your author is giving you, or attempting to give you, something far more definite.

The thirty-two chapters of a novel—if we consider how to read a novel first—are an attempt to make something as formed and controlled as a building: but words are more impalpable than bricks; reading is a longer and more complicated process than seeing. Perhaps the quickest way to understand the elements of what a novelist is doing is not to read, but to write; to make your own experiment with the dangers and difficulties of words. Recall, then, some event that has left a distinct impressions on you—how at the corner of the street, perhaps, you passed two people talking. A tree shook; an electric light danced; the tone of the talk was comic, but also tragic; a whole vision, an entire conception seemed contained in that moment.

But when you attempt to reconstruct it in words, you will find that it breaks into thousands of conflicting impressions. Some must be subdued; others emphasized; in the process you will lose, probably, all grasp upon the emotion itself. Then turn from your blurred and littered pages to the opening pages of some great novelist—Defoe, Jane Austen, Hardy. Now you will be better able to appreciate their mastery. (405 words)(名词性从句、状语从句)

8. Off the Dime

The meaning of *to get off the dime*, as native speakers know, is "to start moving; to stop stalling." But what's the origin? And why hasn't the old slang phrase faded along with the value of the 10-cent piece, in an era when hardly anything can be bought for *a dime a dozen*?

A dime, from the Latin *decem*, "ten", is the smallest and thinnest U.S. coin. In metaphor, it signifies anything especially tiny. When you are driving, and mean to stop at a precise point, not in a general area—you *stop on a dime*.

Thanks to Jonathan Lighter's *Historical Dictionary of American Slang*, we have the activity that coined the phrase. Carl Van Vechter, one of the earliest modern dance critics and author of the 1926 novel *Nigger Heaven*—a title nobody would use today—described the scene in a taxi-dance hall: "Sometimes a couple would scarcely move from one spot. Then the floor manager would cry, *Git off dat dime*!"

To dance on a dime was to grind bodies tightly together in clothed but sexual contact, without moving from that spot; taxi dancers working for a dime (immortalized in the 1930 Lorenz Hart lyric *Ten Cents a Dance*) were exhorted by their bosses to keep the customers moving. Thus, *to get off the dime* came to mean "to get moving." (I get a kick out of finding that out. What a rich language we speak, often without knowing its resonances.)

Dime is still used as a teenage slang synonym for a beautiful woman. This stems from the 1979 movie *10*, starring Bo Derek, and is rooted in "On a scale from 1 to 10, she's a 10." She is now a dime.

Behind a dime is an expression of suspicion. A Southernism in the mid-20th century was "I wouldn't trust him *behind a dime*." A dime is not only small and difficult to hide behind, but also notably thin, as in the phrase *not one thin dime*. Extreme distrust is shown in *behind a dime edgeways*.

Gangsters who wish to rat on their partners in crime with a telephone call to the police or FBI have a linguistic problem. The slang phrase meaning "to inform, betray" used to be to *drop a dime*. However, it has been a long time since a call from a pay phone cost 10 cents; in recent years, the only Mafioso betrayers who used the phrase *drop a dime* were elderly and often short of change. There is as yet no known underworld lingo to express snitching by using a cellphone. "Punch M for Murder" was suggested here this spring. It has been scorned by Mafiosi. (448 words)(直译与意译、遣词用字)

9. Enchantment of the South Sea Islands

The mighty Pacific washes the shores of five continents—North America, South America, Asia, Australia, and Antarctica. Its waters mingle in the southeast with the Atlantic Ocean and in the southwest with the Indian Ocean. It is not on the shores of continents, nor in the coastal islands, however, that the soul of the great Pacific is found. It lies far out where the fabled South Sea Islands are scattered over the huge ocean like stars in the sky.

Here great disturbances at the heart of the earth caused mountains and volcanoes to rise above the water. For hundreds of years tiny coral creatures have worked and died to make thousands of ring-shaped islands called atolls.

The air that sweeps the South Sea Islands is fragrant with flowers and spice. Bright warm days follow clear cool nights, and the rolling swells break in a neverending roar on the shores. Overhead the slender coconut palms whisper their drowsy song.

When white men first came to the Pacific islands, they found that the people living there were like happy children. They were tall men and beautiful women who seemed not to have a care in the world. Coconut palms and breadfruit trees grew at the doors of their huts. The ocean was filled with turtles and fish, ready for the net. The islanders had little need for clothing. There was almost no disease.

Cruel and bloody wars sometimes broke out between neighboring tribes, and canoe raids were sometimes made on nearby islands. The strong warriors enjoyed fighting. Many of the islanders were cannibals, who cooked and ate the enemies they killed. This was part of their law and religion. These savages, however, were usually friendly, courteous, and hospitable. Some of the early explorers were so fascinated with the Pacific islands that they never returned to their own countries. They preferred to stay. (311 words)(词类转换、句子成分转换)

10. Bruce Lee

Bruce Lee was born, according to the Chinese zodiac, during the Hour of the Dragon in the Year of the Dragon. His birth took place during an American tour of Hong Kong's Cantonese Opera Company, in which his father was a comic actor. Known in the family as Little Dragon, Lee was actually sickly and weak; he took up martial arts as a means of self-protection around his tough neighborhoods and soon became agile and versatile. A year after being named the Hong Kong Cha-Cha Champion at eighteen, he returned to the United States, where he studied philosophy and medicine.

On the side, Lee mastered every physical technique of fighting, becoming almost super-naturally good. Eventually he was most often either working out, thinking about it, or teaching others. On the street he practiced kicks on trees and pieces of litter. At the dinner table he chopped at the empty chair next to him; while watching TV he did very slow sit-ups, and even in his sleep he would kick and punch. At parties he did one-finger push-ups and would gladly remove his shirt to show off his "muscles on top of muscles". He believed that concentration was 50 percent of a workout, and "Meditation and Mental Training" always topped his daily to-do list.

Deciding that film was the best way to dispel martial arts' reputation as glorified street fighting, Lee began making his own movies, with himself as the writer, star, director, and choreographer of the fights. In the United States, his movies included *Fists of Fury, Return of the Dragon,* and finally *Enter the Dragon,* considered one of the most commercially successful films ever made.

Lee planned to retire at thirty-five, to spend more time with his family and do something beneficial for society, but he died at thirty-two from a swelling resulting from fluid on the brain. For someone in such superb condition to die abruptly was so strange that rumors have flown ever since. One rumor claims that, like Elvis Presley, Lee is still alive and waiting to return to public life. But his body is buried in Seattle—next to that of his son, Brandon, who also became a movie actor and died suddenly, in 1993 at age twenty-eight, after being accidentally shot during the filming of a violent movie called *The Crow*. (388 words)(遣词用字、结构调整、专有名词)

11. "Winner" and "Loser"

The word "winner" and "loser" have many meanings. When we refer to a person as a winner, we do not mean one who makes someone else lose. To us, a winner is one who responds authentically by being credible, trustworthy, responsive, and genuine, both as an individual and as a member of a society.

Winners do not dedicate their lives to a concept of what they imagine they should be; rather, they are themselves and as such do not use their energy putting on a performance, maintaining pretence, and manipulating others. They are aware that there is a difference between being loving and acting loving, between being stupid and acting stupid, between being knowledgeable and acting knowledgeable. Winners do not need to hide behind a mask.

Winners are not afraid to do their own thinking and to use their own knowledge. They can separate facts from opinions and don't pretend to have all the answers. They listen to others, evaluate what they say, but come to their own conclusions. Although winners can admire and respect other people, they are not totally defined, demolished, bound, or awed by them.

Winners do not play "helpless", nor do they play the blaming game. Instead, they assume responsibility for their own lives. (208 words)(遣词用字、词类转换、结构调整)

APPENDIX A Translation Exercises for Independent Work

12. Versatile Man

It is, perhaps, no accident that many of the outstanding figures of the past were exceptionally versatile men. Right up until comparatively recent times, it was possible for an intelligent person to acquaint himself with almost every branch of knowledge. Thus, men of genius like Leonardo da Vinci or Sir Philip Sidney, engaged in many careers at once as a matter of course. Da Vinci was so busy with his numerous inventions, that he barely found the time to complete his paintings; Sidney, who died in battle when he was only thirty-two years old, was not only a great soldier, but a brilliant scholar and poet as well. Both these men came very near to fulfilling the Renaissance ideal of the "universal man", the man who was proficient at everything.

Today, we rarely, if ever, hear that a musician has just invented a new type of submarine. Knowledge has become divided and sub-divided into countless, narrowly-defined compartments. The specialist is venerated; the versatile person, far from being admired, is more often regarded with suspicion. The modern world is a world of highly-skilled "experts" who have had to devote the greater part of their lives to a very limited field of study in order to compete with their fellows.

With this high degree of specialization, the frontiers of knowledge are steadily being pushed back more rapidly than ever before. But this has not been achieved without considerable cost. The scientist, who outside his own particular subject is little more than a moron, is a modern phenomenon; as is the man of letters who is barely aware of the tremendous strides that have been made in technology. Similarly, specialization has indirectly affected quite ordinary people in every walk of life. Many activities which were once pursued for their own sakes, are often given up in despair: they require techniques, the experts tell us, which take a lifetime to master. Why learn to play the piano, when you can listen to the world's greatest pianists in your own drawing room?

Little by little, we are becoming more and more isolated from each other. It is almost impossible to talk to your neighbour about his job, even if he is engaged in roughly the same work as you are. The Royal Society in Britain includes among its members only the most eminent scientists in the country. Yet it is highly disconcerting to find that even here, as one of its Fellows put it, at a lecture only 10% of the members can understand 50% of what is being said! (425 words)(结构调整、定语从句、状语从句)

13. Thinness and Vainglory

No woman can be too rich or too thin. This saying often attributed to the late Duchess of Windsor embodies much of the odd spirit of our times. Being thin is deemed as such a virtue.

The problem with such a view is that some people actually attempt to live by it. I myself have fantasies of slipping into narrow designer clothes. Consequently, I have been on a diet for the better—or worse—part of my life. Being rich wouldn't be bad either, but that won't happen unless an unknown relative dies suddenly in some distant land, leaving me millions of dollars.

Where did we go off the track? When did eating butter become a sin, and a little bit of extra flesh unappealing, if not repellent? All religions have certain days when people refrain from eating and excessive eating is one of Christianity's seven deadly sins. However, until quite recently, most people had a problem getting enough to eat. In some religious groups, wealth was a symbol of probable salvation and high morals, and fatness a sign of wealth and wellbeing.

Today the opposite is true. We have shifted to thinness as our new mark of virtue. The result is that being fat—or even only somewhat overweight—is bad because it implies a lack of moral strength.

Our obsession with thinness is also fueled by health concerns. It is true that in this country we have more overweight people than ever before, and that, in many cases, being overweight correlates with an increased risk of heart and blood vessel disease. These diseases, however, may have as much to do with our way of life and our highfat diets as with excess weight. And the associated risk of cancer in the digestive system may be more of a dietary problem—too much fat and a lack of fiber—than a weight problem.

The real concern, then, is not that we weigh too much, but that we neither exercise enough nor eat well. Exercise is necessary for strong bones and both heart and lung health. A balanced diet without a lot of fat can also help the body avoid many diseases. We should surely stop paying so much attention to weight. Simply being thin is not enough. It is actually hazardous if those who get (or already are) thin think they are automatically healthy and thus free form paying attention to their overall lifestyle. Thinness can be pure vainglory. (410 words)(正反调换、结构调整)

14. Obscure Characters in Chinese Names

"Ma", a Chinese character for horse, is the 13th most common family name in China, shared by nearly 17 million people. That can cause no end of confusion when Mas get together, especially if those Mas also share the same given name, as many Chinese do.

Ma Cheng's bookloving grandfather came up with an elegant solution to this common problem. Twenty-six years ago, when his granddaughter was born, he combed through his

APPENDIX A Translation Exercises for Independent Work

library of Chinese dictionaries and lighted upon a character pronounced "cheng". Cheng, which means galloping steeds, looks just like the character for horse, except that it is condensed and written three times in a row.

For Ma Cheng and millions of others, Chinese parents' desire to give their children a spark of individuality is colliding head-on with the Chinese bureaucracy's desire for order. Seeking to modernize its vast database on China's 1.3 billion citizens, the government's Public Security Bureau has been replacing the handwritten identity card that every Chinese must carry with a computer-readable one, complete with color photos and embedded microchips. The new cards are harder to forge and can be scanned at places like airports where security is a priority.

The bureau's computers, however, are programmed to read only 32,252 of the roughly 55,000 Chinese characters, according to a 2006 government report. The result is that Miss Ma and at least some of the 60 million other Chinese with obscure characters in their names cannot get new cards—unless they change their names to something more common.

Moreover, the situation is about to get worse or, in the government's view, better. Since at least 2003, China has been working on a standardized list of characters for people to use in everyday life, including when naming children.

One newspaper reported last week that the list would be issued later this year and would curb the use of obscure names. A government linguistics official told Xinhua, the state-run news agency, that the list would include more than 8,000 characters. Although that is far fewer than the database now supposedly includes, the official said it was more than enough "to convey any concept in any field". About 3,500 characters are in everyday use.

Government officials suggest that names have gotten out of hand, with too many parents picking the most obscure characters they can find or even making up characters, like linguistic fashion accessories. But many Chinese couples take pride in searching the rich archives of classical Chinese to find a distinctive, pleasing name, partly to help their children stand out in a society with strikingly few surnames.

By some estimates, 100 surnames cover 85 percent of China's citizens. Laobaixing, or "old hundred names", is a colloquial term for the masses. By contrast, 70,000 surnames cover 90 percent of Americans. (461 words)(遣词用字、结构调整)

15. The Mobile Culture

Technologies tend to be global, both by nature and by name. Say "television", "computer" or "internet" anywhere and chances are you will be understood. But hand-held phones? For this ubiquitous technology, mankind suffers from a Tower of Babel syndrome. Under millions of Christmas trees North and South Americans have been unwrapping cell phones or celulares. Yet to Britons and Spaniards they are mobiles or móviles. Germans and Finns refer to them as Handys, because they fit in your hand. The Chinese, too, make calls on a *shou ji,* or "hand machine". And in Japan the term of art is *keitai*, which roughly means "something you can carry with you".

This disjunction is revealing for an object that, in the space of a decade, has become as essential to human functioning as a pair of shoes. Mobile phones do not share a single global moniker because the origins of their names are deeply cultural. "Cellular" refers to how modern wireless networks are built, pointing to a technological worldview in America. "Mobile" emphasizes that the device is untethered, which fits the roaming, onceimperial British style. "Handy" highlights the importance of functionality, much appreciated in Germany. But are such differences more than cosmetic? And will they persist or give way to a global mobile culture?

As airtime gets cheaper, the untethered masses tend to use their mobiles more. In early 2000 an average user spoke for 174 minutes a month, according to the GSM Association (GSMA), an industry group. By early 2009 that had risen to 261 minutes, which suggests that humanity spends over 1 trillion minutes a month on mobiles, or nearly 2m years. Nobody can keep track of the flood of text messages.

On average Germans—who are fond of saying that "talk is silver, silence is golden"—spend only 89 minutes each month calling others for Handy-based conversation. In contrast, Americans won't shut up. Their average monthly talk-time is a whopping 788 minutes. The chattiest of all are Puerto Ricans, who have by far the highest monthly average in the world of 1,875 minutes, probably because operators on the island offer all-you-can-talk plans for only $40, which include calls to the mainland. In Paris people openly complained when bothered by others talking loudly about intimate matters, but complaints were rare in London. In both places, people tended to separate phone and face-to-face conversations, for instance by retreating to a quiet corner. The Chinese often let themselves be interrupted, fearing that otherwise they could miss a business opportunity. China is distinct because of economics and relatively lax regulation. Many consumers use *shanzhai* ("bandit") phones, produced by hundreds of small handset-makers. Knockoffs are common, with labels such as "Nckia" and "Sumsung". Other innovative manufacturers have developed specialised phones, for instance handsets that can respond to two phone numbers, or models with giant speakers for farmers on noisy tractors. (477 words)(遣词用字、结构调整、定语从句）

APPENDIX A Translation Exercises for Independent Work

16. The Beauty of Science

Judging from the scientists I know, including Eva and Ruth, and those I've read about, you can't pursue the laws of nature very long without bumping into beauty. "I don't know if it's the same beauty you see in the sunset," a friend tells me, "but it feels the same." This friend is a physicist, who has spent a long career deciphering what must be happening in the interior of stars. He recalls for me this thrill on grasping for the first time Dirac's equations describing quantum mechanics, or those of Einstein describing relativity. "They're so beautiful," he says, "you can see immediately they have to be true. Or at least on the way toward truth." I ask him what makes a theory beautiful, and he replies, "Simplicity, symmetry, elegance, and power."

Why nature should conform to theories we find beautiful is far from obvious. The most incomprehensible thing about the universe, as Einstein said, is that it's comprehensible. How unlikely, that a short-lived biped on a two-bit planet should be able to gauge the speed of light, lay bare the structure of an atom, or calculate the gravitational tug of a black hole. We're a long way from understanding everything, but we do understand a great deal about how nature behaves. Generation after generation, we puzzle out formulas, test them, and find, to an astonishing degree, that nature agrees. An architect draws designs on flimsy paper, and her buildings stand up through earthquakes. We launch a satellite into orbit and use it to bounce messages from continent to continent. The machine on which I write these words embodies hundreds of insights into the workings of the material world, insights that are confirmed by every burst of letters on the screen, and I stare at that screen through lenses that obey the laws of optics first worked out in detail by Isaac Newton.

By discerning patterns in the universe, Newton believed, he was tracing the hand of God. Scientists in our day have largely abandoned the notion of a Creator as an unnecessary hypothesis, or at least an untestable one. While they share Newton's faith that the universe is ruled everywhere by a coherent set of rules, they cannot say, as scientists, how these particular rules came to govern things. You can do science without believing in a divine Legislator, but not without believing in laws. (400 words)(上下文语境、综合能力)

17. Saving Lives and Money

An eye for an eye, or at any rate a death for a death, is the type of justice that most states still embrace. Only 14 of the 50 states have banned capital punishment. But that may change with the recession. As state governments confront huge budget deficits, eight more states have proposed an unusual measure to cut costs: eliminate the death penalty.

The states considering abolition, including Colorado, Kansas, New Mexico and New Hampshire, have shifted the debate about capital punishment, at least in part, from morality to cost. Studies show that administering the death penalty is even more expensive than keeping someone in prison for life. The intensive jury selection, trials and appeals required in capital cases can take over a decade and run up a huge tab for the state. Death row, where prisoners facing execution are kept in separate cells under intense observation, is also immensely costly.

A recent study by the Urban Institute, a think-tank, estimates that the death penalty cost Maryland's taxpayers $186m between 1978 and 1999. According to the report, a case resulting in a death sentence cost $3m, almost $2m more than when the death penalty was not sought.

In an age of austerity, every million dollars counts. Proponents of the abolition bills describe the death penalty as an expensive programme with few benefits. There is little evidence that the death penalty deters. In fact, some of the states that most avidly execute prisoners, such as Texas and Oklahoma, have higher crime rates than states that offer only life in prison without parole. There is also the danger that innocent people may be put to death. So far, more than 130 people who had been sentenced to death have been exonerated.

Colorado, one of the states that has introduced a bill to overturn the death penalty, intends to spend the money it will save each year by eliminating capital punishment on an investigations unit. According to Paul Weissman, the state House majority leader and the bill's co-sponsor, around 1,400 murders are still unsolved in the state. Eliminating the death penalty will finance the new unit and leave an extra $1m for other state programmes. Other states are trying to free up funding to help offset their huge deficits. Savings from abolishing the death penalty in Kansas, for example, are estimated at $500,000 for every case in which the death penalty is not sought.

Many other states, including Texas, which last year carried out almost half of all executions in America, have no plans to follow suit. But a prolonged recession may change a few Texan minds. (434 words)(遣词用字、词字增减、结构调整)

18. High Heels—a Woman's Worst Enemy

In department stores and closets all over the world, they are waiting. Their outward appearance seems rather appealing because they come in a variety of styles, textures, and colors. But they are ultimately the biggest deception that exists in the fashion industry today. What are they? They are high heels—a woman's worst enemy (whether she knows

APPENDIX A Translation Exercises for Independent Work

it or not). High heel shoes are the downfall of modern society. Fashion myths have led women to believe that they are more beautiful or sophisticated for wearing heels, but in reality, heels succeed in posing short as well as long term hardships. Women should fight the high heel industry by refusing to use or purchase them in order to save the world from unnecessary physical and psychological suffering.

For the sake of fairness, it must be noted that there is a positive side to high heels. First, heels are excellent for aerating lawns. Anyone who has ever worn heels on grass knows what I am talking about. A simple trip around the yard in a pair of those babies eliminates all need to call for a lawn care specialist, and provides the perfect-sized holes to give any lawn oxygen without all those messy chunks of dirt lying around. Second, heels are quite functional for defense against oncoming enemies, who can easily be scared away by threatening them with a pair of these sharp, deadly fashion accessories.

Regardless of such practical uses for heels, the fact remains that wearing high heels is harmful to one's physical health. Talk to any podiatrist, and you will hear that the majority of their business comes from high-heel-wearing women. High heels are known to cause problems such as deformed feet and torn toenails. The risk of severe back problems and twisted or broken ankles is three times higher for a high heel wearer than for a flat shoe wearer. Wearing heels also creates the threat of getting a heel caught in a sidewalk crack or a sewer-grate and being thrown to the ground—possibly breaking a nose, back, or neck. And of course, after wearing heels for a day, any woman knows she can look forward to a night of pain as she tries to comfort her swollen, aching feet. (373 words)(词字增减、词类转换)

19. Tipping

Tipping is a subject that has long interested and irritated me. Many people think that the word "tip" is an acronym for "to insure promptness". However, this is not possible, I think. Since the practice of tipping began in England in the Middle Ages, scholars have not been able to find any acronyms much earlier than the 20th century. Most scholars track the word "tip" back to the early 1600s, where it originated as criminal slang. It referred to inside information. Therefore, to give another criminal a tip was to give something valuable (information).

The word gradually evolved to the point where, in the late 1700's, it meant to give a monetary gratuity (tip) to someone for service performed. That's where it stayed until the English immigrated to North America.

In America, the three basic occupations that require tipping are waiters/waitresses, taxi drivers, and barbers. The standard tip is now between 15 and 20 percent of the bill, depending on the quality of service.

Why these three particular services deserve this special treatment is a mystery to me. Why am I supposed to tip a waiter for bringing me food when I'm not expected to tip the flight attendant on an airplane for doing the same thing? Why am I supposed to tip a cab driver, but I'm not expected to tip the bus driver? Why am I supposed to tip the barber for cutting my hair but not the dentist for fixing my teeth? I have been a teacher for 39 years. No one has ever tipped me after a particularly successful class or lecture.

The whole concept of tipping doesn't make any sense. I have heard that there are some exclusive and expensive restaurants in major cities in the U.S. where the restaurant does not give the waiters any salary at all due to the large amounts of the tips. In fact, in some instances, I read that the waiters actually pay the restaurant a small fee for the opportunity to collect the large tips.

Also, I was quite surprised to learn that there was actually a website devoted to tipping and related issues (http://www.tipping.org). Some of the invisible and illogical rules of this practice are close to ridiculous.

The tipping problem in many European countries is solved by automatically adding a 15 percent gratuity to the bill. I prefer the Chinese solution: no tipping at all. While I understand why China, as a developing nation, has adopted many western customs, I hope the Chinese are wise enough to never start the unnecessary practice of tipping. The level of service in China is already good enough that it doesn't need anything to make it better. (450 words)(遣词用字、态度语气)

20. The Sokal Hoax

In 1996 Alan Sokal, a physicist at New York University, submitted a paper to *Social Text*, a leading scholarly journal of postmodernist cultural studies. The journal's peer reviewers, whose job it is to ensure that published research is up to snuff, gave it a resounding thumbs-up. But when the editors duly published the paper, Dr. Sokal revealed that it had been liberally, and deliberately, "salted with nonsense". The Sokal hoax, as it came to be known, demonstrated how easy it was for any old drivel to pass academic quality control in highbrow humanities journals, so long as it contained lots of fancy words and pandered to referees' and editors' ideological preconceptions. Hard scientists gloated. That could never happen in proper science, they sniffed. Or could it?

Alas, as a report in this week's *Science* shows, the answer is yes, it could. John Bohannon, a biologist at Harvard with a side gig as a science journalist, wrote his own

APPENDIX A Translation Exercises for Independent Work

Sokalesque paper describing how a chemical extracted from lichen apparently slowed the growth of cancer cells. He then submitted the study, under a made-up name from a fictitious academic institution, to 304 peer-reviewed journals around the world.

Despite bursting with clangers in experimental design, analysis and interpretation of results, the study passed muster at 157 of them. Only 98 rejected it. (The remaining 49 had either not responded or had not reviewed the paper by the time *Science* went to press.) Just 36 came back with comments implying that they had cottoned on to the paper's sundry deficiencies, though Dr. Bohannon says that 16 of those eventually accepted it anyway.

The publications Dr. Bohannon selected for his sting operation were all open-access journals. These make papers available free, and cover their costs by charging authors a fee (typically $1,000-2,000). Policymakers have been keen on such periodicals of late. Since taxpayers already sponsor most academic research, the thinking goes, providing free access to its fruits does not seem unreasonable. But critics of the open-access model have long warned that making authors rather than readers their client risks skewing publishers' incentives towards tolerating shoddy science.

Dr. Bohannon has shown that the risk is real. Researchers can take comfort that the most prestigious open-access journals, such as those published by the Public Library of Science, an American outfit, did not fall for the jape. But plenty of periodicals run by other prominent publishers, such as Elsevier, Wolters Kluwer and Sage, did. With the number of open-access papers forecast to grow from 194,000 in 2011 (out of a total of 1.7m publications) to 352,000 in 2015, the Bohannon hoax ought to focus editors' minds—and policymakers', too. (441 words）（遣词用字、结构调整、增添省略、语气把握）

21. The Misfiring Property Market

Buy land, advised Mark Twain; they're not making it any more. In fact, land is not really scarce: the entire population of America could fit into Texas with more than an acre for each household to enjoy. What drives prices skyward is a collision between rampant demand and limited supply in the great metropolises like London, Mumbai and New York. In the past ten years real prices in Hong Kong have risen by 150%. Residential property in Mayfair, in central London, can go for as much as £55,000 ($82,000) per square metre. A square mile of Manhattan residential property costs $16.5 billion.

Even in these great cities the scarcity is artificial. Regulatory limits on the height and density of buildings constrain supply and inflate prices. A recent analysis by academics at the London School of Economics estimates that land-use regulations in the West End of London inflate the price of office space by about 800%; in Milan and Paris the rules push up prices by around 300%. Most of the enormous value captured by landowners exists because it is well-nigh impossible to build new offices to compete those profits away.

The costs of this misfiring property market are huge, mainly because of their effects on individuals. High housing prices force workers towards cheaper but less productive places. According to one study, employment in the Bay Area around San Francisco would be about five times larger than it is but for tight limits on construction. Tot up these costs in lost earnings and unrealized human potential, and the figures become dizzying. Lifting all the barriers to urban growth in America could raise the country's GDP by between 6.5% and 13.5%, or by about $1 trillion-2 trillion. It is difficult to think of many other policies that would yield anything like that.

Two long-run trends have led to this fractured market. One is the revival of the city as the central cog in the global economic machine. In the 20th century, tumbling transport costs weakened the gravitational pull of the city; in the 21st, the digital revolution has restored it. Knowledge-intensive industries such as technology and finance thrive on the clustering of workers who share ideas and expertise. The economies and populations of metropolises like London, New York and San Francisco have rebounded as a result.

What those cities have not regained is their historical ability to stretch in order to accommodate all those who want to come. There is a good reason for that: unconstrained urban growth in the late 19th century fostered crime and disease. Hence the second trend, the proliferation of green belts and rules on zoning. Over the course of the past century land-use rules have piled up so plentifully that getting planning permission is harder than hailing a cab on a wet afternoon. (466 words）（遣词用字、结构调整、长句切短）

22. You Are What You Eat

That orientals and occidentals think in different ways is not mere prejudice. Many psychological studies conducted over the past two decades suggest Westerners have a more individualistic, analytic and abstract mental life than do East Asians. Several hypotheses have been put forward to explain this.

One, that modernisation promotes individualism, falls at the first hurdle: Japan, an ultra-modern country whose people have retained a collective outlook. A second, that a higher prevalence of infectious disease in a place makes contact with strangers more dangerous, and causes groups to turn inward, is hardly better. Europe has had its share of plagues; probably more that either Japan or Korea. And though southern China is notoriously a source of infection (influenza pandemics often start there), this is not true of other parts of that enormous country.

APPENDIX A Translation Exercises for Independent Work

That led Thomas Talhelm of the University of Virginia and his colleagues to look into a third suggestion: that the crucial difference is agricultural. The West's staple is wheat; the East's, rice. Before the mechanisation of agriculture a farmer who grew rice had to expend twice as many hours doing so as one who grew wheat. To deploy labour efficiently, especially at times of planting and harvesting, rice-growing societies as far apart as India, Malaysia and Japan all developed co-operative labour exchanges which let neighbours stagger their farms' schedules in order to assist each other during these crucial periods. Since, until recently, almost everyone alive was a farmer, it is a reasonable hypothesis that such a collective outlook would dominate a society's culture and behaviour, and might prove so deep-rooted that even now, when most people earn their living in other ways, it helps to define their lives.

Mr. Talhelm realised that this idea is testable. Large swathes of China, particularly in the north, depend not on rice, but on wheat. That, as he explains in a paper in *Science*, let him and his team put some flesh on this theory's bones.

The team gathered almost 1,200 volunteers from all over China and asked them questions to assess their individualism or collectivism. The answers bore little relation to the wealth of a volunteer's place of origin, which Mr. Talhelm saw as a proxy for how modern it was, or to its level of public health. There was a striking correlation, though, with whether it was a rice-growing or a wheat-growing area. This difference was marked even between people from neighbouring counties with different agricultural traditions. His hypothesis that the different psychologies of East and West are, at least in part, a consequence of their agriculture thus looks worth further exploration. And such exploration is possible—for India, too, has rice-growing and wheat-growing regions. (447 words)（遣词用字、增添省略、结构调整）

23. Inventors in Two Ways

In the 19th century, inventors were heroes. The likes of Stephenson, Morse and Goodyear were the shock troops of the Industrial Revolution. Their ideas helped drag humanity from agrarian poverty to manufactured plenty. These days, though, inventor-superstars, while not absent, are fewer and farther between.

That may, in part, be because the process of invention has itself changed since the 19th century. There is no let-up in the growth of the number of patents issued each year, but the introduction of fundamentally new classes of technology seems rarer now than it was in the past. Information technology has certainly transformed the present day. But railways, the electric telegraph, photography, fixed-line telephony, the automobile and the chemical and steel industries each, separately, brought about transformations as big as anything IT has wrought so far. Perhaps the process of invention really was more heroic in Victorian times.

To have an impression that something has changed is not, however, to prove that it really has. For that you need data. And, in a paper just published in *The Journal of the Royal Society Interface*, Youn Hyejin of Oxford University and her colleagues have provided some.

Invention can come about in two ways. Thomas Edison's light bulb, for example, was not so much the product of a metaphorical light-bulb moment of discovery as of the bringing together of pre-existing components—an electricity supply, a heated filament, a vacuum and a glass envelope. None of these things was novel in the 1870s, but in Edison's hands the combination became a patentable invention. In contrast, William Shockley's transistor, invented 70 years later, involved a lot of new physics that Shockley and his colleagues had to work out for themselves. Both devices changed the world, though Shockley's was the foundation on which IT was built. And together they exemplify the two sorts of novelty that exist, in differing proportions, in any successful invention: discovery and recombination.

Most inventions up until now have been based on physics or chemistry. Today's understanding of biology, though, is roughly where that of the physical sciences was in the 19th century. Biology is therefore ripe to yield a clutch of new patent classes—possibly for things (neurological computers? furniture grown from seed?) as unimaginable to present-day folk as the telephone would have been to a soldier at the battle of Waterloo. Then, perhaps, a new generation of heroic inventors will emerge. (399 words)（专有名词、词类转换、插入语、结构调整、长句切短）

24. Prostitution

Street-walkers, kerb-crawlers, phone booths plastered with pictures of breasts and buttocks: the sheer seediness of prostitution is just one reason governments have long sought to outlaw it, or corral it in licensed brothels or "tolerance zones". NIMBYs make common cause with puritans, who think that women selling sex are sinners, and do-gooders, who think they are victims. The reality is more nuanced. Some prostitutes do indeed suffer from trafficking, exploitation or violence; their abusers ought to end up in jail for their crimes. But for many, both male and female, sex work is just that: work.

This newspaper has never found it plausible that all prostitutes are victims. That fiction is becoming harder to sustain as much of the buying and selling of sex moves

APPENDIX A Translation Exercises for Independent Work

online. Personal websites mean prostitutes can market themselves and build their brands. Review sites bring trustworthy customer feedback to the commercial-sex trade for the first time. The shift makes it look more and more like a normal service industry.

It can also be analysed like one. We have dissected data on prices, services and personal characteristics from one big international site that hosts 190,000 profiles of female prostitutes. The results show that gentlemen really do prefer blondes, who charge 11% more than brunettes. The scrawny look beloved of fashion magazines is more marketable than flab—but less so than a healthy weight. Prostitutes themselves behave like freelancers in other labour markets. They arrange tours and take bookings online, like gigging musicians. They choose which services to offer, and whether to specialise. They temp, go part-time and fit their work around child care. There is even a graduate premium that is close to that in the wider economy.

Moralizers will lament the shift online because it will cause the sex trade to grow strongly. Buyers and sellers will find it easier to meet and make deals. New suppliers will enter a trade that is becoming safer and less tawdry. New customers will find their way to prostitutes, since they can more easily find exactly the services they desire and confirm their quality. Pimps and madams should shudder, too. The internet will undermine their market-making power.

But everyone else should cheer. Sex arranged online and sold from an apartment or hotel room is less bothersome for third parties than are brothels or red-light districts. Above all, the web will do more to make prostitution safer than any law has ever done. Pimps are less likely to be abusive if prostitutes have an alternative route to market. Specialist sites will enable buyers and sellers to assess risks more accurately. Apps and sites are springing up that will let them confirm each other's identities and swap verified results from sexual-health tests. Schemes such as Britain's Ugly Mugs allow prostitutes to circulate online details of clients to avoid. (468 words)（遣词用字、词类转换、词语增减、结构调整、长句切短）

25. The Real Jane Austen

"A life of usefulness, literature, and religion, was not by any means a life of event," wrote Henry Austen of his spinster sister Jane. This image of the sequestered author persisted for years. But contemporary scholars have reappraised "dear Aunt Jane" as an independent and worldly-wise woman who wielded a sardonic pen. She continues to fascinate, 200 years after the publication of *Pride and Prejudice*. This is the charm of a new biography from Paula Byrne, a British author, who breathes yet more life into Austen and her works by considering the objects that populated her days.

Each chapter is organized around a single thing. Some are Austen's possessions, such as a topaz cross she received from her brother. Others are simply from the period, such as a barouche (an upmarket carriage), which helps to illustrate how well-travelled she was and how transport indicates status in her novels. In *Northanger Abbey* Catherine Morland finds a trip in Henry Tilney's curricle erotic, whereas she is nonplussed by John Thorpe's gig. Broadly chronological, this thematic approach offers a revealing picture of Austen and a lively social history.

Austen's formative years are the most interesting. Three vellum notebooks contain her "Juvenilia"—the stories and poems she wrote as a teenager. Her "greatest gifts are here in embryo", writes Ms Byrne, clearly relishing Austen's satire and lack of restraint. The young author lampooned famous figures and offered parodies of sentimental novels. But she reserved her choicest words of wit for her sister Cassandra. When they were not living together they corresponded frequently, and Austen often tried out different voices—"gossipy, jokey, affectionate"—to make her laugh.

During this time the movements of family followed the flows of inheritance; a vexatious matter that drives Austen's narratives. Old maids and mothers were often housed by rich cousins; a child might be made heir to childless relatives. An East Indian shawl introduces Aunt Phila—who at 21 sailed to Bengal in order to find a husband—and her daughter, Eliza. A romantic figure, and presumably illegitimate, Eliza first married a man who fell under the guillotine in the French Revolution, and later married Austen's brother Henry. This coquettish cousin is fictionalized as Mary Crawford in *Mansfield Park*. Austen also drew on Henry's militia experience for her depiction of flirtatious redcoats in *Pride and Prejudice*. Her midshipman brothers helped inform references to the navy.

The book's liveliest passages are about city life and romance. Austen frequently visited London and lived in Bath for years. She was probably not a beauty—only one authenticated portrait exists. But her wit and intelligence lured many a suitor. None of them stuck, but many are recalled with mirth in her letters. (449 words)（遣词用字、结构调整、增添省略）

26. A History of Greater and Greater Accuracy

A good unit of measurement must satisfy three conditions. It has to be easy to relate to, match the things it is meant to measure in scale (no point using inches to describe geographical distances) and be stable. In his new book, *World in the Balance*, Mr. Crease, who teaches philosophy at Stony Brook University on Long Island and writes a column for the magazine *Physics World*, describes man's quest for that metrological holy grail. In the process, he shows that the story of metrology, not obvious material for a page-turner, can in the right hands make for a riveting read.

The earliest known units met the first two of Mr. Crease's requirements well. Most were drawn from things to hand: the human body (the foot or the mile, which derives from the Latin *milia passuum*, or 1,000 paces) and tools (barrels, cups). Others were more abstract. The journal (from *jour*, French for "day"), used in medieval France, was equivalent to the area a man could plough in a day with a single ox, as was the acre in Britain or the *morgen* in north Germany and Holland.

But no two feet, barrels or workdays are quite the same. What was needed was "a foot, not yours or mine". Calls for a firm standard that was not subject to fluctuations or the whim of feudal lords, grew louder in the late 17th century. They were a consequence of the beginnings of international trade and modern science. Both required greater precision to advance.

In response the metre, from the Greek *metron*, meaning "measure", was ushered in, helped along by French revolutionaries, eager to replace the Bourbon *toise* (just under two metres) with an all-new, universal unit. The metre was to be defined as a fraction of the Paris meridian whose precise measurement (in *toises*) was under way. Together with the kilogram, initially the mass of a liter of distilled water, it formed the basis of the metric system.

Successful French metrological diplomacy meant that in the ensuing decades the metric system supplanted a hotchpotch of regional units in all bar a handful of nations. Even Britain, long wedded to its imperial measures, caved in. In 1875 *Nature*, a British magazine, hailed the metric system as "one of the greatest triumphs of modern civilisation".

For all its diplomatic success, though, the metre failed to live up to its original promise. Tying it to the meridian, or any other natural benchmark, proved intractable. As a result, the unit continued to be defined in explicit reference to a unique platinum-iridium ingot until 1960. Only then was it recast in less fleeting terms: as a multiple of the wavelength of a particular type of light. Finally, in 1983, it was tied to a fundamental physical constant, the speed of light, becoming the distance light travels in 1/299,792,458 of a second. (484 words) （科技英语、语态转换、结构调整、增添省略）

27. The Power of Pilosity

Blondes are dumber and brunettes more dependable. Or so it is said. But it is redheads who have long been the more feared, revered, loathed and loved; hence the rumour that it takes more than an average dose of anaesthetic to sedate a carrot-top.

Man's fascination with hair is almost as old as humanity itself. But humans have been cutting and coiffing their hair for at least 25,000 years, mostly with the aim of pleasing themselves and distancing or differentiating themselves from others. One of the earliest depictions of styled hair is a paleolithic figurine known as the Venus of Brassempouy, which was discovered in south-west France in 1894.

Middle age and chemotherapy are just two reasons why people lose their hair. Though often painful, at least privately, this is loss via a gradual process and in the case of the latter, is reversible. Examples of voluntary and instantaneous hair loss include styling by punk rockers of the 1980s and the swastika-shaped shavings of neo-Nazi thugs. Either way, the visitor is reminded of what rapid hair loss has meant over time.

Where today parents save first curls as a souvenir of babyhood, in the 19th century it became fashionable to work the hair of a dead beloved into a locket, bracelet or even a ring. One of the most touching pieces in a new show at the Quai Branly museum in Paris is a small curl of blonde hair pasted onto a heart-shaped piece of mother-of-pearl. It was cut from the head of Louis XVI's heir, Louis-Charles, who was born just before the French Revolution and died in the Temple prison two years after his parents were guillotined, having been put under the care of a shoemaker tasked with making him forget his royal origins.

In other civilizations the power of hair lay in its importance as a trophy believed to be infused with the strength or magic of its original owner. From Peru to Gabon, and from India to China, coats, crowns and headdresses of human hair have been made for centuries. It is easy, in these politically correct times, to forget that similar practices were just as common in Europe and America.

The Quai Branly museum may be just six years old, but it is in its way old-fashioned, a throwback to a less timorous time when museums were proud to display human scalps and heads shrunken by Amazon tribes. By exhibiting such items, and putting them in an historical context, it has increased our knowledge and added to an exhibition that is hard to forget. (428 words)（遣词用字、结构调整、增添省略）

28. *Silent Spring* Ignites the Environmental Movement

"Every once in a while in the history of mankind, a book has appeared which has substantially altered the course of history," Senator Ernest Gruening, a Democrat from Alaska, told Carson at the time.

APPENDIX A Translation Exercises for Independent Work

Silent Spring was published 50 years ago this month. Though she did not set out to do so, Carson influenced the environmental movement as no one had since the 19th century's most celebrated hermit, Henry David Thoreau, wrote about Walden Pond. *Silent Spring* presents a view of nature compromised by synthetic pesticides, especially DDT. Once these pesticides entered the biosphere, Carson argued, they not only killed bugs but also made their way up the food chain to threaten bird and fish populations and could eventually sicken children. Much of the data and case studies that Carson drew from weren't new; the scientific community had known of these findings for some time, but Carson was the first to put them all together for the general public and to draw stark and far-reaching conclusions. In doing so, Carson, the citizen-scientist, spawned a revolution.

Silent Spring, which has sold more than two million copies, made a powerful case for the idea that if humankind poisoned nature, nature would in turn poison humankind. "Our heedless and destructive acts enter into the vast cycles of the earth and in time return to bring hazard to ourselves," she told the subcommittee. We still see the effects of unfettered human intervention through Carson's eyes: she popularized modern ecology.

If anything, environmental issues have grown larger—and more urgent—since Carson's day. Yet no single work has had the impact of *Silent Spring*. It is not that we lack eloquent and impassioned environmental advocates with the capacity to reach a broad audience on issues like climate change. But none was able to galvanize a nation into demanding concrete change in quite the way that Carson did.

What was it that allowed Carson to capture the public imagination and to forge America's environmental consciousness? Saint Rachel, "the nun of nature", as she is called, is frequently invoked in the name of one environmental cause or another, but few know much about her life and work. (360 words) （遣词用字、专有名词、直接引语、结构调整）

29. Science Awards

Once a year, on December 10th, Stockholm hosts the dishing out of the Nobel prizes. It is quite a party: the white-tie award ceremony itself, complete with orchestra, happens in the city's concert hall and is broadcast live on television. Some 1,300 lucky luminaries then transfer to the city hall for a banquet, also broadcast (a fashion expert even provides a running commentary on the gowns worn by the women). Finally, students at Stockholm University host a less formal but more raucous after-party for the laureates and their guests. For that, mercifully, the TV cameras are switched off.

The Queen Elizabeth Prize for Engineering, a brand-new award, is a conscious attempt to sprinkle a similar kind of stardust onto engineering, which has long worried that it is seen as a bit of a poor relation to more academic science. At a half-hour ceremony held on March 18th at the Royal Academy of Engineering in London, the prize committee honoured Marc Andreessen, Sir Tim Berners-Lee, Vint Cerf, Robert Kahn and Louis Pouzin, all of whom were instrumental in the development of the modern internet. The Swedish-style pomp and circumstance will come on June 25th, when the queen will host the winners at Buckingham Palace.

While the prominence of the Nobels makes them excellent publicity for the fields they honour—chemistry, physics and physiology or medicine, not forgetting the less scientific endeavours of economics, literature and peace—they miss out large swathes of science. The result has been a proliferation of similar prizes in other fields, many of which are quite open about their intent to mimic the Nobels.

Computer scientists, for instance, aspire to the A.M. Turing Award. The 2012 award, announced on March 13th, went to Shafi Goldwasser and Silvio Micali, both of the Massachusetts Institute of Technology. Mathematicians have the Fields Medal, given every four years to particularly brilliant researchers under the age of 40. They also have the better-remunerated Abel prize (this year's winner, announced on March 20th, is Pierre Deligne of the Institute for Advanced Study in Princeton). Other awards are more catholic. Japan hosts the Asahi and Kyoto prizes, for instance, which honour outstanding contributions in any area of science, alongside prizes for the arts.

Some of the newest prizes on the block come from Yuri Milner, a Russian billionaire, who has attempted to upstage the Nobels by offering $3m to each winner, nearly three times what the Nobel Foundation pays. The Fundamental Physics Prize, given by Mr. Milner's foundation, has so far honoured nine people. As *The Economist* went to press, the next batch was being announced at a ceremony in Geneva. A similar Breakthrough Prize in Life Sciences, this time a joint effort between Mr. Milner, Sergey Brin (co-founder of Google), his wife Anne Wojcicki (who founded 23andMe, a genetics-testing firm) and Mark Zuckerberg (who started Facebook), honoured 11 winners, and paid them each another $3m, in February. (484 words)（专有词语、词类转换、增添省略、结构调整、长句拆短）

30. A Tragic Split

How quickly the unthinkable became the irreversible. A year ago few people imagined that the legions of Britons who love to whinge about the European Union—silly regulations, bloated budgets and pompous bureaucrats—would actually vote to leave the club of countries that buy nearly half of Britain's exports. Yet, by the early hours of June

APPENDIX A Translation Exercises for Independent Work

24th, it was clear that voters had ignored the warnings of economists, allies and their own government and, after more than four decades in the EU, were about to step boldly into the unknown.

The tumbling of the pound to 30-year lows offered a taste of what is to come. As confidence plunges, Britain may well dip into recession. A permanently less vibrant economy means fewer jobs, lower tax receipts and, eventually, extra austerity. The result will also shake a fragile world economy. Scots, most of whom voted to Remain, may now be keener to break free of the United Kingdom, as they nearly did in 2014. Across the Channel, Eurosceptics such as the French National Front will see Britain's flounce-out as encouragement. The EU, an institution that has helped keep the peace in Europe for half a century, has suffered a grievous blow.

Managing the aftermath, which saw the country split by age, class and geography, will need political dexterity in the short run; in the long run it may require a redrawing of traditional political battle-lines and even subnational boundaries. There will be a long period of harmful uncertainty. Nobody knows when Britain will leave the EU or on what terms. But amid Brexiteers' jubilation and Remain's recriminations, two questions stand out: what does the vote mean for Britain and Europe? And what comes next?

The vote to Leave amounts to an outpouring of fury against the "establishment". Everyone from Barack Obama to the heads of NATO and the IMF urged Britons to embrace the EU. Their entreaties were spurned by voters who rejected not just their arguments but the value of "experts" in general. Large chunks of the British electorate that have borne the brunt of public-spending cuts and have failed to share in Britain's prosperity are now in thrall to an angry populism.

Britons offered many reasons for rejecting the EU, from the democratic deficit in Brussels to the weakness of the euro-zone economies. But the deal-breaking feature of EU membership for Britain seemed to be the free movement of people. As the number of new arrivals has grown, immigration has risen up the list of voters' concerns.

Accordingly, the Leave side promised supporters both a thriving economy and control over immigration. But Britons cannot have that outcome just by voting for it. If they want access to the EU's single market and to enjoy the wealth it brings, they will have to accept free movement of people. If Britain rejects free movement, it will have to pay the price of being excluded from the single market. The country must pick between curbing migration and maximising wealth. (498 words)（遣词用字、专有词语、长句拆短、结构调整）

II. C-E Translation

1. 翻译的作用

在人类历史发展的长河中，在世界多元文化的交流、融会与碰撞中，在中华民族伟大复兴的进程中，翻译始终都起着不可或缺的先导作用。所有的国际活动和语言文化交流都离不开翻译。假如这世界有一天没有了翻译，联合国将不复存在，世贸组织将无法运行，一切国际机构都会瘫痪。翻译工作者及其工作就像电线里流动的电流、水管中流动的水流：他们默默无闻地把一个语言文化带到另一个语言文化中，使隔膜变成透明。(187字)

2. 翻译与实践

翻译是一门实践性极强的学问，需要长期下苦功夫才能真正学到手。翻译能力的形成不能单靠学习理论知识、强化技巧训练，而是需要扎扎实实的双语功底及大量的翻译实践。因此，从某种意义上讲，一个人的翻译能力不是课堂上讲出来的，也不是翻译技巧所能造就的，而是要靠自己脚踏实地地干出来。本书正是基于这方面的考虑，为培养和增进读者的英汉互译的实际动手能力而编写成的。(178字)

3. 《毛泽东选集》(节选)

我们中国是世界上最大的国家之一，它的领土和整个欧洲的面积差不多相等。在这个广大的领土之上，有广大的肥田沃地，给我们以衣食之源；有纵横全国的大小山脉，给我们生长了广大的森林，贮藏了丰富的矿产；有很多的江河湖泽，给我们以舟楫和灌溉之利；有很长的海岸线，给我们以交通海外各民族的方便。从很早的古代起，我们中华民族的祖先就劳动、生息、繁殖在这块广大的土地之上。(186字)

4. 《邓小平文选》(节选)

我们的现代化建设，必须从中国的实际出发。无论是革命还是建设，都要注意学习和借鉴外国经验。但是，照抄照搬别国经验、别国模式，从来不能得到成功。这方面我们有过不少教训。把马克思主义的普遍真理同我国的具体实际结合起来，走自己的道路，建设有中国特色的社会主义，这就是我们总结长期历史经验得出的基本结论。(158字)

5. 北京

北京是中华人民共和国的首都，是全国的政治、文化和科技教育的中心，也是全国的交通和国际交往中心。

改革开放以来，首都北京的建设日新月异，发生了巨大的变化。现代化建筑如雨后春笋般相继崛起。2008年奥运会的成功举办给北京带来前所未有的机遇。"爱国 创新 包容 厚德"的北京精神将进一步推动北京的发展，促进中国与世界各国人民的友好交流。

APPENDIX A Translation Exercises for Independent Work

北京科技力量强大，有中国科学院、北京大学、清华大学等世界著名科研机构和高等学府。同时，北京正大力发展高新技术产业，人才密集的中关村被称为中国的"硅谷"。（233字）

6. 长江

长江发源于青藏高原，全长6 300多千米，是中国第一大河、世界第三长河。

长江上游落差大，水流急，有许多高山耸立的峡谷地段。中游的平原地区江面变宽，水流减缓，多曲流、多支流、多湖泊。长江下游地区地势低平，江阔水深，是著名的鱼米之乡。长江入海口，江面宽达80~90千米，水天一色，极为壮观。中国大部分的淡水湖分布在长江中下游地区。

长江流域物产丰富，经济发达。上海、南京、武汉、重庆等大城市都分布在这里。（192字）

7. 黄河

黄河发源于青海省，全长5 400多千米，是中国的第二长河。从地图上看，黄河的形状是一个巨大的"几"字。

黄河上游有许多峡谷，这些峡谷地带水力资源丰富，建有多座大型水电站。

黄河中游经过黄土高原，这里水土流失严重，河水中的泥沙含量大，河水浑浊呈黄色而得名黄河。

黄河下游主要流经低缓的华北平原，这里河道宽阔，水流变缓，泥沙大量沉积，形成了河床比两岸高的"地上河"。（174字）

8. 汉朝

汉朝是中国历史上最重要的朝代之一。汉朝统治期间有很多显著的成就。它最先向其他文化敞开大门，对外贸易兴旺。汉朝开拓的丝绸之路通向了中西亚乃至罗马。各类艺术一派繁荣，涌现了很多文学、历史、哲学巨著。公元100年中国第一部字典编纂完成，收入9 000个字，提供释义并列举不同的写法。其间，科技方面也取得了很大进步，发明了纸张、水钟、日晷（sundials）以及测量地震的仪器。汉朝历经400年，但统治者的腐败最终导致了它的灭亡。（195字）

9. 长城

长城是世界七大奇观之一，是世界上修建时间最长、工程量最大的军事性防御工程，是炎黄子孙血汗与智能的结晶，也是中华民族坚毅、勤奋的象征。它以宏大的气势和壮美的英姿享誉世界，吸引天下的游人，现已被联合国列入世界文化遗产名录。

长城是中国古代用作军事防御的一项宏伟建筑。长城最早大约出现于公元前7~前5世纪。其规模和基础是秦朝奠定的。以后，汉、南北朝、隋、唐、辽金、明、清等朝都曾修筑过长城。（190字）

10. 中秋节

中国人自古以来就在中秋时节庆祝丰收，这与北美地区庆祝感恩节的习俗十分相似。过中秋节的习俗于唐代早期在中国各地开始流行。中秋节在农历八月十五，是人们拜月的节日。这天夜晚皓月当空，人们合家团聚，共赏明月。2006年，中秋节被列为中国的文化遗产，2008年又被定为公共假日。月饼被视为中秋节不可或缺的美食，人们将月饼作为礼物馈赠亲友或在家庭聚会上享用。传统的月饼上带有"寿""福"或"和"等字样。（193字）

11. 丝绸之路

闻名于世的丝绸之路是一系列连接东西方的路线。丝绸之路延伸6 000多公里，得名于古代中国的丝绸贸易。丝绸之路上的贸易在中国、南亚、欧洲和中东文明发展中发挥了重要作用。正是通过丝绸之路，中国的造纸、火药、指南针、印刷等四大发明才被引介到世界各地。同样，中国的丝绸、茶叶和瓷器也传遍全球。物质文化的交流是双向的。欧洲也通过丝绸之路出口各种商品和植物，满足中国市场的需要。（183字）

12. 向世界讲述真实的"中国故事"

"中国是一只沉睡的狮子，一旦觉醒，将会震惊世界。"——拿破仑

"中国这头狮子已经醒了。"——习近平

这是韩国KBS电视台制作的7集纪录片《超级中国》开播时，作品开头的两句话。该片播出后引起很大反响，在韩国迅速掀起了一股"中国热"。与此同时，该片通过网络被越来越多的中国人热传热议，《纽约时报》、CNN、BBC等西方主流媒体相继对此进行报道。

而不为外人所知的是，这部纪录片与清华也有着特别的渊源。该片三位首席编导之一朴晋范（Jinbum Park）2010年毕业于清华大学新闻与传播学院，就读全球财经新闻硕士项目（GBJ）。

朴晋范说："两年的清华GBJ求学经历，让我对中国的现状和未来有了更深入的了解，后来我回到韩国参与了纪录片《超级中国》的创作，希望让韩国人看到印象中不一样的真实的中国。"（328字）

13. 华罗庚

华罗庚少年命运十分坎坷，他的腿因幼时患伤寒症而跛。初中毕业后他辍学在金坛中学当会计。1930年华罗庚在《科学》上发表论文，被清华数学系主任熊庆来教授看到，便安排他在系图书馆做助理员，边工作边学习。他仅用一年半时间就学完了数学系的全部课程，并同时自学了英、法、德语。华罗庚每天除了工作就是学习，休息时间很少，所以短期内就在国际学术杂志上发表了三篇论文。他曾对友人说："人家受的教育比我多，我必须用加倍的时间以补救我的缺失，所以人家每天8小时的工作，我要工作12小时以上

才觉得心安。"

1933年，华罗庚被清华破格提为助教，教授微积分课程。1936年，经学校推荐，他以访问学者身份被派往英国剑桥大学留学。1938年回国，再次被破格聘为西南联大教授。（300字）

14. 蒋南翔

蒋南翔（1913—1988）著名教育家、江苏宜兴人。1952年被任命为清华大学校长，是清华历史上最有建树的校长之一。他一手建立起工程物理、工程化学、工程力学数学、自动控制、精密仪器等新兴科学和技术系科，并提出要把高等学校建设成教学、科研、生产的"三联基地"，依靠教师队伍和职工队伍"两个车轮"发展学校，对清华的发展和国家新兴科学技术的建设起到了重要的作用。作为一位教育家，他一贯强调德智体全面发展的教育方针，要求清华学子练好身体，"争取至少为祖国健康工作五十年"。其主要著述已汇编为《蒋南翔文集》出版。（241字）

15. 二校门

"二校门"即清华最早的校门，始建于1909年。1933年，西院住宅区扩建，园墙外移，同时建造了新的大门（今之西校门）。此后，习惯上即称原大门为"二校门"。梁实秋先生在校读书时，曾对早年校门姿貌写过如下一段描述文字："清华的校门是青砖砌的，涂着洁白的油质，一片缟素的颜色反映着两扇虽设而常开的黑栅栏门。……"

大门拱额上镶嵌着一块大理石，石上镌刻着清末军机大臣兼学部尚书那桐写的"清华园"三个擘窠大字。此门在"文革"动乱初期被拆毁，1991年重建。(209字)

16. 工字厅

工字厅原名工字殿，是古址清华园内的主体建筑，因其前、后两大殿中间以短廊相接，俯视恰似一工字，故得名。现指以工字殿为主体的古式大庭院，其大门正额悬有咸丰皇帝亲书的"清华园"匾额。工字厅共有房屋一百多间，总建筑面积约2 570平方米，院内曲廊蜿蜒，勾连成一座座独立的小套院。工字厅初建时原供皇室贵胄别居休闲之用，建校后成为文化娱乐中心和重要社交场所。1924年印度大诗人泰戈尔访华时就下榻于它的后厅。工字厅大院长时间以来一直是清华大学校机关办公所在地。(215字)

17. 荷塘

沿着荷塘，是一条曲折的小煤屑路。这是一条幽僻的路；白天也少有人走，夜晚更加寂寞。荷塘四面，长着许多树，蓊蓊郁郁的。路的一旁，是些杨柳，和一些不知道名字的树。没有月亮的晚上，这路上阴森森的，有些怕人。今晚却很好，虽然月光也还是淡淡的。

曲曲折折的荷塘上面，弥望的是田田的叶子。叶子出水很高，像亭亭的舞女的裙。层层的叶子中间，零星地点缀着些白花，有袅娜地开着的，有羞涩地打着朵儿的；正如一粒粒的明珠,又如碧天里的星星。微风过处送来缕缕清香,仿佛远处高楼上渺茫的歌声似的。这时候叶子与花也有一丝的颤动,像闪电般,霎时传过荷塘的那边去了。(264字)

18. 杭州风光

杭州位于浙江省北部,钱塘江北岸,大运河的南端,是中国古老的风景名城。蜿蜒曲折的钱塘江,穿过浙西的崇山峻岭到这里之后,江面开阔,景色壮丽。特别是每年中秋前后有钱塘江潮,怒涛奔腾,激流汹涌,蔚为天下大观。

迷人的西湖,位于市区的西面,总面积5.6平方千米。纵贯南北的苏堤和横贯东西的白堤,把全湖分成外湖、里湖、岳湖、西里湖和小南湖五个部分。湖面波光闪闪,湖边茂林修竹,景色四季宜人。西湖又名"西子湖"。北宋苏东坡在咏潮的诗篇中,把西湖比作古代美女西施,西湖就更加名扬四海了。(231字)

19. 豫园

位于上海市南的豫园是著名的古典园林。花园的原主人姓潘,曾是明代四川省的布政史。花园的建造始于1558年,但由于资金短缺,时建时停,20年以后才建成。后来,潘家败落,其子孙急于出售,一些商人得以低价购入。以后豫园与城隍庙合并,成为其"西花园"。鸦片战争和太平天国时期,外国侵略者不只一次在此驻军,因此,历史上豫园屡经灾难,许多原有的风采不复存在。新中国成立以后,在人民政府的关怀下,豫园经历了多次修复。最近一次在1987年,恢复了其东面部分。豫园在1982年被列为国务院重点保护单位,是中国南方最优秀的园林之一。(237字)

20. 温哥华

温哥华的辉煌是温哥华人的智慧和勤奋的结晶,其中包括众多民族的贡献。加拿大地广人稀,国土面积比中国还大,人口却不足3 000万。吸收外来移民,是加拿大长期奉行的国策。可以说,加拿大除了印第安人外,无一不是外来移民,不同的只是时间长短而已。温哥华则是世界上屈指可数的多民族城市。现今180万温哥华居民中,还有一半不是在本地出生的,每4个居民中就有一个是亚洲人。而25万华人对温哥华的经济转型起着决定性作用,其中有一半是近5年来才到温哥华的,他们的到来使温哥华成为亚洲以外最大的中国人聚居地。(230字)

21. 天坛

公共汽车颠簸了一阵,便到达目的地——天坛。我下了车,走进天坛的大门。一刹那间,那公共汽车上的拥挤闷热全被忘却了。

已经是傍晚了,人很少。到回音壁的时候,门已经关了,不能进去。我走到天坛的前面,抬头一看,广阔的天空衬托出金碧辉煌的天坛。一只孤独的乌鸦栖息在穹顶上,嘶哑地叫了一声,拍着翅膀飞了起来。我低头绕天坛走了一圈,然后停下来,站了一会儿,欣

APPENDIX A Translation Exercises for Independent Work

赏着这特殊的气氛。

宏伟的天坛，无声的天空和盘旋着的乌鸦真可入画。凭吊天坛，我触景生情，想到了人类的古往今来，久久不能自已。(270字)

22. 时间

古往今来，"时间"对人来说是个最难捉摸的东西。世上每人每天都有着等量的时间——24小时。并且大家也都一样，只能占有"今天"。一点不假，昨日之日不可留，一去不复返了，而明天，也许要使人们期待着永远也盼不来。这就是说，每个活着的人就只能掌握"今天"——只能掌握此时、此刻。

不过，怎样使用这短暂的24小时，我们每个人都可以各有千秋：我们可以在里面填进去不同的内容，从而得到的结果自然也各不相同。有的人蹉跎岁月，贻误时机；有的人把时间用来为别人造福；有的人则自己努力向上。

你怎样度过你的时间呢？抽空好好考虑一下这个问题准会令你受益匪浅！(266字)

23. 换位

飞机上，一位女士与一名黑人男子的座位挨着，她要求空姐为她换个座位，因为她"不愿意和一个肤色这么难看的人坐在一起"。空姐回答说，飞机已经满员，不过可以到头等舱去看看有没有办法解决。其他乘客看到这一幕都有些不悦，而这位女士却洋洋自得，因为她不必再和旁边的这个"恶心"的人坐在一起了。

几分钟后，空姐回来了，她对这位女士说："很抱歉，本次航班只有头等舱还有一个空位。我已经征得了机长的同意，可以换一下座位。"这位女士露出一副得意的表情，准备离开自己的座位，但此时空姐却对她身边的黑人男子说："先生，您能跟我到您的新座位上去吗？"所有的乘客先是一愣，随即为空姐热烈鼓掌。(280字)

24.《红楼梦》简介

18世纪中叶，曹雪芹的长篇小说《红楼梦》问世，在中国文学发展史上，树立了一座辉煌灿烂的艺术丰碑。

小说以贵族青年贾宝玉、林黛玉的恋爱婚姻悲剧为主要线索，描写贾家荣、宁两府这个封建贵族大家庭的衰亡败落。作者还通过这个家族的社会联系的描写，笔触深入到封建社会的各个方面，生动地展开了封建社会走向衰朽没落这个特定历史时期现实生活的广阔画面。从而，揭示了封建社会必然没落的历史发展规律。

小说的艺术表现，可以说是达到了出神入化的境界。严谨、缜密的结构、生动准确的个性化的语言，特别是鲜明的人物形象，都是非常杰出的。书中出现的人物，粗计多达四百余人。不仅主角贾宝玉、林黛玉和其他10多名主要人物成为人们熟知的艺术典型，而且许许多多次要人物，有的甚至是一笔带过的，也都形象鲜明，栩栩如生。小说的艺术表现，达到如此高的水准，在世界文学名著中，也是极为罕见的。(369字)

245

25. 生命的三分之一

班固写的《汉书》"食货志"中有下面的记载:"冬,民既入;妇人同巷,相从夜绩,女工一月得四十五日。"

这几句读起来很奇怪,怎么一月能有 45 天呢?再看原文底下颜师古做了注解,他说:"一月之中,又得夜半为十五日,共四十五日。"

这就很清楚了。原来我国的古人不但比西方各国的人更早地懂得科学地、合理地计算劳动日,而且早就知道对于日班和夜班的计算方法。

一个月本来只有三十天,古人把每个夜晚的时间算作半日,就多了十五天。从这个意义上说来,夜晚的时间实际上不就等于生命的三分之一吗?

为什么古人对于夜晚的时间都这样重视,不肯轻易放过呢?我认为这就是他们对待自己生命的三分之一的严肃认真态度,这正是我们所应该学习的。(369 字)

26. 诚信

唐代吕元膺任洛阳留守时,有位部下常陪他下棋。有一次,两人正对局,突然来了公文,吕元膺只好离开棋盘到案前去批阅公文,那位棋友趁机偷偷挪动了一个棋子,最后胜了吕元膺。其实吕元膺已经看出他挪动棋子了,只是没有说破。第二天,吕元膺就请那位棋友到别处去谋生。别人都不知道辞退他的原因,他自己也不知道为什么被辞退。临走时,吕元膺还赠送了钱物。

吕元膺之所以要辞掉这位棋友,是由于他从这位棋友挪动一个棋子、搞了一个奸诈的小动作中发现了他的不诚信。诚信,是人生的无形资产,是思想道德的重要组成部分。不诚信的人,不可能做好人,也难处世。与没有诚信的人交往,是十分危险可怕的。(277 字)

27. 师旷论学

晋平公问于师旷曰:"吾年七十,欲学,恐已暮矣。"师旷曰:"何不秉烛乎?"

平公曰:"安有为人臣而戏其君乎?"

师旷曰:"盲臣安敢戏其君?臣闻之:少而好学,如日出之阳;壮而好学,如日中之光;老而好学,如秉烛之明,孰与昧行乎?"

平公曰:"善哉!"(123 字)

28. 寓言三则

A. 自相矛盾

有一个人卖矛又卖盾,有人来买盾,他就夸他的盾说:"我的盾坚固极了,不论什么矛都扎不透它。"有人来买矛,他又夸他的矛说:"我的矛锋利极了,不论什么东西它都能扎透。"

另外一个人问他:"用你的矛扎你的盾,那又怎么样呢?"他就回答不出来了。

APPENDIX A Translation Exercises for Independent Work

B. 狐假虎威

虎求百兽而食之，得狐。

狐曰："子无敢食我也。天帝使我长百兽。今子食我，是逆天帝命也。子以我为不信，吾为子先行，子随我后，观百兽之见我而不敢不走乎？"

虎以为然，故遂与之行。兽见之皆走。虎不知兽畏己而走也，以为畏狐也。

C. 画蛇添足

楚有祠者，赐其舍人卮酒。舍人相谓曰："数人饮之不足，一人饮之有余，请画地为蛇，先成者饮酒。"

一人蛇先成，引酒且饮之，乃左手持卮，右手画蛇，曰："吾能为之足。"未成，一人之蛇成，夺其卮曰："蛇固无足，子安能为之足？"遂饮其酒，为画足者，终亡其酒。(343 字)

29. 全面建设小康社会

我们必须适应国内外形势的新变化，顺应各族人民过上更好生活的新期待，把握经济社会发展趋势和规律，坚持中国特色社会主义经济建设、政治建设、文化建设、社会建设的基本目标和基本政策构成的基本纲领，在十六大确立的全面建设小康社会目标的基础上对我国发展提出新的更高要求。

到 2020 年全面建设小康社会目标实现之时，我们这个历史悠久的文明古国和发展中社会主义大国，将成为工业化基本实现、综合国力显著增强、国内市场总体规模位居世界前列的国家，成为人民富裕程度普遍提高、生活质量明显改善、生态环境良好的国家，成为人民享有更加充分民主权利、具有更高文明素质和精神追求的国家，成为各方面制度更加完善、社会更加充满活力而又安定团结的国家，成为对外更加开放、更加具有亲和力、为人类文明做出更大贡献的国家。

今后五年是全面建设小康社会的关键时期。我们要坚定信心，埋头苦干，为全面建成惠及十几亿人口的更高水平的小康社会打下更加牢固的基础。(400 字)

30. "两个一百年"奋斗目标

事实证明，没有改革开放，就没有中国的今天；没有改革开放，也不会有中国的未来。30 多年来，我们用改革的办法解决了一系列重大问题；今后，我们还将坚持用改革的办法来破解前进道路上的各种困难和挑战。现在，我们确定了"两个一百年"奋斗目标，即到 2020 年国内生产总值和城乡居民人均收入比 2010 年翻一番，全面建成小康社会；到本世纪中叶建成富强民主文明和谐的社会主义现代化国家，实现中华民族伟大复兴的中国梦。我们正在全面深化改革，完善和发展中国特色社会主义制度，推进国家治理体系和治理能力现代化。我们将协调推进经济体制、政治体制、文化体制、社会体制、生态文明体制和党的建设制度改革。我们将以"明知山有虎，偏向虎山行"的政治勇气和智慧，以抓铁有痕、踏石留印的实干劲头推进改革，为中国现代化建设提供强大推动力量，更多更好造福中国人民，为世界带来新的发展机遇。(264 字)

Appendix B Keys to Practice of the Relevant Skill and Exercises

Unit 1

1. 英译汉

拉美人言谈中的谚语

　　谚语是令拉美言谈妙趣横生的通俗话语，是一种浓缩的智慧的结晶。谚语随处可闻。从大学教授到乡野村夫，从市井乞丐到窈窕淑女，谚语不时脱口而出。谚语简洁明快，生动多彩，但往往也不无带刺。

　　听说邻居家那位其貌不扬的千金宣布订婚了，伊梅尔达说：“太太，你知道大伙儿是怎么说的吗：'再丑的罐儿也不愁配个盖儿。'”当伊梅尔达的女婿嚷嚷要去找克扣他工资的老板算账时，她冷冷地盯着他说：“小鱼吃不了大鱼。”

　　一天下午，我听见伊梅尔达和女儿在厨房里争论开了。原来是女儿刚和公婆吵过嘴，她非要女儿去赔个不是。她女儿却偏不依：“可是，妈妈，我就是受不了他们那德行，哪怕是拌了蜜也咽不下呀！他们满嘴讲大话，可是一旦我们需要买点什么，却又穷得不得了。所以今天当他们连买一张新床那么点钱都不肯借给我们时，我只不过讲了你平日说过上百遍的那句话：'既然那么阔，干嘛要叫穷？既然那么穷，干嘛摆阔气？'”

　　伊梅尔达鼻子哼了一声："没家教！难道我没有告诉过你：'舌头闯祸，脖子遭殃'？我可不愿意让人家戳着脊梁骨说我从来不教自己的姑娘要尊敬长辈。快把长裤脱了，换上套裙，去向他们赔个不是吧。你知道你婆婆对女人穿男式长裤是很有看法的。她常唠叨说：'孵出来是只母鸡就别想冒充公鸡！'"

　　做女儿的还想再争一争："可是，妈妈，你不是常说吗，'圣人若烦恼，另向他祈祷。'我明天再去还不行吗？"

　　"不行，不行！要记住：'要是药很苦，赶紧一口服。'孩子，你知道是自己错了嘛。不过，'大门把你关在外，礼物送到门自开。'我炉里正烤着一个蛋糕，本来是给太太晚餐时吃的，我会向她解释清楚的。好啦，乖孩子，赶紧回家，穿上那身粉红套裙，打扮得漂漂亮亮的。等你回来时，蛋糕也就好了，拿去送给你婆婆。婆婆准会高兴，说不定还会向你公公说情，替你们付床钱哩。记住：'手要相互洗，脸要双手洗。'"

APPENDIX B Keys to Practice of the Relevant Skill and Exercises

2. 汉译英

Proverbs

Proverbs are short, pithy sayings that are widely used by common people. Generally passed down by word of mouth, most proverbs reflect the practical experience of the lives of the working people. Similar to the characteristics of idioms, proverbs tend to be oral and easy to understand, thus appealing to all.

To some extent, proverbs may reflect a nation's geography, history, social system, social concepts and attitudes. For example, people inhabiting the coastal areas and making a living on the sea tend to have more proverbs involving marine affairs, such as voyage on the sea, weathering the storm, fisheries, etc. While the proverbs of nomads, as in the case of the Arabs, are closely related to deserts, grasslands, sheep, horses, camels and wolves. A society that esteems the elderly abounds with proverbs that praise the resourcefulness of the old, while a society that reduces women to low status is bound to have many proverbs which despise or disparage women.

After all, people's experience and perceptions of the world are similar in many respects. So, in spite of the fact that the Chinese and English-speaking people have different cultural backgrounds, there is a lot of the sameness or similarity in English and Chinese proverbs.

II
1. 人生道路既铺满鲜花，又布满荆棘。/ 生活总是有苦有乐。
2. 我要丽莎去哪儿她就得去哪儿。/ 我要让丽莎乖乖听我调遣。
3. 他一点儿不显老，面容年轻得令人惊讶。
4. 她再也不愿相信任何鬼男人了。
5. 他是一个神枪手，可这一次却遭到惨败。/ 他遭遇了滑铁卢。
6. 把贵重物品放在显眼处，等于是给小偷发请帖。（直译）/ 应妥善保管贵重物品，以防被盗。（意译）
7. 而中国是一片令人惊讶、日新月异的土地。
8. 他上一部小说写砸了，声望开始一路下滑。
9. 对付这种规模的挑战，我们这样说一点也不夸张："联合我们就能站立/挺住；分开我们就会倒下。（直译）/ 面对一场如此严峻的挑战，我们可以毫不夸张地说："合则生；分则亡"。（意译）
10. 他走在送葬队伍的前头，还不时用一条大手绢抹去脸上假惺惺的眼泪。
11. 还是那句老话：物失方知可贵，病时倍思健康。
12. 卢恩霍普特先生想起一位中国老相识教给他的一句中国谚语："富不过三代"。

13. 这是最美好的时期，这是最坏的时期；这是智慧的年代，这是愚蠢的年代；这是充满信仰的时代，这是顾虑重重的时代；这是光明的季节，这是黑暗的季节；这是富有希望的春天，这是充满绝望的冬天；我们拥有一切，我们一无所有；我们正笔直地走上天堂，我们正笔直地走下地狱。

14. 一张贺卡可以温暖一颗心，握紧一双手，倾听肺腑言，轻拍友人背；它令人喜洋洋，撩得心痒痒，抹去泪汪汪；它给孩子以惊喜，给恋人以温存，给新娘以祝福，给路人以欢迎；它可用以挥手道别，高声喝彩，送上飞吻，也可用以平息争吵，减轻痛苦，提高士气，解除忧虑，开创一种新风尚。

III（供讨论）

1. 匈牙利诗人裴多菲的《自由，爱情》一诗译文 A 为茅盾先生的直译；译文 B 为殷夫的意译，前者准确无误，后者更有诗意。
2. 译文 A 为严复所译《天演论》，译文 B 为现代白话文；比较原文和两个译文，不难看出严复所追求的古雅的文风，是以牺牲"信"为代价的。

Unit 2

1. 英译汉

英国人言谈中的委婉语

英国人或许是世界上最擅长委婉表达的了。委婉语中的精华通常广为人知，在讲话人和听众之间营造出一种愉悦的默契。英国报纸的讣告把这一点做得天衣无缝：尽管谁也不喜欢说死人的坏话，然而很多人喜欢知道有关"离世"者的少许真相。酒鬼可以被形容为"convivial"（欢乐的）或"cheery"（愉快的）人。令人不胜其烦的唠叨可以说成是"sociable"（好交际的）或极度的"ebullient"（热情洋溢）；"lively wit"（生动的机智）则意味着喜欢讲一些残忍无趣的故事。要是说某人"austere"（简朴的）且"reserved"（缄默的），则意味着此人无趣且令人沮丧。要是说某人"did not suffer fools gladly"（对蠢人没有耐心），是指此人脾气火暴。男色情狂美其名曰"享受女性的陪伴"，而女性的好色则是"特别精力充沛"。对一切东西都胃口难控的人可能获得的最高褒奖是"他充分享受了人生"。

这些委婉表达是某一时代所产生的愉快共鸣。在这种时代人们的私生活喜欢带一点保护性谨慎。而今在英国这种谨慎似乎完全不可思议。这给诸如"一个坚定的单身汉"（同性恋者）或某人"私生活因偶尔违规而受拖累"之类的表达留下了想象空间。（对于后者，读者可能会猜测到底是有伤风化的露阴癖、通奸还是易装癖。）

与点关于死人的轶闻只是一个品味问题，因为死者无法起诉。但要撰文形容在世的人则需谨慎（尤其是在英格兰这种以审理诽谤案件为乐的地方）。如"thirsty"（口渴）一

APPENDIX B　Keys to Practice of the Relevant Skill and Exercises

词若用在英国公众人物身上则意味着酗酒；要是说某人"tired and emotional"（又累又情绪化）（这一说法最早出现在讽刺杂志《私家侦探》当中，后成为流行语）就意味着已喝得烂醉如泥。对年轻同事进行"hands-on mentoring"（手把手指导）可暗指风流韵事，但愿不会遇上一个性格"volatile"（反复无常）的人，因为这一字眼意味着暴脾气一触即发。商务活动中记者要是用了"rumbustious"（喧闹的）或"controversial"（有争议的）、"murky"（黑暗的）、"questionable"（可疑的）等字眼，就意味着他们相信其中有非法勾当，而要诉诸法庭却又证据不足。

在英国上层社会，委婉表达是一门精巧的艺术，新来者需尽快掌握。"白厅其他机构"或"我们河对岸的朋友们"指的是情报工作（美国间谍则常说"为政府效力"）。要是某个公务员向部长警告说，做出某决定将会是"courageous"（勇气十足的），就是说这个决定不得人心，会断送其前程；而用"adventurous"（充满冒险的）一词，其程度就严重多了，也即是太疯狂了，行不通。"frank discussion"（坦率讨论）意味着大吵一架，"robust exchange of views"（强有力的交换意见）则是从头到尾吵个不休。

委婉语在英国人的演讲中已积习成性，以至于能讲一口流利英语的外国人有时都可能把握不住一些不起眼的闲谈中所暗示的信号。比方说，"incidentally"（顺便地），其内涵是"我现在告诉你的是此次谈话的目的"；而"with the greatest respect"（以最大的尊重），其潜台词是"傻瓜，你搞错了"。

2. 汉译英

Chinese Buzzwords

Chinese buzzwords usually reflect social changes and culture, and some of them are getting increasingly popular in foreign media. For example, *tuhao* and *dama* are both obsolete Chinese terms, but they get different new meanings now.

The term *tuhao* used to mean rural landlords who oppressed their tenants and servants, while now it refers to people who spend money like water or those who like to show off their wealth. In other words, a *tuhao* is very rich but has no taste. *Dama* was a term for middle-aged women, but now it refers in particular to the Chinese women who rushed for gold when gold plunged not long ago.

Both *tuhao* and *dama* may be included in the latest *Oxford English Dictionary*. So far, about 120 items of Chinese saying have been added to its entries, becoming a part of English language.

II

1. 夜贼需要一点**亮光**来辨识四周，于是**轻步**穿过房间，去**点亮**带有**浅绿色灯罩**的**灯**。
2. "**接来函后**，不到十分钟，我骑马动身了。**到达**坎特伯雷，**换乘**四轮马车进镇，但一场雨**把我浑身淋湿**，**患了**重感冒，一时不能**痊愈**。大约中午**到达**财政部，要做的第一件事，就是**刮脸换衣**。不久，**打听**到在委员会前**树碑**的内情。可是我尚未**得到**答复，不过从送信者口里**获悉**，翌日上午会**得到**的……"

3. 这个国家的全体公民都必须**服从**法律。
4. 支付**随**通货膨胀的变化**而**变化。
5. **在**他们履行其他正式手续的**条件下**，可授予他们一切必要的执照。
6. 酵母在发酵之前，**易受**温度起伏变化的干扰。
7. 就任**须得到**董事会三分之二以上的成员同意。
8. 样品在实验室**经过**一系列的检验，其主要目的在于针对不同情况来决定采取恰当的加工方法。
9. 这种**作用过程**既缓慢又微妙，经常逃过我们的注意。
10. 在资本主义社会，毒品和酒被一些人用作逃避现实的**途径**。
11. 但是人们往往对精巧的**器械**大为惊异，却忘记了制造它的人。
12. 我们国家的缔造者们认为这些真理是不言而喻的，或许这正是他们的**匠心**所在。
13. 随着现代技术的发展，哲学中的**机械论**再度变得盛极一时。
14. 对于社会主义经济**机制**的两种模式需要从市场功能的观点来加以区别。
15. 就像田径队需要一种**器械**（例如秒表）来选拔运动健将一样，社会也需要一种举贤任能的选拔**机制**。

III

1. museum, library, hotel, guest house, embassy, consulate, tea house, restaurant, barber's shop, gymnasium, exhibition hall, cultural center, art gallery, science and technology center, planetarium, photo studio...
2. wine, alcohol, spirits, beer, champagne, cocktail, brandy, whisky, gin...
3. fountain pen, pencil, ballpoint pen, wax crayon, chalk, writing brush, painting brush, electroprobe...
4. radio set, telephone, TV set, tractor, bulldozer, mixer, crane...
5.
   a. He is a worthy son of our country.   b. The crops are doing well.
   c. They are really kind to me.   d. The building is not well built.
   e. This question is easy to answer.   f. Oh, a good seat!
6.
   a. acquire knowledge   b. master a skill
   c. study a foreign language   d. academic records
   e. period of schooling   f. learn from each other
   g. follow the example of Lei Feng   h. emulate others' strong points
7.
   a. present flowers   b. show oneself up

APPENDIX B Keys to Practice of the Relevant Skill and Exercises

    c. show one's skill   d. offer advice (make suggestions)
    e. ingratiate oneself with sb.   f. devote oneself to (dedicate oneself to)
    g. contribute(donate)money and goods

8.
    a. give somebody a book   b. present a gift to somebody
    c. deliver a letter   d. see a visitor out
    e. see somebody off   f. bring somebody an umbrella
    g. lose one's life (get killed)   h. take a child to school
    i. escort somebody home   j. launch a satellite
    k. take part in a funeral procession
    l. hand the criminal over to the court for trial

Unit 3

1. 英译汉

何为天才？

人们给许多拥有不同特质的人贴上"天才"的标签，比如列昂纳多·达·芬奇、鲍比·菲舍尔和托尼·莫里森。他们的成就千差万别，这就引出了这样一个回避问题实质的问题：天才的定义是什么？长久以来，人们一直认为天才与才智等同，其实更适当的说法是创造性生产力。只有把遗传、机遇、努力等因素结合起来，才能产生如此超常的结果。不经过艰苦的努力，谁也不能以杰出贡献问鼎某一领域。但是如果你天赋异禀，成功会来得更快。此外，性格也起一定作用。如果你乐于尝试新鲜事物，还有一些精神变态特征（没错，类似某些连环杀手的特征），比如生性好斗、情感强硬，那么别人就更有可能认为你是天才。

所有天才在一鸣惊人之前，都经历过同样的一般历程。这一历程起始于他们在不考虑实用性的情况下，对一些问题进行无限制的搜索思考。在这一过程中，他们会不断地碰壁，走进死胡同；这让他们不得不退回去从头再来。这种反复尝试、屡败屡战的过程最终能引导他们找到解决方法。对于那些所参与的项目其进展难以衡量，甚至看起来原地踏步停滞不前的人，这种理论格外令人振奋。有时问题本身很复杂，或者需要异常努力才能解决问题，我们可能就不应期望研究呈直线性进展。很多看起来浪费时间、不会取得结果的探索，实际上很可能就是找到一种切实可行的创新解决方案的必由之路。

当然，这种找到解决方案的能力并非人皆有之。真正的创造力和天才取决于未经过滤的世界观，不被先入之见所限制，对新鲜事物更加开放。尤其是少一些概念性的、多一些实际思维方式。比较典型的就是自闭症人士可以通过这种思考方式打开心胸，发现别人错过的一些细节。思想比较开放的人往往将各种视觉元素组成令人震惊的现实主义画卷。譬如一个男孩在大脑损伤后获得了惊人的机械技能。正是脑伤给了他异于常人的眼光，使他得以区分物体的各个部分。

我们学校过于关注帮助潜在后进生，而在培养天才生力军方面投入不足。基于学校的天才教育几乎没有得到联邦资金的支持。如今，美国只有四个州批准了天才教育项目，并提供充足的资金。我们未能及时开发孩子们的天才，使我们所有的人都失去了一大批人才。这些人才包括未来的发明家、具有创造力的思想家、政治领袖以及杰出的艺术表演家。

2. 汉译英

Water Splashing Festival

Water splashing is the main New Year celebration activity of the Dai people. People splash water on others to wash off the dust and dirt of the old year and welcome the coming of the New Year. Water is either splashed gently or fiercely. Gentle splashing is to the elders—people ladle some water and, uttering good wishes while gently pulling loose the collar, pour it down an elder's neck. The one being splashed accepts it with good grace. Fierce splashing has no fixed pattern—people can run after each other and use ladles, basins or even buckets to splash or pour water over each other face to face. The more one is splashed, the happier one is for the many blessings he gets.

II

1. 随着时间的消逝，我对他越来越敬慕。/ 我对他的仰慕之情与日俱增。
2. 他一向反对矫揉造作的英语。
3. 看演出的观众少则几十人，多则数千人。/ 观众人数从几十人到数千人不等。
4. 思想独立的观察家们对你们在这方面所取得的成就给予了很好的评价。
5. 难怪老一辈的许多人一见到它就会想到 36 年前的往事。
6. 目前我国各地对各种消费品的需求量已大大增加。
7. 读遍了关于美国为摆脱英国统治争取独立而进行革命的堂皇纪事，也很难弄清第一个为美国独立捐躯的原来是一个黑人。
8. 我心里十分难受，一头扎进被单和毯子中，像孩子一样哭了起来。
9. 小偷战战兢兢地坦白了所干的坏事。
10. 水手们欢欢乐乐，蜂拥而至，将这两人围成一圈。
11. 我喜爱那洁净的暖风吹拂在我的皮肤上使我陶然欲醉，也喜爱那清凉的流水把我的身体托浮在水面上。
12. 一段时期以来，我注意到了一条普遍规律，不妨说，仪表堂堂的人大抵不是什么社会名流。

APPENDIX B Keys to Practice of the Relevant Skill and Exercises

III

1. In his speech he laid special stress on raising the quality of the products.
2. The adoption of this new device will greatly cut down the percentage of defective products.
3. Socialist revolution aims at liberating the productive forces.
4. They do not know a thing about factory work, nor about farm work, nor about military affairs.
5. The mastery of language is not easy and requires painstaking efforts.
6. On the very night of Mid-Autumn Festival when a bright moon hangs high in the sky, family members would get together, enjoying the silvery full moon.
7. Great changes have taken place since the reform and opening-up in 1978 and the capital has developed quickly. Modern buildings spring up in Beijing like mushrooms.
8. Thanks to the Chinese people's unrelenting and heroic struggle during the last hundred years, imperialism has not been able to subjugate China, nor will it ever be able to do so.
9. Neither the indiscriminate rejection of everything foreign, whether scientific, technological or cultural, nor the indiscriminate imitation of everything foreign, has anything in common with the Marxist attitude, and neither in any way benefits our cause.
10. The successful launching of China's first experimental communications satellite, which was propelled by a threestage rocket and has been in operation ever since, indicates that our nation has entered a new stage in the development of carrier rockets and electronics.

IV

1. 他既不抽烟，也不喝酒。
2. 他失业以后，就很不合群了。
3. 这些问题难以归类。
4. 雨无情地下个不停，我感到惊异。
5. 高血压患者忌服此药。
6. 在决策过程中，他已经不那么抛头露面了。
7. 他讲话时，态度坚定，但面带愁容，时而眼神黯淡。
8. 必须等到有了这些新设备，才能购买这批货。
9. 现在该是我们两国人民为缔造一个崭新的、更加美好的世界而攀登这一伟大境界高峰的时候了。
10. 激光可以应用于许多科学领域，又适合于各种实际用途，因此成了20世纪轰动一时的科学成就之一。

Unit 4

1. 英译汉

从林肯看个人领导能力

在史学家公认的最伟大的美国总统中,亚伯拉罕·林肯通常名列榜首。但林肯将其伟大部分归因于自己是局外人,因为任何明智的人当初都不敢打赌他能成功。他采取了一系列非常大胆的举措,例如派船队向萨姆特堡运送物资,从而迫使南方打响南北战争第一枪——要是换上经验丰富的对手,也许就不会有此举了。而且他还发表了一连串决定国家命运的演讲——除他之外,美国谁也做不出类似的演讲。

因此领导及管理行业欣然接受林肯这位重要人物也就不足为奇了。哈佛商学院的古塔姆·穆昆达所著的新书《不可或缺》以林肯为例,讨论了现代管理学中一个最激烈的争论话题——究竟是局内人还是局外人当老板更好?在金融危机之前,业界的普遍看法强烈支持局内人。但这种看法目前正在转变,这一方面是因为很多局内人把公司管得一团糟,另一方面是因为很多公司正急于四处寻找一种途径来重新激发业务增长。

穆昆达先生将领导分为两类:"筛选出的领导"和"未经筛选的领导"。"筛选出的领导"为众人所熟知:他们是局内人,经历过一系列旨在暴露其优缺点的测验。"未经筛选的领导"则像未知的谜团:有像林肯一样的局外人,他们从未在要职上经过考验;有像温斯顿·丘吉尔一样一度失宠的局内人;有的则和卡尼一样是在业外机构打出自己名声的外来者。"筛选出的领导"选谁其实无关紧要,候选人名单中的任何一个上任都会干得差不多。而"未筛选的领导"则大不相同,偶尔也可能会碰到像林肯或是丘吉尔那样的人才,但更常见的情况是会把局面搞得更糟。

同样来自哈佛商学院的威廉姆·索恩戴克最近也出了一本名为《局外人》的新书。该书对穆昆达关于"未经筛选领导"可能存在优势的论据做了进一步补充。索恩戴克考察了8位公司总裁,他们在掌管公司期间业绩表现超出标准普尔平均值20倍。他发现,所有这8位总裁都是为自己行业带来崭新视点的局外人。《华盛顿邮报》的总编凯瑟琳·格雷厄姆上任时是一位已经多年没有正式工作的遗孀;通用动力公司的总裁比尔·安德斯以前曾是一名宇航员;首都通信公司的总裁汤姆·墨菲在临危受命接手电视台之前从未干过媒体这一行;而伯克希尔·哈撒韦公司的老板华伦·巴菲特则是股神巴菲特。

但每一个局外人的成功都意味着十几例他人的失败。博斯公司的数据显示,2009至2011年共有34.9%的局外人总裁被解职,而局内人总裁中这个比例只有18.5%。这表明如果业务一帆风顺,最好还是避免用局外人。因为把一个好摊子搞砸要比把它做得更棒容易得多。

APPENDIX B Keys to Practice of the Relevant Skill and Exercises

2. 汉译英

Mei Yiqi

Educationalist Mei Yiqi (1889-1962) was born in Tianjin. In 1909, he passed the examination and became one of the first Tsinghua students to study in U.S.A., majoring in electrical engineering at Worcester Polytechnic Institute. In September 1915 he was invited to work in Tsinghua University as a physics professor and was appointed Dean of Studies in 1926. He was appointed president of Tsinghua University in 1931 and did not leave the post until the end of 1948. Under his leadership, Tsinghua University quickly ranked among world famous universities in many aspects in a matter of just a few years. An educationalist himself, he established a complete ideological system of education. His strategy of running the university comprises three parts, i.e. general education (also known as "free education"), professor management (also called "democratic management") and academic freedom (or "the atmosphere of free discussion"). His representative work is *An interpretation of University*, which was published in 1941. And his famous saying "it is great masters, not huge buildings that characterize a university" is still thought highly of by the educational circles even to this day.(And his famous saying "what makes a university famous is not its magnificent buildings, but its reputed scholars" is still popular now in the educational circles.)

II

1. 海洋与其说是分隔了世界不如说是连接了整个世界。
2. 她苏醒过来，看见周围一张张笑脸。
3. 我们居住的星球并不仅仅是一个由惰性物质组成的球体。
4. 瞳孔随光线的强弱变化而缩小放大。
5. 勇敢过度，即成蛮勇；感情过度，即成软弱，俭约过度，即成贪婪。
6. 读书使人充实，讨论使人机智，笔写使人准确。
7. 热情的主人又是切肉，又是倒茶，又是上菜，又是切面包，谈啊，笑啊，敬酒啊，忙个不停。
8. 这种数码相机操作简便，功能齐全，结构紧凑，造型美观。
9. 一条科学假设可以被证明，或被否定，后者可能更为重要。而一首诗，一张画，或一曲音乐却不能。
10. 读史使人明智，读诗使人灵秀，数学使人周密，科学使人深刻，伦理使人庄重，逻辑修饰之学使人善辩。

III

1. Please fill in this form, and give it to me when you have finished.

2. We should advocate the spirit of taking the whole situation into consideration.
3. While eating, take heed that you do not choke; while walking, take heed that you do not fall.
4. Although you may escort a guest a thousand miles, yet must the parting come at last.
5. A fence needs the support of three stakes, and an able fellow needs the help of three other people.
6. It was so cold that the river froze.
7. While the prospects are bright, the road has twists and turns.
8. That theory must go hand in hand with practice is a principle we should always keep in mind.
9. With the weather so close and stuffy, ten to one it'll rain presently.
10. All citizens who have reached the age of eighteen have the right to vote and to stand for election.

IV

And:
1. 太阳一出，草**就**干枯了。
2. 他看了一个钟头的书，**然后**就睡觉了。
3. 他干了这件工作，**并且**干得挺好。
4. 再挪一步，(那么)**就**要你的命。
5. 我上他家去，**而**他却到我家来。
6. 他那么有钱，**却**生活得像个乞丐。
7. 这些零件是用木材或塑料制成的，**而不是**用金属制成的。
8. 锈具有腐蚀性，**所以**能损坏喷射元件。
9. 溶液被用来代替系统中的大量过滤器，**以期**获得最佳去污效果。
10. 化学制品的溅沫会使眼睛发炎，**甚至**会造成永久性伤害。
11. 这就意味着在润滑油进入系统之前就要将其脱水，明智地说，**也就是**要确保润滑油上面的空气干燥。
12. 他分析了压强对温度的依赖，**结果**得出了压强随温度的增高而下降的结论。

When:
1. 我一直待到中午，**然后**就回家了。
2. 你**一旦**过了河，便安全了。
3. **虽然**有车可乘，他通常总是步行。
4. 他**连**听都听不进，我又怎么能说服他呢？
5. 一个人的经验**随**年龄的增长而增长。
6. 你**本**该在学校里的，却为何在这里？

APPENDIX B　Keys to Practice of the Relevant Skill and Exercises

7. 他们需要 5 支晶体管，**可是**只有 3 支。
8. **万一**机器发生什么故障，就把电门关上。
9. 老师离开教室**以后**，学生们就喧哗起来。
10. **每当**那人开口一句"老实说"，我就怀疑他要撒谎。
11. **既然**你知道这样会损坏仪器，怎么还这样干？
12. 我们 6 月初要下乡去，**那时**夏收就要开始了。
13. 我**明明**在总的原则上反对这类行为，又怎能对此事例外呢？
14. 投了保的任何物品，**如果**在保险期内丢失或损坏，保险公司要负责赔偿。
15. 我国的国民经济**只要**真正做到有计划、按比例地发展，就能够实现持续、稳定、高速的增长。

Unit 5

1.　英译汉

以 书 为 友

　　要了解一个人，通常除了可以通过他所交往的朋友之外，也可以通过他所阅读的书籍来认识他。因为一个人就像与朋友有友情一样，与书也有交情。一个人应该经常生活在最佳友伴之中，不管这友伴是书还是人。

　　一本好书可以成为你最要好的朋友中的一员。它过去始终如此，现在仍是这样，将来也绝不会改变。书是所有伴侣中最有耐心、最令人愉悦的一位。它不会在我们身处逆境或悲伤痛苦的境况下背弃我们。它总是给我们以同样的亲切感，年轻时给我们以乐趣和教诲，年老时予我们以舒适与安慰。

　　人们经常会发现由于对同一本书的爱好而产生一种共鸣——正如两个人有时会因同时仰慕另一人而彼此成为朋友一样。古谚云："爱屋及乌。" 但更明智的说法毋宁是："爱吾及书"。书是连接友谊的更真实、更高尚的纽带。人们可以因为喜爱某一作家而同思、同感、同情。他们一道生活在作者的世界中，作者与他们随时相伴。

　　黑兹利特曾这样说过："书沁入心扉，诗人的诗句融入我们的血液。我们年轻时所读之书，年老时仍记忆犹新。我们感受书的情趣，恰如亲历其境一般。书价廉物美，随处可得。我们无不呼吸到书本的芬芳气息。"

　　一本好书往往是人生精华的缩影。因为人的一生主要也就是其精神世界。因此，好书就是美好言辞和高尚思想的宝库，这些言辞和思想铭记在心，会随时随地陪伴并安慰我们。菲利普·西德尼爵士曾说过："以崇高思想为伴者从不感到孤独。"

　　书引导我们进入最优秀的社会群体，将我们带到有史以来最伟大的思想家面前。我们

259

耳闻目睹他们的言行举止，仿佛见到了他们活生生的身影。我们同情他们的遭遇，与他们有乐共享、有难同当，他们的遭遇成了我们的经历，我们感到自己有点像在他们所描绘的情景中扮演角色。

伟人及其崇高思想即使在当今世界也永生不灭。他们的精神永驻书中，传遍世界各地。书是一种逼真的声音，是一种智慧。人们至今聆听其教诲，乐此不疲。因此，我们总是处在已故的伟人的影响之下。先哲们的音容笑貌依然如故，其影响一点不亚于当年。

2. 汉译英

Library of the Foreign Languages Department

With a floor space of 125 square meters the library of the Foreign Languages Department has around 23,000 books in storage. The library consists of 3 stack rooms and 1 reading room, i.e. 1 stack room for English and Russian books, another for English dictionaries and reference books, the third for Japanese, French and German books, and a reading room meant for Chinese and English magazines and periodicals. The library mainly focuses on English linguistic studies and relevant literatures, and concurrently, it keeps a considerable collection of various books in Japanese, Russian, Germany and French. Around 200 Chinese and English magazines and periodical titles are available here.

As a library for special purpose, the library of the Foreign Languages Department plays an important part in the sublibrary of humanities and social science under the Main Library of the University, laying its stress on linguistic studies and language teaching. The management of the library is computerized and is now able to serve the reader via its network.

II

1. 他这个人得寸进尺。
2. 不要自找麻烦。
3. 与人同乐才是真乐。
4. 说有饭大家吃并不完全正确。
5. 他从容不迫，和蔼可亲。/ 他举止不慌不忙，十分友好。
6. 放射线可以引起遗传性疾病。
7. 会引起疾病的细菌称为致病菌。
8. 世世代代以来，煤和石油一直被认为是人员运输的主要能源。
9. 流感病人必须与健康的人隔开，以免疾病传播。
10. 在18种企鹅中，有8种栖息在南极四周。
11. 这些发展中国家，土地辽阔，人口众多，资源丰富。/ 地大物博，人口众多。

APPENDIX B Keys to Practice of the Relevant Skill and Exercises

12. 为了生存，为了自己和子孙后代的衣食住行，人类和大自然不断进行斗争。
13. 冬天是研究树木生长的最好季节；虽然树叶落了，树枝秃了，但树木本身却很美丽。
14. 人类对科学的探索，对知识的寻求，其实际结果是使自己具有抵御天灾人祸的能力。

III

1. He can hardly open his mouth without talking shop.
2. Every river has its upper, middle and lower reaches.
3. He told his parents the whole story exactly as it had happened.
4. People use science to understand and change nature.
5. We must cultivate the ability to analyze and solve problems.
6. These new cars are fast, efficient and handy.
7. For many years there has been serious unemployment in that country.
8. Old and new players should learn from and help each other, to make up for each other's deficiencies.
9. The people of China have always been courageous enough to probe into things, to make inventions and to make revolution.
10. Live or die, we should be loyal to our Party, to our people and to our motherland.
11. I didn't go to town yesterday both because of the nasty weather and the fact that I was not feeling myself.
12. Independence and self-reliance have always been and will always be our basic stand.

IV

1. 一个星期有七天。
2. 谁也没法预料！
3. 据说是这样。
4. 生的是男孩还是女孩？
5. (打电话)我是布朗。
6. 一个人应该尽自己的责任。
7. [谚] 覆水难收。/ 木已成舟，哭也无用。
8. 事实上，我们天黑前就到了那里。
9. 她发现她在写作上很难获得成功。
10. 在古罗马，有贵族、骑士、平民、奴隶……

V

1. 掌上明珠
2. 不晕船(晕船)
3. 昙花一现
4. 保姆(奶妈)
5. 开某人玩笑
6. 扭转局势
7. 承担自己行为的后果
8. 与某人不和
9. 排尿，小便
10. 称职
11. 睡懒觉
12. 不严密

13. 冷热无常，摇摆不定
14. 鲁莽闯祸的人
15. 幕后操纵
16. 孤注一掷
17. 改口
18. 改过自新
19. 处于困境
20. 健康状况良好的人

Unit 6

1. 英译汉

全球大学热

"上帝把我们安全地带到了新英格兰，在那里我们建造了房屋，为自己提供了生活必需品，修建了敬奉上帝的便利场所，设立了文职政府。在完成所有这些之后，我们渴望的下一件事就是推进教育，并延泽子孙万代。"1643年从哈佛学院寄往英国筹措资金的第一本大学筹款宣传册中这样写道。

美国很早就热衷于高等教育，其热情持续至今，因此形成了目前世界最大、财力支持最雄厚的高等教育体系。于是其他国家也模仿美国的教育模式，让更多的高中毕业生接受大学教育，这就不足为奇了。但是，正如我们的特别报告所提出的那样，随着美国的高等教育体系的不断扩散，对高等教育上的忧虑也在日益加剧：花在这方面的大量资金是否真的值得？

美国创造的现代研究型大学是一种牛剑大学与德国研究机构的合体，已成为全球的金本位（黄金准则）。大规模高等教育于19世纪由美国首创，20世纪蔓延到欧洲和东亚，现在已出现在除撒哈拉以南非洲地区的世界各地。2012年之前的20年里，全球的大学入学率（大学学生占适龄人口的比例），已从14%上升至32%；与此同时，入学率超过50%的国家从5个增至54个。大学入学率的增速之快，甚至超过了汽车需求这种最终消费品的增速。人们对学位的渴望无可厚非：在当今时代，学位就是获得一份体面工作的必备条件，也是进入中产阶级的入场券。

广义上讲，有两种方式可以满足如此巨大的需求。一是欧洲大陆的方法，即政府拨款提供资金，大部分院校都拥有均等的资源和地位。第二种是更加基于市场的美国模式，即私人和公共资助并行的混合模式，其特点是办学出色且资金充裕的院校位于顶层，而资金匮乏的院校则处于底层。世界正在朝着美国模式的方向发展。眼下越来越多的国家中的越来越多的大学向学生收取学费。正如政治家们所识，"知识经济"需要一流的研究，公共资源正集中在少数享有特权的院校，因此创建世界一流大学的竞争日趋激烈。

从某种意义上说，这太好了。由于这些顶尖大学的许多发现，才使我们这个世界更安全、更富裕、更有趣。但其费用也在增长。世界经合组织国家在高等教育上的花费通常占GDP的1.6%，相比之下2000年为1.3%。如果美国的高校建设模式持续蔓延下去，这

APPENDIX B Keys to Practice of the Relevant Skill and Exercises

一比例将会进一步攀升。美国在高等教育上的投入为 GDP 的 2.7%。

2. 汉译英

Zhang Guangdou: A Centenarian Wedded to Hydraulics

Zhang Guangdou, a 95-year-old professor of Department of Hydraulic Engineering, Tsinghua University and an engineering educationalist who devotes his wisdom and whole life to China's hydraulics cause, has witnessed and participated in the great development of Chinese water conservancy projects in the 20th century. Founder of the disciplines of hydraulic structure and hydroelectric engineering in China, he is the author of the first textbook *Hydraulic Engineering Structure* in Chinese. He also set up China's first laboratory of hydraulic engineering structure and became the first to have supervised graduate students majoring in this field.

In spite of ups and downs in the past fifty-six years, he has never stopped his steps on the road of the hydraulics study; nor has he ceased to pour his enthusiasm and affection on his students wholeheartedly. Having students all over the world, including sixteen academicians of Chinese Academy of Sciences and Chinese Academy of Engineering, five national master designers and a large number of senior engineers and professors, Professor Zhang Guangdou is going to pass on his following favorite saying to generations of students: "To be a good engineer, one should first of all be an upright person—an honest, patriotic man who serves the people."

II

1. 要知道应该抵消多大重力并需要多大推力才能保持飞行，这很容易。
2. 她非要他讲清楚他的每一分钱都到哪儿去了，他哑口无言。
3. 这种理论的核心是，我们的环境同我们的才能、性格特征和行为即使有什么关系的话，也是微不足道的。
4. 相反，行为主义者认为，成绩的差异是由于黑人往往被剥夺了白人在教育及其他环境方面所享有的许多有利条件。
5. 如果有人敢于公然蔑视世界公众舆论而一意孤行，那他一定是个鲁莽之徒。
6. 由于贵国政府的提议，才得以这样快地重提访问之事，这使我感到特别高兴。
7. 大山沉陷，平原隆起，火焰喷射，周围是一片废墟，这些都有报道。
8. 总统也号召每年的这一天，在东部时间 8：46，也就是当第一架飞机撞上第一座塔楼的时刻全国默哀。
9. 如今人们知道，如果食物中缺少了某些重要的成分，即使其中不含任何有害的物质，也会引起严重的疾病。
10. 你们能不能不分东南西北，建立起一个对付这些敌人的全球联盟，以保证全人类享有更为丰富的生活？你们是否愿意参与这一历史的努力？

11. 游客太多了，这小地方接待不过来。搭班船的、坐包船的、驾游艇的，一批批涌到，从早到晚，络绎不绝，漫步爬上纤路。他们想看什么呢？

12. 这次周年纪念会应该是一个老老实实地评估我们过去失误的时机，同时也应该是一个表达我们有同样决心要做好今后工作的时机。这样，我们就可免遭挫折，并可把这次周年纪念变成一种鼓舞和成就。我相信我的这番话代表了联合国每一位真诚和严肃的代表的心声——今天上午我们听到的发言也使我相信这一点。

III

1. I did not know that he was hospitalized until yesterday.
2. We must get a clear understanding of the things concerned.
3. Their troops advanced by both land and water, and arrived at the front in time.
4. The conference has given full expression to democracy; the atmosphere has been lively and the delegates have enjoyed ease of mind.
5. While crossing the street, he looked right and left, afraid that he might run into some passing car.
6. Only by following the instruction of the Party Central Committee, and mobilizing all positive factors, can we successfully realize the four modernizations.
7. Accumulate more in good years and less or none in years when the crops half fail or totally fail.
8. All of these achievements show that China has taken another solid step forward on the road of building a moderately prosperous society in all respects.
9. This university has 6 newly established faculties, namely, Computer Science, High Energy Physics, Laser, Geophysics, Remote Sensing, and Genetic Engineering.
10. The Chinese mainland is flanked by the Bohai, the Yellow, the East China and the South China seas in the east and southeast, with a total water surface of more than 4.7 mil square kilometers.

IV

1. 我要**重新考虑**自己的结论。
2. 我**谅**你也答不出这个问题。
3. 中国人的纪律性**举世无双**。
4. 最近的一些发现**使**一些老观念成了问题。
5. 他的问题**促使**我们思考。
6. 在敌占区生存**需要**有高超的技术。
7. 他没**肯定说**要进行早期选举。
8. 我**决心要**改善与中国的关系。

9. 我不能一下把话**说死**。
10. 我希望多了解一些情况再**表态**。
11. 我并不抱任何希望你能**承诺**做什么事情。
12. 老板**责成**他做这件事。
13. 他**绝**不会受贿。
14. 他**最**不适合这项工作。
15. 她**最**不喜欢穿比基尼泳装。
16. **怎么也没**想到我会在这个地方见到你。

Unit 7

1. 英译汉

情人节巧克力的传说

　　流行的关于圣瓦伦丁的圣徒传记有好几个版本，但没有一星半点提及他喜欢吃巧克力或者与巧克力有任何关系。这样说是有充分的理由的：古罗马时代上至贵族、下至平民百姓还要过一千年才能知道有那么个中美洲，更不要说品尝什么"遭古力"（xocolatl）的美味了（xocolatl 一词由玛雅语与纳瓦特语混成，意为"热饮"）。

　　可可树原生于亚马孙河与奥里诺科河之间的安第斯山脉。1502 年，克里斯托弗·哥伦布第四次、也是最后一次航海至美洲之后，欧洲人才开始进口可可树的种子。然而一旦西班牙人开始向这种苦涩的饮料中加入蜂蜜或糖之后，巧克力就成了欧洲人提神的饮品，一天之中有事没事都喜欢喝上两口。可可饮料如此深受喜爱，以至于荷兰人、比利时人、法国人和英国人最后都开始在自己新占领的热带殖民地上大面积种植可可树——从而奠定了今天巧克力产业的基础。如今，西非的可可产量占世界的三分之二。

　　暂时回到罗马时代看看。传说罗马时期有几位殉道者统称为"瓦伦丁"，他们因帮助基督徒而遭受迫害，其中一位尤受尊敬。据说此人在在押期间治愈了看守他的狱卒的盲女，并在自己被判决投入狮口之前给她写了一封信，署名"你的瓦伦丁"。他的不幸结局是否发生在公历的 2 月 14 日我们不得而知。

　　且不论这位殉道罹难的传说，就连"圣瓦伦丁"这个节日也和浪漫的爱情毫无关联。直到 14 世纪杰弗里·乔叟写了一首《百鸟议会》之时，二者才真正联系在一起。这首诗是他为庆祝理查德二世与波西米亚公主安妮订婚一周年的纪念日而创作的。乔叟创作该诗用的是生动的中世纪英语（发音有点像现在的泰恩赛德方言）。其中一句这样写道："斯日名曰'瓦伦丁'，百鸟出巢觅夫君"。（"琴之瑟之，瓦伦丁日；颉之颃之，百鸟觅偶。"）有趣的是，当时的理查德和安妮都同为 15 岁。

然而，直到18世纪末，英国年轻的情侣们才开始利用这个机会，通过赠送鲜花、贺卡（被称为情人节卡片）和糖果作为礼物表达他们对彼此的爱。如今，情人节之前的几周是巧克力公司一年中最繁忙的时期。与此同时，随着1840年不列颠群岛统一实行便士邮政，互赠情人节匿名卡片的传统便传播开来。这对很多心存爱慕却羞于表达的人来说是个福音，因为他们再也不用亲自登门来表达爱意了。

2. 汉译英

Modesty vs. Sincerity

"You have a very nice house. It's so spacious." A Chinese who was invited to the home of an American friend complimented him. "Thank you," the host smiled with obvious pleasure and replied in good American fashion, which caused surprise to his guest.

"You speak fluent English, really very fluent," the host said to his guest. "No, no. My English is very poor," the guest replied. Having not expected such a reaction, the host was perplexed.

Was the host's reply immodest? Or was the guest's remark insincere? The answer is no in either case. To Englishspeaking people, praise is to be accepted, generally with a remark like "Thank you." It is assumed that the compliment is sincere, that the praise is for some not unworthy achievement or thing. Therefore, there should be no show of pretended modesty. To Chinese, however, the customary reply to a compliment would be to claim that one is not worthy of the praise, that what one has done is hardly enough. Acceptance of a compliment would imply conceit or lack of manners. So, different reactions in above cases reflect differences in people's expressing habits.

II
1. 新到一个陌生的邻里，越小心越好。
2. 我才不至于蠢到相信你所说的金钱万能呢。
3. 再漂亮的东西，只要仔细观察，也会发现某种缺陷。
4. 我知道此物方枘圆凿，十分不配；但尽管如此，还是勉强顶用。
5. 非洲将西方帝国主义踢出国门并不是为了请进其他新的主子。
6. 双方都认为可以不失体面地接受这个和平方案。
7. 燃料中的所有化学能并非都可转为热能。
8. 外语院校的毕业生并非人人被分配去做翻译工作。
9. 所有这些能量耗散，尽管很大，却都和能量守恒定律无矛盾。
10. 除了太阳的热源以外，所有其他热源都不能把地球的温度升高四分之一华氏度。
11. 动物发出的声音并不都起语言作用。只需以发现蝙蝠的回声定位这个不同寻常的事为例，我们就能知道声音起着严格的功利作用。

APPENDIX B Keys to Practice of the Relevant Skill and Exercises

12. （把标准化测试作为抨击）目标是错误的，因为在抨击这类测试时，批评者不考虑其弊病来自人们对测试不甚了解或使用不当。
13. 读书如果不是为了培养才德和端庄品行，还不如睡大觉好。
14. 事情很少有做不成的：其所以做不成，与其说由于条件不够，不如说由于缺乏决心。

III

1. His absence of mind during the driving nearly caused an accident.
2. Slips are scarcely avoidable when you're new to your work.
3. The meetings were marked by such an absence of lively discussions that at times they were almost on the point of breaking up.
4. That city and the areas around it are an ice-free port and a nuclear-weapon free zone.
5. His lack of consideration for the feelings of others angered everyone present.
6. The days passed quickly, but she worked as hard as ever.
7. Traveling alone, she was sitting still in the corner of the carriage.
8. There are two aspects to everything; to say there is only one is to be aware of one aspect and to be ignorant of the other.
9. It doesn't matter much whether we can come up with new ideas. What matters is that we should not change our policies and should not make people feel that we are changing them.
10. The Chinese government has been advocating the concept of "people-oriented" development, emphasizing the habit of using public transport instead of driving.
11. In China, parents would spare no efforts to help their children regardless of whatever they demand, even help them make important decisions. For they believe that it is for the good of the young.
12. If we fail to analyze it properly and to understand it correctly, we shall become overcautious, not daring to emancipate our minds and act freely. Consequently, we shall lose opportunities. Like a boat sailing against the current, we must forge ahead or be swept downstream.

IV

1. 他们常常吹牛。
2. 那个妇女是妓女。
3. 我要检举那位官员。
4. 那台机器状况良好。
5. 我们将抵制这个计划。
6. 别讨好他们！
7. 她在被告席。
8. 老板解雇了她。
9. 那女学生正值豆蔻年华。
10. 那个老太太安息了。
11. 青年人热恋着那个姑娘。
12. 那老人常忍受不愉快的事。
13. 那人服过三年劳役。
14. 分娩的妇女是他的妻子

15. 我很怕蛇。
16. 我们责令他干那事。
17. 他们撞上他做那个事。
18. 我帮助他渡过难关。
19. 他是议长。
20. 《圣经》在哪儿?
21. 你了解日本漆吗?
22. 我昨天买了一些泻药。
23. 那个人神情沮丧。
24. 别骂他!
25. 那个小男孩是个私生子。
26. 他是个骗子。
27. 他是个巫医。
28. 他买的东西价值连城。
29. 这是一台废弃的机器。
30. 他在此事上公正无私。

Unit 8

1. 英译汉

消失的孪生子

人类一胎多子的情况通常并不常见。尽管如此,据估计在婴儿呱呱坠地之前,每 20 个单胞胎中就有一个丧失了自己的孪生同胞。两胚胎同时受孕,但其中一个未足月就夭折了。

很早之前,人们就知道双胞胎要是在怀孕晚期夭折一个,会对另一个不利。活下来的这个更容易早产、脑瘫,甚至死亡。人们至今也不知道,如果在妊娠头几个月里,其中一个夭折的话,对存活的另一个会有何影响。但英国利物浦大学的彼得·法罗刚刚发表在《人类的繁衍》杂志上的一篇论文表明,影响的确存在。

消失的孪生子会以几种不同的方式显露出来/现形。其中最让人骇异的当是,可能会发现夭折胎儿已完全发育成形的身体部位牢牢嵌在存活的胎儿体内。更常见的情况是,在胎儿降生后,会发现死去的胎儿变成了极小的干尸附在胎盘上。随着超声波扫描的广泛使用,人们越来越多地发现这样的情况:妊娠早期扫描发现了孪生胎,后来却消失了。无论妊娠早期超声波检测的发现,还是(胎盘上)纸状的干尸,这些通常都没有正式记载,甚至不会向产妇提及。所以很难知道早期的双胞胎最终变成单胞胎的频率到底有多高。

但法罗博士要尝试弄清楚(这个问题)。他分析了来自英格兰北部的三组数据。第一组整理核对了婴儿的死亡信息。第二组记录了婴儿先天性疾病的数据。第三组对所有双胞胎、三胞胎等多胞胎的妊娠情况做了登记。

第三组数据非常有价值,因为多胞胎妊娠情况一经超声波检查发现就有了记载,而不是等到出生时做记载。根据这些记载,他发现 138 例在妊娠 16 周之前双胞胎之一夭折、而另一个出生并存活的情况。这些存活胎儿中有 11 个患有先天异常疾病,比如先天性心脏畸形、面裂等。根据这些数据,法罗博士计算出失去其孪生兄妹的幸存婴儿患先天性畸

APPENDIX B Keys to Practice of the Relevant Skill and Exercises

形病的概率是两者均存活情况的 2.4 倍，是从一开始就独享一个子宫的单胎生的婴儿的四倍。他认为当一份血液同时要供给两个胎儿的时候，危害就产生了，而在共用一个绒毛膜的双胞胎妊娠中，这种共享血液供给的情况更为常见。

这一认识是否可以用来帮助存活下来的多胞胎，尚有待讨论。不过，解决问题的关键第一步是锁定问题，而法洛博士似乎已做到了这一点。

2. 汉译英

Genetic Engineering

The term "genetic engineering" was first coined by American science fiction writer Jack Williamson in 1951. Genetic engineering techniques have been extensively applied to various industries in the past 50 years, with some success principally in medical and agricultural fields.

However, some scientists abroad are opposed to genetic engineering for fear that cancerogenic virus or bacteria might be produced, and that the function of normal cells might be disrupted and damaged, and consequently some unknown diseases might occur...

It is known to all that whether a new science is weal or woe to humanity is not decided by the science itself, as the case in atomic energy: it can be either used to benefit human beings or used to make deadly weapons. We believe that if it is properly applied, genetic engineering will certainly become a powerful tool for human beings to conquer and transform the nature.

II

1. 全世界的石油将会用尽，到那时人们将使用通过原子裂变获取的更为方便的动力。
2. 有几种放射性同位素是通过用中子轰击原子核而人造出来的。
3. 应当注意缩短人们在强噪声环境中的停留时间。
4. 有关胚胎干细胞研究的复杂性已经谈得很多了。
5. 多年来，一个名叫古德伊尔的美国人一直在努力寻找一种方法把橡胶做得硬而不黏，但却有弹性。
6. 我们学过，写商务信件要用规范的格式，而不能像个人信件那样随便。
7. 她告诉我，男主人已解雇了她。没有对她说明任何理由，对她的行为也没提出任何异议。而且不许她向女主人申诉。
8. 电视机、宇宙飞船和核动力舰艇对今天的人们来说不是什么新鲜事物，但对于生活于 20 世纪 20 年代以前的人来说，却似乎是不可思议的东西。考虑到这一点，科学发展的速度之快也就显而易见了。
9. 可以认为，腐蚀状态是金属接触湿气、空气和水等介质后形成的破坏性化学侵蚀，而铁生锈只是其中的一个例子。

10. 理论科学分为自然科学和生物科学，前者研究自然界的各种事物及其相互联系，后者探讨的是地球上生物的进化历史和形成条件。

11. 近来我们发现本馆的图书库存正在急剧下降，此事令人关注。现提醒大家注意借书还书规则，别忘了其他同学也需要借阅。今后将严格执行借书规则，凡逾期不还者将照章处罚。

12. 最近查找了卷宗，发现本局并无此信。根据记录，该信于两个月前收到，经研读已寄还贵处。照此看来，贵处似无收信的记录，甚为遗憾。如能查明此信，请即通知本局，不胜感谢。

III

1. Passengers are requested to fill in "Customs Declaration Forms" here.
2. Some things were said here just now which should not have been said.
3. I was astounded that he was prepared to give me a job.
4. The boy who was seriously injured was immediately admitted into the hospital.
5. "One country, two systems" has been adopted to suit China's conditions and is not an expedient measure.
6. The time will come when homes will be heated from a small reactor in the basement.
7. I'm very sorry to say the visit to the museum has to be put off till tomorrow because of the heavy rain.
8. All teachers and students of the department are requested to meet in the conference room at 2∶00 p.m. on Wednesday to hear a speech.
9. If the chain reaction went on without being checked, it could cause a great explosion.
10. With the help of a microscope you can watch the integrated circuits being separated and tested.
11. If the capitalist system is not guaranteed in Hongkong and Taiwan, prosperity and stability there cannot be maintained and a peaceful settlement will become impossible.
12. Other equipment has been devised which is able to break down the noise into various audio frequencies and record the loudness at different frequencies.

IV

1. a red and a yellow dress 各一件；a red and yellow dress 就一件
2. with a child 带一个孩子；with child 怀孕
3. no more useful than 都不管用；not more useful than 不如……管用
4. to the dog 扔向狗；at the dog 砸狗
5. quite properly 严格地讲，他受到了惩罚；punished quite properly 受到恰如其分的惩罚
6. 前一句中的 he 和 Henry 为同一人；后一句中的 he 和 Henry 为不同的两人

APPENDIX B Keys to Practice of the Relevant Skill and Exercises

7. and so he is 他真的疯了；and so is he 他自己也疯了
8. fairly hot 很热，正好喝；rather hot 太烫，不能喝
9. anything but 绝不是；nothing but 只不过是……罢了
10. may as well say so 完全可以这样说；might as well say so 不妨这样说
11. as deeply as I 像我一样深深地冒犯了她；as deeply as me 像冒犯我一样深深地冒犯了她
12. out of question 不成问题；out of the question 成问题
13. continually 不住地，断断续续地；continuously 连续不断地
14. regret to say 遗憾地说；regret saying 因说了……而感到遗憾
15. as a mother 作为母亲；like a mother 像母亲一样
16. to watch the train come in 为了看见火车开入；watching the train come in 偶然看见火车开入
17. I, as well as you, shall not 我和你都不；I shall not...as well as you 我不像你那样
18. The children who wanted to play soccer 孩子中想踢球的人；The children, who wanted to play soccer 孩子们全都想踢球

Unit 9

1.　英译汉

犯罪与贫穷

亚里士多德曾写道："贫穷乃罪恶之源。"他的看法对吗？不可否认，贫穷与犯罪之间肯定有联系。收入拮据或许会迫使一个人行为不端，这一说法听起来似乎可信。但是，斯德哥尔摩卡尔林斯卡研究所的爱米尔·萨里艾斯兰与其同事却对此说表示怀疑。他们在《英国精神病学杂志》上新近发表的一份研究报告对贫穷与犯罪的因果关系链提出了质疑——至少对暴力犯罪、吸毒等诸多问题而言并非如此。

北欧各国公民信息数据库内容丰富，萨里艾斯兰先生和他的团队利用这个数据库，可以对 50 多万个 1989—1993 年在瑞典出生的孩子进行研究。他们查阅了这些人受教育程度、家庭年收入水平以及犯罪记录等方面的信息。研究人员还可以在数据库中确定每人的兄弟姐妹的情况。

在瑞典，承担刑事责任的起始年龄是 15 岁。因此，萨里艾斯兰先生从其研究对象年满 15 岁那一天开始追踪，平均时间为 3 年半。不出所料，他发现成长在收入最低的 1/5 家庭的孩子与收入最高的 1/5 家庭的孩子相比，被判暴力罪的概率很可能为后者的 7 倍，毒品罪概率为后者的两倍。

令他感到惊讶的是，当他在研究那些白手起家由穷变富的家庭时，他发现那些年龄较小的弟妹（他们出生时家庭已比较富裕）在青少年期与他们年长的哥哥姐姐小时候一样，也容易产生不良行为。如此看来，家庭收入本身并不是导致犯罪的决定性因素。

这就显示出两种并非相互排斥的可能性。一种可能性是，家庭文化（家风）一旦形成，便具有"附着性"。说得难听点，孩子可以离开四邻，但身上的邻里印迹却难以磨灭。譬如说，考虑到孩子喜欢效仿他们崇拜的哥哥姐姐，这种说法听起来似乎非常合理。另一种可能性就是下层社会的孩子比上层社会的孩子身上有更多的容易犯罪的基因，也许正是因为无法控制冲动，导致他们的赚钱能力也降低了。

以上两种可能都不是社会改革者所欢迎的。第一种可能表明，仅仅提高人们的收入（尽管从另外一些方面来说这或许是一种好办法），无法解决不良行为的问题。第二种提出了这样一种可能性：代际贫困问题可能会自我强化，特别是在瑞典这样的富裕国家，教育具有筛选作用。许多工作需要高技能，这有利于那些具有自控能力的人，而不利于那些成天靠药物支撑打发日子的人。

2. 汉译英

Eradicating Extreme Poverty

China is playing an increasingly important role in helping the international community in the process of eradicating extreme poverty by 2030.

Since the implementation of reform and opening up in the late 1970s, China has helped as many as 400 million people out of poverty. In the next five years, China will provide assistance to other developing countries in various aspects such as poverty reduction, education development, agricultural modernization, environmental protection, health care, etc.

China has made remarkable progress in poverty alleviation, and it has made unremitting efforts in promoting economic growth. This will encourage other poor countries to cope with their own development challenges. These countries can learn from China's experience in seeking the path of development with their own characteristics.

II
1. 大多数受过教育的人说话或写作时使用的英语就是正确的英语，或如斯威特所说："凡是语言中广泛使用的说法（仅仅这一理由）都可以认为在语法上是正确的。"
2. 他吹嘘说，任何奴隶一踏上英国的土地就获得自由，而他却出卖穷人家六岁的孩子到工厂干活，每天十六个小时，受尽鞭打责骂。
3. 认为自己的思想深奥，不可能表达得很清楚，让任何人都能理解，这是一种虚荣的念头。这样的作家当然不会想到，问题还是出在自己脑子缺乏精确思考的能力。
4. 这并不是说，使用磅秤和使用天平这两种情况在构造原理或工作方式上存在什么差别，

APPENDIX B Keys to Practice of the Relevant Skill and Exercises

而是说与前者相比，后者是一种更精密得多的装置，因而在计量上更准确得多。

5. 我们都认为自己不是机器人，因此能够控制自己的思想。爱伦的贡献在于他准备接受大家的这一共识，并揭示其错误性质。

6. ……但是对于绝大多数受过教育的人过去所深信的所谓人死后另有生命，现今这种观念已经为越来越多的人所怀疑，所以人们对生命的价值认识越来越深刻，其范围也越来越广。

7. 所有美国人受的教育是长大成人后应该追求金钱和权力，而我却偏偏不想要明显是朝这个目标迈进的东西，他对此大为不解。

8. 他在作品里倾诉了自己一生的痛苦和这种痛苦给他带来的一种信念，认为如果受剥削的阶级奋起反抗，世界就会变得更美好。

9. 很久以来，海员中有一种迷信，认为海豚会把快死的人推到水面把他们救起，或者在溺水人周围形成防御队形，保护他们不受鲨鱼伤害。

10. 再者，显而易见的是一个国家的经济实力与其工农业生产效率密切相关，而效率的提高则又有赖于各种科技人员。

11. 例如，测试并不弥补明显的社会不公；因此，它们不能说明一个物质条件差的年轻人，如果在较好的环境下成长的话，会有多大才干。

12. 这种说法从一开始就将讨论引向两个极端，它使人们认为应这样对待动物：要么像对待人类自身一样关切体谅，要么完全冷漠无情。

III

1. I'm afraid that this old radio is beyond repair.
2. Will you see to it that my room is cleaned while I am out?
3. It is well-known that gunpowder is one of the four inventions of the ancient Chinese people.
4. The annual growth target of 7% demonstrates that the government is concentrating on the quality of life rather than the speed of growth.
5. A typical Chinese banquet menu includes cold dishes served at the beginning, followed by hot dishes, such as meat, poultry, vegetables, etc.
6. It was through the Silk Road that the four great inventions of ancient China, i.e. papermaking, gunpowder, compass and printing were introduced to other countries in the world.
7. What's more, Chinese Ministry of Education decides to improve the nutrition of students in less developed areas and provides equal opportunities for the children of migrant workers to receive education in the city.
8. This newly announced project aims at reducing four main pollutants, including exhaust from 5 million motor vehicles, coal burning in surrounding areas, sandstorms

from the north, and local construction dust.

9. China has made remarkable progress in poverty alleviation, and it has made unremitting efforts in promoting economic growth. This will encourage other poor countries to cope with their own development challenges.

10. 100 A.D. witnessed the completion of the first Chinese dictionary which included 9,000 characters, providing interpretation and various ways of writing characters. Meanwhile, great progress was made in science and technology by the inventions of paper, water clocks, sundials and earthquake detectors.

IV

1. 他年纪轻轻，做事却相当老练。
2. 他的生活开销总是入不敷出。
3. 这里的生活支出费用挺低，但乘出租车却贵得要命。
4. 城区很大，交通不便，出行困难。所以出这么点儿钱（坐出租车）还是非常划算的。
5. 他挤公共汽车，身上不是这里擦破，就是那里碰伤，几乎天天如此。
6. 该公司的高层经理人员都来自国家研究机构，这些机构不仅充满官僚主义气息，而且研究经费不足，他们很难在那里待下去。
7. 这是亚洲最具传统色彩的城市之一。浓郁的中国文化给人以亲切欢快之感。这个城市还拥有一座中国艺术和手工艺制品的陈列馆，里面的陈列令人叹为观止。
8. 中国年龄在15至55岁之间的妇女大约有三亿八千万，只要自己的经济条件允许，她们几乎人人都想尽可能把自己打扮得绰约靓丽，这种情形在城市尤为明显。
9. 这个年月，谈情说爱处处都有暗礁。许多单身女子对向自己求婚者既急切地愿以心相许，但又一定要核查对方是否靠得住，于是就纷纷雇佣私人侦探去查清对方的身世经历。
10. 15世纪和16世纪的探索发现了北美洲，又过了100多年，第一艘满载移民的航船越过大西洋驶向现在叫作"美国"的这一领域。
11. 李光耀用了30年时间使一个贫穷的岛国变成了一座井然有序的城市。昔日的棚屋与鸡笼已为锃亮的摩天楼宇群所代替。
12. 每天都有大量报道，谈到人们的饮食和生活方式处处都有险区。这些报道弄得美国人终日提心吊胆。美国人已被一种流行病所笼罩，这个流行病并非是癌症，而是恐惧症。
13. 但是，美国特有的地理条件的影响、不同民族间的相互作用、以及在这片原生状新大陆上维持旧秩序的异常艰难等诸多因素引起了显著的变化。

APPENDIX B Keys to Practice of the Relevant Skill and Exercises

Unit 10

1. 英译汉

舍弃自我

我们生活在人类历史上的一个特殊时代，其标志是每个人的思想与价值观产生了根本的变化。在这样的时代背景之下，我们每个人都必须在内心找到生活中应遵循的理念、信仰与理想。除非我们找到这些理想、坚定不移地坚持它们，否则我们就无法克服我们在这个世界所面临的危机。

我对人充满信心，我相信纯洁无瑕的人性。我愿意倾听人们的心声，帮助他们实现自己的愿望、获取他们需要的东西。当然，也有人行同禽兽，他们残杀无辜、行骗撒谎、破坏成性。但如果不相信人、对人类的未来丧失信心，就会对未来绝望，哀叹今不如昔。我认为每个人都必须有自己遵循的人生哲学。有些人的人生哲学是怀疑一切。他们宣称世界上没有真理，美德不过是自私的巧妙伪装。他们认为人生苦短，生于痛苦，又终将走向坟墓。有些人则宣称人性生就邪恶，生命是历尽苦难净化灵魂的过程，死亡则是对所遭受苦难的回报。

我认为这些人生哲学都是错误的。如何度过自己的一生，这才是人生最重要的课题。世界上没有任何空泛抽象的幸福、美德、道义，没有任何空泛抽象事物，所有这些东西只存在于相信它们、并付诸行动的人身上。只有活着的个体才能每时每刻亲身感受着幸福或痛苦、高贵或低贱、睿智或愚笨，或仅仅活着而已。

问题是：支持个体生命的丰富的人生哲学怎样才能贯穿人生的每一瞬间呢？除非我们舍弃部分自我，除非我们与他人一道生活，理解并帮助他人，否则就会失去人生的根本意义。

世界上有多少追求智慧与美德的人，就有多少通往智慧与美德的路；有多少探求和坚持真理的人，就有多少实在的真理；有多少仁人志士会在生活中奉行并实现这些信念与理想，就有多少信念与理想供人们去追求。

2. 汉译英

Shi Yigong: Regarding the Future of the Country as His Own Responsibilities

In February, 2008, Shi Yigong, a 40-year-old world famous structural biologist and tenured professor of Princeton University in the United States, came back to his motherland. He was granted tenure at Tsinghua University and appointed deputy dean of the Institute of Life Science and Medicine. He said, "In terms of academic research, Princeton University is the most suitable place in the United States. If for the sake of scientific research alone, there is certainly no need for me to come back to Tsinghua. Actually, I didn't come back just for the purpose of doing scientific research; my ultimate aim is educating students—a large number of students. The key to education lies in cultivating the minds, with scientific research as an important link. In my opinion, college students today lack ideals; they lack something that should never be given up under any circumstance. I believe, if properly conducted, there must be a number of students in Tsinghua who bear in mind something beyond their personal interests while striving to pursue their goals. They would regard the country's future as their own responsibilities, which prods them to move ahead. I am sure there will be no lack of such people in Tsinghua. If so, I will be very content with my decision when I retire from Tsinghua 20 or 30 years later."

II

1. 我们每天都要做出选择，其选择结果会影响自己的生活，有时也影响别人的生活。
2. 美国人的许多风俗习惯似乎令初来乍到的游客费解。
3. 19世纪末，美国所有大学已实行学分制，学生们从中受益匪浅。
4. 美国私立学校开设的课程很多，以满足某些学生的各种需求。
5. 勉强躲过洪水劫难的财物，又在火灾多发期被吞噬了。
6. 其实，许多美国人都花得起钱请厨师、雇司机，但他们不那么做。
7. 在博物馆参观的时候，常常可以租用一个小录音机，一面参观，一面听有关展品的录音解说。
8. 盖茨70年代长大成人，具有水门事件年代的人对政治冷漠超然的特点，其心态更接近"唯我的一代"，而不是颓废派；他热衷于个人电脑，将其视为自己这十年的一种极具革命性的动力。
9. 这反映了关于大学教育的另一种理论，其大意是：社会鼓励其成员从事能够获得最大个人或经济收益的职业。身处这样一个社会，如果有选择的话，人们只愿意学习获取成功所需要的知识。
10. 最令女主人失望的是，她花了许多心神和费用来招待客人，可是这位客人只顾津津乐道地与她丈夫谈政治、谈生意，却没注意到香喷喷的咖啡、松软的糕点，或房间内讲究的陈设，而这些却可能是她最感兴趣并最引以为荣的东西。

III

1. Scientists everywhere in the world are looking for the efficient methods to make the air clean and protect it from pollution by all kinds of harmful industrial waste gases.
2. Although the water in a glass looks to be totally motionless to our naked eyes, a great deal of disorderly thermal movement of its countless molecules is going on inside.
3. During the thousands of years of recorded history, the Chinese nation has given birth to many national heroes and revolutionary leaders. Thus the Chinese nation has a glorious revolutionary tradition and a splendid historical heritage.

APPENDIX B Keys to Practice of the Relevant Skill and Exercises

4. We not only need a developed agricultural system with a rational distribution and all-round development of farming, forestry, animal husbandry, sideline production and fishery, meeting the needs of the people's life and expanding industry, but also an advanced industrial system which is complete in range and rational in structure and which meets the needs of consumers and the expansion of the whole national economy.
5. In the next five years, China will provide assistance to other developing countries in various aspects such as poverty reduction, education development, agricultural modernization, environmental protection, health care, etc.
6. China has made remarkable progress in poverty alleviation, and it has made unremitting efforts in promoting economic growth. This will encourage other poor countries to cope with their own development challenges.
7. Not long ago, China obtained the contract for construction of a high-speed rail in Indonesia. It has also signed a contract with Malaysia to provide high-speed trains. This proves that people have faith in China-made products.
8. Tsinghua University, one of the renowned institutions of higher learning in China, is an important base both for bringing up senior professionals of science and technology in China and for promoting the progress of Chinese science and technology. Founded in 1911, it started as Tsinghua Xuetang, a school preparing students for studies in the U.S. After the 1911 Revolution, it was renamed Tsinghua College and then enrolled its first college students in 1925. In 1928, the school was renamed National Tsinghua University. During the Chinese People's War of Resistance Against Japanese Aggression, the university moved to the South to Changsha, and then to Kunming, where it became part of Southwest Associated University by merging with Peking University and Nankai University. In the nationwide reorganization of institutions of higher learning in 1952, Tsinghua University became a university of engineering with multiple disciplines, focusing its emphasis on training qualified engineering personnel, and thus it was reputed as "the cradle of red engineers".

IV

1. 我们打扫干净房间以备大驾光临。
2. 他们正在准备一顿丰盛的饭菜为他接风。
3. 如果我们需要你的意见，我们会向你征求的。
4. 昨晚我听见他鼾声如雷。
5. 当约翰谈起那事的时候，我们感到颇为可疑/有猫腻。
6. 现代语言学是以布龙菲尔德1933年出版的《语言》一书为依据的。

7. 一场越来越渺无希望的革命将人们昨天尚抱有的希望和梦想化为泡影。
8. 在平地的泥浆里跋涉已经是够令人厌恶了，泥浆常常没过踝部。要是上坡路，那就更糟糕。
9. 我们都患了"敦刻尔克喉炎"——凡到过敦刻尔克的人都落下了这样一种嗓子嘶哑的标记。
10. 刚过午夜，驾驶员驾机着陆，差一点儿把飞机毁了。
11. 船及时地调过船头，勉强躲过了近旁一道高耸出水面100英尺的巨大冰墙。
12. 他们要是查出了是谁杀死了这母子俩，必将严惩凶手，绝不姑息。
13. 胡佛以妻子为荣：她能流利地讲五种外语，她安排的食谱据说是白宫有史以来最讲究的。
14. 克劳莱小姐承认，这女孩儿十分天真可爱。她心肠软，心眼实，待人热情，但她的心思令人捉摸不透。

Unit 11

1. 英译汉

何必以心跳定生死

当我得知自己大限将至以后，我的态度就变了。"这是您余生的第一天"这句话对我来说便有了实实在在的含义。对每一个晴空丽日，对鸟语花香，我的感触倍加强烈。平日呼吸轻松，吞食自如，腿脚灵便，一夜安寝到天明——所有这些，我们几曾回味过其中的乐趣？

患病以后，我着手做以前搁置下来的许多事情。我阅读了那些本来打算留到退休后才读的书，而且还写了一本题为《外科手术的艺术》的书。我与妻子马德琳度假更加频繁。我们经常去打网球，劲头十足地玩冰上溜石，还带儿子们去钓鱼。回顾我得癌症后这几年，从许多方面来看，我似乎已经活了一辈子。上次到巴哈马度假期间，我沿着海滩漫步，海浪轻轻抚揉着我的双脚，此时此刻，我蓦然觉得自己与整个宇宙融为一体，尽管我显得多么渺小，就像海滩上的一粒沙子。

虽然我不得不限制自己的医务工作量，但我感到与病人更加心灵相通。每当我走进特别护理室，一种畏怯感就油然而生，因为我知道自己也曾是那儿的一个危重病人。我明白，在经历了被确诊为癌症的极度痛苦之后，仍有可能享受人生，因此，安慰癌症患者便是我莫大的乐趣。一位病人做了喉切除手术，我问他是否想喝冰镇啤酒，并为他端来一杯。这时我看到他眼里闪耀着感激的神情，一股暖流顿时涌上我的心头。

倘若人们意识到人的一生只不过是宇宙的时间长河中转瞬即逝的一刹那，那么以岁月计算的生命就不会像我们所想象的那样重要了。何必以心跳来定生死呢？要是生命依赖于心跳这样一种不可靠的功能,它的确脆弱不堪。而只有死亡才是人们唯一可以绝对依赖的。

2. 汉译英

AIDS

Throughout the world 36 million people are suffering from AIDS, which is more than the whole population of Australia. At present, AIDS is the fourth leading cause of death in the whole world, and the chief culprit in Africa. In Africa, it deprives workers of their jobs, families of incomes and children of their parents. In seven African countries, more than 20 percent of the 15-49-year-old population is infected with HIV: 20 percent in South Africa, 36 percent in Botswana. Zambia cannot train teachers fast enough to replace those killed by AIDS. It is estimated that there will be 40 million AIDS orphans in Africa in 10 years.

Asia remains comparatively untouched. Only Cambodia, Thailand and Burma have infection rates above 1 percent. But the pandemic may be like a typhoon gathering strength off an unsuspected coast. India's HIV rate of "only" 0.7 percent translates to 3.7 million infectious people. China predicts 5 million to 6 million HIV-positives by 2005.

II

1. 又到了每年一度的报税日。室外樱花烂漫,而美国人却无暇赏花,因为他们已经被税表搞得焦头烂额,困在室内动弹不得。
2. 周恩来的房门打开了。他们看到了一位身材修长的人,比普通人略高,目光炯炯,面貌引人注目,称得上清秀。
3. 那是一个金秋丽日,大家与离家出征的青年依依惜别。待到和平降临、层林再度染上秋色,这些青年却青春不再,有的甚至已丧失生命。
4. 猎鹿活动在很大程度上已得到一些地方政府的支持,因为仅在过去的十年中,美国鹿的数量就已翻了一番,在一些州甚至增长了两倍。
5. 为什么如此多的美国人不能如想象中那样幸福呢?我认为原因有二,而两者之间又有深浅之分。
6. 如果一个民族不能自由地决定其政治地位,不能自由地保证其经济、社会和文化的发展,要享受其基本权利,即使不是不可能,也是不容易的。这一论断,在那时几乎无可置辩。
7. 因为在自然界的任何地方都找不到处于游离态的铝,所以直到19世纪铝才为人们所知。铝总是喜欢和其他元素结合在一起,最常见的情况是和氧的结合,因为铝对氧有很强的亲和力。
8. 科学家相信,通过将计算机直接链接人的神经系统,我们可以立即获得感知信息。计算机还可望能模拟人的感觉,这样我们就可以开发出全感虚拟环境,就像科幻影片中的假日场面那样。

9. 据说拿破仑有过这样一句名言："一旦中国醒来,势必震撼世界。"此断言正在得到印证,即便是在中国历来较少触及的领域,如国际象棋、篮球、稀土矿物、网络战、太空探索和核研究等项目亦崭露头角。

10. 绿草萋萋,白云冉冉,彩蝶翩翩,这日子是如此清新可爱;蜜蜂无言,春花不语,海波声歇,大地音寂,这日子是如此安静。然而这一切又并非安静,因为万物均以其特有的规律和节奏在运动:或动,或摇,或震,或起,或伏。

III

1. One is never too old to learn.
2. How can you catch tiger cubs without entering the tiger's lair?
3. So long as the green hills remain, there will never be a shortage of firewood. (While there is life, there is hope.)
4. No one was in the room; only the ticking of a clock could be heard.
5. Suddenly a dog began to chase after her, scaring her almost out of her wits.
6. Whenever a problem crops up, tackle it right away; don't let problems pile up and then try to settle them at one go.
7. Backwardness must be recognized before it can be changed. One must learn from those who are more advanced before he can catch up with and surpass them.
8. In its inner harbor, the broad and wide seawater is calm and deep. Vessels of 10,000 tons can enter or leave the port with ease and 50,000-ton freighters can call at or depart from the port with the flood tide.
9. It is said that Xi'an reflects China's history of 2,000 years, and Beijing, 1,000 years. To know China's history in the latest 100 years, you'd better look at Shanghai—the epitome of modern and contemporary China.
10. In order to adapt to the needs of socialist construction, Tsinghua University set up a Graduate School in 1984 and then Continuing (Adult) Education School in 1985 since reform and opening in 1978. The curricula and the structure of the departments and disciplines have been constantly readjusted so as to keep abreast with the upsurge of the worldwide technical renovation, the development of modern science, the new trend of cross-disciplines and comprehensive research which emerges as a result of social progress. A number of departments of hi-technology and new specialties have been set up, and in addition to the newly established disciplines of science, economics and management, liberal arts, the university has rehabilitated School of Science and School of Law, established School of Economics and Management, School of Humanities and Social Sciences and School of Information Science and Technology. Then Academy of Arts and Design was merged into the university and School of Medicine was founded. The university now comprises 65 undergraduate specialties, 7 specialties for the

second bachelor's degree, 271 Master's programs, 252 Ph. D. programs, of which 38 are of first-grade disciplines, and 37 postdoctoral programs. The university covers an area of 392. 4 hectares, with a total floor space of 2,496 milliom square meters. The university library boasts a collection of 3.72 milliom books and periodicals. The total number of faculty members and staff is 7,186, of whom 1,262 are professors, 1,814 associate professors, 37 academicians of the Chinese Academy of Science (CAS) and 34 of the Chinese Academy of Engineering (CAE) respectively. The students number 31,643, of whom 14,608 are undergraduates, 9,783 master's degree students and 7,252 Ph. D. candidates.

IV

1. 我不是那种让感情统治理智的人。
2. 激光用于医学领域尚处于发展的初期。
3. 我希望我方这一让步能打开局面。
4. 这位使得全世界人们发出阵阵笑声的人自己却饱受酸楚。
5. 他留下一封短信，对我表示欢迎；那信写得热情洋溢，文如其人。
6. 你瞧，小伙子年轻漂亮，脑瓜里却空空如也。
7. 你这样急急忙忙没头没脑去干什么？
8. 我倒挺想出去吃午饭。不过，你知道，我手头没几个钱啊。
9. 战争期间，他还是一个初出茅庐的外科医生，于是参加了巡回医疗队。
10. 此人体壮如牛，脾气也十分暴烈。
11. 他起早睡晚，精力迅速消耗。
12. 他在这一领域的成功使其前辈们的论点黯然失色。
13. 我们要完全掌握集成电路工艺，必须经过三个阶段。
14. 这个国家异常美丽，但要把它从敌人手中夺回来也异常困难。
15. 有时候，我晚上行走在大街上，感到自己已到了山穷水尽的地步，只好横下心孤注一掷。
16. 相互竞争的利益集团有时为了一些枝节问题或仅仅为了一个字眼而争论得面红耳赤，剑拔弩张。
17. 这一谋杀残酷、蹊跷、干净利落，连警察局的办案老手葛莱斯也思忖了好久，感到无从着手。
18. 工业化国家和发展中国家之间的差距，即富国与穷国之间的差距越来越大。发展中国家还是发展不起来。

Unit 12

1. 英译汉

三种人的纽约

大致说来有三种纽约。首先是那些土生土长的男男女女的纽约，他们对这座城市习以为常，认为它有这样的规模和喧嚣，乃自然与必然之事。其次是乘公交车上下班的人的纽约——这座城市白天被如蝗的人群所吞噬，晚上又给吐出来，天天如此。第三种是外来人的纽约，他们生于他乡，到纽约来寻求机缘。在这三种充满骚动的城市中，最了不起的是最后一种——作为最终归宿和奋斗目标的城市。正是由于这第三种城市，纽约才有了高度紧张的禀性、诗情画意的风度、对艺术的无私奉献和无与伦比的卓然成就。上班族给纽约带来了潮汐般的永不宁静，本地人保证了纽约的稳固和发展，而外来人则赋予纽约以激情。无论是从意大利来到贫民窟开小杂货店的农夫，还是为了躲避邻居的侮蔑目光，从密西西比州某小镇跑出来的年轻姑娘，或是从玉米地带满怀酸楚，拎着手稿来纽约的小伙子，情况都没有什么两样：每个人都怀着初恋的激情拥抱纽约，每个人都以冒险家的新目光来审视纽约，每个人散发出的光和热都足以令爱迪生联合电气公司相形见绌。

上班族是天下最怪异的人。他们栖身的郊区实质上本身没有什么活力，无非是日落归来睡觉的地方而已。住在马马罗内克、利特尔内克、蒂内克，到纽约上班的人，除极个别情况外，对这座城市大都了无所知。他们所知道的无非是火车汽车到站离站的时间以及去快餐店应当走哪条路。这些人成天伏案工作，从没有片刻闲暇徜徉在暮色之中，从来不会偶然走到公园观景塔前，观看池塘中突兀而起的垒石、沿湖垂钓米诺鱼的男孩、漫不经心地躺在突出的岩石上的女孩。他们根本不曾在纽约东游西逛，绝不会偶然遇见什么。因为他们下了车就上车，其间没有半点空余。他们伸手探入曼哈顿的钱包，从中摸出几个子儿，但却从未聆听过曼哈顿的鼻息，从未在醒来时见到曼哈顿的早晨，也从未在曼哈顿的夜幕中进入梦乡。

2. 汉译英

Shanghai

Located on the estuary of the Yangtze River, Shanghai is a historic city famous for its culture and tourism, the biggest center for China's economy, trade, finance and culture. Before the establishment of People's Republic of China in 1949, Shanghai was called "paradise for adventurers", a city with the lopsided development of industry and commerce. Today, with its transport lines extending in all directions, Shanghai has become the largest port in China, the largest transportation hub in East China. It is not only the starting point of Hu-Ning (Shanghai-Nanjing) and Hu-Hang (Shanghai-Hangzhou)

APPENDIX B Keys to Practice of the Relevant Skill and Exercises

railways, but also an important aviation center of China, and one of the international aviation ports. With its advanced commerce, Shanghai is a super large comprehensive trading center of China, and one of the international economic, financial and trading centers. The successful host of World Expo 2010 Shanghai has attracted participants in around 200 countries and international organizations, and more than 70 million tourists at home and abroad. The theme "Better City, Better Life" has left a rich spiritual heritage for the world.

II

1. 有的河水流湍急，有的河流速缓慢，有的大河出海口有好几处，有的河带着大量冲击土入海，有的河清澈见底，有的河的水量在一年中的某些季节较少，而在某些季节里却多得多，有的河可利用其动力大量发电，有的河承担着大量的交通运输。

2. G&C 梅里亚姆公司大概是世界上最大的字典编纂者。它声称这项编纂工作耗资 350 万美元，300 名学者为此辛勤工作长达 27 年，对搜集到的语言中最大量的词语例证作了编辑加工。难道它声称的所有这些是为了欺骗和愚弄人民吗？

3. 20 世纪初，生产技术条件开始产生深刻的变化和极大的改进。但在当时的技术条件下，燃料、材料、安全着陆、推进装置，特别是电子计算等一系列的问题都过于复杂，难以解决，制造不出登月运载工具，因此直到 20 世纪后期才揭开月球的秘密。

4. 为了保证全体会员国拥有加入本组织后应获得的权益，所有会员国应一秉诚意，履行依照本宪章所承担之义务。

5. 美国人如果想要成为真正的爱国之士，就必须努力探求他们之间的共同之处，努力探求在这个国度里值得珍惜和恪守不渝的究竟是什么。如果他们做不到这一点，那么他们的所谓爱国主义充其量只是一场自我炫耀的午后大游行。

6. 计算机语言有低级的也有高级的。前者比较详细，很接近于特定计算机直接能懂的语言；后者比较复杂，适应范围广，能为多种计算机所自动接受。

7. 复杂的官僚机构乐于维持现状，因为既然没有发生明显的重大危机，则维持现状可以驾轻就熟；而且根本不可能证明另一种处事方案可以产生远胜于现行方案的结果。大多数伟大的政治家都曾陷入与其外事机构中的专家进行永无休止的纷争之中，这似乎不是偶然的事。因为政治家见地博大，与专家们那种力求少冒风险的倾向针锋相对。

8. 此刻，他在夏日的树林中漫游，林间是一片幽暗的深绿，真比十一月里那灰蒙蒙的一派萧煞凋零还显得更加暗淡无光。即使待到中午时分，也只能在没风时看到斑斑点点的阳光，洒在从来没有干过的、到处都是蛇在爬行的地上。那里有毒蛇、水蛇，还有响尾蛇，这些蛇身上也有灰暗的斑纹，因此只有在它们蠕动的时候，才能看得出来。他回营地的时间越来越晚。一天，两天，到第三天，当他走过小木桩围着的木畜棚时，已是薄暮时分了。这时山姆正忙着把牲口赶进棚里准备过夜。

9. 这种公正的精神，至少在私立公校中被视为最神圣不可侵犯的传统而深入人心。这种精神在人们的供职上，尤其是在属地统治上，对于英国民族是很有用的。当统治属地时，英国的官员抱着一种显然的愿望，要想公正地处理土人与欧人间的争执，而希冀得到公平的解决，使英国人处在海外的异族文化中，因缺乏同情的理解而格格不入的情形多少获得了一点儿补偿。

10. 如果条件许可的话，我们还可以采取最后的手段，那就是身居国内而向国外求医进行诊断和治疗。用专业术语来说，也就是电视卫星诊断。与面诊相比，比如说与在一个设备不良，医务人员水平不高的医院进行诊断（特别是诊断那种急性、重症或是医师认为病因不明的病例）相比，电视卫星诊断无疑是一种可以利用的非常有效的医疗手段。

III

1. The refrigerators of 112 and 145 liters manufactured by our plant are noted for their graceful styles, reliable quality, low noise, low power consumption, easy operation and safety.

2. A well-equipped and well-manned nuclear-energy lab is badly needed at present. Such a lab, of course, must be advanced in technology and built in accordance with the principle of security and protection as well as in the spirit of meticulous discretion.

3. We have been in the silk garment trade for 50 years. The products find a ready market in 50 countries and regions. They are made of high quality pure silk, soft and smooth, an easy fit in the latest style. Fast to washing and sunlight, the silk garment is a must for ladies of good taste. Contact us for more information.

4. "There is no royal road to learning except diligence with great concentration." This saying reveals a truth that on the road to attain one's goal of learning, there is neither shortcut to take, nor smooth journey to go on. If one wants to acquire profound knowledge, he must be both diligent and dedicated, which are two essential and inseparable conditions for success.

5. History has proved that man's understanding of natural resources and his tapping and utilizing of them, as well as his capability of making tools of production to make use of these sources, are very important signs to indicate the developing level of social productive forces. And to some extent, these, too, have decided the basic structure and developing pattern of a given society.

6. Starting from 1978, China has embarked on a new journey of transforming from a planned to a market economy, from cloistered up to opening up, from exclusive self-sustaining to integration into globalization. By following a path of building socialism with Chinese characteristics in an independent and self-reliant manner, we have scored glorious achievements that attracted worldwide attention.

7. From the Opium War and the First Sino-Japanese War after the 1840s, China's War on Foreign Invaders in 1900 to the Japanese War of Aggression against China in

APPENDIX B Keys to Practice of the Relevant Skill and Exercises

1930s, China was subject to the butchering of the then strong powers in the West and East and their extremely barbarian economic depredation. This, coupled with feudal corruption and years of successive civil strife and chaos, led to the loss of China's sovereignty and the horrendous suffering of her people, her national strength failing and people barely surviving.

8. Information technology is a hi-technology developed on the basis of microelectronics, computer and modern communication technology, with the functions of information collection, transmission, procession and service. Nowadays 500 million electron elements can be integrated on a chip of 8 inches, each with the width of merely 0.2503 micron; the processing speed of the computer may be as fast as approximately 100 million times per second; and the virtual technique of computer will greatly widen the scope of the application of information technology.

IV

1. "这是布什总统的命令。""我才不管它什么布什、布头、布片呢。"(管它什么布什、布八、布九呢。)
2. 如果我妈妈知道此事,一定会气得火冒三丈、死不瞑目。
3. 众院议长吉姆·赖特于昨日在华府挥泪认输。
4. 在与艾滋病的斗争中,每取得一点儿进步就加大了一分希望,有助于造出消灭这种疾病的魔弹。
5. 这个文件就是我们走向绞架的通行证,再没有退路了。我们要是不紧紧团结一致,就必然会一个个被绞死。
6. 关于我,母亲总是以特有的克制口吻说:"这小鬼头,他甚至连书本都不消打开——门门都是优秀,真是个活脱脱的爱因斯坦。"
7. 布朗先生是个非常正直的人。那天,他脸上颇有病容。近来他一直情绪低落。我见到他时他正在默默沉思。希望他能早日恢复健康。
8. 好吧,伙计们,就是这话!开始行动吧!马上出发,以迅猛之势投入竞争。给他们点儿厉害瞧瞧!我们的决策明晰精确、丝丝入扣。不要一味地退却防守!噢,对了,我们可不希望出现家贼,更不愿队伍中藏有内奸。另外,在实施策略时要留有余地,切勿陷入尴尬境地!尽管承诺一切:新型交易、公平交易、公正交易。只要做成第一笔买卖,随后的生意就会像骨牌效应一样源源不断。总之,最关键的一点就是卖、卖、卖!

Unit 13

1. 英译汉

人造细胞问世

包括索斯塔克在内的许多生物学家认为生命在早期阶段比较简单：现在由脱氧核糖核酸 (DNA)、核糖核酸 (RNA) 和蛋白质完成的繁多任务全都由 RNA 单独完成。但即便在今天，RNA 分子的作用不仅是信使，而且还担负着蛋白质构建块氨基酸的采集和运输功能。它们也可以像蛋白质一样催化反应。于是 RNA 大体上既可以充当细胞的基因材料，又可以提供它的自组装机制。

如果这一想法正确，构建细胞可能就只需用膜将物质定位，外加一些 RNA、一些供合成更多 RNA 的成分，以及一种能源即可。能源的形式是富能量分子三磷酸腺苷 (ATP)，而 ATP 正是现有细胞用以将能量从产生处运送到耗用处的物质。索斯塔克博士已制造出一系列的"核酶"（这一术语在业内指代具有催化作用的 RNA)，而其中一些由 ATP 提供能量。尽管他目前尚未创建一个可以自我复制的系统，但那是他的目标。

索斯塔克的细胞要是果真开发成功，将会与生物学家所熟悉的基于蛋白质和 DNA 的生命相去甚远。这在有些方面甚至会比文特尔博士的成就更伟大，因为它是真正从零开始创造的生命。不过其实用意义并不太大，因为这种生命非常原始，甚至不及普通细菌。

而索斯塔克在哈佛的同事乔治·切奇却梦想构造一个极其实用却未被文特尔博士实现的东西：核糖体。文特尔的捷径——启动一个细菌的尸体——意味着新造的细菌必须依赖于死去受体的核糖体来制造其基因组所描述的蛋白质。但它也具有用于合成自身核糖体的基因，而随着时间的推移，它也会这样做，同时稀释掉让它启动的那些遗留物质。按文特尔博士的计算，一旦 JCVI-syn 1.0 经过 30 次分裂，所有原始细胞的痕迹都将消失。但这并不解决这一问题：在开始的时候，新细胞需要老细胞基因的产物来帮助自己繁衍。

切奇博士正在从头开始构建核糖体——由数十个蛋白质和 RNA 成分组成的复杂玩意儿。他已经成功地合成了其中的全部 RNA 成分，以至于当它们与天然核糖体蛋白质混合时，能构成可运作的核糖体。白手起家制造蛋白质更为困难，因为其形状是决定其功能的关键，所以目前尚不清楚他是否会费心去这样做。

2. 汉译英

English for Science and Technology

English for science and technology (EST) refers to English used in scientific books, papers, textbooks, technical reports and academic lectures in natural science and engineering. Unlike average English that is characterized by sentimental thinking and emotional coloring, EST does not use rhetoric means such as metaphor and hyperbole.

APPENDIX B Keys to Practice of the Relevant Skill and Exercises

Instead it describes the objective world in accurate and clear logical thinking, so as to reveal the laws of nature. As a kind of written language, EST requires rigorous, simple writing style without stringing together ornate phrases, nor considering the reading effect. Its lexical meaning is constant and stable, of international feature. According to statistics, more than 70% of EST vocabulary comes from Latin and Greek. With the development of technology and the increasing development of global economic integration, EST will play an even more important role in international communication.

II

滚珠轴承、实验台、运载火箭、气压式缓冲器、拖拉机履带片、锤式打桩机、球阀、模板、自动穿孔器、螺旋钻、衰变子体、同类金属、异体组织、离子溅射泵、叠影、垫块（板）、桐油、橡胶淀带、整形外科、防毒面具、急救、救火车、防滑链、饮用水、抗药性、肺活量

工字梁、环形圈、丁字尺、折尺、三角尺、八面体、人字屋顶、十字缝、拱坝、凸轮轴、锥形浮标、槽钢、U 形（马蹄）螺栓

III

1. 生物化学研究有生命的有机体内的化学过程，涉及诸如蛋白质、碳水化合物、脂类、核酸及其他生物分子之类细胞成分的结构与功能。
2. 早期的集成电路的研制可追溯到 1949 年，当时德国西门子公司的工程师维尔纳·雅可比申请了一项类似集成电路的半导体放大设备的专利，在一个 2 级放大器电路中的一个共衬底上安装了 5 个晶体管。
3. "克隆"一词源于希腊语，为"主干，分支"之义，指的是让一种新植物从细枝中创生出来的过程。在园艺界，直到 20 世纪末这一词一直拼写为 clon，后来加了一个结尾字母 e，以标明元音字母 o 是一个长音而不是短音。
4. 电机工程是一个非常广泛的领域，可以包括对各类电气和电子系统的设计和研究，如电路、发电机、电动机、电磁/机电设备、电子器件、电子电路、光纤、光电器件、计算机系统、电信和电子产品等。
5. 目前所知最著名的高速磁悬浮技术的商用经营是在中国上海由德国建造的磁悬浮列车初始运行段 (IOS)。将旅客运送到机场的一段 30 千米 (18.6 英里) 的路线只需 7 分 20 秒，达到每小时 431 千米 (268 英里) 的最高速度，平均每小时 250 千米 (160 英里)。
6. 《科学引文索引》最初是 1960 年由尤金·加菲尔德创办、美国科学信息研究所 (ISI) 出版的引文索引，目前为汤姆森·路透科技信息集团所拥有，范围覆盖从 1900 年至今全世界 6 500 多种知名的及重要的刊物，包括生命科学、临床医学、物理化学、农业、生物、兽医学、工程与技术等 150 个学科。
7. 光纤材料广泛用于光纤通信，与其他通信形式相比其传输距离更长，传输带宽（数据传输率）更高。之所以用纤维而不用金属导线，是因为前者的信号传播损失较少，而

且不受电磁干扰。纤维还用于照明，并可以捆绑成束用以传送图像，因此可用于查看狭小空间。

8. 纳米技术可以创造许多具有广阔应用范围的新材料、新设备，如在医学、电子、生物材料和能源生产等方面。另一方面，与引入任何新技术的情况一样，纳米技术也引起了许多类似的问题，包括人们对有关纳米材料的毒性和环境影响的关注，纳米技术对全球经济的潜在影响，以及这一技术最终会导致世界末日的种种猜测。

IV

1. 1827 年，他以《数学方法处理的电流链（电路）》为标题撰文发表了这些成果。
2. 当他通过自己耐心的试验满意地证明了讲课中所作的解释时，他那种欣喜无比的自豪感简直难以形容。
3. 科学的发现与发明，并不总是会对语言产生与其重要性相当的影响。
4. 他满头白发，十分凌乱——简直像通了电似的根根直立。
5. 对超导体在电器应用上的重要性怎么估计也不会过高。
6. 所有的情绪都是由思维产生的，或者说来源于"认识"。"你现在有这样的感觉是因为你此刻有这样的思想。"
7. 后来，他发现在太阳西部的边缘上有一群黑子，过了好一会儿，黑子渐渐消失，出现在太阳东部边缘，最后又恢复原位。
8. 新方法将溶剂用量减少到四分之一。
9. 指示灯熄灭，以表示操作终止。
10. 如果一个托架应当被设计为能支撑 1 000 磅而设计者却将它设计为能支撑 100 磅，那么肯定会出现事故。

Unit 14

1. 英译汉

版 权

版权是一种合法权利的体现，旨在保护创造性作品，防止该作品在未经允许的情况下被他人复制、演出、展出或传播。版权拥有者具有这样一些专有权：复制受版权保护的作品；根据版权保护作品制作其他作品；将保护作品的拷贝出售、出租或借给公众使用；在公众场合演出以及公开展出受版权保护的作品。版权拥有者的以上种种基本专有权也有例外的情况，这往往要根据作品的种类以及他人怎样使用作品而定。

版权法中"作品"一词指的是以固定形式存在于有形媒介中的原作者的创作物。这样，能受版权保护的作品就包括文学作品、音乐作品、戏剧选集、舞蹈、照片、绘画、雕刻、

APPENDIX B　Keys to Practice of the Relevant Skill and Exercises

图形、广告、地图、电影片、电台和电视节目、录音片断以及计算机软件程序等。

版权不保护某种想法或概念，只对作者表达想法或概念的方法加以保护。例如，要是某科学家发表了一篇文章，阐述生产某种药品的新的制作过程，那么版权可以阻止他人抄袭该文章，但不能制止任何人用上述过程配备药品。要想保护上述制作过程，该科学家就必须获得专利。

版权是对作品创造者实行的一种法律保护。最初仅仅限于对书籍方面，而今已扩大到对各种杂志、报纸、地图、戏剧、电影、电视节目、电脑软件、绘画、图片、雕塑、音乐作品、舞蹈动作设计等类作品的保护。实质上，版权保护的是知识或艺术财产。

版权这种财产与众不同，因为它旨在为公众所利用，为公众所享受。如果一个读者买一本有版权保护的书，这本书就归其所有。但是如果他将此书复制出售或散发，那便属非法。因为这种权利属出版商、作者或拥有其版权的人所有。

2.　汉译英

Documentation

Documentation refers to printed non-book or non-periodical materials that cover a wide range of fields. In terms of branches of learning, documentation may fall into various subfields such as medical documentation, technical documentation (e.g. software documentation, product specifications, data sheets, or a patent), legal documentation, administrative documentation, historical documentation, etc. It may also mean any communicable material (such as text, video, audio, etc.) used to explain some attributes of an object, system or procedure. Documentation is often used to mean engineering documentation or software documentation, which is usually paper books or computer readable files (such as HTML pages) that describe the structure, components, or operation of a system/product. Common types of computer hard-ware/software documentation include online help, FAQs, how-tos, and user guides.

II

1. 合同

从法律上讲，合同是一种对签约各方都具有约束力的协议。合同的要点如下：（1）双方同意；（2）一种合法的报酬，在大多数情况下，不一定是金钱报酬；（3）签约各方均具有合法的签约能力；（4）不具有欺诈或威胁性；（5）签约主题不得具有非法性或违反公共准则。

一般来说，合同既可以是口头的，也可以是书面的。不过，为了便于执行起见，有些合同必须采用书面形式，并须签字。这些合同包括不动产的出售和转让合同，对执行计划失败（miscarriage）拖欠债务或对他人的违约（default）做出保证、负责赔偿的合同，等等。

2. 报告

堪培拉，ACT2600

Acme 电子有限公司

总经理

总经理先生：

您于 1998 年 6 月 20 日指示，要我对 HILLCREST 街 153 号公司房舍需修整翻新的事宜向您报告。为此，我于 6 月 25 日视察了该处房屋，现向您书面汇报如下：

（1）分公司经理室的墙壁需要粉刷油漆。

（2）空调设备需要尽快维修。

（3）接待厅地毯严重磨损，需要更新。

（4）房舍后门的锁很不牢实，需要更换成结实的"单闩锁"。

（5）公司办公室需要加装一部电话。

综上所述，请您指示公司维修部对上述前四项进行维修，并请电话公司利用现有电话线路为办公室另安装一部电话。

您忠实的

维修工程师

C. S. 斯宾塞

3. 作者须知

用于宣读和编入文摘的论文将根据作者提交的摘要选出。摘要以及任何所附插图必须限制在一页之内，其规格为 A4 纸或 210×297 毫米。

寄稿附函须包括主要作者的完整邮政地址和传真号码。所有摘要的收稿截止日期为 1992 年 12 月 6 日。

请将摘要寄送大会技术委员会主席。（地址略）

技术委员会在对所收文摘进行审阅以后，无论接受其论文与否，都将于 1993 年 3 月 6 日之前通知作者本人。所有论文都必须用英语写成。

论文全文的长度应在 4 页以内，在此阶段即索取，收件截止日为 1993 年 5 月 8 日。论文摘要将根据作者所提供的复制论文资料进行直接编辑，并提供给与会者。

4. 商标

商标由美国联邦商业部的专利与商标局登记注册。当商标拥有者申请注册时，该局将检验申请是否符合联邦法律。检验的重要项目之一是该商标不能混淆于以前在美国已登记注册或使用过的商标。根据 1996 年的商标修订法，驰名商标拥有者可以设法禁止他人使用类似的商标，即便是将该商标用于非相关的产品也不行。政府在批准注册的同时，要将商标公布于官方报纸，以便能够听到各种不同的相反意见。商标一经正式注册，便可连续使用 10 年。只要该商标仍在继续使用，就可以每隔 10 年重新注册。商标拥有者一旦获得联邦正式注册，便可在自己的商标旁注上 ® 符号。

任何人使用与已注册的商标类似的标记，由此可能会混淆顾客识别力的做法叫作侵权，被侵权人可就此行为向州法院或联邦法院提起诉讼。法院在确定某商标是否有侵权行为时，

APPENDIX B Keys to Practice of the Relevant Skill and Exercises

要对相关商标从声音、外形以及意义等方面进行比较,还要比较其商品及服务的相似性。其他相关因素还包括:有争议的双方的商品是否通过类似的销售渠道售给类似的顾客,以及商标的知名度等。商标侵权不同于专利侵权或版权侵权。商标侵权的唯一界定标准是看它是否可能会混淆顾客的识别力。在法院判定某商标侵权之后,通常最好的处置办法是禁止侵权者使用该商标。

5. 文献

文献(希腊语 bibliographia,"写书"之意)源于"写书"或"抄书"的含义。18世纪中叶以来,此词逐渐变为"一系列书籍"或"其他形式的书面的材料"之意,或此类书单的编写技巧。文献通常要提供某些信息,如作者、书名、版本以及出版日期和出版地等;也可以包括书的字体、书的尺寸大小以及其他一些物理特点等信息。文献往往附有注释,也就是说,简短地注明论述的主题,或对书的实用价值加以评论。文献对学者和以书籍为职业的专业人员来说,如图书收藏者、图书馆管理员以及书商尤其显得非常重要;对所有的严肃读者来说,又是十分有用的信息源。

文献可分为两大类型:分析型文献(有时也被称为批评型文献)和描述性文献。分析型文献是将书视为客体,它以书的物理特性为依据(例如,纸张的种类和印刷的特性)来确定作者,或判断不同文本的可靠性。

本文所涉及的描述性文献是对出版物的系统列举。它又可分为通用的或一般的文献和选择性文献。一般文献可以列出若干题目的作品,这些作品在不同的国家发表于不同的时间。选择性文献可能会限于某一特定题材、特定来源国、特定作者,或是有特定目的、特定读者的书籍。

III

1. Contract

   ...

   Midterm Termination of the Contract: Neither party shall terminate this contract without reasonable cause prior to the agreed date of expiration. If party B wants to terminate this contract, he/she must hand in a written application one month before leaving China. Part B shall not stop working without part A's consent. Party A shall cease to pay party B his/her salary two weeks after its consent to party B's application and cease to provide party B and the family with relevant benefits concerning living conditions. All the traveling expenses for return shall be borne by party B.

   If part B violates the laws and decrees of the Chinese government party A is entitled to terminate the contract. Party B shall be paid regularly for one month after the termination of the contract. Party B shall be arranged to leave the country within this period. The cost of the economy air ticket(s) and the cost of the luggage for a limited amount according to regulations incurred by party B and the family within China shall be paid by party A. The international traveling expenses shall be borne by party B.

Party A is entitled to terminate the contract if party B fails to do the job well. Within one month after the termination of the contract, party A shall arrange for party B and the family to leave. The cost of the economy air ticket(s) and the cost of the luggage for a limited amount according to regulations incurred by part B and the family shall be paid by party A. Any other cost shall be at party B's expense.

If, owing to poor health, party B has been absent from work two months in succession with a doctor's leave certificate and is still not able to work, party A is entitled to terminate the contract prior to the agreed date of expiration and shall arrange for party B to leave within one month in accordance with B's physical condition. The cost of the economy air ticket(s) and the cost of the luggage for a limited amount according to regulations incurred by party B and the family shall be paid by party A.

This contract is written in Chinese and in English, both texts being equally authentic.

2. Patents

In America, the first patents for inventions were issued in 1642 by the colonial governments. The first U.S. patent laws were enacted by Congress in 1790 under the authority of Article 1, Section 8, of the Constitution. The Patent Act of 1790 was administered by a commission composed of the secretary of state, the secretary of war, and the attorney general of the U.S. The basis of the present patent system is the act of July 4, 1836. Many legislative enactments have modified the original patent law. The most important of these is the act of July 8, 1870, and the subsequent act of July 19, 1952, which revised and codified the patent laws and which, with amendments, constitute the patent law in force at the present time. In 1849 the Patent Office became a part of the Department of the Interior; it was transferred by executive order of the president to the Department of Commerce in 1925. On January 2, 1975, the name was changed to Patent and Trademark Office.

3. Indexes and Abstracts

Two types of documents, indexes and abstracts, contain catalogs and bibliographies of original materials. Indexes include any of countless bibliographies of currently published material, usually of articles in periodicals. Sometimes libraries have taken the initiative to create these finding aids for journal articles. For example, the U.S. National Library of Medicine has produced Index Medicus, a monthly listing of current articles from some 3,500 biomedical journals throughout the world. In other cases, scientific societies have taken the initiative. Early in the 20th century, the American Chemical Society began to prepare indexes and abstracts to help chemists obtain information about the literature in their field, and the Institute of Physics in the United Kingdom took a similar responsibility

APPENDIX B Keys to Practice of the Relevant Skill and Exercises

for physics. The long series of indexes published by the H. W. Wilson Company of New York City and covering many different fields is well known and widely used in other countries, though their coverage is mainly limited to American publications. This national focus has resulted in similar efforts in other countries, such as the *Current Technology Index* (British) and the *British Education Index*.

Unit 15

汉译英

Motivation Statement

In my memory, I have never seen my father seeing a doctor since my childhood in the past 20 years—not because he is very healthy and strong, but he couldn't afford it at all. As a girl from a poor family in a rural area, I know quite clearly that for most of the rural residents there is no other way to cope with an ailment except putting up with it, while when a severe disease comes along, it is no less than a disaster to the whole family.

The moment I got to know the programme of Erasmus-Mundus of Health and Welfare, my father came to my mind. In the past, every time when I went back home on vacation, I would see my aged poor dad suffering from multiple illnesses. Coughing ceaselessly all day in senile weakness, he struggled against a bad fate in vain. Seeing his physical status, I could do nothing but ask him to take care of himself. I felt so conscience-stricken and so painful that my heart ached as if it were stabbed with a knife. Virtually, instead of a private family trouble of my own, it is a social problem for hundreds of millions of Chinese rural residents who are excluded from the welfare of medical and health care.

It reminds me of C. Wright Mills, a famous American sociologist who prominently made sociology the study of the public issues that derive from the private troubles of people. In the past years I have kept all the private troubles in my mind and never confided it to anyone, even to the closest friends. Now the programme offers me an opportunity to connect my private troubles with an issue of public concern. For the first time in my life, I was considering I might do something for folks like my father.

Obviously, the programme of Erasmus-Mundus Master is of profound realistic significance. Since the adoption of the reform and openingup policy in the late 1970s, Chinese government has insisted on a market-oriented medical reform. As the result of marketization, the vital significance of pubic sanitation welfare is ignored to a large extent, which leads to a series of unfair phenomena. A striking evidence is that rural residents do not have basic medicare. Therefore, how to draw successful medicare experience from advanced countries and integrate it with China's reality so as to create a public medical system that can benefit all Chinese people, particularly those rural residents who account for the major part of the whole Chinese population is the urgent desire from the public and it is also the responsibility of our generation. It is universally acknowledged that European medicare system has gained remarkable achievements. It is the system that we should pay attention to and learn from. On the other hand, China's exploration and experience in medicare will be of inspiring value to European countries.

The programme provides me with an opportunity to get a better understanding of European public medical systems, while my four-year college studies have laid a solid foundation for me to obtain such an opportunity. In the first two years of my college life, I accepted general education of humanities and social sciences, including sociology, political science, economy, history and philosophy. This comprehensive background enables me to have wider horizons which most Chinese students do not possess. Then in the third year, I took philosophy as my major from which I have dramatically developed and enhanced my reflective spirits and critical thinking. Furthermore, as illustrated in my CV, I have actively participated in academic field research, which makes me experience the practice of the methodology of social science.

As an old Chinese saying goes, "All is ready except for the east wind to raise the sail." And now the ship carrying my dream is ready to sail. What I need is an opportunity which enables me to fulfill the prospective study in Europe. I hope in a few years I, as a goodwill messenger could bring the most advanced ideas of medical welfare back to my motherland. By then I will, together with millions of my likeminded friends, devote ourselves to China's health welfare cause and build a fair, sound, efficient health welfare system that may benefit all people over the country, no matter in urban or rural areas.

II

Curriculum Vitae

Personal Information

Name: Wang × ×

Address: Room 212A, Zijing Dormitory, Building No.5, Tsinghua University, Beijing, P. R. China

Phone: 86-15101146× × ×

APPENDIX B Keys to Practice of the Relevant Skill and Exercises

E-mail: prongs@gmail.com

Education

Aug. 2013-present	Department of Hydraulic Engineering, Tsinghua University, P. R. China (GPA: 88.5/100; Ranking: 12/68)
Sep. 2010-Jun. 2013	Wuhan Foreign Languages School (Senior High)
Sep. 2007-Jun. 2010	Wuhan Foreign Languages School (Junior High)

Services & Activities

Sep. 2015-Jun. 2016	Vice President of SAST (Students' Association for Science and Technology), Department of Hydraulic Engineering, Tsinghua University
Apr. 2016	Volunteer of Tsinghua University Centenary Celebration
Sep. 2014-Jun. 2015	Member of Xinghuo Forum, SAST, Tsinghua University
Apr. 2015	Volunteer Teacher for Xiaojiahe Primary School, Beijing, China
Mar. 2014-Jun. 2014	Member of the Student Union, Department of Hydraulic Engineering, Tsinghua University
Sep. 2013 - present	Member of the Tsinghua University Chinese Orchestra

Research & Job Experience

Aug. 2016	Internship at MVA Transportation Consultancy Corporation
Mar. 2016-Jun. 2016	Teaching Assistant of Introduction to Transportation Systems
Oct. 2014-Jun. 2015	Participator of Development and Improvement of Filling Device for Geotechnical Centrifuge

Honors & Awards

Top Grade Scholarship from Huigu Company (2015)

2nd Prize in Hydraulic Science & Technology Competition, Tsinghua University (2015)

3rd Place in Summer Social Practice Team, Tsinghua University

Language Proficiency
TOEFL: 109/120 (Mar. 2016)
College English Test Band 6: 583/710 (Dec. 2014)

III

Recommendation Letter

Dear Sir or Madam,

    I am writing this letter to recommend my student Ms Li Hong for studying at your university. Ms. Li Hong was enrolled in Chinese Department of Tsinghua University without taking the National University Entrance Examination in 2009, due to her excellent high school academic record. Later on, she was admitted into the initial experimental class of liberal arts—a special class aimed at laying solid foundation for the students who are supposed to be accomplished scholars with thorough and profound knowledge of Chinese and Western cultures, both ancient and modern. They not only have to have a good command in traditional Chinese culture and literatures in virtually every historical period, but also the representative literary works and theories of the West. Ms Li Hong has gained outstanding achievements in the extremely challenging studies and has been awarded university scholarship for prominent students every semester. Meanwhile, she is assiduous at writing. In spite of heavy academic engagement, she has published a lot of literary works in her spare time. In 2012 alone she published two novels—a milestone in her career of literary writing.

    Furthermore, Ms. Li takes an active part in social work. She served as student leader in the university Student Union and has been a leading cadre of her class all these years. Besides, she performed the duty of Chinese instructor respectively to the students of Hong Kong Baptist University (December, 2010) and Cheng Cheng College, Japan (March, 2011).

    Therefore, with great pleasure I recommend Ms. Li Hong to your graduate program and expect her to gain even greater achievement at your university.

    Sincerely yours,

XU × ×
Professor of Chinese Department,
Tsinghua University

APPENDIX B Keys to Practice of the Relevant Skill and Exercises

IV

Personal Statement

Dreams open the door of the future, and perseverance makes them come true.

There have been many dreams in my mind since my childhood. The first of them came from my parents, who taught me a lot and ushered me to a fantastic world of science.

My intense interest now is civil engineering, a subject that combines engineering science with construction technology and social value. It provides me with a good opportunity to express my idea and display my creativity. And at the same time I obtain from it the pleasure of achievement and immense satisfaction. I hope I will become a prominent professor or scholar in this field someday, and I am trying my best to prepare for it.

Under the teachers' instructions, I've made steady progress in my studies and scientific research in the past few years. I have taken all the courses in civil engineering, including mechanics, concrete structure, steel structure, high-rise building, anti-seismic structure, experimental methodology, etc., thus laying a solid theoretical foundation. I am particularly fond of various courses of experiment, for they not only reveal the secrets of the Nature, but also teach me how to think rigorously and scientifically. In the process of studying I have realized that if I want to have a thorough knowledge of the civil engineering, the most important is to touch upon some related fields, such as architecture, project management and environment, etc. So I have chosen some kernel courses of related subjects and am rewarded with good training.

Seeing the widespread use of the computer in scientific research, I have studied FORTRAN and C++. I have made quite a few programs to be used in actual design and experimental work. Thanks to these programs, I am now able to do my research work with ease.

Civil engineering is oriented to application. Keeping this in mind I used to practice in some building sites, construction companies and architecture institutes at weekends or on my holidays. The experience has helped me a lot in comprehending theoretic knowledge with actual designing. Last year, I participated in the construction of SIEEB (Sino-Italian Environment and Energy Building), an engineering project of peculiar shape dotted with multiple joints of different materials. During this period I learnt how to apply theoretic knowledge to actual construction of engineering project.

To acquire more practical experience, I have made a point of designing my own work. I am one of the best student designers for the work of concrete structure designing and steel structure designing. I won the top prize for comprehensive representation and the best structure analysis prize in the 10th Structure Design Competition of Tsinghua University, and a first prize for comprehensive representation and the best prize for structure analysis in the 2nd Structure Design Competition of Beijing. I had the honor of taking part in the 2nd National Structure Design Competition as a member of Tsinghua University team.

I have also engaged in the development project of civil engineering and projects of other disciplines. I have attended lots of lectures, many of which are delivered by some Academicians of Chinese Academy of Engineering and celebrated professors abroad, through whom I get familiar with the latest achievements and the current trend of the engineering science in the world.

It seems to me that there are two major branches in the future of civil engineering. One is the microcosmic theory of materials, which will lead to the development of analysis methods and structure materials. The other is the design and construction of huge architectures, such as super-high-rise buildings and super-span bridges. In my opinion, either of them is very challenging; and either entails painstaking efforts.

I will be very glad to continue my studies in civil engineering and other related subjects. As NUS University has a worldwide reputation for its PhD program of civil engineering, it has long been my goal of pursuit. If my request is granted, I will endeavor to make greater progress in my studies. I am confident that I will be excellent in the field of civil engineering.

Unit 16

1. 英译汉

哪些语言最适合发微博？

这条长 78 字符的英语微博写成中文只需 24 个字。这一优点使中文成为理想的微博用语，因为微博信息通常被限制在 140 字以内。尽管推特作为世界上最著名的微博服务，有着 1.4 亿活跃用户，但在中国推特受到屏蔽，而中国本土的新浪微博，则有着超过 2.5 亿的注册用户。在印第安纳大学从事社交媒体研究的唐硕（音译）先生称，中文非常简练，所以大多数中文微博都不会超过 140 个字符的上限。

日语同样也很简洁：俳句迷很容易用推特的方式，将俳句这种由 17 字音组成的短诗迅速发出，虽然韩语和阿拉伯语需要稍大的字符空间，但推特用户一般会省略韩语词汇中的音节；而阿拉伯语推文也会惯常地省略元音部分。去年，阿拉伯地区的推特业务如雨后春笋迅速增长，虽然这可能要归功于遍布中东的民众起义而非语言的特点。据一家总部位于巴黎的社交媒体动向调查公司 Semiocast 的数据，目前阿拉伯语已经成为推特上第八大

APPENDIX B Keys to Practice of the Relevant Skill and Exercises

常用语言，每天有超过两百万条阿拉伯语推特发布。

在众多语言中，罗曼诸语言通常显得较为冗长啰嗦。因此西班牙语和葡萄牙语作为推特上除英语外最常用的语言，有一些"招数"来减少字符数。譬如巴西人用"abs"代替abraços（拥抱），"bjs"代替beijos（亲吻）；讲西班牙语的人从来不需要用第一人称说"我走"（只用动词"voy"表示）。然而，非正式英语则更是简便。非正式英语可以去掉人称代词，无需准确的发音，尽情使用完善的缩写文化。也门政府发言人穆罕默德·奥巴沙同时用英语和阿拉伯语发推特，他说"英语的首字母缩写无与伦比，比如用DoD三个字母可以表示 department of defence（国防部）"。

推特用户在全球迅猛增长使得英语推特使用总量从2009年的2/3下降到了目前的39%，但是通用多国语言的推特用户仍然青睐英语，因为它使用广泛。许多说阿拉伯语的革命者在"阿拉伯之春"行动中使用英语来向更多听众传播信息，有时候甚至用自动翻译服务来进行宣传。直到最近的一次升级之前，阿拉伯语、波斯语和乌尔都语的用户在使用井号(#)标签时都会遇到麻烦（在文字前面加上井号#以标明推特的主题）。有些人选择用英语来避开政府的审查。

尽管英语的通用性和灵活性使得英语获得了霸权地位，推特同时也在帮助那些使用范围小、苦苦挣扎的语言。巴斯克语和盖立克语使用者使用推特来与距离遥远的其他人（巴斯克语和盖立克语使用者）进行联系。美国密苏里州圣路易斯大学的凯文斯坎内尔教授发现推特上用了500种语言，并建立了一个网站来追踪这些语言的动向。据说澳大利亚土著语言Gamilaraay目前全世界仅有三人使用，其中一人正在使用推特以便于复兴这种语言。

2. 汉译英

Innovation in China

Innovation in China is flourishing at an unprecedented rate. In order to surpass developed countries on science and technology as soon as possible, China has sharply increased its research and development fund. Chinese universities and institutes are actively carrying out innovative researches, which cover various fields of high technology, ranging from big data to biochemistry, new energy, robots, etc. They are also cooperating with science and technology parks throughout the country, so as to commercialize their fruits of innovation. In the meantime, Chinese entrepreneurs are also making pioneering efforts to innovate their products and business models, so as to adapt to the changing consumer market at home and abroad, and their growing demands.

II

1-10　Versions A: word-for-word translation, very stiff and unintelligible；
　　　　Versions B: translation of actual meaning, better rendition with readability；
　　　　Versions C: translation of original flavor, better rendition of the three versions,

with idiomatic Chinese expression

III

These three English versions are virtually word-for-word correspondence with the original Chinese. The problem is the readability for native English speakers: What we Chinese consider vivid, lifelike and idiomatic may seem dull, exaggerated, or even ridiculous to them on account of either cultural gap, (as shown in passage 1), different social and political background, (as shown in passage 2), or their preference for certain writing styles and wording (as shown in passage 3). These questions are open to discussion.

Appendix C: Keys to Translation Exercises for Independent Work

I. E-C Translation

1. 论读书

读书可以怡情,足以傅彩,足以长才。其怡情也,最见于独处幽居之时;其傅彩也,最见于高谈阔论之中;其长才也,最见于处事判事之际。练达之士虽能分别处理细事或一一判别枝节,然纵观统筹、全局策划,则舍好学深思者莫属。读书费时过多易惰,文采藻饰太盛则娇,全凭条文断事乃学究故态。读书补天然之不足,经验又补读书之不足,盖天生才干犹如自然花草,读书然后知如何修剪移接,而书中所示,如不以经验范之,则又大而无当。有一技之长者鄙读书,无知者羡读书,唯明智之士用读书,然书并不以用处告人,用书之智不在书中,而在书外,全凭观察得之。读书时不可存心诘难作者,不可尽信书上所言,亦不可只为寻章摘句,而应推敲细思。书有浅尝者,有可吞食者,少数则须咀嚼消化。换言之,有只须读其部分者,有只须大体涉猎者,少数则须全读,读时须全神贯注,孜孜不倦。书亦可请人代读,取其所作摘要,但只限题材较次或价值不高者,否则书经提炼犹如水经蒸馏,淡而无味矣。读书使人充实,讨论使人机智,笔记使人准确。因此不常作笔记者须记忆特强,不常讨论者须天生聪颖,不常读书者须欺世有术,始能无知而显有知。读史使人明智,读诗使人灵秀,数学使人周密,科学使人深刻,伦理使人庄重,逻辑修饰之学使人善辩:凡有所学,皆成性格。人之才智但有滞碍,无不可读适当之书使之顺畅,一如身体百病,皆可借相宜之运动除之。滚球利睾肾,射箭利胸肺,慢步利肠胃,骑术利头脑,诸如此类。如智力不集中,可令读数学,盖演题须全神贯注,稍有分散即须重演;如不能辨异,可令读经院哲学,盖是辈皆吹毛求疵之人;如不善求同,不善以一物阐证另一物,可令读律师之案卷。如此头脑中凡有缺陷,皆有特药可医。(王佐良译)

2. 美国总统林肯葛底斯堡演讲词

87年以前,我们的先辈们在这个大陆上创立了一个新国家,它孕育于自由之中,奉行一切人生来平等的原则。

现在我们正从事一场伟大的内战,以考验这个国家,或者说以考验任何一个孕育于自由而奉行上述原则的国家是否能够长久存在下去。我们在这场战争中的一个伟大战场上集会。烈士们为使这个国家能够生存下去而献出了自己的生命，我们在此集会是为了把这个战场的一部分奉献给他们作为最后安息之所。我们这样做是完全应该而且非常恰当的。

但是，从更广泛的意义上来说，这块土地我们不能够奉献，我们不能够圣化，我们不能够神化。曾在这里战斗过的勇士们，活着的和逝去的，已经把这块土地神圣化了，这远不是我们微薄的力量所能增减的。全世界将很少注意到、也不会长久地记得我们今天在这里所说的话，但全世界永远不会忘记勇士们在这里所做过的事。毋宁说，倒是我们这些还活着的人，应该在这里把自己奉献于勇士们已经如此崇高地向前推进但尚未完成的事业。倒是我们应该在这里把自己奉献于仍然留在我们面前的伟大任务，以便使我们从这些光荣的死者身上吸取更多的奉献精神，来完成他们已彻底为之献身的事业；以便使我们在这里下定最大的决心，不让这些死者们白白牺牲；以便使国家在上帝福佑下得到自由的新生，并且使这个民有、民治、民享的政府永世长存。

3. 意义深远的葛底斯堡演讲

盖提斯堡演说大手笔名副其实，既值得纪念，又便于记忆。亚伯拉罕·林肯用区区270个词，发表了一篇如同散文诗一般的无与伦比的政治演说。他在葛底斯堡战役所在地为国家士兵公墓哀悼致辞所做的这篇"简短讲话"完全没有偏离纪念美国阵亡将士这一主题。但是，在不到3分钟的时间里，他的讲话升华到了内战意义、自由本质和国家希望的高度。林肯甚至不是这场活动的主要发言人。他的讲话排在著名演说家、政治家爱德华·埃弗里特之后，而后者的讲话持续了两个多小时。当时，埃弗里特的演讲更受大家青睐。

林肯的演说是这么开头的："八十七年前，我们的先辈们在这个大陆上创立了一个新国家，它孕育于自由之中，奉行一切人生来平等的原则。"这一犹如圣经般宏大庄严的开场白气息中掩藏着在当时的战争苦难中相当激进的一项主张。因为仅仅在几个月前，就在林肯所站的地方爆发了一场血腥大战，联邦军击败南方军，在这一战役中获胜。双方都有数千名将士牺牲。1863年11月的这个星期四下午，我们很难看清葛底斯堡战役究竟是为何而战。而林肯给出了清晰的答案：这不仅仅是为了宪法原则而战，更是为了平等、生命、自由和对幸福的追求而战——所有这些理念早在1776年的《独立宣言》中就记入了史册。南方同盟紧紧抓住宪法不放，声称合法权利在他们这一边。而林肯用一句话就表明，道义在北方联邦军一方。

但是，葛底斯堡演讲真正感人之处在于它远不只是一个政治声明，它也是一种谦卑的表达。这篇演讲承认了这种方式的不充足之处。但林肯确实成功地为逝者增添了色彩。他呼吁活着的人将自己奉献给逝者所追求的崇高事业，"我们要从这些光荣的死者身上吸取更多的奉献精神，来完成他们已经完全彻底为之献身的事业。"林肯在几年前曾谈到过类似的主题，但他之前的演讲从没有像那天那么精辟有力。

但不是所有人都欣赏这次演讲。有些听众认为林肯那天声音过于尖细，甚至带点刺耳的感觉。《泰晤士报》的通讯记者认为林肯的演讲"荒唐可笑"，评论说"没有什么演讲比这更无聊更陈腐了"。林肯本人在演讲中谈及奉献之前曾说："世界将不大会注意、也不会长久记得我们在此说过什么。"在这一点上，他可预言错了。

4. 西方哲学史

　　教皇势力之衰落，始于15世纪以前。到15世纪，更有多种原因，促其衰落，政治与文化，均呈急剧变化。火药用于争战，中央政府因之以强，拥据领地之公侯因之而弱。法王路易十一与英王爱德华四世联富商以制诸侯，息纷争而致治。意大利于15世纪末，遭北方兵祸，然在此之前近百年间，实丰足昌盛文化发达之邦。此一新文化，崇希腊，法罗马，恶中古之僧侣，创人本主义之文明。凡建筑，凡文学风格，悉以古之巨作伟构为师。(15世纪中)君士坦丁堡为土耳其所占。自希腊罗马之衰，古文化残存于世，仅君士坦丁堡一地。既陷，寓居于君士坦丁堡之希腊学人，相率流亡意大利，意大利倾慕希腊人文之学者，迎为上宾，达迦玛绕好望角抵印度，哥伦布西行发现新地，而世界为之扩大。哥白尼立日中心说，而宇宙为之扩大。所谓君士坦丁大帝册封诏，学者证为数百年前赝物，儒林腾笑，教廷威信坠地。拜占庭学者西行，西方学者得读柏拉图原作，识其真谛，此与读僧侣篆疏之本，迥然不同。昔者，人间是烦恼悲泣之地，居尘世者，必升入天堂，始离苦海。今者，人间亦有乐趣：享盛誉于邦国，创文艺之美，猎奇于远方，皆人间乐事。雕刻绘事，诗歌词章，赏心悦目，奔进汹涌，美不胜数。几百年中绝欲弃智、攻苦食淡之说教，已置脑后。虽然，即在意大利，衰亡之中古思想仍有挣扎。萨方那罗拉，修身鄙世之僧人也；达·芬奇，无艺不精之大艺人也，而二人生于同年，同是本时代之人。大体言之，旧日之种种恐怖，今已失去恐怖；新获得之精神解放，使人陶醉，陶醉虽仅一时，然恐怖已驱除矣。此时也，精神解放，为之雀跃，为之欢庆，现代世界于焉诞生。(许国璋译)

5. 词呀！多义的词！

　　行了 (It works)，这两个字可以是对一项导弹工程或一项提高班组效率的计划的最终肯定，也可以用来对父辈未竟的极复杂的项目的满意回答。这两个字也可用以表示比例适当的混合物放进密封瓶罐后所发生的反应。有的人在锅炉厂 (works) 挣钱糊口。正是手表的机件 (works) 使之发出嘀嘀嗒嗒的声音。大多数人为生活而工作 (work)。哪一个青少年不会为了使用汽车而说服 (work on) 老爸呢？小船可以穿破 (work) 冰原航行，军队跋涉穿越 (work) 沼泽，举步维艰。

　　物理学家赋予 "work"（功）一词以精确的含义，而冶金学家用这个词来论及各种各样的加工过程。开坯、棒材或板材的轧制、棒材、毛坯或半成品的锻造、棒材穿轧成管、线材模拉、板材槽拉、型锻、锤锻以及挤压成型等，所有这一切过程均属金属加工 (working)，而生产出来的产品则称为金属加工件（"worked" metals）。冶金学家所说的加工 (work)，是指改变金属形状但不改变体积的任何操作过程。锤子敲弯钉子是受到加工 (worked)，再把钉子敲直是进一步的加工 (further working)。制造汽车缓冲板、牙膏管或铝质安全帽等都是严格的金属深加工 (severe working) 的通例。在所有金属零件中，只有铸件和烧结产品可归于成品类，在生产过程阶段无须经过一个或几个所谓的加工工序 (working)。

6. 20世纪最重要的讲话

元旦这天，中国各家报纸都刊登了邓小平的一篇6 000字的讲话，我们由此了解到他迈出了多大的一步。讲话的内容标志着中国几千年仇外历史的终结。

这篇讲话最终有可能被认为是20世纪最重要的一次。因为在讲话中，占人类总数四分之一的国家的这位最高领导人宣称，中国在20世纪正在加入世界其他国家(除了阿尔巴尼亚以外)的行列。

邓说："任何国家要发达起来，闭关自守都不可能。我们吃过这个苦头，我们的老祖宗也吃过这个苦头。"邓一反几千年来官方对长城以外世界的敌视态度，坦率地说："闭关自守把中国搞得贫穷落后，愚昧无知。"

承认这一点着实令人吃惊，这同中国几千年来执行的政策大相径庭。这种政策可以追溯到明代以前直到秦代，当时修筑了长城，旨在将马背上的野蛮人挡在关外的荒野区域。

邓的意思是：不放弃马克思主义，但是只要资本主义的观念有道理，就采纳，因为"开放伤害不了我们"。由较年轻的领导人带头进行的经济改革是国家安全最重要的保障，因为只有经济实力雄厚，才能购买炸弹、导弹和飞机。

如果中国在20世纪设法赶上世界上其他国家，21世纪可能会属于中国。他们有人力、有人才，他们训练有素，纪律严明。他们的工业潜力也令人生畏。

21世纪，人们可能会普遍接受这样一种说法，发表了有史以来最重要讲话的戴牛仔帽的人不是罗纳德·里根，而是一位80岁的中国人。

7. 应该如何读书？

应该如何读书？这个问题很简单，因为既然书分类别，如小说、传记、诗歌，那我们就应该有所区别，从中吸取其应该给我们的正确东西。但是很少有人向书索取它所能真正给我们的东西。最通常的情况是，我们总是模模糊糊、心不在焉地看书。对于小说，要求它真实；对于诗歌，要求它虚构；对于传记，要求它恭维奉承；对于历史，要求它强调我们的偏见。倘若我们在阅读时能排除以上这些成见，那将是一个极好的开端。我们应该尽量去适应作者，不要对作者发号施令，要成为他的同行或伙伴。假如你一开始就踟蹰不前，对作者持保留和批评的态度，那么你就无法从书中获得最充分的益处。但是，要是你完全敞开思想，那么，篇首一些迂回费解句子中那些细枝末节、难以觉察的微妙暗示与线索将带你进入一个与众不同的人性境界。你要是沉浸于作者的境界，熟悉这一境界，那么你很快会领略到作者正在或力图传递给你的东西远远不限于这些文字内容。

我们先以小说的读法为例。一部32章的小说，作者努力把它打造成建筑物一样有形态、可控制的东西。然而，字句不是砖瓦，更令人难以触摸：与眼观实物相比，阅读的过程更长、更复杂。或许理解小说家创作要素的最快捷方法不是阅读，而是写作——亲自去体验一下遣字造句的种种困难和危险。那么，就来回忆一下给你留下深刻印象的某一事件吧。比如说，在马路的拐角处，你从两个正在谈话的人身旁走过。树影摇曳，灯光闪烁，谈话的声调亦喜亦悲——整个景象、全部意念似乎都融汇于这一瞬间。

但是，要是你企图用文字来重建上述景象，你会发觉，原来完整的景象一下分裂成千百个互相矛盾的印象。这些印象有的要抑制，有的要强调，在这期间，你对情绪本身可能会把握不住。这时，不妨搁下手中几页模糊、散乱文字，去阅读某位大小说家（如笛福、珍妮·奥斯丁或托马斯·哈代）作品的开篇几页。这样你就能更好地欣赏他们的精湛手法了。

8. 动起来

正如以英语为母语的人士所知，"get off the dime"的意思是"开始行动，停止犹豫"。但是它源于何处？而且为什么这条陈旧的俚语没有随着10美分硬币的贬值而消亡？尤其是在当今这个时代，几乎没有任何东西能够一毛钱买一打。

Dime(10美分硬币)一词源于拉丁语decem，即"10"的意思，是美国硬币中最小最薄的一种，在隐喻修辞中，表示极小的玩意儿。开车时，你要是想把车准确地停在某一点，而不是一个大概的区域，那就是 stop on a dime(停在一角硬币上/停车很到位)。

多亏乔纳森·赖特的《美国俚语历史词典》，我们得以找到产生这条短语的行为。最早的现代舞评论家之一，1926年的一部小说《黑鬼的天堂》(现在谁也不会用这个标题了)的作者卡尔·范·维切特，描述了娱乐舞厅中的这样一个场景："有时候，一对舞伴几乎停在原地不动，这时舞场经理就会大叫道：别磨磨蹭蹭！"(Git off dat dime！)

To dance on a dime (一角钱上跳舞/凭一角钱跳舞)是指两个人的身体紧紧地贴在一起，虽然穿着衣服，却有着性接触，几乎在原地不动。那些为了挣得一角钱的陪舞女郎(1930年劳伦斯·哈特的抒情诗《10美分一曲舞》使其名垂千古)在老板的敦促下让顾客不停地跳动。因此，to get off the dime(从一角硬币上离开)便有了"动起来"的意思。(这个发现给我以极大的乐趣。我们的语言多么富于变化啊！常常给人以意外的反响。)

Dime这一字眼至今仍用于青少年俚语，为"漂亮女人"的同义词。这词源于1979年波·德里克主演的一部名叫"十"的影片。片中有这么一句台词："从1到10按等级打分，她是10分"。这一来她就"十分"(dime)漂亮了。

Behind a dime (在一角钱后面)是一种表示怀疑的说法。20世纪中期有一句南方方言："我绝不相信他在一角钱后面"(我对他极不信任)。一角钱不仅很小，很难把东西藏在后面，而且特别薄，例如短语 not one thin dime (不及一角薄币/一点也不)。因此"极端的不信任"就表示为 behind a dime edgeways。

在犯罪活动中想出卖同伙的歹徒在打电话给警察局或者联邦调查局时会遇到语言保密问题。过去曾一度用 drop a dime(投一角硬币)的说法来表示"告发、出卖"这一俚语。不过，10美分打一次收费电话已是很久以前的事了。最近几年，黑手党告密者中仍使用"投一个角币"这一短语的仅限于那些年老且守旧的人。目前还没有听说通过手机告密的黑社会隐语。今春曾有人提出"摁M键表示谋杀"。但对这一说法黑手党成员却嗤之以鼻。

9. 迷人的南太平洋诸岛

太平洋气势磅礴，滚滚波涛拍打着五洲海岸——北美洲、南美洲、亚洲、大洋洲和南极洲。太平洋在东南方与大西洋汇合，在西南方与印度洋相接。然而，浩瀚的太平洋最精美之处不在其大陆海岸，也不在沿海诸岛，而是在远离陆地的海域：富有神奇色彩的南太平洋诸岛像天上的繁星一样散布在广阔的海面上。

在那里，由于地心引力的剧烈干扰，一道道山脉、一座座火山升出水面。千百年来，微小的珊瑚虫在这里繁衍、死亡，形成了数不胜数的叫作环礁的环状岛屿。

散发着鲜花和香料芬芳的微风轻轻地吹拂着南太平洋诸岛。白日明媚温暖，夜晚清澈凉爽。滚滚浪花拍打着海岸，发出永不休止的轰鸣。头顶上空，纤纤椰树沙沙作响，轻声哼着令人昏昏欲睡的催眠曲。

白人首次登上这些太平洋海岛时，发现生活在那里的人们都像孩子一样欢快。男子身材高大，妇女婀娜多姿，似乎对世上的一切都不用操心。他们茅舍门前长着一丛丛椰子树、面包树；海洋里鱼鳖成群，张网可得。岛上的人几乎不需要穿什么衣服，也几乎见不到任何疾病。

邻近部落之间有时会爆发残酷的血战。他们有时乘独木舟去攻击附近的岛屿。这些强悍的勇士乐于战斗。岛民中的许多人都有吃人的习俗。他们把杀死的敌人煮熟吃掉。这种习俗是他们的法律和宗教的一部分。然而，这些野蛮人通常是友善、谦恭和好客的。一些早期的探险家因为太迷恋这些太平洋岛屿而不再返回自己的国家。

10. 李小龙

按中国的 12 生肖，李小龙出生在龙年龙时。他父亲是香港粤剧团的一名丑角，而他就是在他父亲随团到美国巡演的时候出生的。虽然在家里大家都叫他小龙，但他实际上体质很弱，而且还多病。为了对付周围那些凶悍的邻居，他选择习武作为自我防卫的一种方式。他很快就变得身手敏捷、武艺非凡。他 18 岁时还拿过香港恰恰舞冠军。一年后，他回到美国攻读哲学和医学。

此外，李小龙还精通各种格斗技巧，几近炉火纯青的地步。他最终形成了这样一种生活方式：不是自己构思、设计武术技巧，就是教别人习武。在大街上他冲着树木或废弃物练踢腿；在午餐桌上他会对着邻座的空椅砍砍劈劈；看电视时他缓慢地做仰卧起坐；甚至是在睡觉的时候也要伸伸拳、踢踢腿。在舞会上他会用一个指头撑地做俯卧撑，并且很乐意脱去衬衣，展现他"无与伦比的肌肉"。他深信在体育锻炼中全神贯注是成功的一半，而"冥想与精神训练"总是列在他日程安排的首位。

武术向来被认为是美化了的街斗，而李小龙认定电影是用以消除这一偏见的最好方式。他开始制作自己的电影，既当编剧、演员又当导演和动作设计师。在美国，他的电影作品有《精武门》《猛龙过江》和《龙争虎斗》——最后这部影片被认为是有史以来最成功的商业片之一。

APPENDIX C Keys to Translation Exercises for Independent Work

　　李小龙原打算在 35 岁淡出，希望能多花点时间陪家人并做些对社会有意义的事，但却在 32 岁时死于脑水肿。一个精力旺盛正处于事业巅峰的年轻人突然猝死，自然令人感到奇怪，流言蜚语也就不胫而走。一个说法是说李小龙和猫王普雷斯利一样仍然活着，等着有一天再重返公众生活。而实际上他的遗体已经埋葬在西雅图了——与其子李国豪之墓相邻。李国豪也是一个电影明星，1993 年猝死，时年 28 岁。在拍摄暴力影片《乌鸦》时，他随着一声枪响意外倒地身亡。

11. "胜利者"与"失败者"

　　"胜利者"与"失败者"这两个词有许多含义。我们说某人是胜利者，并不意味着他击败了其他人。对我们而言，不管是作为个人还是社会的一员，胜利者都能真正地承担责任。他们诚信可靠、反应灵敏、待人诚恳。

　　胜利者不会献身于某一抽象概念，想象自己应当是什么样的人；相反，他们是什么就是什么，从不把精力用在矫揉造作、虚伪迎合、操纵他人之类的事上。他们知道真正的爱和假装的爱之间的区别，知道什么是真正的愚蠢、什么是假装的愚蠢，什么是真正的博学、什么是假装的博学。他们不会用面具伪装自己。

　　胜利者不畏惧独立思考，不畏惧运用自己的知识。他们能从众多纷杂的说法中找出事情的原委，而不会假装对所有问题都知道答案。他们聆听他人，分析别人的话，最终得出自己的结论。胜利者尽管也佩服并尊敬他人，但他们不会被别人所完全限制或击败，不会被别人所束缚或慑服。

　　胜利者不会佯装无助，也绝也不会玩推诿的把戏。相反，他们会承担起自己的人生责任。

12. 多才多艺的人

　　在过去的时代中，许多杰出人物都异乎寻常地多才多艺，这也许并不是偶然的。就在距今不远的时代，一个聪明人还有可能熟悉几乎每一个门类的知识。因此，列奥纳多·达·芬奇和菲利普·西德尼爵士这样的天才人物就被认为自然是要同时从事许多方面的工作的。达·芬奇从事于众多的发明，忙得几乎没时间完成他的绘画；32 岁就战死沙场的西德尼不仅是一个伟大的军事家，也是一个才华横溢的学者和诗人。他们很接近文艺复兴时期对理想人物的要求——"万能的人"，即精通一切的人。

　　今天，我们极少听说某个音乐家刚刚发明了一种新潜水艇。知识领域被分了又分，分成无数个范围狭窄而且互不通气的部门。受人崇敬的是专家；而多面手非但不受人钦佩，反而常常不为人所信服。当今世界是精通业务的"专家"的世界，这些专家须将自己一生的大部分时间用以研究某个十分狭小的领域，这样才能与同行竞争。

　　随着专业化程度的提高，各门知识的边界正在以前所未有的速度被压缩。但这种压缩是付出了相当大的代价才做到的。现在一个科学家离开了自己的专业，比一个傻子强不了多少，正像一个文学家对科技方面的重大进展几乎一无所知一样。这是现代才有的怪现象。同样，专业化也间接地影响到了各行各业中的普通人。以前由于感兴趣而从事的许多活动，现在常常绝望地放弃了。专家们说，这些活动需要技巧，得付出毕生的精力才能精通。如果你能在客厅里欣赏到世界上最杰出的钢琴家的演奏，自己干吗还要学钢琴呢？

　　渐渐地，人们相互间的交往变得越来越少了。你简直不可能同你的邻居交谈工作上的事，哪怕他的工作与你的相差无几。英国皇家学会的会员都是国内最优秀的科学家。然而正如一位会员所言，令人深感不安的是，在皇家学会举办的讲座中，仅有百分之十的会员能够听懂所讲内容的百分之五十！

13. 瘦身与虚荣

　　"女人的钱再多也不多，女人身材再瘦也不瘦。"这句经常被认为是已故温莎公爵夫人说的话从很大程度上体现了我们时代的奇怪精神。瘦被视为这样一种美德。

　　这种观点的问题在于有人实际上想以此为生活准则。我自己就幻想能够套上瘦小的时装。因此，我一生中的大部分时间都在节食——这真是糟糕极了。再说，有钱也不是什么坏事，但这种情况不会发生在我身上——除非一个不知其名的亲戚突然死在某个遥远的国度，给我留下了千百万美元的遗产。

　　我们在何处背离了生活常规？什么时候吃黄油成了一种罪过？稍稍多一点赘肉不是令人厌恶，就是毫无魅力？所有的宗教都有特定的禁食日，暴食是基督教不可饶恕的7大罪行之一。然而，直到前不久，大多数人都还存在吃不饱的问题。在有些宗教团体中，财富曾被视为可能得到拯救和道德高尚的象征，而肥胖则是财富和康乐的象征。

　　今天恰恰相反。我们已转向以瘦为美德这一新标志。其结果便是肥胖很糟——哪怕是稍稍偏重也不行——因为这意味着缺乏道德力量。

　　对健康的关心使我们对瘦身也越发痴迷。的确，我国目前体重超标的人比以往任何时候都多。在许多情况下，肥胖与心血管疾病危险的增加息息相关。但是这些疾病既同超重有关，也与我们的生活方式及高脂肪饮食不无相关。相关的消化系统癌变的危险可能更多的是来自饮食而不是体重问题——脂肪太多、纤维缺乏。

　　这么看来，问题的关键不是我们的身体太重，而是锻炼不够，吃得也不科学。锻炼对强健骨骼、保持心肺健康都很必要。低脂肪的均衡饮食也能帮助身体避免多种疾病。我们绝对不应该再把这么多的注意力放在体重上了。仅仅瘦是不够的。如果那些变瘦了或本来就瘦的人认为他们自然就健康，因而不注意调整自己的整个生活方式，这实际上很危险。瘦身可能纯属一种极度的虚荣。

14. 中国姓氏中的生僻字

　　"马"这个表示一种动物的汉字，也是中国的第十三大姓——共有近1 700万人姓"马"。要是许多姓"马"的人聚在一起，尤其是有人同名同姓，就会造成无尽的混乱，而名字相同是对很多中国人来说屡见不鲜。

　　但马骉骉(三个马字并列，音 cheng) 就没有这方面的麻烦——她那嗜书的爷爷为她的起名找到一个妙招。(马骉骉的爷爷饱读诗书，为解决这一常见问题找到一个巧妙的方法。)26

APPENDIX C Keys to Translation Exercises for Independent Work

年前孙女出生时,爷爷搜肠刮肚,翻遍了满书房的中文字典,目光突然落到一个读音为"cheng"的汉字上:骉。这个字的意思是奔驰的骏马,看起来就像"马"字,不同的是三个"马"字紧连,并列写在一起。

对于马骉骉和千百万其他中国人来说,家长们渴望赋予子女个性亮点(凸显个性)的心愿与中国官僚机构企盼秩序的意愿形成了强烈的冲突。为了努力使中国十三亿公民庞大数据库现代化,中国公安局一直在尝试用一种可供计算机读取的新身份证来代替人人随身携带的手写身份证。这种新一代身份证上有彩色照片,嵌入了微型芯片,很难伪造,而且可以在机场之类的一些重要安检场所进行扫描识别。

然而,2006 年发布的一份政府报告指出,公安局的电脑系统设置仅能识别大约 55 000 个汉字中的 32 252 个。这样一来,马小姐以及大约 6 000 万名字中带有生僻字的中国人将不能获得新身份证——除非他们将自己的名字改为较为常见的汉字。

而且上述情况似乎会变得越来越糟。不过在政府看来,情况会越来越好——因为至少从 2003 年起,中国政府就一直在致力编写出一套规范汉字表,以便于人们日常使用,其中包括为子女命名的汉字。

上周有一家报纸报道说,今年晚些时候将发布这套汉字表。此举将有效地遏制用生僻字命名的现象。一名主管语言文字的政府官员告诉国家新闻机构新华社,新的汉字表列出的汉字将超过 8 000 个。虽然这一数目远远少于现有数据库可能包括的汉字,但这位官员表示,这些字足以"覆盖任何领域的任何概念"。中国目前使用的常用汉字大约有 3 500 个左右。

一些政府官员指出,中国家长为子女取名就像为漂亮服装配时髦服饰,费心挑选最生僻的字眼,甚至不惜凭空捏造汉字。这类情况太多了,以至于各种五花八门的名字泛滥失控。许多中国夫妇仍为能从丰富的中国古典文献中找到一个与众不同且讨人喜欢的名字而引以为荣,因为在一个姓氏少得惊人的社会里,标新立异的名字从某种程度上将有助于子女引人注目。

据估计,中国有一百个姓氏覆盖了全国总人口的百分之八十五。老百姓 (laobaixing),也即是"老用的一百个姓氏"(old hundred names),便是一个泛指广大民众的词语。对比而言,美国有七万个姓氏覆盖了全国总人口的百分之九十。

15. 移动电话文化

无论从本质上还是称谓上看,科技往往都具有全球性特征。在任何地方一提到"television""computer"或"internet",别人可能都能明白你的意思。但手提电话呢?对这无所不在的科技产品,人类却患上了"巴别塔"综合征。每到圣诞节,南北美洲的人们在无数圣诞树下打开的圣诞礼物叫作"cell phones"或"celulares"。不过对英国人和西班牙人而言,却叫作"mobiles"和"móviles"。德国人和芬兰人将其叫作"handys",因为这种电话可以拿在手中;中国人也用这玩意儿打电话,称之为"shou ji"(手机);日本人则称其为"keitai"(携带),大意为"可随身携带之物"。

这同一物体称谓上的不一颇为发人深省。10年之间，移动电话对于人类已成了鞋一样的必需品。而之所以没有一个全世界统一的称谓，是因为其名字的起源赋有深厚的文化内涵。"cellular"（蜂窝状的）说明了现代无线网络的建造方式，表明美国的科技世界观。"mobile"（可移动的）强调的是不受束缚，这正好适合昔日大英帝国那种漫游无拘风格。"handy"（手边的）则突出了其实用功能，而这一点德国人非常重视。但这些称谓差异仅仅是表面现象吗？这些差异会长期存在，还是会让位于全球移动电话文化？

由于电讯资费越来越便宜，广大民众越来越倾向于使用自己的移动电话。根据全球移动通信协会(GSMA)的统计数字，2000年年初，一般用户每月通话时间为174分钟；而到了2009年年初，这一数字上升为261分钟。这表明世界范围内，人们每月使用移动电话通话总计1万亿分钟，相当于近200万年。至于海量的短信，就无从统计了。

德国人通常的口头禅是"开口是银，沉默是金"——他们月均使用手机谈话时间只有89分钟。与德国人相反，美国人总是滔滔不绝，其月均通话时间高达788分钟。最爱煲电话粥的是波多黎各人，他们以月均高达1 875分钟的通话时间位居世界首位。究其原因，可能是因为运营商为这个小岛上的居民提供了花费仅为40美元的包月服务，想怎么打就怎么打，拨美国大陆的电话也不另收费。在巴黎，如果受到他人大声谈论私事的打扰，人们会公开抱怨。而在伦敦就鲜有类似抱怨。无论在巴黎还是伦敦，在与他人面对面交谈时如果电话响了，人们往往会停止交谈，走到安静的角落去接电话。中国人通常愿意受电话干扰，生怕错过任何商机。中国的情况很独特，主要是经济方面的原因以及法规的不严。许多消费者使用小作坊生产的山寨手机，这类厂商在中国数以百计。打着"Nckia""Sumsung"之类牌子的翻版仿制品司空见惯。一些具有创新意识的制造商已经开发出专业的手机，如双卡双待手机，或为开拖拉机的农民生产的大功放手机。

16. 科学之美

从我认识的科学工作者（包括伊娃和鲁斯）和从书中读到的科学家的经历来看，只要去探寻自然法则，不用多久，就能与美不期而遇。一位朋友说，"我不敢肯定这就是夕阳西下时的那种美，但感觉上两者是相同的。"这位朋友是位物理学家，长期致力于破译天体内部的必然变化。他回想起第一次领悟狄拉克的量子力学等式和爱因斯坦的相对论等式时的兴奋感，"它们太美了，你一眼就可以看出它们必定是正确的，或至少是接近正确。"当我问及是什么能使理论变得美丽时，他回答说：" 简洁、对称、精确、有力。"

自然界为何会与我们觉得美的理论相一致？这一问题远未明了。正如爱因斯坦所言，宇宙最不可理解之处就在于它是可以理解的。人类，一种生活在一个微不足道的星球上的两足动物，历史并不久远，竟能测算光速，揭示原子结构，并估算黑洞的万有引力，这是多么不可思议。我们远未能通晓万物，但我们确已对自然界的运作规律所知甚多。一代接着一代，我们苦苦思索出各种公式并加以检验，发现它们与自然界的吻合达到了令人惊讶的程度。建筑师在薄纸上绘图，而按照图纸而建的建筑却能经受住地震的考验。我们将人造卫星发射到轨道上，并通过它在各大洲之间反射信号。我输入这些文字所用的计算机体

APPENDIX C Keys to Translation Exercises for Independent Work

现了成千百种对这个物质世界运作方式的真知灼见，屏幕上闪现的每一个字母都是对这些见识的证实；而我注视屏幕时所透过的镜片则遵循了由艾萨克·牛顿率先详细论述的光学原理。

牛顿相信，他在通过辨析宇宙结构模式来探索上帝的神力。我们这个时代的科学家们多半已摒弃了创世主这一概念。他们认为这是毫无必要，或至少是无法验证的假说。当他们与牛顿一样，坚信宇宙万物均由一套合乎逻辑的规则所制约时，作为科学家，他们不能断言这些规则具体是如何左右事态的。不相信上帝的法规照样可以从事科研，但不相信自然法则却不行。

17. 废除死刑，节省开支

以眼还眼，杀人偿命，无论如何，这种做法仍然是美国大多数州所信奉的司法审判。50 个州中只有 14 个明令禁止死刑——但这一状况许会随经济的衰退而改变。由于各州政府面临巨额财政赤字，又有 8 个州已经提议采取非常规的手段来削减开支：废除死刑。

正在考虑废除死刑的各州包括科罗拉多州、堪萨斯州、新墨西哥州和新罕布什尔州，它们已将是否废除死刑的争论从道德层面转移到开销成本上——至少在某种程度上是这样。研究表明，对犯人实行死刑比判终身监禁的花费要高很多。一件死刑案子，从精心遴选陪审员到一次次审判和上诉，其过程可费时长达 10 年以上，令州政府债台高筑。而死刑犯还必须关在一间间严加看管的单人牢房里，对死囚区的管理也需要一笔不菲的开支。

一家名叫"城市学会"的智库最近做的一项研究表明，1978 年至 1999 年期间，实行死刑花费了马里兰州纳税人大约 1.86 亿美元。根据他们的报告，办一个最终宣判为死刑的案子的平均费用为 300 万美元，比不采用死刑的案子几乎多花费 200 万美元。

在眼下这种经济紧缩时期，动辄上百万美元可真不是一笔小数，实在是太重要了。废除死刑提案的支持者们认为死刑花费高昂却收效甚微——鲜有证据表明死刑（对犯罪）起了震慑作用。事实上，在热衷处死囚犯的那些州——比如得克萨斯州和俄克拉何马州——其犯罪率比那些只监禁犯人而没有假释的州高多了。而且，执行死刑还有误杀无辜的风险。迄今为止，已有 130 多个被判处死刑的人后来被证明无罪。

科罗拉多州已推行废除死刑法案，它打算把每年因废除死刑而节省下来的钱用来成立一个调查小组。据州众议院多数派领袖、废除死刑提案的发起人之一保罗·威斯曼提供的数据，该州还沉积了约 1 400 起未破的谋杀案。废除死刑将给新的调查小组提供更多的资金，还可以给州里的其他项目余留 100 万美元。其他各州也在尝试腾出资金以填补巨大的财政赤字窟窿。比如，堪萨斯州估计能从每个不执行死刑的案子里节省出 50 万美元。

而别的其他一些州目前尚无跟风的计划（其中包括去年执行了全美几乎一半以上死刑的得克萨斯州）。不过，一场旷日持久的经济衰退或许会改变一些得克萨斯人的想法。

18. 高跟鞋——妇女的死敌

在全世界的百货商场和壁柜里，它们正在翘首以盼。它们的外表似乎相当诱人：款式

311

多样、质地紧凑、五颜六色。但它们完全是当今时装业最大的骗局。它们是何物？它们就是高跟鞋——妇女最凶恶的敌人(无论穿鞋者知道与否)。高跟鞋意味着现代社会的衰败。时装神话使女性相信，穿高跟鞋使人更漂亮、更成熟，但实际上，一穿上高跟鞋，各种磨难就接踵而至，周期或长或短。为使世界免除不必要的身体和心理上的痛苦，妇女应该同高跟鞋制造业作斗争，拒穿高跟鞋，不买高跟鞋。

当然，为公平起见，也必须看到高跟鞋也有积极的一面。首先，高跟鞋极有利于草坪透气。凡是穿高跟鞋在草坪上走过的人都知道此言不虚。只需穿着这宝贝鞋在院子里走一圈，就完全没必要再请修剪草坪的专业人员了，因为走这一圈会形成大小合适的孔眼为草坪供氧，而且周围还不会留下乱七八糟的土块。其次，高跟鞋颇具抵御敌人进攻的用途。鞋上那双锋利、致命的高跟能轻而易举地吓退迎面而来的敌人。尽管高跟鞋有上述种种实用好处，但仍然有一个不争的事实：穿高跟鞋对身体健康有害。随便与哪个足病医生聊聊，你就会知道他们的业务大部分来自穿高跟鞋的妇女。我们知道，高跟鞋可以引起脚掌畸形和脚趾甲破裂等足病。穿高跟鞋所造成的剧烈的背疼、扭伤或踝骨骨折的风险比穿平底鞋的人高出2倍。穿高跟鞋还会遇到鞋跟卡入人行道裂缝或阴沟栅中拔不出来的危险，使人跌倒在地——其结果可能不是摔破鼻子就是摔伤背或脖子。当然，在脱下穿了一天的高跟鞋之后，任何妇女都知道她们所盼来的是一个痛苦之夜——因为她们得试着揉揉那双肿胀变形疼痛难忍的脚以减轻痛苦。

19. 小费

长期以来，小费一直是让我既感兴趣又十分恼火的事。许多人以为小费"tip"一词是"to insure promptness"(确保及时)的首字母缩写。不过，以我看来这是不可能的。自从中世纪在英格兰开始形成付小费的习俗以来，学者们还未能找出任何早于20世纪的首字母缩合词。多数学者对"tip"一词的起源追溯到17世纪初，认为它源于罪犯的黑话，指"内部消息"。所以，给别的罪犯一个"tip"，也就是给他某种有价值的消息。

后来"tip"这个词的含义逐渐演变，到18世纪末，意思就变成了"给某人赏钱"(即小费)，以奖赏所提供的服务。这个词的意思从此不变，直到英国人移居北美，也将它带到那里。

在美国，从事三种底层职业的人需要付给小费：男女服务员、出租车司机和理发师。现在小费的付费标准为账单的15%~20%，付多付少取决于服务质量。

为什么偏偏这三种服务就应该受到特殊对待，对我来说是一个不解之谜。为什么餐馆服务员为我上菜，我就应该给小费，而飞机乘务员提供同样的服务，就不必给？为什么我应该给出租司机小费，而不必给巴士司机？为什么理发师为我理发，我应该给小费，而牙医为我补牙就不必给？我当了39年教师，即便我课上得很棒，讲座非常成功，也从没人给过我小费。

付小费这套观念毫无道理可言。我听说，美国大城市一些高档奢华餐馆根本就不给服务员开工钱，因为他们可以获得大量的小费。我还读过一些报道，说是在有些情况下，服务员实际上反而要上交餐馆一小笔钱，以感谢餐馆为他们提供了获取丰厚小费的机会。

非但如此，还真有这么一个专门探讨小费和相关问题的网站 (http：//www.tipping.org)，我得知后很是惊讶。付小费的做法隐而不见、不合逻辑，有些规则近乎荒谬。

欧洲的许多国家采取自动加收 15% 酬金的办法解决付小费问题。我倒更喜欢中国的办法：压根儿就没有小费。虽然我也理解作为发展中国家，中国为什么接受了许多西方习俗，但我希望中国人更明智一点：付小费完全没有必要，千万不要开这个头。中国的服务水平已经很不错了，无须再锦上添花。

20. 索卡尔假论文骗局

1996 年，纽约大学物理学家艾伦·索卡尔将一篇论文投寄给探讨后现代主义文化研究的重要学术期刊《社会文本》杂志。杂志通过同行评审，确保该研究符合发表标准，于是对该文大加赞赏。但是，当编辑部按时发表了此文之后，索卡尔博士却披露说，论文是随意杜撰的，故意"瞎编胡扯"。这一后来被称为"索卡尔假论文"的骗局，证明在自诩高雅的人文期刊，一篇文章只要它包含大量的花言巧语，迎合评阅人和编辑的思想偏见，是多么容易就能通过学术质量审查。自然科学家幸灾乐祸，对此嗤之以鼻：这种情况不可能发生在理科领域，对吧？

可叹之至，正如本周《科学》杂志上刊载的一篇报告所示，答案是否定的：理科领域也可能会发生类似情况。一位名叫约翰·博汉农的哈佛大学生物学家兼科技新闻工作者，杜撰了一篇自己的"索卡尔假论文"，描述从地衣中提取的化学药品如何明显减缓癌细胞生长的过程。然后他用一个虚构的学术机构假名，将这份研究投稿给世界各地的 304 家由同行评审的期刊。

尽管这项研究的实验设计、验定及分析结果都漏洞百出，但它符合其中 157 家的基本要求，只有 98 家表示拒绝。（其余 49 家要么没做回复，要么没能赶在《科学》杂志付印前审完论文。）仅有 36 家给出反馈意见，暗示他们已注意到论文的不足之处。不过博汉农博士说，其中有 16 家最终还是接受了该论文。

博汉农博士故设圈套所选定的出版物都是开放性期刊。这些期刊提供免费论文，并通过收取作者一笔费（通常为 1 000~2 000 美元）来用弥补出版开销。政策制定者们一直热衷于近来这些期刊。有一种流行的想法思想是，既然纳税人已赞助大多数学术研究，所以提供可免费使用的成果似乎也不无道理。但是这种开放获取模式持的批评者早就提出过警告，让作者而不是读者成为自己的客户会冒风险，造成怂恿出版商出台一些激励机制来容忍伪科学。

博汉农博士表明，上述风险确有其事。研究人员可以感到安慰的是，最负盛名的开放性期刊，如那些由一家美国机构"科学公共图书馆"出版的那些期刊就不会上这类当。但很多其他著名的出版商，如爱思唯尔、威科集团和塞奇旗下的期刊就容易上当。预计 2015 年出版的可供开放获取的论文的数量会从 2011 年的 194 000 篇增长到 352 000 篇（出版物总数为 170 万）。有鉴于此，博汉农恶作剧对于加强编辑审稿、促使政策制定者深省，应当具有很好的警示作用。

21. 失灵的房地产市场

掏钱买地吧，因为不会再造更多土地了。马克·吐温曾这样建议道。事实上，土地并非真的稀缺：全美国的全国人口迁入得克萨斯州也绰绰有余；每家可坐享一英亩以上的土地。推动土地价格一路飙升的是激增的需求与有限的供给之间的矛盾，主要发生在像伦敦、孟买、纽约之类的大都市。在过去十年间，香港地产的价格已飙升了150%。伦敦中心的梅费尔区的住宅房产可高达每平方米高达55 000英镑（82 000美元）；曼哈顿的住宅房产一平方英里值165亿美元。

即便是在上述这些大城市，土地的稀缺也是人为造成的。对建筑物的高度和密集程度的规控限制了供应，助推了房价。伦敦经济学院的学者们最近在一次分析当中预估，伦敦西区对土地使用的条例导致了写字楼价格上涨了800%；在米兰和巴黎，这类法规推动土地价格上涨了约300%。大部分巨额资产之所以被土地所有者所掌控，是因为想要新建办公楼、通过竞争来挤掉暴利几乎已不可能。

这种失灵的房地产市场付出的代价很大，主要是因为它对个体住户的影响甚大。高昂的房价迫使务工者搬到一些房价较便宜但生产力较低的居住地。据一项研究结果显示，要不是因为对建筑业的严格限制，旧金山湾区的就业率应该是现在的五倍；再加上收入损失和尚未挖掘的人才潜力损失，这一数据使人震惊。如果能扫清美国境内所有限制城市增长的阻碍因素，那么国家GDP将会增加6.5%~13.5%，即约1万亿~2万亿。很难想象要是去掉其他众多的类似影响的政策，会产生多大的影响。

两个长期运转的趋势导致了这样一种断裂的市场。一个是城市这个全球经济增长这台机器的中心齿轮的复苏。在20世纪，交通成本大幅下降，削弱了城市的吸引力；到了21世纪，数字革命使城市重新恢复了吸引力。科技和金融业之类知识密集型产业繁荣兴旺，靠的是人才聚集、集思广益、技术分享。其结果是诸如伦敦、纽约、旧金山此类的大都市经济和人口都出现了反弹。

从历史上看以前这些大城市具有自己的扩展能力，可以接纳想来就来的人，但现在这种能力尚未得到恢复。这有其充分的理由：19世纪末无节制的城市增长滋生了犯罪和疾病。因而产生了第二种趋势：绿化带和城市分区法规激增。在20世纪整整一百年，土地使用的规章制度堆积如山，要想得到一张建设许可证困难重重，其难度不亚于雨后的下午叫出租车。

22. 人如其食 / 以食见人

东方人与西方人思维方式不一样，这一说法可不只是什么偏见。过去的二十年里，许多心理学研究都显示，在精神生活方面西方人比东亚人更具个性、更注重分析和抽象思维。为了解释这一现象，研究者们提出了以下几种假说。

其一是认为现代化发展促进了个人主义的发展，但这一假说在第一道坎就受挫：日本是一个超现代化国家，但其国民保持了集体主义的观念。其二是认为如果一个地方传染病越肆虐，那么与陌生人交流的风险就越大，因而造成当地族群变得内向。这一说法比第一种也强不了多少。欧洲曾遭受的瘟疫之虞，大概比日本或韩国都多。尽管中国南方是臭名昭著的传染病之源（流感大流行常常源于此），但对于这个泱泱大国的其他地区来说，这种说法却站不住脚。

这就引起了弗吉尼亚大学的托马斯·托尔赫姆和他的同事们把目光转向第三个假说：差异的关键在于农业。西方的主食是面食，而东方是大米。在农业机械化之前，种水稻的农民必须比种小麦的多花一倍的劳作时间。为了有效地安排劳动力，尤其在插秧和收割时节，相距甚远的各国水稻种植群体（譬如印度、马来西亚和日本）都逐渐形成了各种劳动合作交换机制，这就使邻里可以错开彼此的务农日程，在农忙的关键时期展开互助。因为在近代以前，全世界几乎人人都是农民，所以认为这种集体观会支配一个社会的文化和行为的这一假说是有一定的道理的。而且有证据表明，这种观念可能是如此根深蒂固，以至于直到今天，尽管大部分人不以农业谋生，但对界定他们的生活方式仍旧起着很大作用。

托尔赫姆意识到这个假说是可以测试的。中国有大片地带，尤其在北方，是以小麦而不是水稻作为主要作物。如他在《科学》杂志的论文所言，他和他的团队借此对该理论的构架进行充实。

该团队从中国各地集中了近1 200名志愿者，向他们提问并评估他们的个人主义或集体主义程度。志愿者的答案与他们来源地的富裕程度几乎没什么关联，而托尔赫姆把该因素看作地区现代化程度或公共医疗水平的代表。然而，答案却与来源地种植水稻或小麦的问题表现出显著的相关性。这种差异甚至在有着不同农业传统的邻县之间也有体现。他的假说认为，东西方的心理学差异至少部分可归因于农业差异，因此值得进一步探索。而这样的探索是可行的——因为印度同时既有水稻地区，也有小麦地区。

23. 两类发明家

在19世纪，发明家是英雄。像史蒂芬生、莫尔斯和古德伊尔之类的发明家是工业革命的天降神兵。他们的想法帮助人类从农耕的贫困跨越到制造业的富足。虽然当今世界发明家并不缺乏，但是发明巨星却越来越少，相距的时间间隔越来越大。

这在一定程度上可能是因为自从19世纪以来发明过程自身的改变。每年发布的专利数量的增长并没有减少，但是引入的根本性全新技术似乎比过去减少了。诚然，信息技术确实改变了当今社会，但是铁路、电报、摄影、固定电话、汽车以及化工、钢铁业等，每一项技术都分别带来了毫不亚于信息技术迄今为止所带来的那么大的变革。也许维多利亚时代的发明过程真的比其他时代都更壮烈。

但是，光有某些状况改变了的印象，并不能证明它真的就改变了。对此我们需要数据。牛津大学的云·叶金和她的同事发表于《英国皇家学会期刊·界面》的论文中就提供了一些相关数据资料。

发明大致可通过两种方式产生。比如，托马斯·爱迪生发明电灯泡，与其说是发现了一种灯泡的隐喻契机，不如说是把早已存在的各个部件聚合到一起——一个电源、一节加热灯丝、一个真空管以及一个玻璃外壳。这些部件在19世纪70年代都不是什么新玩意儿，但是在爱迪生的手里，这些组合变成了一个可申请专利的发明。与此相反，威廉·肖克利70年之后发明的晶体管涉及许多新的物理现象，需要肖克利和他的同事亲自动手解决。上述两大发明都改变了世界（尽管公认肖克利的晶体管是后来创建的IT的基石）。它们一道例证了两种不同程度地存在于任何成功的发明中的创新点：发现和重组。

迄今为止大多数发明都是基于物理或化学。而今天我们对生物学的理解大致还停留在19世纪的物理学水平。因此，生物学已成熟到可以产生一系列新的专利分类的时候了——也可能产生一些新东西（譬如神经计算机科学？由种子长成的家具？）这些东西就像当年电话会在滑铁卢战役投入使用那样令现代人无法想象。那么，此时可能会出现新一代发明家的壮举。

24. 网络时代的皮肉生意

站街女、路边驱车求欢者、张贴着丰乳肥臀广告的公用电话亭——这就是卖淫这一下流行当中的常见字眼。长久以来，各国政府之所以想将其视为非法行为，或是将其限制在有营业执照的妓院或是"容忍范围"内进行，这就是其中的一个原因。在这一问题上，邻避主义与清教徒和社会改良者同心协力。在清教徒看来，卖淫女是上帝的罪人；而社会改良者认为她们是受害者。但是，实际情况千差万别，不可一概而论。有的卖淫者的确是非法贩卖、压榨剥削或是暴力行为的受害者；施虐者应该为他们的罪行被关进监狱。但是，对于众多的卖淫者来说，不管是男性还是女性，性工作也是工作。

本报从未觉得"卖淫者都是受害者"这一说法言之有理，而且这种说法正随着网络性交易的增多，越来越难以站住脚。个人网站的出现意味着性工作者可以推销自己并创立自己的品牌。点评网站给商业性交易带来的是值得信赖的客户反馈，这在以前是没有的。这种转变使得该行业越来越像是一种常规的服务产业。

这一行业可以像一个普通的行业那样接受分析。根据我们对一个大型国际网站有关其19万名女性卖淫者在价格、服务和特色等方面的分类数据显示，男人确实更喜欢金发女，这使得她们的收费比红发女高出11%。被时尚杂志所热衷的骨感女比胖妞更有市场，但骨感女不如健美女郎。卖淫者的日常行为与其他劳动力市场中自由职业者并无二致。她们安排行程，并接受网络预订，如同临时客串的音乐人一样。她们在提供何种服务以及是否提供专业化服务方面是有选择的。有的是临时的，有的是兼职的，有的还得调整工作时间以便照看孩子。另外，这个行业甚至也像广泛的经济领域的其他行业一样，大学毕业生要加价。

卫道士会对卖淫业的网络化趋势痛心疾首，因为这会让性交易更加火爆。买春的和卖春的会发现，见面和交易更方便了。新的供给方会加入到这个正在变得更加安全少了些俗气的行业。新客户会自己想办法找到妓女，因为他们可以更容易找到他们想要的服务并确认这些服务的质量。皮条客和老鸨也应发抖。因为互联网会削弱他们的造市权。

但是，除此之外，别的所有的人都应该欢呼。对于第三方来说，如果性交易是在网上安排好，然后在公寓或者旅店房间中进行的话，不像在妓院或者红灯区内进行那么令人讨厌。更重要的是，网络会让卖淫变得更安全，这是以往的任何法律都做不到的。如果卖淫者另有办法进入市场，皮条客就不大有可能那么暴虐了。专业性网站会让买卖双方更精确地评估风险。正在大量涌现的各种应用程序和网站会让买卖双方确认对方的身份，交换得到认可的性健康体检结果。诸如英国的"丑陋的面孔"之类网站的方案会允许卖淫者与客户在网上交流双方都想避免的各种细节。

25. 还原一个真实的简·奥斯汀

"她的一生虽裨益他人，与文学和宗教为伴，却并无任何大起大落，"对终身未婚的妹妹，亨利·奥斯汀这样评价道。简的这种隐居作家形象持续了多年。然而当代的学者重新评价了他们"亲爱的奥斯汀姑姑"，把她视为笔锋辛辣、深谙尘世智慧的独立女性。《傲慢与偏见》问世两百年后，她依然令人着迷——这就是英国作家宝拉·伯恩新近为奥斯汀所著传记之魅力。作者从简·奥斯汀所处年代的流行物品入手，为简·奥斯汀的生平及其作品注入了新的活力。

传记的每一章都围绕着一件物品展开。有些是奥斯汀的私人收藏，例如她从哥哥那儿得到的一个黄宝石十字架。而另一些物品则是那个时代的代表物，如四轮四座大马车（一种高档马车），足以展现她游历之广，以及交通工具在其作品中代表的身份地位。在《诺桑觉寺》中，凯瑟琳·莫兰觉得坐亨利·蒂尔尼的双马双轮马车旅行很是新奇撩人，而面对约翰·索普的轻便双轮马车时却不知所措（感到为难/陷于窘境）。作者用这种大刀阔斧按时序展开的主题式记传方式，为我们揭示出简·奥斯汀的形象，勾勒出一段鞭辟入里的社会图景。

奥斯汀写作的成型期最耐人寻味。三本羊皮纸笔记记录了她的"少女之作"——她在青少年时期写的故事与诗歌。伯恩女士很欣赏此时的奥斯汀式讥讽语调和无拘无束风格。她写道，奥斯汀"无与伦比的天赋萌发于此"。此时年轻的奥斯汀嘲讽当时鼎鼎有名的人物，戏谑感伤小说，却把连珠妙语全留在写给姐姐卡桑德拉的信件中。当姊妹俩不住在一起时，便频繁通信。奥斯汀经常试图用"嚼舌的、诙谐的、亲切的"等各种不同语气博得姐姐一笑。

这一时期，在继承了大笔遗产之后，奥斯丁的家庭几度迁居，也正是这种搬迁所造成的种种困扰促成了奥斯汀的叙述风格。在奥斯汀的笔下，老姑娘和单身母亲们往往寄居在有钱的堂亲家中，孩童可能会成为膝下无子的亲戚的继承人。一条东印度围巾引出了费拉阿姨和她女儿伊莱扎的故事——为了觅得一位丈夫，费拉阿姨21岁去了孟加拉。而伊莱扎这位浪漫人物可能是个私生女。她第一次结婚不久丈夫就在法国大革命中上了断头台后，后来又嫁给了奥斯丁的哥哥亨利。这个轻佻妖冶的表亲后来被编写成《曼斯菲尔德庄园》里玛丽·克劳福德的原型。奥斯汀还从哥哥亨利的民兵生涯中汲取素材，在《傲慢与偏见》里描绘了轻浮的英国军人形象。她那些曾有过海军经历的兄弟们则为她描写海军生活提供了相关的参考资料。

本书最精彩逼真的篇章是描述城市生活和浪漫轶事。奥斯汀频繁地出访伦敦，并旅居巴思多年。从仅存的一张得到认证的照片可看出，她可能并非美貌动人，但她的聪明才智吸引了众多的追求者。尽管最终无一人与简白头偕老，但在简的书信中，他们给她留下的回忆大都充满欢声笑语。

26. 度量史话：日益精确的"公尺"

一个好的计量单位必须满足三个条件：便于直接测量、与所测对象比例匹配（如用英寸来描述地理距离就没有意义）、稳定。克利斯先生现为长岛纽约州立大学石溪分校的哲学教授、《物理学世界》的专栏作家，在《悬而未决的世界》这本新书中，他描述了人类对于计量"圣杯"的不懈探求。他的笔下所展现的计量学史话显然不是引人入胜的阅读素材，但有对其感兴趣的读者会爱不释手。

人们所熟知的最早的计量单位很好地满足了克利斯先生所提出的前两个要求。这些计量单位大多数来源于触手可及的东西，如：人体（比如，"英尺"源于英语的"脚"；英里，源于拉丁语 milia passuum，即 1 000 步）和工具（比如桶、杯）。其他一些计量单位则较为抽象。中世纪法国使用的 journal（源于法语 jour，即"白天"的意思）是一个计量面积的单位，相当于一个人用一头牛在一天所耕地的面积，就像英国使用的"英亩"，或者德国北部以及荷兰这一地区使用的"摩根"（morgen）一样。

但是没有任何两只脚、两个桶或两个工作日是完全相同的。我们需要的是"一只抽象的脚，既不是你的，也不是我的"。17 世纪末，人们对严格的度量标准的呼声越来越高，这种标准既不受各种社会波动的影响，也不受制于封建领主的一时心血来潮。这是国际贸易以及现代科学的兴起的结果——两者都需要提出更加精确的度量标准。

为此，我们迎来了来源于希腊语 metron（意为"测量"）的 metre（米）——引入这一长度单位的是法国的革命者，因为他们急于用全新的通用的单位来取代波旁王朝的 toise（突阿斯，稍小于 2 米的一个长度单位）。他们把公尺的长度规定为经巴黎的子午线长度的一定比例，而当时对这条子午线长度的精确测定（以"突阿斯"为计量单位）尚未结束。与此同时产生的还有千克（公斤）这个单位，它最初是指的一公升蒸馏水的质量，正是这个单位奠定了公制的基础。

法国计量外交的成功意味着在接下来的几十年中，公制逐渐取代了各地混乱不堪的计量体系（少数几国除外）。即使此前一直坚持使用其皇家单位体系（英制）的英国，最后也只好认输，改用公制。1875 年，英国《自然》杂志将公制誉为"现代文明最伟大的胜利之一"。

尽管公制体系取得了外交上的成功，但"公尺"本身却未能兑现它最初的承诺。因为将其与子午线或其他的自然基准挪定并非易事。因此，直到 1960 年之前，"公尺"这个单位的度量都一直明确地参照一块独一无二的铂铱块来确定。此后它才被改造成更为稳定的模式，即某种特定类型光的波长的倍数。最终在 1983 年，它被绑定到光速这个物理常量，即一公尺等于光在 1/299 792 458 秒所通过的距离。

27. 毛发的魔力

金发女郎有些傻气，而深褐色头发的女人比较可靠。据说还确有这么一说。但长期以来，让人敬畏不禁、爱恨交加的却是红发女郎。因此有传言说，给红发妞做麻醉都得多上点麻药。

人们迷恋头发的历史几乎和人类自身一样悠久。不过，至少两万五千年以来，人类就一直不断在修剪、打理自己的头发，主要是为了取悦自己、疏远别人或是让自己显得与众不同。最早的一件刻画发型的作品是1894年在法国西南部出土的旧石器时代小雕像，被称为"布拉瑟普的维纳斯"。

上了年纪和化学疗法仅仅是人类脱发的两个原因。尽管脱发通常很痛苦（至少私下如此），但这是一个渐进的过程，而且如果因化疗而脱发，头发还是可以再长出来的。也有一些出于自愿、干脆利落剃掉自己头发的例子——包括20世纪80年代的朋克摇滚歌手以及在头上剃出反"卍"字记号的新纳粹暴徒。无论出于自愿还是被迫，都会让观众会想到突然的脱发久而久之究竟意味着什么。

今天，有些父母会把婴儿的初生髦发（胎毛）保留下来作为纪念收藏；而在19世纪，时髦的做法是把辞世的至亲的头发嵌进盒式吊坠、手镯，甚至嵌进戒指里。巴黎凯布朗利博物馆新展品中最感人的一件是粘在一块心状珍珠母上的一小髦金发。这是从国王路易十六的继承人路易-夏尔头上剪下来的。路易-夏尔生于法国大革命前夕，后来父母被送上了断头台，而他被送给一名鞋匠抚养，鞋匠的任务就是让他忘记自己的皇室出身。两年后，路易-夏尔死于圣殿塔监狱。

而在其他一些文明中，头发的魔力在于它作为战利品的重要性——认为头发中注满罹难者（死者）的力量或魔力。从秘鲁到加蓬，从印度到中国，数百年来人们一直在用头发制作外衣、头冠和头饰。在奉行政治立场正确的这些时代，我们很容易忘记一点：类似的做法在欧美也同样司空见惯。

凯布朗利博物馆可能只有六年的历史，但它的展览方式却有些守旧，回到了过去那种较为大胆的时代：以展出人类的头皮和亚马孙部落的干骷髅头为荣。通过展出这些物品，将它们置于某一历史背景下，这一展览让观众增长知识、开阔眼界，令人难以忘怀。

28.《寂静的春天》点燃了环保运动

"在人类历史上，每当一部作品偶尔问世，就会使历史进程大为改观，"阿拉斯加民主党参议员欧内斯特·格鲁恩对卡森曾这样说道。

《寂静的春天》问世于50年前的这个月。虽然卡森的初衷并不是出于这方面的考虑，但她对环保运动的影响之大，超过了自19世纪亨利·大卫·梭罗以来的任何人。梭罗是一位最负盛名的隐士，写过《瓦尔登湖》一书。《寂静的春天》提出了合成农药，尤其是滴滴涕有害这样一种自然观。卡森认为，这类农药一旦进入生物圈，不仅会杀死虫子，而且其作用还会不断拓展到食物链，直接威胁鸟类和鱼类群体，最终可能会导致儿童患病。

卡森获得的大量数据和案例研究并不是什么新玩意儿，因为相当长一段时间以来，科学界就知道这些研究结果。但卡森是将各种数据整合一起展示给公众的第一人，并做出了旗帜鲜明、意义深远的结论。通过这种做法，卡森这位平民科学家催生了一场革命。

《寂静的春天》一书迄今已售出 200 余万册，书中对"如果人类为害自然，自然势必会祸害人类"这一概念提出了强有力的例证。"我们无视自然、破坏环境的行为恶果已渗入地球的大循环体系，迟早会给人类自身带来危险，"卡森告诉小组委员会说。通过卡森的目光我们依然可以看到肆无忌惮的人为干预的严重后果：卡森向民众普及了现代生态知识。

要说现在情况有什么不同的话，那么自从卡森提出环保问题以来，环境问题已经变得更为严重，时间更为紧迫。然而，没有任何作品能产生《寂静的春天》那么大的影响。这并不是因为我们缺少雄辩口才、缺乏充满激情的环保主义者的能力，难以在气候变化等问题上达成广泛的共识，而是没有一个能够激励一个国家要求的具体变化的方式，就像卡森所做的那样。

是什么因素使得卡森能够抓住公众的想象力，开拓出美国的环保意识？答案在于被称为"大自然修女"的瑞巧·森特。森特这一名字经常出现在一个个环保事业的活动中，但其生平和事迹却鲜为人知。

29. 科技奖项种种

每年的 12 月 10 日，诺贝尔奖各学科奖项在斯德哥尔摩颁出。其颁奖晚会真可谓盛况空前：市政音乐厅举行的颁奖典礼本身就十分庄重，清一色西装白领，加之管弦乐队助阵、电视实况直播，就更显热闹非凡。颁奖结束，约 1 300 位有幸与会的杰出人士移师宴会厅共进晚宴，其场景也实况播出（一位时装专家甚至还会对赴宴女嘉宾的着装进行连续不断的评论）。最后，斯德哥尔摩大学的学生会为获奖者及宾客举办一场余兴晚会，其氛围轻松随意、喧嚣刺耳。谢天谢地，晚会的后半截实况直播会切断电源。

另一个全新的奖项叫作"伊丽莎白女王工程奖"，旨在刻意让工程领域也沾上一点光。因为长期以来工程这门学科一直担心自身被认为比更具学术性的理科略逊一筹。3 月 18 日，伦敦皇家工程学院举行了半小时的授奖仪式，评委会将本届工程奖颁予马克·安德森、蒂姆·伯纳斯-李爵士、温特·瑟夫、罗伯特·卡恩和路易斯·普赞，表彰他们五人对现代因特网的发展做出的卓越贡献。瑞典式的堂皇仪式将于 6 月 25 日举行，届时，女王会在白金汉宫宴请诸位获奖者。

尽管声誉赫赫的诺奖为嘉奖的各学科领域打造出绝佳的宣传效果，包括化学、物理、生理学或医学等领域，还没忘记经济学、文学、和平贡献之类没多少科学成分的诺贝尔奖项，但是却遗漏掉其他许多大片领域。其结果是其他领域的类似奖项激增，其中很多奖项毫不掩饰其模仿各项诺奖的意图。

比如，计算机科研人员渴望获得的奖项是"图灵奖"。3 月 13 日揭晓的 2012 年图灵奖授给了麻省理工学院的沙菲·戈德瓦塞尔和西尔维奥·米卡里。数学界有"菲尔兹奖"，每四年一次授予 40 岁以下的青年才俊。数学界还有奖金更高的"阿贝尔奖"（本届奖项于 3 月 20 日授予普林斯顿高级研究所的皮埃尔·德利涅）。另外还有一些更为宽泛的奖项。比如，日本设有"朝日奖"和"京都奖"，奖励任何科学领域中的杰出贡献人员，包括文科类奖项。

眼下颁发的几个最新奖项出自俄罗斯富豪尤里·米尔纳的捐赠。这位亿万富翁试图超越诺奖，为每位获奖者奖励 300 万美元——这一数额几乎是诺奖基金会给出的三倍。米尔纳基金会设立的基础物理学奖迄今为止已授予 9 人。在本期《经济学人》付梓时，该奖正在日内瓦举行授奖仪式。与之类似的是"生命科学突破奖"，该奖由米尔纳先生、Google 联合创始人谢尔盖·布林及其夫人、基因测试公司 23andMe 的创始人安妮，以及 Facebook 创始人马克·扎克伯格共同出资，于今年二月授予 11 人，付给每位获奖者 300 万美元奖金。

30. 脱欧的悲剧

从难以想象到覆水难收，这一切的发展是多么的迅速。一年前几乎没有人能想到，众多喜欢抱怨欧盟的英国人（他们讨厌其规章制度愚蠢、预算庞大、充斥浮华官僚主义等种种问题），竟然真的会投票退出这个购买了他们将近一半出口的国家俱乐部。然而，到了 6 月 24 日凌晨，选民们显然不顾经济学家、盟友和本国政府的警告，作为欧盟成员 40 多年之后，他们即将大胆迈入未卜前程。

英镑汇率跌至 30 年来的新低，道出了来日的滋味。随着信心暴跌，英国很可能会进一步陷入经济衰退。经济长期缺乏活力意味着就业机会减少、国家税收缩水，并最终导致经济进一步紧缩。这一后果也将动摇脆弱的世界经济。多数投票支持留欧的苏格兰人现在可能也更热衷于从英国独立出去，就像他们在 2014 年差一点就成功了那样。海峡对岸，法国国民阵线等疑欧派将把英国人的愤然退出视作一种激励。而欧盟这个帮助维持欧洲和睦长达半世纪之久的机构，则遭受了沉重打击。

要应对国家从年龄、阶层到地域划分的各类人群之间产生的裂痕，短期内的善后工作需要灵活的政治手腕；但是长期来看，可能需要重新划分传统政治斗争界线，甚至重划英伦四区的边境线。这将会带来一段长期有害的不确定局面。没人知道英国会何时或以何种条件离开欧盟。尽管退欧支持者们一片欢腾，留欧支持者们相互指责，但是有仍两个问题凸显出来：对英国和欧洲来说退欧意味着什么？接下来又会发生什么情况？

投票"离开欧盟"实际上是一次对"权势集团"愤怒的宣泄。每一个人——从贝拉克·奥巴马到北约和国际货币基金组织领导人都曾敦促英国人拥抱欧盟。他们的恳求被选民们断然拒绝，不仅是因为选民们拒绝接受他们的主张，还因为通常意义上的"专家"的价值不被选民承认。受到公共开支削减影响最多并且未能享受英国繁荣果实的大量英国选民，现在已陷于愤怒的民粹主义而不能自拔。

英国公民们提出了许多拒绝欧盟的理由，从布鲁塞尔的民主赤字到欧元区经济体的疲软。不过导致英国留欧失败的关键原因看起来是欧盟内部的人口自由流动。随着流入人口的增长，移民问题已经引起了选民们的担忧。

因此，脱欧的一方向其支持者承诺，既保持经济繁荣又控制移民。但英国人不可能仅仅通过投票就实现这样的结果。如果他们想进入欧盟的单一市场并享受它带来的财富，他们就必须接受人口自由流动。如果英国拒绝人口自由流动，那么它就将付出被欧盟单一市场排除在外的代价。英国必须在限制移民和最大化财富这两者之中择其一。

II. 汉译英

1. The Function of Translation

Translation has always played an indispensable role in the long history of human development. It serves as the forerunner in communication, amalgamation, and collision of multiple cultures, as well as in the course of the national rejuvenation of the Chinese people. All international activities and communications of languages and cultures could not be performed without translation. If there were not translation someday, the United Nations would not be able to operate any longer, nor could WTO function well, and all the international organizations would be at a standstill. Translators and their efforts are just like that of the current in the electrical wires or the stream in the pipelines: They quietly bring one language and culture into another, clearing up misunderstanding.

2. Translation and Practice

Translation is a branch of learning that entails a great deal of practice and the mastery of translation needs prolonged practice and painstaking effort. One's translation ability cannot be developed from theoretical knowledge and intensified skills alone. It needs a good grounding in bilingual knowledge and plenty of translation practice. To some extent, one's translation ability is not obtained from the classroom, nor is it derived from translation skills. Rather, it is acquired only after one's down-to-earth practice. This textbook is compiled based on the above consideration, with a view to train and enhance the translation abilities on the part of the reader.

3. An Excerpt from the *Selected Works of Mao Zedong*

China is one of the largest countries in the world, her territory being about the size of the whole of Europe. In the vast country of ours there are large areas of fertile land which provide us with food and clothing; mountain ranges across its length and breadth with extensive forests and rich mineral deposits; many rivers and lakes which provide us with water transport and irrigation, and a long coastline which facilitates communication with nations beyond the seas. From ancient times our forefathers have laboured, lived and multiplied on this vast territory.

4. An Excerpt from the *Selected Works of Deng Xiaoping*

In carrying out our modernization programme we must proceed from Chinese realities. Both in revolution and construction, we should also learn from foreign countries and draw on their experience. But the mechanical copying and application of foreign experience and models will get us nowhere. We have had many lessons in this respect. We must integrate the universal truth of Marxism with the concrete realities of China, blaze a path of our own and build a socialism with Chinese characteristics—that is the basic conclusion we have reached after summing up long historical experience.

5. Beijing

Beijing, the capital of the People's Republic of China, is the political, cultural, scientific and educational center of the country, and the center of transportation and international exchange as well.

Great changes have taken place since the reform and opening-up in 1978 and the capital has developed quickly. Modern buildings spring up in Beijing like mushrooms. The successful Summer Olympic Games in 2008 has brought Beijing an unprecedented opportunity. And Beijing Spirit, i.e. Patriotism, Innovation, Inclusiveness and Virtue, will definitely promote further development of Beijing and promote friendly communication between Chinese people and people all over the world.

Beijing has a strong potential in science and technology. It boasts a number of world famous scientific research organizations and institutions of higher learning such as the Chinese Academy of Sciences, Peking University and Tsinghua University, etc. At the same time, Beijing is making efforts to develop hi-tech industries. Its Zhongguancun district, where a galaxy of talents are gathered, is reputed (as) China's Silicon Valley.

6. The Yangtze River

The Yangtze River originates from the Qinghai-Tibet Plateau. With a length of more than 6,300 km, it is the longest river in China and the third longest river in the world.

The upper reaches of the Yangtze feature big vertical drops, with torrents and many gorges flanked by towering mountains. It gets to the plain area in the middle reaches of the river. Here the river broadens and the flow slows down. This part is characterized with many crooked streams, branches and lakes. Known as the famous land of fish and rice, the lower reaches of the Yangtze River are low and flat, and the water is broad and deep. At the spot where the Yangtze enters the sea, the river is 80 to 90 km wide, and the water and sky blend into a mixture, presenting a grand view of extraordinary splendour. Most freshwater lakes of China are scattered along the middle and lower reaches of the Yangtze.

The drainage area of the Yangtze River is rich in products and the economy is well developed. Many metropolises like Shanghai, Nanjing, Wuhan and Chongqing are distributed along the river.

7. The Yellow River

Originating from Qinghai Province, the Yellow River, the second longest river in China, is over 5,400 km. Seen from the map, the Yellow River lies in the shape of huge Chinese character "几".

Along the upper reaches of the river there are many gorges with abundant water resources, and large-scale hydroelectric power stations have been built there.

The middle reaches flow through the Loess Plateau, where there is a serious problem of soil erosion. This part of the river contains large amounts of sand. The water there is turbid and assumes yellow colour, hence the name "the Yellow River".

The Yellow River flows through the North China Plain in its lower reaches, where the river broadens, the flow slows down, and the mud and sand accumulate to form a "suspending river", with the riverbed higher than the surrounding land.

8. The Han Dynasty

The Han Dynasty was one of the most important dynasties in Chinese history that made remarkable achievements during its reign. It was the first to open its doors to other cultures. Foreign trade flourished during this period. The Silk Road initiated by Han Dynasty led all the way to the West Asia and even to Rome. Various forms of art prospered, with the emergence of a lot of literature, history and philosophy masterpieces. 100 A.D. witnessed the completion of the first Chinese dictionary which included 9,000 characters, providing interpretations and illustrations of various ways of writing styles. Meanwhile, great progress was made in science and technology. Paper, water clocks, sundials and earthquake detectors were invented. The reign has lasted for 400 years. However, the corruption of the rulers eventually led to its downfall.

9. The Great Wall

One of the seven wonders in the world, the Great Wall is the largest piece of military defensive engineering in the world which took the longest time to be built, repaired and extended. The Great Wall stands for the crystallization of the blood, sweat and wisdom of Chinese people and also a sign of their persistence and diligence. It is known for its incomparable grandeur, attracting tourists from all over the world. UNESCO lists it as one of the world cultural heritage sites.

The Great Wall is a remarkable military defensive architecture in ancient China. Its genesis dates back to 700 B.C. to 500 B.C. It was in the Qin Dynasty that the Great Wall really began to take shape. Since then, a number of dynasties such as Han, South and North, Sui, Tang, Liao, Jin, Ming and Qing, successively contributed to the construction of the Great Wall.

10. The Mid-Autumn Festival

Since ancient times, it has been a custom for the Chinese people to celebrate the mid-autumn harvest season, similar to that of celebrating Thanksgiving in North America. The custom of observing Mid-Autumn Festival came into vogue around the early Tang Dynasty all over China. It is on the fifteenth day of the eighth lunar month—a festival for the people to worship the moon. On the very night when a bright moon hangs high in the sky, family members would get together, enjoying the silvery full moon. In 2006, the Mid-Autumn Festival was listed as China's cultural heritage. In 2008 it was designated as a public holiday. The mid-autumn moon cake is regarded in China as an indispensable delicacy that is commonly presented as a gift among friends, or shared at family gatherings. Traditional moon cakes are usually decorated with such Chinese characters as *Shou* (longevity), *Fu* (blessing), *He* (harmony), etc.

11. The Silk Road

The world-renowned Silk Road is a series of routes connecting the East and the West. Named after ancient China's silk trade, it extended more than 6,000 kilometers and played an important role in developing civilizations in China, South Asia, Europe and the Middle East. It was through the Silk Road that the four great inventions of ancient China, i.e. papermaking, gunpowder, compass and printing were introduced to other countries in the world. Similarly, Chinese silk, tea and porcelain spread all over the world via the Silk Road. As the result of a two-way exchange of material culture, Europe also exported various goods and plants through the Silk Road to meet the needs of the Chinese market.

12. Telling the World a Real "Chinese Story"

"China is a sleeping and when China wakes up, she will shake the world," Napoleon said.

"In fact, the lion of China has awoken," says Xi Jinping.

Super China, a seven-episode documentary which was made by Korean Broadcasting System (KBS), started with these two remarks. After it's broadcasted, the documentary evokes a strong response and sets off an upsurge of learning about China. Meanwhile, the documentary is spread widely and causes heated discussion among more and more Chinese people on the Internet. Many of the Western mainstream media, such as *New York Times*, CNN and BBC subsequently covered this news.

However, what is unknown by many people is that this documentary has a special relation with Tsinghua University: Jinbum Park, one of the three chief directors, was a student of the program, Global Business Journalism (GBJ), and graduated from School of Journalism and Communication in Tsinghua in 2010.

"Two years' experience of studying in GBJ program in Tsinghua enables me to know more about China's current situation and future. Afterwards, I returned to South Korea and participated in the production of *Super China*, hoping that it will bring South Koreans a real China which is different from their impression of the country," Jinbum Park said.

13. Hua Luogeng

Lame with typhoid in his early childhood, Hua Luogeng led an adolescent life full of frustrations. Upon graduation from a junior middle school, he discontinued his studying and worked as an accountant at Jintan Middle School. In 1930, Hua Luogeng got a thesis published in *Science*, which was accidentally noticed by Professor Xiong Qinglai, director of the Department of Arithmetic of Tsinghua University. Professor Xiong arranged for him to work as a part-time assistant librarian in his department. In a matter of one and a half year Hua completed all required courses of his department; at the same time he got a good command of English, French, and German through self-studying. Hua's daily schedule was divided between work and study, with little time for rest. So in a short period of time he had three papers published in journals abroad. Hua Luogeng once said to his friends: "I have less school education than others, so I have to double my efforts to make up my lost time. While others work 8 hours a day, I must spend more than 12 hours. Only in this way can I feel at ease."

In 1933, Hua Luogeng was promoted assistant, teaching Calculus, which broke the conventional promotion regulations in Tsinghua. In 1936, he was recommended by Tsinghua University to study as a visiting scholar in Cambridge University, U.K. He came back to China in 1938 and was engaged as a professor of Southwest Associated University, getting an exceptional promotion again.

APPENDIX C Keys to Translation Exercises for Independent Work

14. Jiang Nanxiang

A famous educator, Jiang Nanxiang (1913-1988) was born in Yixing, Jiangsu Province. He was appointed president of Tsinghua University in 1952, and is considered as one of the most successful presidents in the university history. He made an overall plan of founding a number of departments and disciplines of burgeoning science and technology in Tsinghua, such as Department of Engineering Physics, Department of Engineering Chemistry, Department of Engineering Mechanics Mathematics, Department of Automatic Control, Department of Precision Instruments, etc. He also put forward the concept of building the university into "three-in-one" base, i.e. the combination of teaching, research and production, pushing forward the development of the university by relying on "two driving wheels", i.e. university faculty and the staff. His efforts were of great significance to the development of Tsinghua University and the construction of the new science and technology in China. As an educator, Jiang used to put much stress on the education guideline of developing in an all-round way—morally, intellectually and physically. He exhorted Tsinghua students to build up a good physique, and "strive/endeavor to serve the motherland in good shape for at least 50 years". The major parts of his writings are included in *Collected Works of Jiang Nanxiang*.

16. The Second Gate

The Second Gate, built in 1909, is the original school gate of Tsinghua University. In 1933, the west residential area was expanded and the campus got enlarged. At the same time a new school gate was built (now called the West School Gate). Since then, the original gate is conventionally called "the Second Gate". When studying in Tsinghua University, Mr. Liang Shiqiu described the old school gate as follows:

"The school gate of Tsinghua University, coated with white paint, is made of gray bricks. It is shrouded in plain white, reflecting against two leaves of black barrier which are invariably standing ajar..."

On the plaque of the arch of the gate there is a piece of marble, engraved in which are three big eyecatching Chinese characters "Qing Hua Yuan", inscribed by Na Tong, a high official of the late Qing Dynasty. The gate was demolished in the initial stage of the Cultural Revolution and was not reconstructed until 1991.

17. Gongzi Ting (H-shaped Courtyard)

Gongzi Ting (H-shaped Courtyard), originally called Gongzi Dian (H-shaped Palace), is the main structure of ancient Tsinghua Garden. It is so-called because the whole structure, with the front palace and the rear palace connected by a short corridor, assumes the form of the Chinese character "工" when viewed from above. Now it refers to the whole ancient-styled courtyard, with Gongzi Dian as its main building. On the gate there is a plaque with an inscription "Qing Hua Yuan" by the Emperor Xianfeng. Gongzi Ting contains more than 100 rooms, covering a total floor space of about 2,570 square meters. Inside the courtyard there are zigzag corridors interlocked into separate small yards. It was originally built to entertain the royal family. After the establishment of Tsinghua School, it was turned into a cultural and entertainment center and an important location for social activities. Famous Indian poet Tagore stayed for a time in the rear hall of the yard during his visit to China in 1924. The whole courtyard has been the locus of the administrative offices of Tsinghua University ever since its foundation.

17. Lotus Pond

A path paved with coaldust zigzags along the lotus pond, so secluded as to be little frequented in the daytime, to say nothing of its loneliness at night. Around the pond grows profusion of luxuriant trees. On one side of the path are some willows and other trees whose names are unknown to me. On moonless nights, the place has a gloomy, somewhat forbidding appearance. But on this particular evening, it had a cheerful outlook, though the moon was still pale.

On the uneven surface of the pond, all one could see was a mass of leaves, all interlaced and shooting high above the water like the skirts of slim dancing girls. The leaves were dotted in between the layers with white flowers, some blooming gracefully; others, as if bashfully, still in bud. They were like bright pearls and stars in an azure sky. Their subtle fragrance was wafted by the passing breeze, in whiffs airy as the notes of a song coming faintly from some distant tower. There was a tremor on leaf and flower, which, with the suddenness of lightning, soon drifted to the far end of the pond.

18. Scenic Hangzhou

Hangzhou, an ancient renowned city for its picturesque scenery, is situated in northern part of Zhejiang Province, along the northern bank of Qiantang River and at the southern terminus of the Grand Canal. After winding through high mountain ridges of the western part of Zhejiang, Qiantang River becomes wider with majestic scenery. Especially round the Moon Festival every year, one can enjoy the raging tidal billows, which are a most spectacular natural phenomenon.

Lying in the west part of the city, the charming West Lake covers a total area of 5.6 square km. Divided by Su causeway and Bai causeway, the whole lake falls into five

APPENDIX C Keys to Translation Exercises for Independent Work

sections: Outer Lake, Inner Lake, Yue Lake, West Inner Lake and Minor South Lake. With glistening water and luxuriant trees and bamboo groves along its bank, the West Lake has attractive landscape all the year round. Su Dongpo, a celebrated poet of the Northern Song Dynasty (960-1127A.D.), once in a poem compared the Lake to an ancient Chinese beauty named Xizi. Hence comes the name—Xizi Lake. Since then the West Lake has enjoyed a high reputation in the whole country.

19. Yu Yuan Garden

Yu Yuan Garden, located in the southern part of Shanghai, is a famous classical garden. The original owner of the garden, surnamed Pan, was once the governor of Sichuan Province during the Ming Dynasty. Construction of the garden started in 1558 but went on and off for lack of money. It did not come to completion till twenty years later. When the Pans went into a decline, their descendants were eager to sell the garden, so some businessmen bought it at a low price. Later it was incorporated into the City God Temple to become its "West Garden". During the Opium War and the Taiping Revolution, foreign aggressors stationed their troops in the garden once and again. As a result, the garden experienced repeated devastation and lost much of its original grandeur. Thanks to the people's government, Yu Yuan Garden has gone through many renovations since liberation, with the most recent one carried out in 1987 to restore its eastern part. The garden, placed under the special protection of the State Council since 1982, ranks one of the best gardens in the South of China.

20. Vancouver

Vancouver's prosperity is attributed to the wisdom and diligence of the people living in Vancouver, including the contribution made by multiethnic groups. Being a vast, underpopulated country with a land area larger than that of China and a population of less than 30 million, Canada has been practicing for long the state policy to accept immigrants from all over the world. We can even say that all Canadians are immigrants except the Indians and the only difference between them lies in how long they have lived in the country. Vancouver is one of the few multiethnic cities in the world. Among its 1.8 million residents, half were not born locally and there is on average one Asian out of four local people. Moreover, the 250,000 overseas Chinese there have played a decisive role in the city's economic transition. Half of these Chinese came to the city in the past five years and their arrival has made Vancouver the largest overseas Chinese community outside Asia.

21. Temple of Heaven

The bus bumped along for a while and then reached its destination—the Temple of Heaven. I got off the bus and walked through the main gates. In a moment, the crowded and stifling bus was entirely forgotten.

It was already dusk and there were few people. When I arrived at the Echo Wall the doors were already closed and I couldn't get in. I walked up to the Temple of Heaven and looked up. The vast sky set off its brilliance. A solitary crow was perching on the dome. It cawed hoarsely, flapped its wings and took off. I lowered my head and walked round the Temple of Heaven. Stopping, I stood for a while, appreciating the unusual atmosphere.

The magnificent Temple of Heaven, the soundless sky and the whirling birds all could have appeared in a scenic picture. That day I went to see the Temple of Heaven I was moved and thought of the past and future of humankind for a long, long time.

22. Time

Time is one of the greatest riddles of the ages. Everyone in the world has the same amount of it—twentyfour hours—each day. We are all alike, too, in only having today. Yes, yesterday is gone, tomorrow may never come—so every living person has today, this hour, this minute at his disposal.

We do, however, differ greatly in the ways we use this little measure of time; we differ in what we put into it and therefore of course in what we take out of it. Some idle away their chances, others use them to benefit other people or to try to move onward in life.

It is always worthwhile to pause and ponder over what you do with your own time.

23. An Episode on the Plane

A woman passenger seated next to a black man on the plane asked the stewardess to change her seat because she "would not sit beside a guy whose skin was of an ugly color". The stewardess replied that all the seats were occupied but she would go and have a look at the first class compartment. In spite of other passengers' disapproval of her behavior, the woman felt elated, for she wouldn't have to sit beside such a "repulsive" person.

A few minutes later the stewardess came back and said to the woman, "I'm sorry that there is only a vacant seat in the first class compartment. I've consulted the captain and he has agreed to make some rearrangements about the seat." The woman was delighted at it and was about to leave her seat when the stewardess turned around and said to the black man, "Would you please follow me to your new seat, sir?"

All the passengers, puzzled at the stewardess' remark, soon saw the light and burst into a warm applause.

APPENDIX C Keys to Translation Exercises for Independent Work

24. On *A Dream of Red Mansions*

The mid-18th century novel *A Dream of Red Mansions* by Cao Xueqin (approx. 1715-1763) is a monumental work in the history of Chinese literature.

Taking as its main theme the tragic love between a young aristocrat, Jia Baoyu, and his cousin, Lin Daiyu, the novel depicts the decline of a once great Manchu family. In describing in detail the social milieu of this aristocratic household the author presents a vivid panorama of everyday life and mirrors the progressive enfeeblement of feudal society in a given historical period, thus revealing the developing pattern of feudal society which is doomed to decline.

The artistic achievement of the novel, so to speak, has attained an unimaginable sublimity. It is outstanding for its rigorous and balanced structure, vivid and precise depiction of the language of each individual, and above all, the striking images of the characters that number over 400. Not only wellknown heroes and heroines such as Jia Baoyu, Lin Daiyu and other 10-odd major figures are lifelike, the array of secondary characters, even those appearing only briefly, are clearly drawn in realistic touch. The artistic achievement of the novel is so extraordinary that even among world famous literary works it is rare to find its counterpart.

25. One-Third of Our Lifetime

In the chapter "Foods and Goods" of *The Chronicles of the Han Dynasty,* the great historian Ban Gu says: "In winter people stay indoors. Women get together to spin hemp threads at night. They manage to work forty-five days a month."

It sounds strange. How come there are forty-five days in a month? Let us look at its annotations given by Yan Shigu: "They gain half a day's time every night and, therefore, they have forty-five days in a month."

Now it's clear. Our ancestors had learned, earlier than the westerners, how to calculate workdays accurately and reasonably. They had also learned how to calculate day shift and night shift as well.

It is common knowledge that there are only thirty days in a month. Counting the time of one night for half a day, our forefathers managed to extend the month by fifteen days. In this sense the night time gained amounts to one-third of our lives, doesn't it?

Why did the people in the past set such great store by the night time? I think this is proof of their positive attitude toward the onethird of their lives. This is exactly what we should learn from them.

26. Importance of Being Honest

A subordinate of Lv Yuanying, a minister in Luoyang of the Tang Dynasty often came to play chess with him. One day some urgent governmental documents arrived when they were playing chess. Lv excused himself to go to his desk to attend to them. His playmate took advantage of this and stealthily moved a piece, and as a result Lv lost the game. As a matter of fact, when he came back to the game, Lv noticed that one of the pieces on the chess board had been secretly moved during his absence, but he didn't say anything about it. The very next day Lv asked that man to seek a living at some other place. No one else, not even the man himself knew why he was dismissed. Before leaving, Lv Yuanying presented him some money as well.

Lv's reason to quit the subordinate is obvious: this man played a treacherous trick which betrayed dishonest personality. As an intangible asset to human life, honesty is an important ingredient of the ethics. Dishonest people are not likely to be upright persons, nor could they get along well with others. Therefore, it is awfully dangerous to be with such people.

27. Shi Kuang's Advice on Learning

Lord Jinping asked Shi Kuang, a blind musician for advice: "I am seventy years old and want to learn. I am afraid it is too late for me."

Shi Kuang replied: "Why not light a candle?"

Lord Jinping said: "How dare you play joke on your lord?"

Shi Kuang said: "I am a blind man and dare not tease my lord. I have heard of such a saying: one who loves to learn when young is like the rising sun; to learn in one's middle age is like the sun at noon; to learn in one's later years is as bright as a lighting candle. Which do you prefer: walking with a candle or stumbling in the darkness?"

Lord Jinping said: "Oh, I see. You are right."

28. Three Fables

A. The Spear and the Shield

Long ago there was a man who sold spears and also shields. When someone came to buy a shield he would praise his shields and say, "My shields are extremely strong. No spear can pierce through them."

If someone came to buy a spear he would also laud his spears, saying, "My spears are extremely sharp. They can pierce through anything."

Another person asked him, "If we use one of your spears to pierce one of your shields,

APPENDIX C Keys to Translation Exercises for Independent Work

what then?" The man could not answer.

B. Tiger in Tow

A tiger, on the hunt for animals to devour, caught a fox.

"You cannot be so bold as to eat me," said the fox, "I am sent by the heavenly god to rule over the animal kingdom. If you eat me you will be going against a heavenly mandate. Do you think I am lying? Let me go first and you follow behind. We'll see whether any animal is so brave as not to flee when they see me."

The tiger agreed to the plan and accordingly went with the fox. All the animals who saw them fled. The tiger, under the impression that they were afraid of the fox, was unaware that he himself was the cause of their flight.

C. The "Finishing" Touch

In the Kingdom of Chu, an aristocrat, after offering sacrifices to his ancestors, bestowed a flask of wine on the hangerson who worked for him. They discussed among themselves.

"The wine is not enough for several and too much for one person. Let us each draw a snake on the floor and the first one that finishes his drawing drinks the wine."

A man finished his drawing first. He took the wine and was about to drink it when, with the flask in his left hand, he drew with his right hand, saying, "I can even add legs to my snake."

Before he finished, another man completed his drawing and snatched the flask from him.

"A snake does not have legs. How could you add legs to it?"

With these words he drank the wine. The one who added legs to the snake eventually lost his wine.

29. Building a Moderately Prosperous Society in All Respects

In keeping with changes in domestic and international situations and in light of the expectations of the people of all ethnic groups for a better life, we must follow the trend and laws of economic and social development, uphold the basic program consisting of the basic objectives and policies for economic, political, cultural and social development under socialism with Chinese characteristics, and set new and higher requirements for China's development on the basis of the goal of building a moderately prosperous society in all respects set at the Sixteenth Congress.

When the goal of building a moderately prosperous society in all respects is attained by 2020, China, a large developing socialist country with an ancient civilization, will have basically accomplished industrialization, with its overall strength significantly increased and its domestic market ranking as one of the largest in the world. It will be a country whose people are better off and enjoy markedly improved quality of life and a good environment. Its citizens will have more extensive democratic rights, show higher ethical standards and look forward to greater cultural achievements. China will have better institutions in all areas and Chinese society will have greater vitality coupled with stability and unity. The country will be still more open and friendly to the outside world and make greater contributions to human civilization.

The following five years will be a crucial period for building a moderately prosperous society in all respects. We must enhance our confidence and work hard to lay a more solid foundation for success in building a moderately prosperous society of a higher level in all respects to the benefit of over one billion people.

30. Our Two-centenary Goals

What has happened shows that without reform and opening-up, China could not have come to where it is today, nor can it have a future. Over the past 30 years and more, we have resolved a series of major issues through reform. Going forward, we will continue to meet the various difficulties and challenges through reform. We have put forward our "two-centenary goals", namely, to double the 2010 GDP and per capita income of urban and rural residents and complete the building of a society of moderate prosperity in all respects by 2020; and to build a modern socialist country that is prosperous, strong, democratic, culturally advanced and harmonious and realize the Chinese dream of great national renewal by the middle of this century. We are now comprehensively deepening reform, improving and developing the system of socialism with Chinese characteristics and modernizing the state governance system and capacity. We will promote reform of the economic, political, cultural, social and ecological systems and the Party's development system in a balanced way. We will advance reform with the political courage and wisdom of "venturing into the mountain despite the fact there might be tigers there". When we step onto the stone, we will leave our footprints on it; and when we clutch a piece of iron, we will leave our handprints on it. This is the spirit we will uphold in pushing forward reform. By so doing, we strive to provide a stronger driving force for China's modernization, bring more and greater benefits to the Chinese people and create new development opportunities for the world.

Bibliography 参考文献

Hawkes, David. 1980. *The Story of the Stone*. London: Penguin Books.
New York Times. 2002-2010.
Newmark, Peter. 2001. *A Text Book of Translation*. 上海：上海外语教育出版社．
Nida, Eugene. 1993. *Language, Culture and Translating*. 上海：上海外语教育出版社．
Snow, Helen Foster. 1984. *My China Years: A Memoir*. New York: Morrow.
The Economist. 2008-2017.
Time. 1998-2010.
wikipedia http://en.wikipedia.org/wiki.
Yang, Xianyi & Gladys. 1994. *A Dream of Red Mansions*. 北京：外语教学与研究出版社．
安危，杜夏 译．1986. 我在中国的岁月——海伦·斯诺回忆录．北京：中国新闻出版社．
陈福康．1992. 中国翻译理论史稿．上海：上海外语教育出版社．
陈复庵 译．1981. 阿丽思漫游奇境记．北京：中国对外翻译出版公司．
丁树德．1996. 英汉汉英翻译教学综合指导．天津：天津大学出版社．
杜承南，文军．1994. 中国当代翻译百论．重庆：重庆大学出版社．
方梦之，马秉义．1996. 汉译英实践与练习．北京：旅游教育出版社．
冯庆华．2002. 实用翻译教程．上海：上海外语教育出版社．
冯树鉴．1995. 实用英汉翻译技巧．上海：同济大学出版社．
冯伟年．1996. 高校英汉翻译实例评析．西安：西北大学出版社．
郭建中．2000. 当代美国翻译理论．武汉：湖北教育出版社．
郭著章，李庆生．1996. 英汉互译实用教程．武汉：武汉大学出版社．
韩其顺，王学铭．1994. 英汉科技翻译教程．上海：上海外语教学出版社．
胡庚申等．2000. 文献阅读与翻译．北京：高等教育出版社．
黄龙．1986. 翻译技巧指导．沈阳：辽宁人民出版社．
黄龙．1988. 翻译学．南京：江苏教育出版社．
黄雨石．1988. 英汉文学翻译探索．西安：陕西人民出版社．
江镇华．1984. 英文专利文献阅读入门．北京：专利文献出版社．
金隄．1989. 等效翻译探索．北京：中国对外翻译出版公司．

金岳霖.1983.知识论.北京:商务印书馆.
靳梅琳.1995.英汉翻译概要.天津:南开大学出版社.
井升华.1995.英语实用语大全.南京:译林出版社.
李瑞华.1997.英汉语言文化对比研究.上海:上海外语教育出版社.
李亚舒等.1994.科技翻译论著集萃.北京:中国科学技术出版社.
连淑能.1993.英汉对比研究.北京:高等教育出版社.
林相周.1988.英语理解与翻译100题.上海:上海译文出版社.
刘宓庆.1985.文体与翻译.北京:中国对外翻译出版公司.
刘重德.1991.文学翻译十讲.北京:中国对外翻译出版公司.
吕瑞昌等.1983.汉英翻译教程.西安:陕西人民出版社.
彭启良.1980.翻译与比较.北京:商务印书馆.
钱歌川.1972.翻译的技巧.台北:台北开明书店.
外国语.上海外国语大学学报.1995—2000.
王泉水.1991.科技英语翻译技巧.天津:天津科技出版社.
许国璋.1991.许国璋论语言.北京:外语教学与研究出版社.
许建平.2008.研究生英语实用翻译教程.北京:中国人民大学出版社.
许建平.2009.大学英语实用翻译.北京:中国人民大学出版社.
许建平.2011.成功留学写作指南.北京:外语教学与研究出版社.
张克礼.1993.英语歧义结构.天津:南开大学出版社.
张培基等.1980.英汉翻译教程.上海:上海外语教育出版社.
张志公.1982.现代汉语.北京:人民教育出版社.
中国翻译.中国翻译工作者协会会刊.1996—2010.
中国翻译工作者协会.1984.翻译研究论文集(1894—1983).北京:外语教学与研究出版社.
钟述孔.1983.英汉翻译手册.北京:商务印书馆.